V   2009

On Architecture

ON ARCHITECTURE

COLLECTED REFLECTIONS ON A CENTURY OF CHANGE

ADA LOUISE HUXTABLE

Walker & Company
New York

Published by Walker Publishing Company, Inc., New York

All papers used by Walker & Company are natural, recyclable products made from wood grown in well-managed forests. The manufacturing processes conform to the environmental regulations of the country of origin.

"The Tall Building Artistically Reconsidered," reprinted by permission from *The Tall Building Artistically Reconsidered*, (New York: Pantheon Books/Random House, Inc., 1984).

"The Way It Never Was" reprinted by permission from *The Unreal America: Architecture and Illusion*, (New York: The New Press, 1997).

Photograph credits:
Corbis: pages 16, 108, 189, 271, 299, 368; Library of Congress/Prints and Photographs Division: pages 49, 204, 262, 303, 373, 406; Yale University Department of Art and Architecture: pages 53, 57; Michele Lee Amundsen: page 64; The Museum of Modern Art, New York: page 103; Getty Images: pages 161, 178, 244, 254, 287, 295

LIBRARY OF CONGRESS CATALOGING-IN-PUBLICATION DATA HAS BEEN APPLIED FOR.

ISBN-10: 0-8027-1707-1
ISBN-13: 978-0-8027-1707-8

Visit Walker & Company's Web site at www.walkerbooks.com

First U.S. edition 2008

3   5   7   9   10   8   6   4

Typeset by Westchester Book Group
Printed in the United States of America by Quebecor World Fairfield

Contents

PART VII. TASTE AND STYLE

PART VIII. STRICTLY PERSONAL

Introduction

CRITICS ARE NO MORE CLAIRVOYANT than their fellow mortals. Those of us who write for newspapers have little time to consider the long term or the larger implications of our work, nor are editors known for welcoming such digressions. We are focused on the moment, looking for the next big thing; it is the immediate news peg or upcoming trend that matters. Sometimes we are so busy fighting a defensive rearguard action for an old revolution that we miss the signals of a new one. This has been particularly true for the champions of modernism, a crusade that never seemed to end even as the ground shifted radically under its practitioners' feet.

Pressing deadlines, we are not given to abstractions, but this does not mean that we are without passionately held convictions or a personal point of view. I was once asked by a distinguished French journalist, "Just what polemical position do you write from, Madame?" and when I failed to produce an appropriate polemic and replied that I wrote from crisis to crisis it was clear that I had failed to measure up to his expectations. I could have said that I wrote from a sense of entitlement, in the belief that everyone deserves, and has a right to, standards of quality, humanity, and yes, even art, because art elevates the experience and pleasure of the places where we live and work. As critics, we do our best to explain and uphold those standards and to hold faulty feet to the fire. As journalists, we report the news, which runs the risk of instant obsolescence.

As I sorted through hundreds of columns and articles in the *New York Times*, the *Wall Street Journal*, and the *New York Review of Books* to choose what appears in this book, a picture emerged that was much more gratifying, I confess, than I had hoped for or expected. With the hindsight of the twenty-first century, I began to notice a pattern that told the story of an extraordinary evolution of architecture and culture in the five decades of the twentieth century that I have been privileged to witness and record. What could have been an exercise in nostalgia turned out to be an exercise in discovery. I was writing at a historic moment, observing an amazing century of change, documenting an architectural revolution, watching a remarkable scenario unfold. Looking back, it seems that I had been looking forward all the time.

The theme that runs through all of this writing is the transformation of the modernism that pervaded every intellectual and cultural aspect of the twentieth century into a new way of thinking and building. Inevitably, the topicality and immediacy of many of these pieces has faded. Some hot-button issues no longer have the urgency of their original publication. Do-or-die controversies dissolved over the decades. A recent online response to an architecture blog, signed Harry, gave a "shocking" Philip Johnson building that was the buzz of the 1970s its ultimate putdown and place in history: "Remember when the AT&T now Sony Chippendale tower was a scandal? Ho-hum."

I have included items never reprinted before because it is clear to me now that they are part of the larger story. Many more familiar columns were not chosen, but subjects that still seem like landmarks, or milestones, or express enduring values, have been retained. Some endure in spite of me, and for all the wrong reasons. My reservations about the architectural worth of Edward Durell Stone's 2 Columbus Circle in New York, built by Huntington Hartford in 1964 as his Gallery of Modern Art, and the case I made for its conversion by the Museum of Arts and Design after a long period of deterioration and neglect, have been blown off by preservationists in full nostalgic cry for the impossible and unreasonable. The name "lollipop building," from my original description of it as a "little die-cut Venetian palazzo on lollipops," has stuck, even if my arguments haven't, and may prove to be my only claim to immortality. As a case history, however, it is a perfect example of how wrong the preservation movement is going today in its evaluation of the buildings of the recent past.

I felt that it was important for every piece in this book to appear as originally published, without the layers of interpretation or reevaluation that subsequent decades have added. Nothing has been changed, edited, or updated, because the issues can only be understood in their original context. There are some obvious omissions. I have not devoted space to preservation, although I was an active participant in that hard-fought battle, because its success is a matter of record and I do not need to repeat the well-known achievements that have established it firmly in our cities and our lives. Admittedly, the war is never won, and we are faced today with a new crisis: a modernist heritage that is under threat, without the scholarship or the standards that are needed to resolve it. Nor have I included anything on sustainable or green architecture, because I believe that building for climatic and human needs should be a given, intrinsic to any design utilizing the remarkable technology that has revolutionized construction today. The literature is overwhelming; it needs no cheering section here.

The reviews and articles chosen for this book represent only a fraction of what I have written over the years; at best this is a spotty history, a very rough guide to a movement inspired as much by the miraculous tools of computer and structural technology and intense generational and societal change as by the perceived failures or deficiencies of modernism. It is all quite low-key. There is no revelatory blast; no moment of epiphany; no trumpet flourish announcing the ways in which modernism was being rejected or redefined, how everything it preached and practiced was being questioned, or how this led to a radical shift in the art of architecture comparable to any of history's great redefining aesthetic upheavals.

"The Way We Were" looks back briefly at the decades covered in this book with a few randomly selected pieces meant to suggest the nature of the times. "The Way We Built" presents a selection of some of the iconic images and structures of the twentieth century, when modernism was fully embraced by the establishment for its skyscrapers, corporate headquarters, and public and cultural buildings, even as countercurrents were flowing underneath. "Modernism and Its Discontents" brings that rebellion to the surface, while "Reinventing Architecture" and "Rewriting History" deal with the new work and ideas as they appeared. These later sections include those architects who refused to play by modernism's rules and had enormous influence on the state of the art, as well as practitioners and styles banished by modernism as counterproductive to its radical purity and revolutionary intent. Revisionism was rampant, and as controversial as it seemed at the time, it has all been absorbed into a productive mainstream.

I don't think I lost my compass; the pieces neither protest nor fail to acknowledge change, nor do they offer uncritical admiration of what seemed the irresistible leading edge at the time. Tempting as it is to be part of a glamorous in-crowd, I have never joined architectural groupies of any persuasion. As an architectural historian, I have not bought into anyone's belief systems, including modernism's most admirable and often faulty illusions. I have a built-in skepticism of dogma and its more pretentious theoretical justifications, and a scholar's interest in the evolution of creative thought and style.

Now to answer the question I am most frequently (do I sense, hopefully?) asked: Do I think I was ever "wrong"? Sorry to disappoint, but my opinions have not really changed; I called the buildings like I saw them, and I feel pretty much the same way now. My judgments have all been made in the immediate context of their time, measured against some pretty timeless standards—something hindsight, with its rewriting of history, often prefers to ignore. Simply put, I was there; I know what happened. Neither am I a good building's fair-weather friend, abandoning it if it has gone out of style, nor am I capable of elevating a bad building to newly discovered significance through some previously unperceived and often invented attributes. When a perfectly dreadful mid-twentieth-century office tower in London that I once described as looking as if it had been run up on giant knitting needles is given protected status, I can only wonder, "What are they thinking?"

Occasionally I have second thoughts. I was, perhaps, too kind to Renzo Piano's revisions for New York's Pierpont Morgan Library. Because I am easily snookered by an elegant design, something Piano always delivers, I suspended my unease about how the library's unique personality and quirky charm had been sacrificed, albeit handsomely and efficiently, to a coolly rational unifying plan and what is rapidly becoming a generic museum model. Now let me see, if this is a Gutenberg Bible, it must be the Morgan. As museums have expanded and multiplied on their way to becoming the social, cultural, and economic status symbols of our time, they have, like airports, become almost indistinguishable. Frank Gehry's Bilbao Guggenheim of 1997 changed the museum landscape forever, but it also established the museum as an iconic structure and a model that would be blindly followed by business-dominated museum boards unwilling to invest in anything less than an iconic look-alike by a tiresomely familiar name.

Hindsight gives greater weight to some buildings and events, while downgrading others. Robert Venturi's "gentle manifesto," *Complexity and Contradiction in Architecture*, published in 1966, was a shot across the bow of modernism that seems even more significant today. This small, slim volume, with its plea to reexamine history and the environment, opened the door to a whole new range of thought and practice, from the best and worst of postmodernism to the most extreme forms of expression today. Venturi and his wife and partner, Denise Scott Brown, continued to unsettle accepted conventions by praising the "dumb and ordinary," telling us to learn from Las Vegas, and suggesting that Main Street was almost all right. Their mantra, "inclusive rather than exclusive," denied the practice of filtering out whatever displeased our preconditioned aesthetic responses. If accepting the past was unthinkable, acknowledging the existence of the expedient world of the twentieth-century strip mall and suburbia was worse; this was heresy, but heresy was reality. Nor is it inconsistent with the century's rapid and continuing change that even the Venturis' vision was superseded as Vegas morphed and malls mutated and architecture, once the rarified province of artists and intellectuals, became one of the priciest and most popular marketing tools of an expanding supercapitalist age that had no use for the dumb and ordinary and instead invented globe-hopping starchitects.

I am more than ever convinced that the postmodernism that took over in the 1970s with so much hoopla was a blip in the process, but an absolutely essential blip as a generation rebelled against the faith of its fathers—although rarely, if ever, have so many stand-up one-liners, inside jokes, and ill-digested knockoffs of history produced so many really bad buildings. I am just as sure that some of its most egregious exercises in bowdlerized trivia will be lovingly embraced by future preservationists.

By the end of the century, with taboos broken and technology showing the way, the art of building had evolved into a galaxy of new styles, from high-tech marvels to computer-generated undulating blobs. For all who forged boldly ahead, however, there were others who remained locked into the ideals and beliefs of a rigid and righteous modernism, even as younger architects were kicking over its lingering traces. Modernism became history when the preservationists moved in.

What is truly fascinating is the way reputations have gone up and down over the years. Each generation sees what it wants to see, writes its own script to fit its own needs, relevant to its own worldview. If you wait long enough, what is admired will be relegated to history's dustbin, and if you wait even longer, it will be rescued and restored. Stick around, as they say on TV. Paul Rudolph's 1971 Art and Architecture building at Yale is a stunning example of how the generational love-hate process works. I thought it was an extraordinary building then, with its powerful, brutalist forms and complex interlocking levels, and I think it is extraordinary still. But the multilayered interiors that made it so spatially intriguing frustrated a faculty and students used to warehouse-style studios, and as modernism bashing became the fashion, increasing indignities were visited upon it, from the rejection and destruction of those spaces by the architecture students' construction of favela-like mini-slums within them, to a still-mysterious fire. More than thirty years later, Yale has undertaken a full-scale, respectful restoration of the building, calling it "a masterpiece of space, light and mass." It will be known as Paul Rudolph Hall.

Boston's competition-winning City Hall, designed by Kallmann, McKinnell and Knowles in 1962 at the height of the brutalist style, is at the bottom of the cycle. Everybody in Boston hates it and the mayor wants to demolish it. Admittedly, there is nothing cozy and lovable about the uncompromising drama of the building's rough concrete forms, but it has been ill-served to a degree remarkable even for politicians, who have a notoriously bad eye for architecture as anything but patronage or real estate and a preference for Howard Johnson Georgian once removed. I am convinced that there are whole bureaucracies devoted to the painstaking sabotage of any good government building they get near. Not quite lost in the mists of political time is the unrealized plan of another mayor, Abe Beame of New York, to demolish the equally despised Tweed Courthouse for a little colonial cupcake with a cupola on top. Déjà vu, anyone? Boston's old City Hall, long unloved, was eventually saved and reused. But only a massive cultural shift will save this City Hall, a building consistently misused and misunderstood. As originally designed, it had a dignity and openness that belied Boston's notoriously convoluted politics. I admired the building then, and I admire it now.

Who could have imagined that the palatial headquarters built by corporations like Connecticut General and American Can, exemplars of modernist luxury dominating the twentieth-century suburban landscape, would be abandoned and sold off as real estate to developers for McMansions? Or that the General Motors building that brought mediocrity and a dismal, redundant plaza to the most elegant part of New York's Fifth Avenue would be redeemed by the Apple store's magic crystal cube on a newly elevated plaza, turning disaster into triumph? When I agitated to have the concrete bunker against the Hudson River planned for New York's Javits Convention Center redesigned in glass, I never anticipated that it would turn out to be a lump of black coal. In architecture, the Law of Unexpected Consequences applies.

Time also plays surprising tricks. It is inconceivable to me that Alvaro Siza and Rafael Moneo, indisputably in the top rank of today's most talented international practitioners, critically acclaimed and universally admired by their peers, are passed over on institutional short lists in favor of those who play a more provocative and publicity-wise game. Because the practiced excellence of their subtle, sophisticated work lacks the instant "wow" required for the competitive, can-you-top-this stakes, it fails to push the right buttons for those whose knowledge does not extend beyond trophy names. Similarly, the aggressively theatrical solutions of Jean Nouvel have eclipsed the delicacy and refinement of Christian de Portzamparc, who combines sensuous references to mid-twentieth-century form and color with stylish twenty-first-century solutions of striking originality.

The diagrid façades and space-frame-covered courts of Norman Foster, the high priest of high tech, are proliferating on a scale previously unimaginable. Impeccably executed, commercially viable, and utterly predictable, they are blanketing the world with the twenty-first century's equivalent of the twentieth century's universal curtain walls of Skidmore, Owings & Merrill. What was big business then is even bigger business now. It also never occurred to me that engineering advances would finally remove all the traditionally observed height restrictions from tall buildings, and I certainly did not envision an age of Skyscrapers Gone Wild. Supersized, contorted, totally out of context, setting new benchmarks in the race to claim the slippery title of world's highest and most ostentatiously vulgar building, they make futurism look like something by Emily Post.

What pleases me most is that the masters who gave modernism its name and form not only refute all this ghastly overreaching, they look better than ever. Discipline, restraint, and rigor have a lot to recommend them. These were gigantically talented architects who pioneered a to-tally new kind of building and a radical new aesthetic based on the epochal changes in materials and construction brought about by the industrial revolution. Even those whose work seems farthest from the source are quick to acknowledge their debt. Richard Meier's admira-tion of Le Corbusier has always been clear; postmodernists like Robert Venturi give Alvar Aalto his due. What is emphasized by this generation, however, are not the obvious signposts of modernism, but features more relevant to their own needs and perceptions, like implicit connections to historic precedents and attention to the setting and the land.

Rereading the pieces I wrote about these twentieth-century giants, I see genius, and courage, and great works of architecture that endure. I also see qualities that set their work above and apart from today's prac-tice, when "attitude" and a challenging novelty are bringing architec-ture to a discomfort level of fashionable edginess that may be claiming its first architecture victims. At a time of superchic hard-edged mini-malism, Alvar Aalto's soft-edged humanism invites us to experience the skill with which his buildings include people and nature, and the time-less pleasure that gives us. Louis Kahn elevates our own humanity in buildings that speak to our dignity and worth. And faced with so much excess in our lives and our world, Mies van der Rohe still gives us the relief of the precise and perfect elimination needed to reach the bones of beauty, reminding us that indeed, less can be more.

In the short piece that opens this collection I suggested that it was time for a book on "The Joy of Architecture" to celebrate the pleasures of this remarkable art. It took about thirty years, but Alain de Botton's *The Architecture of Happiness*, published in 2006, fills the bill. This lovely book is devoted, in large part, to finding one's comfort zone, showing us how easily we can understand the art and design of our en-vironment. But comfort has never produced the departures that mark the turning points of art and history, and we are in the turmoil of his-toric change and out of our comfort zone right now. We need to stretch beyond the familiar to appreciate the power of this new work to expand and enrich our sense of self and place. Architecture is remaking our world. It is important to understand how and why this is happening if we are to be beneficiaries, rather than casualties, of the process. Its re-wards are personal and universal in a way no other art can match. Its joys are common to us all.

Preface

The Joy of Architecture

EVERY AGE CUTS AND PASTES HISTORY to suit its own purposes; art always has an ax to grind. Classical Rome became the Renaissance in the eyes of the fifteenth century. Every great artist is re-created in the chosen image of a particular time. No "historic reconstruction" is ever really true to the original; there is neither the desire nor the courage to embrace another era's taste. We keep what we like and discard what we don't. In the recent past the nineteenth century has been disdained except for a limited interpretation tailored to modernist taste and beliefs, for a fascinating, if somewhat hobbled, history.

Fortunately, great art contains enough to satisfy each generation's needs, and there is always pleasure in the process of rediscovery. The news is that the academy wasn't all bad, and the action wasn't only in the world-class cities; Peoria and Dubuque may have been in the mainstream after all. The realization is growing that a great deal has happened outside the conventional centers of power and culture and there is a whole world of architecture between New York and San Francisco and beyond Charleston and Savannah, lost in the shadow of the Chicago skyscrapers. It has been there all along, but the tendency has been to write it off and out of the history books.

The immediate gain is for architectural scholarship. We are undoubtedly suiting our own biased vision again, but we are achieving a richer and broader mix, enlarging experience and aesthetic response. The emphasis is on the material that is the most troubling to modernists—the kind of sentiment and ornament in Frank Lloyd

1

Wright's work, for example, that the nineteenth century admired and the twentieth century banished. Bypassed achievements and unfamiliar or unsettling aspects of familiar work are being explored enthusiastically.

In a curious way, the door has been opened for serious study, not just by revisionist scholarship, which has been operating quietly for some time, but by the relaxation of conventional "received" standards. This includes the fashionable vogue for nostalgia and camp; the trivia of the recent past has become an enormously popular stylistic dig. No earnest and involved intellectual justifications are offered for the vigorous pursuit of the novel and the new; the objective is pure perverse delight in artifacts bound to shock those whose values are being challenged. There is nothing so far out, the new taste makers seem to be telling us, that it cannot be embraced. There is nothing so antimodern that it cannot be accepted. There is nothing so totally rejected that we cannot admire it now, and if that means rewriting history, we will do so.

But the game is not a scholarly one alone. As with so much else in our determinedly hedonistic society with its emphasis on short-term satisfactions, the consistent theme is pleasure. There is so much more to see, to experience, to understand, to enjoy. There are worse ways of pursuing today's liberated sensibility. *The Joy of Architecture* must be on some publisher's list by now.

New York Times, February 5, 1978

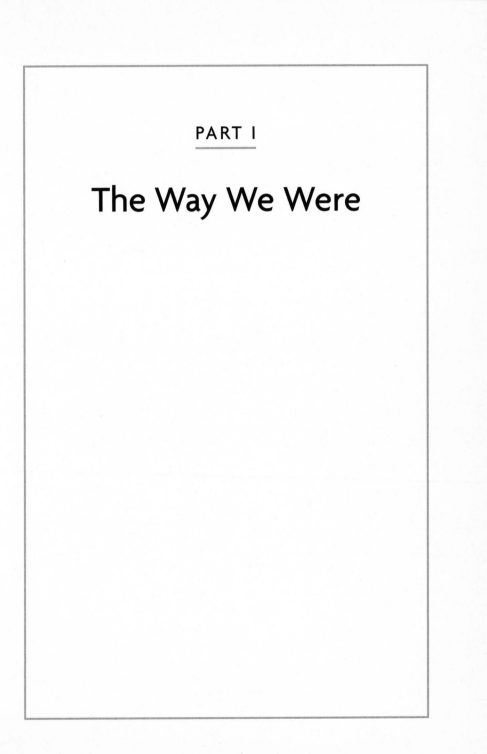

PART I

The Way We Were

THE SIXTIES

Modernism: USA

WANT TO KNOW THE SCORE FOR American architecture in the twentieth century? Go to the Museum of Modern Art any time through September 6 to see Modern Architecture, U.S.A., the selective survey of building achievement in this country from 1900 to 1965, arranged by Arthur Drexler, director of the Department of Architecture and Design, and cosponsored by the Graham Foundation for Advanced Studies in the Fine Arts.

The museum, of course, is the outstanding scorekeeper of our time. It not only keeps the score but occasionally calls the shots. Understand, then, that you will see only the best, according to the museum's lights, since the exhibition presents just seventy-one buildings for those sixty-five years, a microscopic sampling by any standard.

But the best is good enough. The sampling has been done not only with an astute eye, but with a commendable tolerance of diverse styles and trends. The picture that emerges is therefore definitive, on a quality level. It shows the twentieth century in the United States as a period of solid, stimulating, wide-ranging accomplishment in the building arts, with high points that have become international landmarks.

This is the museum's fourth survey of the American building scene, at approximately ten-year intervals. The first was its introductory architecture show in 1932, the pristine bombshell by Philip Johnson and Henry-Russell Hitchcock that defined The International Style. That exhibition, which relied heavily on European examples by necessity, introduced modern architecture to the United States.

Pioneering and proselytizing, its message fell on not very fertile

5

ground. But it was, like the museum itself at that time, avant-garde, radical, electrically prophetic; the bearer of winds of change. (Ah, the excitement of those days—how quickly innovation becomes nostalgia!
Has success spoiled the Museum of Modern Art?)

The second survey, in 1944, was Built in U.S.A., Since 1932. That
show, which this writer remembers as a kind of indoctrination, relied
heavily on houses, or the private sponsorship of enlightened individuals
who were "with it" and had the means and belief to commission the
new work. It was still a small, exclusive club. The modern movement
was austerely and firmly intellectual; the property of the initiated; not
yet for the masses. But the museum, as usual, was an excellent propaganda showcase.

By the time the third show, Built in U.S.A., Postwar Architecture,
was presented in 1953, the modern movement had arrived. But it still
belonged to a kind of architectural aristocracy.

Its monuments were uncommon buildings like the trend-setting
Lever House by Skidmore, Owings & Merrill, the first glass tower to
breach Park Avenue, and Saarinen's General Motors Technical Center
in Detroit, a Versailles of modern industry. To put it bluntly, the hacks
had not yet jumped on the bandwagon in any sizable quantity.

The museum continued to point the way by the severe selectivity of
its standards.

With the present exhibition there is a subtle but significant change
in the museum's role. It cannot pioneer in the old sense. Modern architecture is here to stay. It is no longer a crusade; it is the structural
norm, the speculator's tool, the routine designer's rubber stamp, the
only practical way to build.

The museum maintains its function as the fingerer of quality, but it
has espoused the role of historian rather than of groundbreaker.

The show covers the whole century. All the avant-garde works that
originally shocked and stimulated are here.

There are the pre–World War I California houses of Greene and
Greene, the beginnings of a native, rustic style, and of Gill and Schindler,
with their almost clairvoyant cubist purity.

Breuer's bi-nuclear houses in the East share space with the growing
West Coast manner of Harris and Yeon in the thirties and forties. Neu-
tra and Gropius represent the influential landmarks of the transplanted
International Style at the same time.

With the mise-en-scène established, half of the show is devoted to the last fifteen years. Mies van der Rohe emerges as the star of the fifties and the source of a burgeoning commercial style of glass-walled simplicity. The emphasis shifts from domestic daring to corporate splendor and the espousal of modern architecture by the business establishment.

The late fifties and sixties show a definitive move away from the rigors of the International Style, with an explosion of decorative and historical tendencies in the work of Johnson, Yamasaki, and Stone. Finally, there are the fireworks of the most recent innovators: the theatrical experiments of Rudolph and the smoldering, quiet revolution of Kahn.

Through it all, the creative force of Frank Lloyd Wright pulsates as a kind of American leitmotif from beginning to end.

The museum's job has been simply to record, and to separate the gold from the dross. It has done this with its usual taste and competence, and the conclusion is that there is a gratifying amount of construction of 14-karat quality in American building today.

The exhibition is full of glorious virtuoso performances. In the art of architecture, the United States scores high.

But if this country is ahead on buildings as individual works of art, it is woefully behind on architecture as total environment. It has failed completely to deal with the critical problem of controlling the urban explosion through design, of planning the man-made environment for beauty, efficiency, and order. This is the great architectural challenge of the twentieth century.

In this area, Europe, not America, points the way. European architects have been concentrating on frontiers of design on the community and environmental scale. In close-up, their work may frequently be less attractive and imaginative than U.S. counterparts, but they are not evading the basic issues. These must be dealt with if architecture is to remain the most vital and meaningful art of our time.

The museum show contains some splendid, isolated things. But it is concerned primarily with brilliant nonessentials. For American architecture, this is victory by default.

New York Times, May 23, 1965

World of the Absurd

INEVITABLY, 1967 ENDED AND 1968 BEGAN with news about cities. Athelstan Spilhaus (a name with an authority of its own) saw the old year out by telling the American Association for the Advancement of Science that old cities are obsolete. Out with the old, in with the new, was his message; the new would be a four-billion-dollar Experimental City to rise in Minnesota, using advanced, multilevel techniques of transport, construction, communication, and organization. Ten Minnesota industries and three federal agencies have put together three hundred thousand dollars for preliminary studies.

Also in the news as the old year died was the fact that city life and city problems had come to Antarctica. In some kind of record for nest-fouling, urban sprawl has turned McMurdo Station into an urban horror in a brief ten years. This may be a standing backjump record for ruining the environment.

"A smoking garbage dump and junkyard litter the shore of a once picturesque inlet; power lines from the nuclear plant deface the stark, windswept and lifeless hills that so awed and impressed explorers 50 years ago," a reporter noted. The answer? A McMurdo redevelopment program, naturally.

THE NEW YEAR will see megalopolis, the urban smear that is staining the entire American Northeast and blurring city boundaries everywhere, relentlessly on its way to ecumenopolis, or a totally urbanized world, according to planner Constantinos Doxiadis. (The Greeks had a word for it and still do. Any trend or truism dressed up in classical etymology becomes a charismatic concept for the intellectually susceptible. It has the authority of a sermon from the Acropolis.)

Ecumenopolis may take a little while, but we'll get there. We may get to the moon first, of course, although only one thing is sure about that and none of the scientific prognostications mention it. When we get there, we'll make a mess of it.

Meanwhile, back at the foundations and universities, studies of the city proliferate, and the new year promises more. In a brilliant review of a compilation of papers by urban experts collected under the title *Taming*

Megalopolis, planner and architect Clive Entwistle envisions "continuing and increasing and ever more expensive 'research' projects to the horizons of urban space and post-graduate time."

The pinned butterfly of urban phenomena, the dissected and annotated crisis, with enough academic verbiage attached, substitutes handily for solutions. Few studies have the jolting pertinence of a Moynihan analysis of the Negro family in American society. Most are pretentious and fatiguingly detailed enshrinements of the obvious or ordinary, properly impressive to those who are awed by Greek-root words. "Before the buzz of refined scholarship," Entwistle concludes, "the decision makers, engineers and politicians stand abashed and emasculated."

The new year, not surprisingly, will produce still another research group, this time on the highest federal level—an Institute for Urban Development to process problems and trends.

"TREND IS NOT destiny," warns Lewis Mumford in one of his periodic blasts on the urban scene from his sanctuary in the nonurban hills of New York State, quoting Albert Mayer's book, *The Urgent Future*. "Progress," says the *New York Times* editorially, is an idea that needs to be "challenged."

All of which makes it quite clear where we are in 1968. We are obviously in the world of the absurd. The black urban comedy continues to be played out in the research institutes, and the black urban tragedy goes on in the ghettos while Rome, and Detroit and Newark, burn.

Disaster is charted as destiny and objective, scholarly truth. Progress consists of making the same mistakes, but on an Olympian scale. Research builds abstract monuments to itself. Funds are made available for "prototype studies" while untouched problems take their toll of the human heart and the urban world. In government agencies, policy set at the top is reversed by bureaucracy at the bottom.

We pollute the country with the refuse of the affluent society. In Washington, D.C., it has been found that there is more gold per ton of fly ash in the refuse dumps than in commercial mines. At McMurdo we have the apotheosis of absurdity: We have destroyed the environment while studying it. The reality of the world of the absurd can't be touched by anything in the imagination of man.

There is hope, of course. We can press that precious garbage into construction blocks and build with them, according to promising new processes, rather than face slow strangulation from the detritus of prosperity. Eventually we may be able to move to Minnesota. We can enter the research cloisters in handsome parts of the countryside where megalopolis waits to spring.

But at some point we are going to have to resolve a basic conflict. There is a current credo of it's right and it's real because it's what's happening, baby, and all we have to do to be with it is to feel it, and documentation is the ultimate revelation. This may open new polemical horizons for the intellectual and new creative doors for the artist, but it is suicidal stupidity as an attitude toward the world we live in.

What's happening in cities happens to a large extent out of greed, self-interest, ignorance, and foul-up. The few happy environmental accidents that occur, the occasional lessons in the vitality of an unregulated urban mix as against the defective sterility of much planning, are no argument for the abdication of judgment, morality, opinions, objectives, and ideals. These are square words and square concepts, but also square necessities.

FOR RESPONSIBILITY AND action we substitute the high-level makework of scholars. It is a face-saving, if not city-saving, evasion. For value judgments we embrace an esoteric, half-baked, admiration for the natural chaos of "the scene." The administrator, politician, or planner who holds convictions enough to battle for solutions—and solutions are always partial, imperfect, debatable, and without guarantees—must be an extraordinary combination of gutter tough and intellectual visionary. He does it, surprisingly in an age of cynicism, because he cares.

The twentieth century is a time of mind-blowing, psychedelic change, in both values and environment, much of it as valid and fascinating as it is painful and confusing. An understanding of this fact, too, must be used, like research, to help create a viable quality of contemporary urban life.

Abdication or rejection is not the answer. Neither is the fashionable acceptance of the existential status quo, unless crime, disease, pollution, slums, and human misery are also acceptable answers for our time.

New York Times, January 14, 1968

THE SEVENTIES

Forward, Backward, Sideways

LAST YEAR, MODERN ARCHITECTURE was declared dead, but this year, it refused to lie down. The building of the year was definitely an establishment edifice in the heroic modern tradition. It was I. M. Pei & Partners' new East Building for the National Gallery of Art in Washington, D.C., designed for establishment clients Carter Brown, director of the museum, and Paul Mellon, its benefactor, with other members of the Mellon family and trust, to provide a home and setting for the established masterworks of modern art. It is a smashing establishment success.

In fact, it has been so highly praised (including here) and so popular with a vast public, that it is already very unpopular with those who find conservative, moneyed, safe art and architecture anathema. There are dissident murmurings about the vast skylit court and its surrounding galleries being the ultimate shopping mall for consumer culture, as if such central skylit spaces and peripheral circulation were not also characteristic of a notable number of historical building types.

This might be called the putdown of the year. But it is hard to downgrade a building in which space, structure, and art all work together for a definitive statement of a major aesthetic ideal of the twentieth century. If the postmodernists want to bury that ideal, they couldn't pick a better place.

For the nonbuilding of the year, I nominate Philip Johnson and John Burgee's AT&T Building, which has certainly had the most publicity of 1978. This is an interesting building, for all the wrong reasons. It is fascinating to see just how far it is possible to stretch a weak idea; a tiny concept has been turned into a monument by sheer size and scale.

MR. JOHNSON HAS put together some currently fashionable features that appeal to his educated eye and mind—a Lutyens oculus here, a pop art pediment there—in what is supposed to be the spirit of the new eclecticism. As noted before, the design fails to achieve that creative life and synthesis that marks a successful eclectic work, or even a successful work of architecture; it has neither genuine quirkiness nor real style. In spite of some passing shock value, this is a dull building—a pedestrian pastiche pulled together by painstaking, polished details.

The event of the year was the unveiling of the Temple of Dendur in the new Sackler Wing designed for it by Kevin Roche John Dinkeloo and Associates, at the Metropolitan Museum. The Egyptian temple is tiny and delicate, and the Sackler Wing is big and barren. It is like putting a desert flower in a gymnasium. *Poverina.*

The trend of the year is the return of ornament. Ever since Adolf Loos thundered that ornament was crime, decoration has been barred by the modern movement. Closet ornamentalists may now come out. The Cooper-Hewitt Museum, in the combination of the timely, the scholarly, and the provocative that has become its hallmark, held a twentieth-century ornament show this year that was a feast for the eye. Every bit of it broke taboos. The section on ornament in architecture not only revived some buried reputations, but also made it quite clear that the decorative urge had never really died; it was merely subverted into structural systems that were ornamental in themselves, and into building shapes much closer to abstract sculpture than to their programmatic or functional rationale.

Sneaky stuff, ornament. Now if someone can only figure out how to produce a still undetermined kind of decoration within the current constraints of costs and skills, we'll have a new style. At least, we now have a fresh eye.

THE DECISION OF the year was the Supreme Court's upholding of the constitutionality of New York City's landmarks law in the Grand Central case—and by extension, of other landmarks legislation throughout the country. Not only was the terminal spared, but the status of landmark buildings was confirmed and clarified in a way that considerably strengthened the nation's heritage.

The anticlimax of the year was anything at all about postmodernism, which was mainly preoccupied with continuing to give modernism its lumps. And the postmodernist confrontation of the year was in the pages of the *Times Literary Supplement*, between Charles Jencks, author of *The Language of Post-Modern Architecture*, and Reyner Banham, author of numerous books on modernism.

In this war of words, Banham accused Jencks and the postmodernists of not being able to reject modernism totally, and Jencks replied that Banham, and other modernists, simply cannot get rid of their hang-ups long enough to see the new, enlightened eclecticism, which welcomes everything the modernists discarded, as all-inclusive — even of modernism. Banham called Jencks silly, and Jencks called Banham silly. Phrases such as "postgraduate wierdos" (the Jencks camp) and "Vacuum Cleaning Period" (Banham's machine aesthetic) were lobbed. To date, postmodernism has produced better phrasemaking than architecture.

The portent of the year is that construction has begun again in New York City, just as if there were no fiscal crisis. Developers are busy devising the most remarkable ways of building on top of, around, and in between the city's best addresses, to meet a resurgent demand for luxury housing and offices.

Predictably, the city is being taken again, with the hefty tax abatements that were meant to be given as encouragement to building when there was no building at all, now going to construction that is clearly able to get top dollar in the booming commercial market. Only in New York would that advantage be given to buildings that have already milked the zoning dry for extra bulk and size. If half the ingenuity being brought to bear on breaking the city's zoning for more profitable blockbusters was turned to the city's finances and operation, the result could be a miraculous urban rebirth.

The cliffhangers of the year are Westway and Radio City Music Hall. Will they, or won't they, be built, or saved? As usual, the forces of good and evil are lined up blindly on both sides, each according to its own definition, while some of the fanciest numbers in history attest to more or less traffic and pollution for Westway, and more or less profit or loss for Radio City. You pick your figures to suit your cause. But beyond the slippery statistics is the unparalleled land planning opportunity for Manhattan that may never be properly realized even if Westway is built — and which should be the heart of the debate but is not — and the resolution of Radio City as something more in the city's future than a sentimental aesthetic artifact or a real estate opportunity.

If all this is too much, how about the joke of the year? Consider architect Stanley Tigerman's *Invitation to the Sale of One-Way Tickets on the Titanic*. This is the title of his visual one-liner, a pasteup of Mies van der Rohe's Crown Hall in Chicago, elegant symbol of the heroic period of modernism, upended in the ocean as it takes the final plunge into the sea. Woe to the architect left rearranging the deck chairs. Happy postmodern 1979.

New York Times, December 31, 1978

THE EIGHTIES

Breaking the Rules

THE ART OF ARCHITECTURE IS ALIVE and well; it is neither in the doldrums, nor retreating into the neoconservatism of the new aesthetic Right, nor suffering from creative block. If its practitioners seem to be subject to fits of pettiness and pique, that might most charitably be attributed to growing pains as modern architecture matures and moves toward a more complex style, or styles, and the beliefs and values of orthodox modernism collapse. The art of building at this moment is full of angst and uncertainty. But it is also showing all the signs of a very lively art in a provocative period of development and change. It is easy to believe that a significant chapter is being written in its history.

Architecture-at-a-crossroads has become a favorite theme of the popular cultural press; the state-of-the-art articles are advertised interchangeably as a crisis or a breakthrough. Actually, practice at the level where styles are set and trends are put in motion has been moving away for some time now from the strict, single-line, reductivist aesthetic that the world has come to know as modern architecture. This has been accompanied by the regrets and alarms of those who have been dedicated to that aesthetic for the last half century, and the hosannas of those who were neither born into, nor a practicing part of, the modernist revolution.

In this atmosphere of ferment and change, there is an explosion, not only of new building, but of exhibitions, books, and professional journals—suave, glossy publications with a heavy emphasis on the new theories and practice of architectural design and the rediscovery of periods and styles long out of favor with the modernists. Architecture and planning schools are being restructured in a way undreamed of in the sixties; policies and curricula are being painfully reshaped for the eighties. The excitement everywhere is aesthetic and polemical; and the emphasis is on the art of building, as much as or more than the act of building, or even with the building itself. In those rare cases where

Staatsgalerie, Stuttgart

theory and practice meet, the results are expansively published in the international press.

There is absolutely no way to view the architecture of the eighties as static, reactionary, or out-of-steam. Even the rediscovery of history—so long outlawed by the modernists—is infused with the spirit of radical change. The "retreat" to the past is either a total break with modernism or a new and unprecedented kind of eclecticism. This is taking the form of a return to a literal, impeccable classicism, as in the work of Allan Greenberg, its forms updated by subtle twists of use and meaning. Or it can draw on history and the vernacular for very personal and broad manipulations in a contemporary context. The Venturis, for example, have established the canons of pop culture as a system of signs and symbols which they translate into refined details. Michael Graves organizes a historical stream of consciousness into buildings that can be viewed as fantasies or follies, depending upon one's hang-ups about what a building should look like. His tend to have small, square windows, outsized keystones, and totemic volutes, colored Pompeian red and green.

Carrying conservatism full circle to radicalism, the brothers Léon and Robert Krier have renounced the forms, materials, and construction methods of modern society to embrace traditional, preindustrial building types and urban configurations. Their drawings, which are far more visionary than nostalgic, are as exquisite as they are unsettling, and their influence is international. In the work of the Italian architect Aldo Rossi, the familiar can become sinister, calling up totalitarian and surrealist images. When traditional or historical references are distilled to their most abstract essence, they are treated as "typologies," or ideal solutions, in the projects of such architects and teachers as Giorgio Silvetti, Diana Agrest, and Lauretta Vinciarelli, or the poetic and allegorical exercises of John Hejduk. Each group has its devout and faithful followers, who are highly critical of all the rest. But make no mistake — not all of this activity moves the art of building onward and upward. Architecture is not escaping the dead ends, the enchantment with trivia, the narrow, narcissistic vision of an incompletely educated generation that has invaded other arts. An art in turmoil churns up a lot of activity, but there is no guarantee of the quality of the product. It is not always easy to separate the significant from the silly or self-indulgent.

Criticism is not doing the job. That is not surprising at a time when being part of the action is more important than asking questions about its meaning and value. The media has created a false culture of celebrityhood and cost, fed only by the more sensational, entertaining, and superficial aspects of the arts. Publicity is its own reward. In architecture, publicity seems to be the lifeblood of a grab bag of practice that has been dubbed postmodernism, whose adherents had been working the international lecture and exhibition circuit with generous press coverage. Much of what they are saying is a useful contribution to a larger debate, but a good deal of their work, for this reviewer, at least, is problematic. It is a frankly surface style, in which the structural rationale of architectural design is given short shrift for trendy historical, vernacular, or decorative references applied with a kind of aesthetic shorthand that is supposed to indicate wit, irony, and symbolism to the initiate. But for every case in which these allusions produce interesting effects, there are other annoyingly fussy examples that prove nothing except that it is easier to tart up a building than to design a good one.

Postmodernism's most highly publicized practitioner is Philip Johnson, and the postmodernist skyscrapers of the Johnson-Burgee office are about to loom large on numerous city skylines. The pedimented AT&T Building rising in New York is only the first of a group that will clothe standard structural frames and commercial plans in Gothic, guildhall, or deco disguises. The paper dolls of one's childhood come to mind, with cutout wardrobes of fashions to be attached by paper tabs. Edward Durell Stone was the first to play this evocative, decorative game; postmodernism delivers its corn on a much classier and more erudite level.

For those who like their buildings straight—or straighter—there is the architecture of high technology, such as the work of Foster Associates in England, or of Helmut Jahn of C. F. Murphy Associates in Chicago. This school takes modernism's "machine art" about as far as it can go, carrying the aesthetic of glass, steel, plastic, and glorified hardware to its most dramatic and exotic conclusion.

Surely nothing could better exemplify the extremes of the present architectural moment than two public buildings going up in this country right now. The Portland Public Service Building of Portland, Oregon, by Michael Graves, and the State of Illinois Center at Chicago by Helmut Jahn, are polar opposites. The first is a competition-winning, postmodernist exercise of romantic classical persuasion; the second is a spectacular glass-and-metal sweep of high-tech, hard-edged geometry. Here is the summation of the stylistic schizophrenia of the eighties.

Tradition and modernism are curiously allied in the work of a British architect who has been a consistent leader of the profession. James Stirling has moved from a high-tech style of the sixties to a preoccupation with isolated and overscaled historical details in his most recent buildings in Europe and the United States. The combination of the two vocabularies looks like space-age classicism, and the mixed feelings set up by its calculated ambiguities are deliberately invoked.

One factor ties all of this diversity and debate together: the desire to pursue all possibilities for a richer and more varied kind of architecture. The sense of exploration and experiment, using all of history and technology as source material, is the leading spirit of the new work. It is hard to realize that, to the present generation, modern architecture is as much a part of history as the Renaissance; today Le Corbusier and Palladio are equally open to interpretive borrowings. Among those who choose to stay with the forms of modernism, the firm of Gwathmey Siegel makes the International Style more stylish still, and Richard Meier explores new meanings and relationships. Meier's just-completed building for the Hartford Seminary floats like an elegant white flagship in a Connecticut field.

Everyone is interpreting or reinterpreting something. But the essential relationships of structure and style—when they are not just being ignored—are expressed with a formalism, complexity, and sophisticated, intellectual artfulness that go far beyond anything done earlier in this century. This is today's architectural frontier.

Is this extraordinary vitality producing great work? Probably not, or at least, not yet; and surely not in terms of the fully resolved aesthetic that creates masterpieces. But it is an active and exhilarating time, and we are about to see a great deal more of this stimulating, disturbing, provocative, and promising building. This is a very different kind of modern architecture than we have learned to love or hate.

New York Times, September 6, 1981

THE NINETIES

The New Architecture

I

THERE IS A NEW PILGRIMAGE POINT in Santiago de Compostela, the near perfect city in the far northwest corner of Spain that has drawn supplicants and scholars for centuries to its great cathedral and extraordinary architecture. Although a modern intervention seems almost unthinkable in a city of such intimate scale and splendid historical style, the recently completed Galician Center of Contemporary Art by the Portuguese architect Alvaro Siza slips gracefully into its sacrosanct surroundings. It took a brave architect to accept the challenge, and a very good one to pull it off. The building is at once radical, beautiful, and timeless.

The Santiago museum does much to define the state of architecture today. It clearly puts the theme-park world of postmodernism behind us. Nor is there any pretense to a false historical humility. The building's sharply angled forms and almost unbroken horizontal planes make a strong case for the enduring validity of modernism. And yet the building is as respectful and *contextual*, if one may use that overworked and misused term, as it is *modern*, another word that has come to beg all meaning and definition, although it can still be understood in its historical sense as something distinctly of its own time. Siza's modernism contains bold departures and subtle complexities that highlight a shift in concept and style—a new way of seeing and building that signals a significant change in the philosophy and practice of architecture. This is the work of a master who has left almost everyone else behind.

THE SANTIAGO PROJECT is referred to in Siza's office as a work of "preservation/transformation"—an interesting dualism that collapses past and future together. Intended as the catalyst for the restoration of a neighborhood on the edge of the city's historic center, the museum occupies a roughly triangular site that narrows to a twenty-one-degree angle at its tightest corner for a striking, wedge-shaped plan: Two L-shaped sections converge and interpenetrate at their closest point. But the new building does not so much occupy the site as it is skillfully inserted into it; from a distance one does not see it at all. What is most remarkable as one approaches is its quality of extreme horizontality, the easy way it seems to fit into the urban landscape. Yet the long, low, granite façade is neither passive nor recessive; it possesses a dynamism that prefigures the surprises awaiting within the bold exterior forms.

Nothing is conventional about this building—not even the way one enters up a short flight of steps that leads to an angled portico at the structure's small, sharp end. Nor is this entrance as understated or inconspicuous as its size and location might indicate; there is an almost reverse high drama in the subtle precision with which the stair meets and stops the long portico that sweeps along the building's main façade. Inside, the reception area with its sleek, serpentine counter is an oasis of cool white marble. Where the structure's two sections merge, they form a triangular atrium sky-lit at the top, placed slightly to one side— rarely is anything straight ahead in this building—flanked by temporary exhibition galleries and an auditorium. Three shallow corner steps rotate the visitor diagonally down from the reception area into the first of a series of irregularly shaped temporary exhibition spaces. A central spine of stairs, ramps, and corridors slashes straight across the angled plan.

The stairs lead up to three large, handsomely proportioned permanent exhibition galleries. But these are not the formal, monumental stairs of the beaux arts tradition evoked by Robert Venturi and Denise Scott Brown for their museums in London and Seattle; as you go up Siza's stairs you are offered views of low-walled balconies with partially glimpsed galleries behind them; these shifting planes and suggestive spaces—neither quite open nor closed—are constantly modified by variations in natural and artificial light. Vistas appear that Dr. Caligari might have envied, although there is nothing sinister here, only delight.

At the top of the stairs one is confronted by the point of a double corridor that divides diagonally for public galleries and private offices. To merely describe this scissorslike split can hardly convey the effect of its knife-sharp diverging paths. We become very conscious of how the radical rearrangement of the familiar revises our expectations and revolutionizes our vision. Siza's rigorously and artfully conceived forms and dimensions—for example, the way one emerges from a long, low gallery to a sudden explosion of height and light—make us respond to our surroundings with an intensified awareness. We are immersed in a powerful and profound experience of architectural space.

ALL OF SIZA'S buildings are full of revelations that seduce with their visual and poetic force. Since the camera records these views as pure abstraction, the architect's office carefully labels photographs "top" and "bottom." In the Santiago museum one has constant surprises: A sharply angled room or gently curving passage, an elegantly sculptured stair, a dramatic wash of light from a suddenly revealed source; each discovery becomes a palpable aesthetic encounter.

Siza's style has been defined by the Italian architect and critic Vittorio Gregotti as "radical minimalism," but that does not begin to explain the complex interrelationships that are smoothly combined into a deceptively simple whole. Rooted in modernism, Siza transcends it. His departures from received doctrine have coincided with the liberating forces of postmodernism. But he heartily dislikes the postmodernist style of cribbed classical fragments, of skyscrapers with broken pediments at the top or stretch columns at the base, their machinery dressed in historical drag. He uses the clean, bare, reductive vocabulary established by the modern movement for a minimalism that expands, rather than restricts, architectural possibilities. Siza starts where the modernists left off.

Although he is clearly indebted to the rich local tradition of simple geometric forms and eloquently expressive masonry of his native Portugal, his remarkable walls also draw on twentieth-century architecture. All of his work pays homage to Le Corbusier—once having seen the magical union of space and light of the church at Ronchamps, who could avoid it?—but he explores possibilities in his own way. Siza's buildings are a fugue of orchestrated views and events. His strict geometry is the expressive vehicle for a much more fluid, plastic, and kinetic approach than modernism ever achieved, with enormous dramatic effect. Space has not been handled so theatrically since mannerism. Façades have not been composed so surprisingly since Hawksmoor.

II

Alvaro Siza is not alone in pushing the boundaries of conventional practice. Among today's established architects are two practitioners of particularly strong personal styles equally dedicated to the exploration of new directions: Frank Gehry in the United States and Christian de Portzamparc in France are pursuing similar goals in distinctly different ways. Siza makes his headquarters in Porto, Portugal; Portzamparc practices in Paris; and the peripatetic Gehry, who is by far the best known of the three, is based in Los Angeles. Gehry has already achieved the kind of popular recognition that has made his dramatic compositions a familiar trademark. Siza seems to be an acquired taste still restricted to the cognoscenti. Portzamparc has been less well known outside of France until his selection for the Pritzker Architecture Prize last year brought a deluge of publicity. Their buildings are international events.

What is common to all is the process of design which begins inside, breaking the building down into its component parts for a searching analysis of their functional rationale. Architecture is no longer conceived as the making of a formal "container," as it has developed over centuries of stylistic evolution. These architects think first of the interior space and second of the enclosure; they handle space not as finite form, but as fluid and open-ended; for the user, it becomes a serial rather than a static event. The significance of this approach is that the building's interior space and other elements can be redesigned and reassembled in a variety of unconventional configurations, with a greater awareness, and sometimes radical reinterpretation, of the relationship of use and form.

The paths people take through a building make movement an essential part of its design. The connections between places are now as important as the places to which they lead. Frank Gehry's recently completed building for the Vitra Furniture Company in Basel offers a striking example. The connection between the two parts of the structure—the sales offices and administration headquarters—is a series of bridges crossing an open atrium at different floor levels. In a conventional building one would simply get off an elevator on separate floors. Here the passage from one section to the other is a calculated transition that not only is notable in itself, but also serves to characterize the transfer between two areas that are totally unlike in use, look, and feel. The process of getting there has great drama and its own rewards.

Conceiving the exterior enclosure of these new spatial relationships becomes a free exercise in style, a matter of personal preference in this time of pluralistic taste and expression. This fact, rather than chaos in the profession or competing claims of correctness, explains much of the diversity of architecture today. Far more important is the expansion of the art of architecture itself. To its conventional definition as a three-dimensional, spatial art a fourth dimension has been added: an aesthetic of experiences in time, of responses dependent on the passage from one part of the building to another. Interlocking, layered views are seen simultaneously and sequentially. The eye and the body are invited, and required, to register perceptions and sensations of an actual and aesthetic complexity rarely encountered before. It is creative change of this magnitude that defines the history of art.

THESE BUILDINGS MUST be visited personally. Photographs are more than usually misleading; what one sees in pictures are the strange shapes and stylistic mannerisms that merely hint at the strategies beneath. Gehry's eccentric piles of richly colored sculptural shapes may seem arbitrary or about to tumble over, oblivious to the laws of gravity and order; but this is a precisely calibrated disorder, sedulously studied and arranged. An unrepentant modernist, he is pursuing a fundamental inquiry into the art of building and the expanded forms this may take. Portzamparc, also based in modernism, turns the modernist aesthetic into a much more evocative, romantic, and referential idiom, invoking the shapes, images, and colors of the fifties with unabashed élan. His roofs soar, swoop, and hover with a lively retro wit; his affectionately reconstituted details in aluminum, tile, and concrete recall Morris Lapidus's "architecture of joy," the showy style of the Fontainebleau and Americana hotels in Miami in the sixties. Although Portzamparc was an active participant in the student protests in Paris in the sixties, when Miami architecture would have been considered the ultimate frivolous irrelevance, he sees nothing odd or anachronistic about combining this flamboyant hedonism with his continuing sociological concerns. Both a sophisticated stylist and sensitive urbanist—qualities usually considered antithetical in modernist practice—he is a skilled planner with an acute understanding of the nature of public and private places. Siza's work, which depends on the exacting organization of its minimal components, is the most abstract of the three and has immense poetic rigor. It is also the hardest to imitate; great talent is required to resolve complex needs while using forms of such absolute, elemental purity.

III

What Siza, Gehry, Portzamparc, and others are doing today is, in a sense, reinventing architecture. They are stretching the limits of the art, much as mannerism and the baroque stretched the principles of the Renaissance, forever altering its vocabulary and range. Portzamparc's work is, perhaps, the most easily misunderstood. It would be simple to dismiss it as theater, to call it a younger generation's clever appropriation of recent history for its popular evocative and decorative appeal. To do so one must overlook the logic and originality of his plans, the expert and effective way in which his solutions flow and function, his sure grasp of scale and proportion, his superior sense of urban amenity, his lyrical use of light and color. In addition to Miami-modern redux, there are echoes of Oscar Niemeyer and Roberto Burle Marx in the undulating curves of his work that transform Corbusian austerity into Latin American exuberance. Given cultural distance and a European perspective, these sources become more than fashionable sentimentalism; Portzamparc transforms his obvious delight in Arplike free forms and giant cones and candy colors into a pop monumentality that moves serious high camp into serious high art.

Make no mistake about its seriousness. The French take their pleasures very seriously; French chic is a high art form. But unlike so much French architecture, where the chic is skin-deep, this is genuinely innovative work with an impressive range of dramatic invention. Only a seriously assured architect could carry it off. Official French taste tends to favor modish displays of real and faux engineering—whether it's Piano and Roger's muscular Centre Pompidou or I. M. Pei's suave pyramid at the Louvre. The current rage of Paris is Jean Nouvel's polished glass and steel headquarters for the Fondation Cartier, where style and client are perfectly matched for a dazzling display of impeccable, glistening cachet. This kind of work is greatly preferred to a *humanism*—another loaded word—that delights in subjective and evocative images.

But Portzamparc is not alone in persistently incorporating personal stylistic icons in his work—James Stirling had his lighthouses, and Aldo
Rossi has his haunting skeletal stairs and lonely lookout towers.

At fifty, Portzamparc has not yet perfected the art of self-presentation
usually cultivated by the celebrity architect. Trailing a well-worn rain-
coat that is somewhat more, or less, than Armani-casual, wearing a fashionably beat-up fedora and a permanently distraught air, he is just as
likely to exhaust a visitor with a tour of earnest and highly commendable rehabilitations of social housing as to show off his star turns. But
when one gets to them, they are breathtaking.

TEN YEARS HAVE passed since the start of construction of the first part
of his competition-winning design of 1985 for the Cité de la Musique in
the redeveloped district of La Villette. The second half of this very large
complex in the Parisian outskirts is being completed only this year. One
of Mitterrand's *grands travaux*, this national conservatory for music and
dance is more interesting than many of the other projects to come out
of that imperial effort. Like Siza's museum, there is nothing conventional about this building. The conservatory, already in use, contains
both classrooms and performance facilities. As you enter through a dramatic, multistoried space, you have a full view of the main stair and the
tiered balconies that form open corridors around it on all floors. The
building is partly underground, but one is not aware of this because of
the visible top-to-bottom interior flooded with natural light. The vistas
out from the large glazed areas are spectacular—across to the cone-
shaped organ recital hall that is part of the complex, or up to an undulating canopy that connects two sections, its curve pierced by a huge
oculus through which one sees the sky. Art deco railings, high-style furniture, and beguiling colors banish any institutional air.

The second structure includes Paris's major new concert hall, which
opened on January 14. The experience of this building starts outside,
with a stunning public act. Visitors step down through several entrances into a roofed but open court; one can arrive from the park, the
street, or the conservatory across a connecting plaza. The court serves
as a collecting point for pedestrian traffic, which then moves along a
curving, covered promenade leading to, and circling, the concert hall.
If one doesn't enter the hall or wishes to proceed to the museum, studios, or, finally, to an exit to the street, one follows the narrowing sweep

of the curving path to its end. As the corridor unfolds, walls change in hue; Portzamparc is also a painter, with an artist's eye for what color does to a place and the people in it.

In no way is this a traditional promenade in the City Beautiful sense; it relies on the drama and mystery of movement as well as on traditional monumental scale and architectural form. The space is intriguingly ambiguous in its open and covered, public and private nature; the nearly circular path never quite reveals what lies beyond. Inside the large concert hall—one of numerous performance and practice spaces in both buildings on which Pierre Boulez has been an active collaborator—an array of colored lights instantly imbues the handsome wood panels with Hollywood glamour, a feature dear to Portzamparc's heart.

His School of Dance for the ballet of the Paris Opera at Nanterre is also a competition-winning design. Under the French system, the architectural commissions for all large public buildings are awarded by state-run competitions, with construction by state authorities. This system yields conspicuously mixed results: The Bastille Opera is one of the grander disappointments of the *grands travaux,* and the much revised quartet of glass towers for the Très Grande Bibliothèque is more notable for bombast than for reason. Materials, finishes, and details are frequently a casualty of a division of labor between the state construction agency and the architect's office in the provision of working drawings. But the system allows younger architects in France to have an equal chance at the larger commissions almost universally given to older and more experienced practitioners elsewhere. In this case, the logic and lyricism of Portzamparc's ballet school design survive any defects of execution.

The building is, quite literally, the sum of its individual parts—a characteristic of much of the new architecture. It consists of three distinct areas—the dance studios, a classroom and administration section, and student dormitories—connected by a glass-walled entrance area that gives access to all of them. These separate parts are shaped and disposed by circulation patterns based on the acoustic isolation of the studios, the social orientation of classrooms and offices, and the privacy of the dormitories, which take the form of a connected, serpentine wing, narrow and sinuous, that curves across the landscape like a tail.

The central feature and dramatic focus of the building is a soaring, full-height spiral stair that serves the dance studios. There is constant movement up and down this spiral, and along the mezzanines that alternate with studio entrances on different floors. The wide bridges across this open, central space become lounges that tie the activities together and also provide a place for the dance students to pause between them.

Portzamparc is becoming famous or notorious, depending on one's point of view, for his "ski boot" office building designed for the Crédit Suisse bank in Lille, one of those "images" that editors rush to publish and architects love to promote. He is not immune to the unremitting French infatuation with "googie," or gimmicky modernism, where outrageousness passes for inspiration. But his buildings succeed because they address fundamental concerns—the needs and pleasures of the body and spirit—that all great architecture serves and turns into art. And he has something that other architects recognize instantly, the single-minded application of a rich poetic creativity.

IV

If, like Frank Lloyd Wright, Portzamparc seems to shake designs out of his sleeve, Gehry's search for form is a painstaking one. His slow, anguished choices seem to involve as much public suffering—displayed engagingly to anyone who closely follows his work—as private investigation. He has chosen a particularly difficult path, walking a thin, treacherous line between architecture and sculpture, pursuing the tantalizing prospect of a union of the two that will maintain their integrity while transforming their intrinsic natures. This constant balancing act between experiments-on-the-edge of architecture that renew it and the potential disaster of architecture for sculpture's sake can enlarge the art of building magically or diminish it disastrously, enrich it or empty it out. Gehry is pushing the very idea and definition of architecture to its limits in a dangerous but exhilarating game.

To this creative challenge he adds a dedicated search for new materials, and a fresh eye for the older, more ordinary ones that add unconventional color and texture to his buildings. Much has been made of his elevation of common, unloved plywood and chain-link fencing to starring roles in his early work; today he is more likely to use elegant and expensive copper sheathing. But this attention to surface is essential to his inventive aesthetic. His best buildings offer unusual perceptions and heightened pleasures hard to imagine before. No facile art, it requires uncertain moves into unprecedented territory, accompanied by relentless self-criticism. One misstep and all is lost. Gehry loves the challenges, and even the risks, and continues to produce extraordinary work.

At Weil am Rhein in Germany, where the Vitra Furniture Company has commissioned an international roster of star architects to design a custom collection of buildings, Gehry has constructed a furniture museum in which the utilitarian is elevated to high drama and fine art. The visitor climbs an encircling ramp through a sequence of display spaces that lead to a double-height, sky-lit gallery at the top, where daylight pours down stark white walls, spilling into the galleries below. The trip is exhilarating. Presented as the history of the modern chair, this exhibition is its apotheosis as well. Solitary or in groups, on pedestals and platforms or suspended in air, chairs are haloed, enthroned, and enshrined.

The new Vitra headquarters building just across the Swiss border in Basel is perhaps Gehry's boldest and most colorful composition yet. Like the museum and the other Weil am Rhein spectaculars, it was commissioned by Vitra executive Rolf Fehlbaum, one of Gehry's most enthusiastic admirers. The chapel-like executive offices were not furnished when I saw them last year. Their walls glowed red or gold with natural light from skylights and strategically placed openings. (Le Corbusier's Ronchamps again: How pervasive and lasting is the influence of that icon of modernism!) Altars would have seemed as suitable as desks and chairs.

I FOUND MYSELF an uneasy admirer of these spaces, trapped between acceptance and rejection, fascinated by their superb drama and put off by the way their uses were made subservient to an overwhelming but gloriously willful aesthetic. Gehry's evocative, sense-filling environment is a personal statement of great conviction and power. It still works in a wonderful and scary way.

But one begins to wonder. Has the task of analyzing how we use buildings in order to revise how they are designed become less important than the invention of pure form? Functions seem increasingly allocated to the idiosyncratic spaces that we see essentially as dramatic exterior sculpture, or are related only tenuously to them. Is Gehry being trapped by popular acclaim and prodigious publicity into a spectacular stylistic formalism? Will this process continue to lead to new and useful transformations of architecture or to a sublime dead end? No doubt he searches for his solutions as diligently and conscientiously as ever. Carried to extremes or copied by others, the results can become arbitrary or self-indulgent. At what point does such a forceful personal aesthetic threaten the delicate and essential equilibrium between art and life that makes architecture such a risky and rewarding art? Can the responsibility for keeping that balance be ignored? Does it matter when the architect is so gifted and the product so outstanding? These are questions I suspect Gehry wrestles with constantly, and even the most sympathetic viewer can hardly avoid them.

His recently completed American Center in Paris, located on the city's outskirts in Bercy, raises other questions. In the interest of architectural diplomacy Gehry used Paris's traditional, creamy limestone to face his unusual façade—a characteristic collagelike jumble of canted and disjointed shapes. My initial response was to respect his judgment. But an uneasy feeling persisted; the conventional skin gives a strangely muffled effect; something seems to be suffocating behind that respectful camouflage, struggling desperately to get out. We miss the vivid and varied colors and materials that are such an important part of his exploratory forms. This is the trap and fallacy of "contextualism" into which so many architects jump or fall—the masquerade of matched materials, the cosmetic cover-up of architectural maquillage. The center was dedicated recently in a bravura gesture—a dazzling, empty package constructed while there is a serious shortage of funds for programs and maintenance. Walking through this mute symbol of American culture was a ghostly and sobering experience.

V

In Portugal, Siza's Architecture Faculty for the University of Porto also awaits people and activity. A controversy over moving a road that caused years of construction delays appears to have been as much a matter of political and academic infighting as of planning policy; moving the road would have sabotaged the design, and at last it was avoided. In all of Siza's projects, site and structures are conceived together; here, two facing rows of buildings are linked by circulation and landscaping; the paths people will use to move among them and the outlook along the way are basic elements of the design.

One row consists of four rectangular pavilions that march in a straight line across the land; "matching" but unequal, they vary in their heights and shapes; the size and placement of their window openings make a subtle balance of solids and voids. In partial use now, these pavilions contain classrooms with spectacular river views. The variations of their taut, abstract volumes play off against one another and the setting. Opposite this row, and joined to it by a fifth, offset building, is a long, low structure that completes the composition and contains most of the school's other activities—auditorium, library, exhibition space, lecture rooms, and student facilities.

Connecting ramps run the full length of all the buildings—an organizing device that provides essential circulation and supplies Siza's characteristic horizontal emphasis. The separate pavilions are joined by an outside ramp, or walk, at ground level; the long building has a continuous ramp inside, treated as a glass-walled corridor that parallels the walk across the way. They are linked above and below ground. Sometimes the ramp runs flat, sometimes on an inclined plane, as it leads to classrooms and communal spaces. At one point it loops off dramatically into a semicircular exhibition area. There is always a view of the land and the other buildings. When both parts of the complex are completed and functioning, the ramps will set the whole into a kind of contrapuntal motion. Half a world and centuries away, the tradition of Jefferson's University of Virginia with its lawn and ranges has been radically updated.

Siza's kinetic and sculptural sense of space is prefigured in a small gem of an entry to an earlier building for the Architectural School completed in 1985. A glass entrance door is placed asymmetrically at one corner of a U-shaped structure that has been bent into acute, rather than ninety-degree, angles. This door opens directly onto a short flight of steps that proceeds from the point of the angle and widens almost imperceptibly to a doubly curved upper level where corridors start on both sides. With such deceptively simple sleight-of-hand-and-eye, Siza marries mannerism and modernism in one astoundingly elegant little stair. This spectacular work comes from a seemingly unspectacular man—soft-spoken, chain-smoking, politely professorial, he is a study in brown: brown beard, brown business suit of indeterminate cut, brown tie of indistinct pattern. Wearing the perfect conservative camouflage, he is beyond fashion.

VI

Important architectural change is not an instinctive or unpremeditated act; in all of this work, theory has a significant, if questionable, role. Architects tend to be coattail philosophers, adopting and bowdlerizing intellectual trends as they go out of style; their connection to the world of fashionable ideas is tenuous, their application disturbing. The architectural avant-garde is always alert to the newsworthy possibilities of a radical stance; a shot of revolutionary obscurantism can launch a four-star architectural attraction. Nothing is more seductively appealing than being terminally iconoclastic—a lot of mileage can be gotten out of insisting that there should be no architecture at all.

Theory can redefine architecture or derail it. Literary and philosophical borrowings "appropriated" and force-fed into this pragmatic, problem-solving art become, at most, barely recognizable and, at worst, dangerously irrelevant. Deconstruction, building as "text" or "narrative," contextualism, chaos theory, all have had their day and devotees. The result has been much pretentious and tortured reasoning, a few striking tour de force buildings of baffling beauty and equally spectacular impracticality, and a lot of gorgeously indecipherable drawings of stupefying complexity. A few notable examples of work driven by theory become transient landmarks or textbook illustrations; the rest make it to the New York Times Style pages, where styles go to die.

Structures that defy gravity and common sense by looking as if they are about to fall down or fly apart are as carefully composed and put together as Palladian villas. The London-based Iraqi architect Zaha Hadid's sleekly handsome, superbly crafted, and dizzily angled "deconstructivist" fire station for the Vitra Company in Weil am Rhein may set a record for both the number of its foreign visitors and the number of working drawings the design required. Like so many first buildings by talented architects, this one tends to overreach its purpose. Faced with spending a lot of time living life on a slant where right angles are taboo, one hopes the firemen have learned to lean—to go with the flow. Hadid is spectacularly gifted; her works on paper are breathtakingly beautiful; but theory and reality need to come together in more constructed work. Her competition-winning design for the Cardiff Opera House in Wales—currently embroiled in battles of politics and taste—is a superb, mature design; it would be a tragic mistake not to build it.

A young Spanish practitioner, Enric Miralles, has constructed an arresting house by extrapolating the sightlines of the natural features of
the building site into two different kinds of geometries that collide in
the plan. The overlapping patterns of this elaborate projection of "context" have resulted in rooms of unusual shape and location that seem to
impinge and intrude on one another in an intriguing way. Writing
about the house in the *Journal* of the Royal Institute of British Architects in February 1994, John Welsh noted a "criss-crossing of circulation
routes corresponding to the complexity of any family": an arrangement
that leaves "simple bourgeois, suburban logic" far behind. We are a
long way from Levittown and the "dumb and ordinary" lessons that the
Venturis once told us we should learn there.

THERE ARE ALWAYS architects who seek ways to achieve revelations
that will break through custom to new kinds of vision and design, to new
definitions of art and use. The objective is discovery, to reconstitute the
familiar in a freshly revealing way and, ultimately, to achieve a greater
conceptual and aesthetic range. The hope is not to rehearse familiar
pleasures and encourage feelings of pride in having for oneself what others have had; but to find a route to changes in viewpoint and perception
that will heighten experience and enlarge sensibility through an expanding set of visual and visceral signals derived directly from the art of
design.

Architects relish theoretical discourse; it is part of the climate of the
times. Some, like Siza, Gehry, and Portzamparc, absorb what serves
their needs and go their own way. Today, everyone is free to follow a personal path and muse. The English architect Norman Foster is a master
of fine-tuned, exquisitely honed minimal technology. In his choice of
materials and structure he uses, with remarkable eloquence, a fastidious
aesthetic that derives from engineering but quietly makes it clear to the
viewer (as with the 1991 exhibition rooms of the Royal Academy of Arts
in London) that a series of highly intelligent choices have been made.

In France, Jean Nouvel treats the same technological aesthetic as
high-tech fantasy; the brilliant, hard-edged image is so diligently pursued that it can override structural logic or necessity. In his exquisite
glass and steel Fondation Cartier building, transparency is emphasized
even to the conceit of a cable-supported clear glass wall surrounding
the building at the street line; here high tech comes close to haute

couture. Foster and Nouvel use similar technology with a dramatic difference; both are equally admired. But it is the Dutch architect Rem Koolhaas who is taking the engineering aesthetic through the thickets of theory into an imaginative exploration of ways to make material and structure serve unprecedented ends. Like Koolhaas, Siza, Gehry, and Portzamparc represent this more adventurous kind of creativity.

BUT COMPARISONS ARE invidious; there are no longer any rules; it hardly matters what philosophy drives the design or what vocabulary is being used. The perennial architectural debate has always been, and will continue to be, about art versus use, vision versus pragmatism, aesthetics versus social responsibility. In the end, these unavoidable conflicts provide architecture's essential and productive tensions; the tragedy is that so little of it rises above the level imposed by compromise, and that this is the only work most of us see and know.

Today, when so much seems to conspire to reduce life and feeling to the most deprived and demeaning bottom line, it is more important than ever that we receive that extra dimension of dignity or delight and the elevated sense of self that the art of building can provide through the nature of the places where we live and work. What counts more than style is whether architecture improves our experience of the built world; whether it makes us wonder why we never noticed places in quite this way before.

The test, finally, is the manner in which ideas, vocabulary, and structure are employed, how far these instruments of exploration carry architecture into new uses and sensory satisfactions, how well they move building beyond current limits. What matters is whether this work serves and satisfies us, in the personal and societal sense, and ultimately, how this process engages and reveals necessity and beauty in the visual language of our time. There are architects today creating buildings on the edge of this extraordinary art. That this can happen in a culture of the transient, the shoddy, and the unreal, deserves recognition and celebration.

New York Review of Books, April 6, 1995

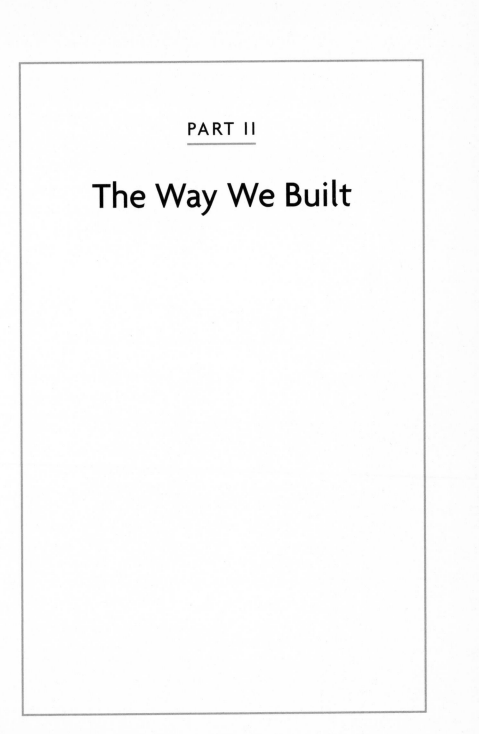

PART II

The Way We Built

Twentieth-century
Icons and Images

Pan Am: The Big, the Expedient,
and the Deathlessly Ordinary

THE CITY'S MOST MONUMENTAL ADDITION since the Empire State Building—the one-hundred-million-dollar Pan Am Building—made its official debut with brass-band ceremonies worthy of a presidential inauguration.

In other development news at the same time, announcement was made of the sixty-acre plan for New York's Civic Center in the City Hall–Foley Square area. Federal and city agencies have since been engaged in a deadlocked *vendetta*—to borrow James R. Hoffa's useful word—over changes that New York has requested in the federal government's previously designed structures to fit into the city's belated plan. Federal resistance, backed by irrefutable arguments of money and time, is nibbling away at the original concept with predictable bureaucratic compromises. ("We went to Washington to ask for a banquet," said New York public works commissioner Peter Reidy, "and they gave us a bag of peanuts.")*

The Avenue of the Americas continues its transformation with some of the most glossily impersonal façades of the city. On Columbus Circle, Edward Durell Stone's little seraglio for Huntington Hartford's Gallery of Modern Art is more suggestive of houris behind its pierced marble

---

* For the results, see *The Federal Government Lays a Colossal Architectural Egg*, p. 105.

screen than art. This is a provocatively misplaced pleasure pavilion transplanted from some Shalimar garden to a Manhattan traffic island.

Of these new buildings, Pan Am has by far the greatest impact on the city scene. Criticism, which has been plentiful since the building's inception, is directed largely at its physical and sociological implications: the effect of seventeen thousand new tenants and 250,000 daily transients on the already overcrowded Grand Central area and its services, and the unresolved conflicts and responsibilities of the city and private enterprise in the control of urban densities and master planning.

But now that the building is functioning, something else becomes distressingly apparent. Bigness is blinding. A one-hundred-million-dollar building cannot really be called cheap. But Pan Am is a colossal collection of minimums. Its exterior and its public spaces, in particular, use minimum good materials of minimum acceptable quality executed with a minimum of imagination (always an expensive commodity), or distinction (which comes high), or finesse (which costs more). Pan Am is gigantically second-rate.

This is no Michelangelesque masterwork from the late and latter-day Medici, promoter Erwin Wolfson, but a super economy package with the usual face-saving gimmick: painting and sculpture in the lobby. In its new role as an architectural cover-up, the builders of New York are turning good art into a bad joke. Pan Am's one effective aesthetic feature is its brutality. In afternoon sun, from lower Park Avenue, its patterned mass rises with striking power behind the dwarfed familiarity of Grand Central's proper academic façade. Its one functional plus is the pedestrian throughway that its lobby and connections provide from Grand Central Terminal to Forty-fifth Street.

At best, Pan Am is an impressive demonstration of the number of square feet (2.4 million) of completely standard rentable office space that can be packed into one income-producing structure, a lesson in how to be mediocre without really trying. For its bulk, its importance, its effect, and its ballyhoo, it had an obligation to be much better. Size is not nobility; a monumental deal does not make a monument. This is a prime example of a New York specialty: the big, the expedient, and the deathlessly ordinary. Build we must, but on the record it is questionable if we are building for a better New York.

New York Times, April 14, 1963

CBS: Eero Saarinen's Somber Skyscraper

THE FIRST OBSERVATION THAT ONE MUST make about the new CBS headquarters that rises somberly from its sunken plaza at Sixth Avenue and Fifty-second Street is that it is a building. It is not, like so much of today's large-scale construction, a handy commercial package, a shiny wraparound envelope, a packing case, a box of cards, a trick with mirrors.

It does not look like a cigar lighter, a vending machine, a nutmeg grater. It is a building, in the true, classic sense: a complete design in which technology, function, and aesthetics are conceived and executed integrally for its purpose. As its architect, Eero Saarinen, wanted, this is a building to be looked at above the bottom fifty feet; to be comprehended as a whole.

CBS is Saarinen's only skyscraper and only work in New York. It is the first of the city's landmark skyscrapers to be executed in reinforced concrete, and one of the first to use an exterior bearing wall rather than the usual skeleton frame-curtain wall formula. It served as a demonstration model for the new zoning when it was being formulated in 1960–61, with the Saarinen office helping to develop realistic land coverage ratios to permit the plaza-surrounded sheer tower. As such, CBS set the shape and standard for New York building today.

It does all of this with distinction for a figure estimated at not too far above the speculative norm of about twenty-four dollars a square foot, and well below the luxury building price of forty dollars upward. Like ABC next door, CBS could simply have taken space offered to it in a conventional investor's building which would then have been named for it, but the company was seeking something special. It got good value and good looks.

And yet the reaction to the building is extremely mixed. The dark dignity that appeals to architectural sophisticates puts off the public, which tends to reject it as funereal.

There is certainly nothing seductive about CBS. But its sober solidity is in a noble architectural tradition. The Strozzi Palace, as a historic example, is an awesome masterpiece of forbidding, stony strength. It is doubtful, of course, whether the Medici were as friendly as Chase

Manhattan, and today people want friendly banks, and friendly buildings. Quality and presence are more usual requisites for great architecture; there are few friendly buildings on the list.

The first fault, therefore, is in the public eye. Thoroughly corrupted by what might be called the American Product aesthetic—applied equally to buildings and possessions—it takes bright and shiny as synonymous with new and good. Surrounded by tinsel and tinfoil, it finds CBS's somber restraint gloomy, and gloom is not part of the American way of life.

The spurious glitter of much of the new Sixth Avenue surrounding CBS eclipses Saarinen's sober subtleties.

The second fault is in the building. The failure to carry through its distinctive style and concept consistently into all of its major interior spaces accounts for a curious deadness. Deadness and darkness are easily equated. This abrogation of style that ruptures aesthetic continuity is particularly damaging in the ground-floor area occupied by a bank, which forms the entire Sixth Avenue street façade and one third of the ground floor. It continues in office interiors. The result is a first-rate work of architecture that just misses coming alive as a unified work of art.

But it is still an extraordinarily impressive structure. The strong, straight shaft is sheathed in dull Canadian black granite and gray glass and set back twenty-five feet from the building line to take up 50.8 percent of the block-long, two-hundred-foot-deep site. It rises severely from its depressed plaza for thirty-eight stories and 491 feet. On winter days, the wind seems to whip around it with extra force and chill. No frills; no nonsense; no tricks; no pretty come-on with art and flowers.

Approached from outside, the granite-faced, triangular poured-concrete columns appear first as overlapping, faceted fins of solid stone. As one's perspective changes, they open to reveal glass, then close slowly, massively again.

Their module is five feet; five feet of wall or column and five of glass, for a particularly felicitous scale. The relationship inside offers superbly calculated framing of the inexhaustible miracle of New York views.

These columns are neither as simple nor as solid as they seem. Rising uninterrupted from ground to top, they have a dual purpose: as a bearing wall and as conduits for services. From the second floor level they are hollow for ducts, and sheared flat on the interior. At the ground floor, they are solid and fully diamond-shaped inside and out, and almost as impressive as the columns of the Parthenon.

What is involved here are the complexity of structure and service of the modern high-rise building and its relationship to visual aesthetics, a problem that separates the men from the boys and good buildings from bad. CBS solves it with maximum logic and minimum ambiguity.

The difference between CBS and its neighbors, however, is the basic difference between building and architecture. It is in the fact that most of New York's mammoth commercial structures are no more than weatherproof containers of rentable square footage, or candy-wrapped bulk space.

In contrast, CBS is all one architectonic piece. The outside perimeter of columns and an interior service core support it. Between, there is a thirty-five-foot ring, or "square doughnut," in Saarinen's words, of flexible, totally open office space, uninterrupted by columns or corridors. It all fits together in an economical scheme that unifies structure, planning, and aesthetics. It makes the "whole thing" that Saarinen envisioned.

But in New York, buildings are rarely whole things, and CBS, unfortunately, is no exception. This can be blamed partly on the untimeliness of Saarinen's death just before construction, which led to a double switch of firms for interiors, and partly to the accepted practice of separating container from contained in the design of the city's business quarters.

Credits list Carson, Lundin & Shaw as "interior architect" (sic) and Florence Knoll Bassett as interior designer. The inside of CBS is a solid-gold corporate cliché; a lavish cocoon, complete to standardized concealed wastebaskets and accredited and almost as equally standardized abstract art. Interchangeable from Sixth to Third avenues. The building has been turned into the anonymous, vacuum-packed commercial shell that it was never meant to be. And CBS does not become, as Saarinen had hoped, a whole and "soaring thing." It is a great building, grounded.

New York Times, March 13, 1966

The Whitney's Bold New Look

AT THE MOMENT, THE MOST DISLIKED building in New York is undoubtedly the Whitney Museum. It seems that almost everyone's feelings have been violated by this brashly unconventional structure on the suave upper reaches of Madison Avenue. Still, it fascinates. One of its most serious preopening security problems was keeping the curious out, and on Tuesday evening the interior and its contents, at least, were endorsed enthusiastically by a crushingly chic crowd of first-nighters. Like that fine old saying about sin, first the Whitney repulses; then it intrigues; and finally, it is embraced.

This reviewer embraced it in print on September 8. It is understood that this is not the only way to build a museum, even on that awkwardly small, corner plot. But it is an excellent way, and there can be no quarrel with an unusual design that is justified by imaginative, but practical planning, in which the primary requirement of maximum exhibition space is beautifully ordered and separated from efficiently organized services.

This is what the architect, Marcel Breuer, and his associate, Hamilton Smith, have done by the use of the building's controversial, inverted setbacks, which permit, on that scanty site, a sunken sculpture court and an extra glass-walled story below grade, with exhibition floors increasing dramatically in height and dimension as they rise. The top gallery, seventeen feet high and the full 125-foot depth of the land, with its single Martian eye, is subdivided for the present show, but open, it could provide one of the most smashingly suitable settings for large-scale contemporary sculpture in the city.

"You start with the client's program," Mr. Breuer observes. "That's not architecture, but it's the groundwork. Architecture grows out of it."

Unfortunately, it does not just grow. Architecture is the painstaking clarification and organization of that functional program into a distinctive and aesthetically viable physical form. This is exactly what most buildings that line the streets of New York, including some with major pretensions, are not. Nor does it work the other way round—pick a striking form and push in the functions—although this is becoming increasingly common practice, or malpractice, today.

Good architecture is still the difficult, conscientious, creative, expressive planning for that elusive synthesis that is a near-contradiction in terms: efficiency and beauty. And beauty, as at the Whitney, is not always in the eye of the beholder. We still cling tenaciously to that timelessly appealing, fallacious definition of the Greeks; the beautiful is good, and the good is beautiful. The good and the beautiful today are often harsh, strong, severe, and bold (the new brutalism, in architectural language), although—and this is the kicker—there is the same underlying care, taste, and sensitivity in the adjustment of elements as in the most refined, traditional practice of art. If there are any basic ground rules for architecture-watchers, they should be, first, don't look for something pretty; and second, look again.

The materials of the Whitney are magnificent, and they have been used with a sure hand. The flame-treated gray granite employed outside and in, unpolished and polished, is one of the handsomest stones to be seen in New York. The unfinished concrete used with it for the sculptural element of the entrance bridge, the service wing at the south, and the enclosing end walls, has programmatic and aesthetic justification. Concrete aggregate walls and teak and bronze fittings inside, all meticulously crafted, are deliberately understated luxury, detailed with exemplary finesse.

The Whitney offers several architectural lessons. In addition to its virtues of thoughtful planning and sensitive artistry in the use of materials, it is an effective demonstration of the fact that the anonymous, flexible exhibition space most directors want need not be reduced to the lowest barn, warehouse, or factory common denominator. Inevitably, museum space has a sameness, partitioned and lit with uniform technological care, totally dependent on the quality of its displays.

But with all of the Whitney's flexibility and mechanical marvels, a sense of architecture remains. Breuer's open space is defined by the character of its hung, concrete grid ceilings, bluestone, slate, and teak floors, the design of permanent features, such as elevator walls and stairwells, and those odd, trapezoidal windows that offer occasional exotically framed glimpses of the ordinary world.

He never smothers with the conventional trappings of pseudoglamour and he offers convincing evidence that new buildings need not be routinely finished inside with the sleekly monotonous, expensive packaged excellence of the contemporary corporate cliché. The style here is suave-brutal; a curiously anachronistic aesthetic that stimulates, provokes, and unsettles, and produces some of today's best new buildings. But once its displays have been installed, this interesting structure in its own right becomes, simply, a museum.

In addition to a museum, the Whitney wanted, and got, a landmark; a distinctive, recognizable structure on the New York scene. Yet it has not achieved this status at the expense of its pleasantly elegant, if architecturally undistinguished, surroundings.

One of the Whitney's more significant lessons, this time in urban design, is that the new and different is not necessarily destructive, and the timid and traditional does not necessarily preserve and protect. Done badly, one can be as vicious an environmental violation as the other. The answer is completely in the spirit and quality of the architecture.

New Yorkers, conditioned by the Guggenheim, will probably accept the Whitney fairly quickly. In doing so, it is to be hoped that they will recognize that the Guggenheim is an objet d'art, inside and out, with its staff battling endlessly to make it a workable museum, while the Whitney is a workable museum raised to the level of architectural art. It will be a constant challenge to its directors to match the uncompromising standards, sophisticated expertise, and thoroughly professional excellence of the building.

New York Times, October 2, 1966

General Motors: A Mixed Marble Bag

THE GENERAL MOTORS BUILDING has opened to huge crowds and what might be called mixed reviews. To the public at large, it's a smash. Some professional responses are less enthusiastic.

The gap between the two is the difference between I-know-what-I-like and serious judgment of the building's form and functions, and its impact on the New York scene. Any structure that rises fifty conspicuous

stories on one of the city's prime sites with a make-or-break urban relationship to the elegant and focal small plaza that sets the tone of Fifth
Avenue must be looked at as more than just a building. General Motors,
its associated developers, the Savoy Fifth Avenue Corporation, and the
architects, Edward Durell Stone and Emery Roth & Sons, consider it
more than just a building. It must, therefore, be judged as architecture
and urban design.

Behind the marble cladding and bay windows, architecture, like the
proverbial thin man in the fat man's body, is signaling wildly to get out.

Under their seven-eighths-inch marble veneer, those fifty-story
diamond-shaped piers are actually hollow, bearing concrete columns
carrying service ducts, a functional design solution that frees the building's periphery of columns behind the windows and integrates services
with structure. The rest of the structure is steel. The silhouette, head-
on, is a slim, soaring shaft.

Beneath the curious mixture of small-town department store and
styling section décor is the kind of breathtaking skyscraper shell, balanced in space, that modern technology makes possible. You could
wrap it in brown paper, instead of Georgia marble, and it would still be
impressive. General Motors, however, prefers marble.

Without the screens, gimmick lights, and revolving and stationary automobiles, the high-ceilinged, glass-walled lobby would have striking architectural scale. Liberated of looped gold "drapes" that cover the
thirty-foot windows and obscure the unparalleled view for a kind of
GM-Hilton look, and without the carved-border gold area rugs that even
amateur decorators gave up years ago, the main floor would be a handsome architectural space.

In other words, relieved of all the schmaltz that both client and architect seem to feel is necessary to disguise and diminish one of the great art
forms of our age (they fight the natural elegance of the contemporary
skyscraper with overlays of low-level corn and pseudograndeur all the
way), a building of clear, contemporary beauty might have emerged.

Indications of those elements of structure, space, and light that are
basically and essentially architecture are still there. Inside Edward
Durell Stone, there is an architect signaling to get out.

Inside the building, there is wall-to-wall marble. The Parthenon has
come to General Motors. Pentelic marble by the ton from the same
Greek quarries that supplied the Acropolis lathers the lobby walls; the

rejects are upstairs. It is good to keep thinking of the Parthenon, or one begins to think of luxury lavatories. Here and there, on the high walls and around elevators, the marble is chamfered and incised.

In the General Motors offices above the ground floor, architecture and interiors part company completely. (GM has the first twenty-six floors, and the rest is rental space at the city's highest rates.) The architects did not design these work areas; they are the product of the GM staff, headed by Ervine Klein, and the interiors firm of J. Gordon Carr & Associates.

The ground-floor showrooms and the executive offices have been done by LeRoy Kiefer of the Detroit styling staff.

The building's twenty-foot interior column module is ignored by the module set for the office space. The columns, therefore, appear strangely and frequently in the corners of reception areas and just beyond corridor walls.

One of the basic battles of skyscraper design has been to develop systems that integrate the column into modular office schemes, and when one sees these offices one understands why. It is a matter of aesthetics and logic. But GM gains some square footage this way, even if it looks as if it had to make the best of a building over which it had no structural or design control.

The twenty-fifth, or executive, floor simply abdicates the twentieth century. The top executive offices are furnished in conventional reproductions of "traditional" pieces. No antiques have been purchased, and there has been no art program.

At present, smoothly illustrative oils of geese flying and barns in snow with a few mistily impressionistic landscapes are being fetched in by staff on a trial-and-error basis. One recalls the Chase Manhattan Bank's art program for its headquarters building, which set up a museum-caliber advisory board to select a fine collection.

Which brings us to the question of style, that stamp of individual or corporate taste that makes waves in its surroundings, for better or worse. In its early days, automotive taste was touchingly buckeye. Measured by the General Motors Building, it is now pretentiously ordinary. One wonders if this taste should have been turned into a monument.

The style might be called Throwback Classicism or Furniture Store Posh. Mr. Stone has been called a classicist manqué. In spite of much propaganda to that effect, he is really a modernist manqué and a good one, who simply fruits it up.

General Motors states proudly that the building cost (unspecified) was 20 to 25 percent less than that of comparable luxury structures in New York.

Asked whether that meant that GM was poorer than Union Carbide or other corporate builders, the response was stunned silence. Asked why it was good to build a monument cheap, the reply was that the pressing of economies was "sound business practice." It does not look as if any money was saved on marble.

The still incomplete sunken Fifth Avenue shopping plaza is a promising urban device. But here its lower level only partly ameliorates the disruption of a previously perfectly scaled open space of singular sophisticated graciousness. This, and the influx of crowds—both factors considered when the Hartford café was vetoed for the south end of Central Park—have effected the dissolution of one of the last of the city's quality environments.

The crowds slam the showroom car doors from nine A.M. to nine P.M. The lady of the Fountain of Abundance and her dwarfed parklet look shabby genteel. General Motors has brought a new style and a new kind of abundance to Fifth Avenue. It has the best address in town. It has not given the city its best building.

New York Times, October 1, 1968

Boston's New City Hall

"WHATEVER IT IS, IT'S NOT BEAUTIFUL," said the Boston cabdriver taking the visitor to the new City Hall. "What would you call it, Gothic?" asked another. Which about sums up the architectural gap, or abyss, as it exists between those who design and those who use the twentieth century's buildings. The new $26.3-million Boston City Hall has been an object of international attention and debate since the architects, Kallmann, McKinnell & Knowles, won the competition for its design in 1962. A week of festivities marking its opening starts Saturday, with the official dedication on Monday. The move is virtually complete from the 1862 Civil War City Hall a few blocks away.

Boston can celebrate with the knowledge that it has produced a superior public building in an age that values cheapness over quality as a form of public virtue. It also has one of the handsomest buildings around, and thus far, one of the least understood. It is not Gothic. ("No kiddin'," said the cabdriver.) It is a product of this moment and these times—something that can be said of successful art of any period. And it is a winner, in more ways than one.

Not only cabdrivers are puzzled by the unconventional structure. Cultural and community leaders who are also society's decision makers and a public with more and higher education than at any time in history also draw a blank. Too bad about that architecture gap. It has a lot to do with the meanness of our cities.

Boston's new City Hall is a solid, impressive demonstration of creativity and quality—uncommon currencies in today's environment. A powerful focus for the new government center that has replaced the sordid charms of the old Scollay Square, it makes a motley collection of very large, very average new buildings around it look good. It confers, in a kind of architectural status transferral, an instant image of progressive excellence on a city government traditionally known for something less than creativity and quality. That is an old trick of architecture called symbolism.

They call it the new Boston, but inside the new structure Councilors Saltonstall and Timilty work side by side at old desks moved from the old City Hall that suggest the old politics. The City Council gave itself

Boston City Hall

a raise but voted down the twenty-four-thousand-dollar, room-size, horseshoe installation that would have completed the council chamber and accommodated all its members in the new style.

The mayor, Kevin White (ambivalent about the building), and the City Council (mixed reactions from approval to acute denunciation) are fighting over space now used as an exhibition gallery. Tradition dies hard in Boston.

The building will survive the councilors' objections and the mayor's ideas of decoration. Its rugged cast-in-place and precast concrete and brick construction, inside and out (the new brutalism, for those who like stylistic labels), is meant to be impervious to the vicissitudes of changing tastes and administrations.

The monumentality of this public building—and it is magnificently monumental without a single one of those pompous pratfalls to the classical past that building committees clutch like Linus's blanket—is neither forbidding nor austere.

It is an "open" City Hall. At ground level, it is meant to serve as a concourse to other parts of the city, and there are views of the city from every part of the structure. The visitor is made aware of the city in a very special way—of its history, in the architects' sensitively glass-framed vistas through deep concrete modular window reveals of adjoining Federal brick buildings and Faneuil Hall and the granite Quincy Market and waterfront to the east, and of its burgeoning growth in new construction to the west, north, and south.

This appropriate and finely calculated sense of historic continuity is no small architectural achievement.

Today's buildings rupture historic scale, and this one was placed in the heart of historic Boston. But there is no "style-dropping" here. The architects have neatly disposed of Preservation Fallacy Number One. There are none of the overblown vestigial traditional details or "recalls" considered "appropriate" in such situations, milked of architectural meaning and offered as pious ligaments between old and new to create caricatures of both. This is subtle, dramatic, respectful homage to the past by an uncompromising present. It is a lesson in proper preservation philosophy and aesthetics.

There is also a lesson in that basic element of building, the use of space. The entire structure is conceived as a progression of functional and hierarchical spaces. Its striking exterior reflects this arrangement.

This is not space as a container. See any office building for that. It is space molded to function, form, and expressive purpose. The striking irregular shapes and surfaces that show the functions and mechanical services, all of which are more commonly hidden behind flat walls and ceiling slabs, are part of the visual and sensuous impact.

The building is a hollow rectangle around a court. Its focus is the lobby, which rises a dramatic nine stories on two sides to skylights, and centers on a platform of ascending brick steps. This is a space equally satisfactory to connoisseurs of the art of architecture and the art of sit-ins, and that is exactly what the designers had in mind as public architecture.

Above the lobby are the Council Chamber and offices and the mayor's quarters. These large, ceremonial rooms are visible outside as rugged projections on the building's east and west façades, and as strong, broken wall planes inside, within the soaring skylight shafts. The upper levels are office space. This also shows clearly on the outside, as a massive, stepped "cornice" at the top.

The building stands, not in isolation, but on a still-unfinished fan-shaped brick plaza of stepped levels that will embrace the neighboring structures. This promises to be one of the more impressive of today's urban spaces.

It is as certain as politics and taxes that without the national competition that was held for this building nothing like it would have been designed or constructed. Mr. Kallmann and Mr. McKinnell were young and unknown as architects when they won. The usual route of public building commissions is through political patronage or to familiar, established names.

The architects have devoted seven years to the project, working with the Boston firm of Campbell, Aldrich & Nulty, and with LeMessurier Associates as structural engineers. Virtually no changes have been made in the prize-winning design. The result is a tough and complex building for a tough and complex age, a structure of dignity, humanism, and power. It mixes strengths with subtleties. It will outlast the last hurrah.

New York Times, February 4, 1969

It's So Peaceful in the Country

ONE OF NEW YORK'S WORST-KEPT secrets and best-manipulated statistics is the exodus of major corporations. City Hall shivers for its tax base with every new company count.

Where do the corporations go? To the country, even as you and I, when and if we can. What do they get? That can best be illustrated by one of the newest and most architecturally distinguished corporate additions to the country scene, the American Can Company.

AMERICAN CAN HAS moved its headquarters to 175 acres of spectacularly beautiful wooded and rocky land in Greenwich, Connecticut, not far from another corporate exurbanite, IBM. While the building was in construction last summer, the company transferred 2,200 employees from the office building at 100 Park Avenue in Manhattan. (Shiver.) This represents its central, administrative operation. American Can is a giant with 54,500 employees in areas from the United States and Canada to American Samoa, with subsidiaries, affiliates, and licensees in twenty-three countries. That's not corporate peanuts.

The new plant has a setting of idyllic splendor. It was designed by Gordon Bunshaft of the firm of Skidmore, Owings & Merrill, the country's notable purveyors of good architecture to corporate clients whether their taste runs to sylvan campuses or city skyscrapers. It offers comfort, efficiency, and structural grand luxe, tastefully controlled. And it is a triumph of environmental consideration.

THE IMPACT OF such a plant on its surroundings is considerable. Communities that previously welcomed tax benefits on this corporate scale have been taking a hard look recently at some of the problems raised. Studies have been made of how much new revenue is offset by new demands for increased facilities and services and an enlarged administrative burden. There is a rising concern with ecology and conservation.

In Greenwich, apparently, if local officials and corporate executives shadow-boxed at all, it ended in a marriage dance. For benefits received—zoning was changed from residential to commercial—American Can worked to make its host community happy.

American Can Company Headquarters

All of American Can's traffic is taken off local roads as quickly as possible by a sweeping four-lane highway that enters and serves its own property. The corporation has built its own sewage disposal plant. Water comes from its own wells. Neighborhood views are unspoiled. Since Greenwich land is expensive and zoning is restrictive, it is unlikely that new housing on a mass scale can adjoin the new plant to bring expansionary problems. You may read whatever sociological message you want into this, and it will not be irrelevant. But these are the current facts.

The building is a beauty. A lot of people would call that irrelevant, but they shouldn't. American Can has not participated in the Rape of the Environment.

It costs a lot of money to be environmentally considerate, and the real American Can construction figure isn't even available. First, there is the least possible coverage and destruction of the site. What the architect has done is to bridge a ravine and a stream with his building, in effect, creating a dam. Most of the structure has been dropped into this ravine, and the building itself is the dam. With one level partly below ground, five beneath that, and three above ground, nine floors look like a three-story building. Nothing has been leveled, almost every tree has been spared, and a lake has been created at the end of the ravine.

Second, with between one and two thousand people commuting by car daily, there are no visible automobiles. Repeat, no asphalt parking seas. Five of those underground levels are a sixteen-hundred-car parking garage. No one need put foot on the site. One enters and leaves on wheels.

ONE LARGE AND one small building are constructed in this fashion, connected below ground. The large structure, 525 by 255 feet, with three administrative floors above its parking podium, is the general headquarters operation. The smaller structure, 165 feet square, is a one-story executive building, also on a parking podium inserted into the slope of the land.

Both buildings are stunning structural bravado. And now, if I may borrow a shopworn phrase, let me make one thing perfectly clear. Structural bravado does not mean whizz-bang visual effects such as fins, curves, and other eye-stopping gimmicks. That kind of flash is a cheap substitute for the real thing, and you can see its corporate fall guys in nearby Stamford.

What it means is the use of unprecedented modern structural techniques for a rational combination of functional purpose and dramatic architectonic effect. But effect does not come first. And it is not faked. It derives from appropriateness. The use of structure at American Can is to bridge that ravine and provide large, clear-span floors with a practical working module.

This is done with poured-in-place concrete walls, columns, and girders, and precast double-tee beams on office floors of the main building to make thirty- by sixty-foot bays. Two vertical spines contain elevators and services, and between them at ground level is an open, landscaped central court 95 by 195 feet, making the building into Mr. Bunshaft's favorite shape—the squared, or rectangular, doughnut. The span and strength of the construction are impressively, handsomely evident.

THE CONCRETE FINISH is a grayish granite aggregate exposed by sandblasting; the precast tees are white. Recessed windows are of gray glass, with muted incandescent lighting at the perimeter to keep the building from being a beacon at night. On a recent winter day, the gently mounded white curves of snow swept against the strong gray concrete planes next to jagged outcroppings of gray and black rock and the black tracery of bare trees. There was the combined power and delicacy of a Japanese wash drawing.

The supremely elegant executive *tempieto* is framed by huge, 165-foot long, post-tensioned beams that provide sixty-foot spans. After erection, when the steel inside the beams was tightened (in a very elementary sense, that is what *post-tensioned* means) to make the beams enormously strong, the exposed ends of the steel were covered with a jeweler's touch—polished stainless steel caps. This may be understated overreaching, but it is pretty breathtaking stuff, structurally and visually.

On to the main office building interiors, alas. Structurally they are excellent, with exposed beams permitting an integrated lighting and air-conditioning system that allows higher than normal ceilings in most of the work areas. These work areas are serenely and efficiently organized around the central court. Higher-echelon offices ring the edge of the building, with views of the site. If the gentlemen in these outer offices are kind enough to leave their doors open, everyone else can see part of the carefully conserved view. But the court is pretty, too.

There is high-intensity red carpet throughout. If you like insistent red carpet, fine. If it gives you a headache, stay away. It must be said here that SOM furnishings sink deeper and deeper into a familiar, formalistic rut. At American Can, it is no less deadly because it is red, white, and blue. I suppose you could stand up and salute.

BACK IN NEW YORK, there is slush and crime in the streets. Disturbing questions enter one's head. What part of a workforce does a commuter's country-club plant set in Greenwich's restrictive zoning serve? What does it do for larger considerations of regional planning? After how much captive pastoral beauty does one crave the lively, bad vibes in town? Defectors are few, according to American Can's low turnover figure. After all, you can get out of your car or leave the cafeteria with its lovely lake views and humdrum food for a scenic walk to the carefully preserved swamp or the sewage plant. And you can breathe the air, which is fully conditioned and artificially controlled in a sealed building all year round.

New York Times, January 17, 1971

The Building You Love to Hate

THIS IS A BIT OF REVISIONIST HISTORY. It is the story of the rehabilitation of the Yale Art and Architecture Building.

The Art and Architecture Building has been a symbol and cause célèbre in the revolution of the consciousness of man. When Paul Rudolph's celebrated structure burned on the Yale campus two years ago it became a supersymbol. While the official verdict was accident, not arson, it was generally assumed that either an act of God or an act of man had destroyed, with uncanny prescience for the moment and the mood, a monument that embodied the despised establishment standards and values that the radical young were rejecting on moral and social grounds.

*　*　*

Yale Art and Architecture Building

AS HAPPENS WITH symbols, it had become an object of hate. And as happens with hate, violence struck, and some called it just. It had become, in fact, the building you love to hate. Its destruction was looked on with an attitude approaching awe. The proof of its wrongheadedness was supposedly in the burning. It was offered as a lesson to those architects lacking in consciousness, who would finesse their deeper social responsibilities to impose their vanity on man.

Not anymore. The day of rehabilitation has come. The instrument of rehabilitation is, of all things, a calendar published and distributed several times a year by the Yale School of Architecture. The final 1971 segment for November and December bears a drawing of the Art and Architecture Building and two messages.

The first announces the appointment of Herman Spiegel as dean, a position vacant since the expiration of Charles Moore's term last year. The second concerns the building. It is a deeply felt statement by the student editor of the calendar, Henry Wollman, involving much more than a report on reconstruction since the fire. It reinstates the structure in the architectural pantheon with the skill of a Soviet manifesto raising reputations from the dead.

Never have a building's fortune and reputation gone up and down so far and so fast. During construction, the A & A, as it became known, was one of those word-of-mouth pilgrimage points for architects. When it was finished in 1963, it was an object of almost universal praise. Critics, including this one, welcomed it.

This column called it "willful, capricious, arbitrary, bold, brilliant, beautiful and highly controversial." We held that the architect "occasionally sacrificed practicality . . . and often contrived means for his ends," but judged it a powerful and handsome generator of excitement that would be influential for decades. With a peculiar premonition we remarked that if the students responded to the challenge of their environment, they should never think, or see, quite the same again.

That happened, but not the way we thought. After the bouquets of the opening, the building proved, in use, to be full of bugs. There were serious functional faults. A strong design, in intent and result, it forced its occupants to live with it on its own terms. There was nothing formless, and very little that was flexible, about it. The students reacted to the challenge of the environment all right; they rejected it in no uncertain terms.

THE PAINTERS AND sculptors, in cramped, poorly lit, and ventilated studios, rejected it totally. The architecture students, unwilling to be bound by Rudolph's atelier ambience—he had been dean of the school when he designed it—attempted to reshape the spaces for their own philosophical needs. When this observer visited again, they had built, inside of those spaces, what can only be called a rat trap of enclosures and semienclosures that resembled nothing so much as those tar paper and cardboard Depression villages of the thirties. It was expression of a sort, and expression was paramount. Denial of Rudolph's style and spaces was essential. They were, of course, irrelevant.

Although there was a great deal wrong with the building in terms of physical facilities and working spaces, it was also a legitimate experiment in enlarging architectural experience and expression.

The two aspects, however, became immutably tied in students' minds as evil, and it was not long before the structure was being reviled for more than its real, or imagined, errors. In the oversimplification and slick superficiality of revolutionary rhetoric, it became the archetype of the imposition of a false value system by an architect on an antipeople ego trip. In the architectural division of the revolution, that was the cardinal sin.

If you remember Yale at the height of the movement, it was a busy place. The air was full of adrenaline. Much of the spirit of change was, and is, necessary and admirable, and some essential rethinking of aims and objectives has been done. But paranoia was not absent. There were the usual threats, including an ambiguous reference to destruction by fire. Then, mysteriously, the building burned. Student work was lost. Classes had to be disbanded and moved. The school was in a state of dislocation and shock.

That was two years ago. In the reconstruction, some of the building's physical faults have been corrected, and changes have been made in the art and architectural quarters. The building has apparently risen from the ashes, in more than one sense.

"BURNT, CLOSED, WALLED off, in tumult, A & A carried a legacy of confusion and overwhelming sadness during the restoration process," the calendar tells us. And then comes the kicker, the surprising reevaluation. "But not even the holocaust of fire could in any ultimate way tear the heart from this monument of American architecture, this presence on the Yale campus. The terrifying, ferocious nobility and grandeur that are so much the fabric of this building remain.

"It is, for these reasons, not an easy building to live with. Physically it is often uncomfortable. Fundamentally, however, it is the emotional demands of this building that are the most difficult. In this sense the cliché 'the building is too strong' rings true: too difficult to live the humdrum student life; too aware of itself; too much concerned with an ideal; not concerned enough with the reality of everyday.

"YET SOMEHOW WE manage to live with it; richer because of it. We are aware that we are in confrontation with more than structure, more than function. We are aware of the fact that we are in confrontation with the heart of monumental architecture, a statement of human spirit and a material manifestation of an ideal of human culture."

That was what we meant in 1963. How quickly time and passions pass. How the human condition and consciousness change. How arbitrarily are reputations made, destroyed, and revived. How short is history today.

New York Times, December 12, 1971

The Meier Superstyle

THE ATHENEUM, NEW HARMONY, INDIANA

ON THE BANKS OF THE WABASH RIVER, not far from the cornfields of Indiana, stands a gleaming white structure that is as radical an addition to the rural American heartland as Le Corbusier's Villa Savoie was to the French countryside at Poissy half a century ago.

Called the Atheneum, the building is the visitors' center for the historic town of New Harmony—the Indiana village that played a uniquely important role in nineteenth-century social idealism, religion, and science. This Atheneum is not, as one would expect, a classical place of learning; the name draws more from New Harmony's intellectual heritage than from the building's present functions. It is a reception and orientation center built around a series of exhibits and presentations through which the visitor is channeled. By the time the journey has been made from the ground floor to the rooftop terrace for views of the river and town, one has also become familiar with the story and spirit of New Harmony. At the same time, one has been exposed to an extraordinary series of architectural impressions in which the sense of the past is heightened, both physically and poetically, by the experience of the present.

This latest building by Richard Meier & Partners—public, open, dealing in movement and process made visible—is the perfect vehicle for the architect's evolving personal, intricate, and highly sophisticated style. It carries his rigorous explorations of geometry and space about as far as they can go.

Middle America has mixed feelings about the Atheneum—a controversy that extends into professional ranks. There are those who call it inappropriate for the setting and the purpose, who find its striking forms just as strikingly out of place. But there are also those who consider the building a significant step beyond the accepted ways of composing architectural space for a whole new range of perceptions and experiences. The matter of suitability is bound to be an extremely subjective judgment. But I think the nature of the building should be weighed against the history and character of New Harmony, which is a very special kind of American town, and the unconventional approach to preservation that has guided its restoration.

New Harmony was founded, planned, and built by a religious sect, the Harmony Society, led by George Rapp from 1814 to 1824. As organized and orderly as its small straight grid of streets, the community prospered in its industries to become the affluent "wonder of the West." In 1825, Rapp decided to move closer to eastern markets. The town was sold, lock, stock, and barrel, to the Welsh-born social reformer and industrialist Robert Owen. Owen had visions of New Harmony as a Utopian community—one of those admirable nineteenth-century experiments in social idealism. He brought together a group of eminent naturalists and educators, who were to create a model of egalitarian excellence. The Utopian ideal soon failed, but New Harmony became an important center of scientific research from 1825 to 1860. Owen's descendants were distinguished scientists, active in the geological mapping of the West and the founding of such national institutions as the Smithsonian.

Of the two phases of the town, the spiritual and scientific—both so typical of the nineteenth-century New World—there are only spotty remains. But the size and configuration have stayed essentially the same. There is no single, cohesive character or style, however, and no richly uniform period architecture. What the town offers is a remarkable continuous history, with fascinating fragments of each of its phases from its founding to the present, and a sense of the character of a special place. Its preservation philosophy emphasizes the interpretive presentation of what was once there as well as what has survived, using everything from early nineteenth-century split-log houses to Victorian gingerbread. There is no arbitrary "cut-off date"; there is no attempt to create a homogeneous "place museum." Under the direction of Ralph G. Schwarz, president of Historic New Harmony, Inc., a combination of physical rehabilitation and skilled interpretive presentation has brought the community back to life in more ways than one; the past is being preserved as part of the present on a revitalized economic base of commerce and tourism.

The Atheneum can be seen as New Harmony's twentieth-century capstone—designed in the same spirit of creative inquiry and experiment

as the town itself. Located at the northwest outer limit of the town, near
the curving river's edge, the building stands on a low grassy podium above
a flat green field that is flooded yearly by the Wabash. A traditional split-
rail fence separates the site from the older historic section. To me, the
building is suitable, quite aside from its unusual architectural interest. I
see the choice as one between a legitimate artifact of our own time and a
spurious or debatable, and ultimately, quite arbitrary, "suitability," since
there is no real "New Harmony style" or even any overriding vernacular. I
do not see the point of inventing one. Given the choice of such a fabrica-
tion, and a design of contemporary beauty and brilliance, I would opt for
the latter.

The building is actually conceived as a circulation system. A reception and orientation area with computerized tour ticketing facilities
leads to exhibition galleries, a theater, and observation terraces. Visitors
follow a central ramp up to the theater and exhibition levels within a
high open space that extends from the ground to the sky-lit roof. Because the ramp winds up on a five-degree diagonal grid, the interior is
simultaneously perceived in different ways as the visitor ascends; the
twist almost seems to set the building in motion. Everything that does
not need to be enclosed, such as the theater, is not only visible, but visible from many levels and points of view. And as one moves, each view
yields still more intricate patterns of a staggered and overlapping geometry of floor levels and indoor and outdoor spaces and outdoor vistas.
There is a constant counterpoint of stairs, with an inner core containing a spiral stair as a sculptural object; that it is primarily for viewing is
emphasized by the fact that this is the one area off-limits to the public.

Surprisingly, there is no sense of disorientation. It soon becomes evident that this striking interior is totally integrated with the purpose of
the building—to tell the story of New Harmony. As that story and its artifacts are revealed along the visitor's route, so are corresponding views
of the town, through glass walls or between white metal panel screens,
or from the outdoor terraces. Standing in front of the model of the first
New Harmony, for example, it is possible to see out to the fence-
enclosed field of early split-log structures—also visible on the model—
which have been moved back to their original site after numerous
relocations. Thus they are seen both in the context of the present and of
the nineteenth-century town.

There is a remarkable fusion of architectural means with the programmatic result. But it is not possible, of course, to be aware only of this process. At the same time, one is also intensely aware of the building. Never background, it fulfills its purpose while it plays skillfully with a new aesthetic, advancing conventional modernist practice provocatively, beyond established limits. Meier does not deny or reject modern architecture in any way, as is the fashion now; he uses its vocabulary and achievements to move into a new phase of exploration of those things that architecture has always been about: the controlled and purposeful manipulation of light and space, and the rewarding relationship of pragmatic and sensuous purpose. This is the kind of development that has always marked the change from one period of art to another. The point can be made that the creative spirit of this building is not far from the pioneering heritage of New Harmony. Frontiers are where you find them.

New York Times, September 30, 1979

THE HARTFORD SEMINARY

Any visitor to the new headquarters of the Hartford Seminary in Hartford, Connecticut, will have no trouble recognizing the building. This glistening white structure makes its immaculate presence so inimitably clear that there is no question about which building one has come to see. It is just as clearly the work of Richard Meier, who has developed this clean but complex style with dedicated consistency through a series of recent buildings that have already achieved a special significance on the international architectural scene.

Meier's work, which began in the sixties with a number of well-publicized, snowy houses of intriguing formal geometry, took on major importance with the larger challenge of the Bronx Developmental Center built from 1970 to 1976 in New York (clad in silvery aluminum rather than white panels) and the New Harmony, Indiana, Atheneum of 1975–79. The recently opened Hartford Seminary building will be followed by additions to the Museum of Decorative Arts in Frankfurt, Germany; the High Museum of Art in Atlanta, Georgia, and an office building in Paris. From concept to completion, every project from the office of Richard Meier & Partners receives worldwide, exhaustive analysis in the architectural press.

Hartford Seminary

It should be said immediately that this attention is justified; Meier is surely one of the most accomplished practitioners of a difficult art in a period of controversial transition. This work is assured and brilliant on both the technological and design levels. And while these transitional times encourage diverse solutions—the historial contextualism of Kallmann, McKinnell & Woods's building for the American Academy of Arts and Sciences reviewed here last week is an example of another approach—Meier's work is moving modern architecture beyond its established achievements into a new realm of formal and functional expression.

The recent institutional structures have given the architect far more scope than the houses that established his reputation. As exquisite as those dwellings were, and are, their demanding aesthetic can make severe claims on clients whose living habits are less than totally in tune. Many of Meier's ideas and images have seemed compressed into his earlier structures; the tension between angled and orthogonal planning, for example, sometimes adds confusion to complexity. The New Harmony Atheneum was almost too small to contain its wealth of visual and spatial effects. The Hartford Seminary, which is actually no larger than the Atheneum, refines and simplifies some of those themes and organizes them into a resolved and mature work that confirms the architect's attachment to a meticulously evolving style.

As spectacular as these gleaming white structures are, Meier does not create stage-set architecture. The drama of these buildings is not to be confused with the cutouts or add-ons of the false fronts and pseudohistory currently in vogue. His designs grow out of a strong commitment to the essential relationships of plan and structure. This steel-framed, three-story, twenty-seven-thousand-square foot building is made up of intricately linked spaces and volumes derived equally from the plan and program and an acute awareness of its aesthetic and symbolic values.

The plan itself is surprisingly simple. The ground floor consists of a central entrance flanked by a library and bookstore on one side, and meeting room and chapel on the other. The second and third floors contain classrooms, conference rooms, and offices. How the plan is handled, however, is not simple. It is conceived three-dimensionally, with the volumes of the larger, public spaces threaded vertically through the structure, and a circulation system that emphasizes the experience of those spaces at many levels. The white porcelain-enameled steel panels of the exterior set the building's three-foot module.

As in Meier's other buildings, much of this can be "read" on the exterior, where a precise and elegant "code" of architectural components graphically indicates interior uses. The "box" on the wall to the right of the entrance, for example, turns out to enclose a chapel worthy of its exterior abstract sculpture. It also creates the structure's L-shaped plan. Glass block indicates a stair tower. A shallow screen wall suggests an entrance arcade.

But these functions and features are revealed gradually, through studied relationships of solids and voids. The screen wall through which one passes into a partially enclosed court on the way to the entrance provides a cloistered serenity. Other shallow screen walls establish a pattern of receding and advancing planes; sometimes they extend beyond the building's corners to create modifications of space in much the same manner as the devices of mannerism modulated the formal spaces of the Renaissance.

Once inside, views of the outside are never lost; indoors and outdoors are played off against each other with courts, roofs, balconies, and terraces connected by bridges and walkways. Even interior spaces are suggested or revealed through glass walls and partitions. Balconies become viewing platforms of space for art's sake.

At a time when modern architecture is being questioned and rejected, Meier is loyal to the vocabulary of modernism. He uses it in a way, however, that transcends historical precedents. He is much indebted to Le Corbusier and Aalto, whom he obviously admires, but he carries these references to new stages of interpretation only possible at this particular moment of hindsight and technological development.

His effects are achieved through the careful interplay of solidity and transparency, of screen walls and openings, and the complex interlocking of volumes. They are enriched by the interraction of spaces perceived simultaneously and sequentially, at different levels, and the way they are given subtle and luminous life through the sources of daylight. This gives new and extended meaning to Le Corbusier's famous definition of architecture as the calculated play of forms in light.

That is exactly the kind of building that the president of the seminary, John Dillenberger, and his trustees wanted. In the last decade, the Hartford Seminary has moved from being a training college for the ministry to much broader, interdenominational educational and community activities meant to serve both the clergy and the lay public. There have been no resident seminarians since 1972. The new program needed only one building, and it was hoped that the new structure could express the seminary's changing spirit and functions. The old buildings, a Gothic Revival group that the seminary had occupied since 1927—its fourth home since it was founded in 1834—were sold to the University of Connecticut Law School.

The new Hartford Seminary stands close by them, a pristine presence in a level green field about a large city-block in size. Its break with tradition has caused considerable local controversy. But it does not upstage its handsome stone neighbors; white, after all, is not an unfamiliar New England color, and it pays them the compliment of superior design quality and suitable scale. New and old coexist nicely, without false obeisances of style.

Interestingly, the chapel was not originally included in the program. It was added as a result of the architect's persuasive arguments that it would provide a symbolic focus for the building, and while it bears out this belief, it has also provided an irresistible architectural opportunity. In a sense, it is the key to the design. This high, white-walled, glowing, sky-lit space is constantly transformed in color and mood by clouds and the course of the sun. If it is more coolly intellectual and hard-edged, less gently or deeply sensuous than comparable chapels by Le Corbusier and Aalto, it is still a very special place. Meier's disciplined, rigorous, highly intellectual work achieves a large measure of lyrical beauty. The Hartford Seminary is a dazzling structure on the leading edge of the building art.

New York Times, September 27, 1981

Order in the Courthouse

ON THE WAY FROM THE DOMED AND colonnaded courthouses of the nineteenth century, with their marbled rotundas, paneled courtrooms, and classical evocation of a noble jurisprudence, to today's bottom-line design and construction, something got lost with the architecture—the authority and majesty of the law.

It is a fact of congressional life that government buildings are routinely treated as legislative favors to be doled out to architects, developers, and contractors who have demonstrated their loyalty to the party or otherwise endeared themselves to their Washington representatives. Government construction as pork is a hallowed tradition that has kept public building in this country at a deplorable level; the most impressive thing about these predictably pedestrian structures is the lucrative contracts available through the right connections. There have been times when the sights and the standards are raised, but even with the best intentions quality goes up and down with yo-yo-like regularity.

We are in an "up" period right now. In response to a notoriously overburdened criminal justice system, this country is in the middle of a courthouse building boom. As luck would have it, this coincides with one of those times when a special effort is being made by the Public Buildings Service of the General Services Administration, the agency responsible for the construction and maintenance of public buildings, to upgrade the level of federal design. The courthouse project, an eight-billion-dollar, thirteen-year plan for 160 new and renovated court-houses, is the largest federal building project since the WPA programs of the Depression-era New Deal.

The acknowledged centerpiece of this ambitious program stands quietly on Boston Harbor—the recently completed, $220-million United States Courthouse by the architect Henry Cobb, of the New York firm of Pei Cobb Freed & Partners—a ten-story, 765,000-square-foot building that occupies 4.5 acres of South Boston's Fan Pier in a neglected waterfront area currently undergoing radical redevelopment. Buildings by Henry Cobb tend to be very quiet indeed. There are no architectural fireworks, high-wire acts, or wild flights of fancy; this is not an extravaganza or tour de force like the Bilbao Guggenheim Museum or Paris's Centre Pompidou, intent on breaking barriers and making waves.

Mr. Cobb is an almost painfully thoughtful designer whose every deliberate move is the result of a measured intellectual effort. Sometimes you wish he were less meticulously controlled, but his assiduous perfectionism creates a solid, studied excellence that wears well. He sets standards. The Boston courthouse is a superior building rationally and elegantly conceived and carried out. Contrary to the inevitable, hard-to-kill rumors that circulate if anything built by the government dares to look good, the building was brought in on budget and on time, and the cost was reasonable compared to commercial construction of equivalent quality. Its innovative, superbly functional plan and handsome courtrooms and inviting public spaces stand as a model of concept and execution, something rare in the annals of federal design.

Just don't expect anything seductive or flashy. This is not a drive-by building, as they say in the real estate business, that sells itself at first sight. For one thing, its back is on the street, and its most dramatic feature, a seven-story, curved and canted, all-glass wall, faces the harbor on the other side. Today's courthouse is less a temple of justice than a very large office building with an administrative and bureaucratic presence that overshadows its judicial functions. The offices of the Boston courthouse present their bulk to the approaching viewer. The large street wall is disconcerting; its scale defeats the carefully modulated details that tend to disappear at a distance. As other buildings go up, however, this façade will be less overwhelming than when it stands alone.

In keeping with Mr. Cobb's preference for dignified restraint, there is no grand gesture at the entrance, no muscular modernism or colonnaded flourish as in the past. One goes in through a corner of the building under a brick arch reminiscent of Louis Sullivan; the same rosy, water-struck New England brick and Maine granite trim are used inside and out. Directly ahead, in the somberly handsome brick entry hall, are steps that lead to a light-filled, white-walled rotunda rising through the building to a sky-lit drum at the top. This luminous space is lined with solid color panels by Ellsworth Kelly that enrich the architect's austere vocabulary. The nonpublic uses of the building include the extensive security system, prisoners' detention center, and marshals' quarters: the life of the law that goes on behind the scenes. These functions are invisibly wrapped around the reception core on the ground floor. Three skillfully separated circulation systems serve the building's three constituencies—the public, the prisoners, and the legal professionals.

The public can proceed to elevators to the courtrooms or continue beyond this central core to a breathtaking open space fronted by the angled glass wall of the harborside façade—four hundred feet long and ninety feet high, it offers stunning views of the water and the Boston skyline. The wall curves back to embrace a waterfront park that connects to a harbor promenade. This atrium, or great hall, runs almost the entire length and height of the building. All the public floors open onto this light-filled space with balconies that serve as corridors. Ranged along these balcony-corridors are the courtrooms, their entrances marked by partial brick vaults that define their presence. There are twenty-seven double-height, wood-paneled courts in the building; they differ only in subtle changes of color and the pleasing, stenciled decoration of their shallow, domed ceilings. The two-story space that surrounds each courtroom contains the judges' chambers and jury rooms with windows and views.

If the building is exceptional, so is the process that brought it into being. Two concerned and knowledgeable federal judges dedicated themselves to the project from the start, Justice Stephen G. Breyer, now on the Supreme Court, and Justice Douglas P. Woodlock, for whom this building has been a one-man crusade to bring dignity and humanity to the judicial process. Their point man in Washington was the chief architect of the Public Buildings Service of the GSA, Edward A. Feiner, who is deeply committed to improving the quality of federal design.

The ideal they all shared was that this should be a "people's court," open to the public and used by the community. The design redefines today's courthouse as a useful and accessible place; it deals with the alienation and intimidation of the impersonal and off-putting administration of justice reinforced by the shoddy mediocrity of the setting in which it usually takes place. Local area lawyers of the Boston Bar Association have raised funds for community programming. Art shows, concerts, symposia, and dinners are already being held in that impressive atrium with its spectacular views.

It is not hard for lawyers and judges accustomed to bad light and bad air, showers of soot in the courtrooms and shackled prisoners in the halls, to like this building. The problems of its "break-in" period, like the too-perfect acoustics that make private bench conferences or confidential lawyer-client conversation difficult, are minor and correctible. The *Massachusetts Lawyers Weekly*, in its coverage of the project, noted that "a courthouse is not just another office building. It represents the core values on which this country was founded." The editor concluded that "a society that spends billions on sports stadiums and skyscrapers" does not need to demolish its core values. We rest our case.

Wall Street Journal, March 9, 1999

Libraries in London and Paris

YOU'VE GOT TO BE FRENCH TO LOVE the new National Library—the Bibliothèque Nationale de France that is the last of the *grands travaux,* or great works, bequeathed to Paris by the late president François Mitterrand. You've got to love the kind of rationalism that strains logic to the breaking point and turns reason upside down for a pharaonic presence that the French, with their inborn assurance about who they are in the hierarchy of national cultures, find neither irrational nor chilling. Known popularly as the Très Grand-Bibliothèque, or TGB, which, as a British journalist has noted, translates into the fairly ordinary sounding "very big library," it is anything but ordinary in cost, concept, and execution.

Love it or not, you've got to admire the French for the way they officially embrace the most mind-bending schemes, with a take-no-prisoners and spare-no-expense single-minded dedication to an image and an idea. By law, all public commissions in France must be awarded by competition, a process that favors big, bold plans and star turns over subtler solutions. Construction of French architect Dominique Perrault's prize-winning design—four 128-foot-high L-shaped glass towers in the form of "open books" at the corners of an enormous rectangle roughly the size of the Grand Palais—began in 1989; in a feat of faith and expedited imperialism, one quarter of the structure was opened to the public this year. The building's overpowering scale and style has many admirers. Mr. Perrault himself describes its strict modular geometry and stylishly sleek space-age fittings as the work of a lonely visionary exploring the far side of the future. Others see the building as an extravagant throwback to a passé, monolithic modernism in *Star Wars* guise. The result has all the humility and humanity of Versailles.

If you've got to be French to love the TGB, then you've got to be British to hate the new British Library, which has been thirty-five years in design and construction, with a history of political obstruction and government mismanagement all the way. Led by a press with a notoriously well-developed instinct for the jugular, library bashing has become a kind of national sport in the UK, with Prince Charles weighing in early and predictably with the judgment that the benign classic modernism of

British architect Colin St. John Wilson looked like "an academy for secret police." Labor and Conservative governments chopped up the
project and cut and withheld funds. The National Audit Office, a
public-expenditure watchdog, issued a scathing indictment of escalating costs and construction errors. The London-based magazine *Ac-
countancy* scored the government's "parsimony and lack of vision." The
process lumbered on, and the scattered collections, including those of
the beloved round reading room of the British Museum, are finally being moved to the new site on Euston Road next to St. Pancras Station,
with the opening scheduled for this fall.

Unlike the French, I do not love the Très Grand Bibliothèque. But I
admit that it knocks me out as much as it turns me off. It is the most
awesomely perverse building I have ever seen. Nor, like the British, do
I hate the British Library, which even they are beginning to realize is a
good building—handsome and humane—not an easy achievement
when you're dealing with a gross floor area of more than 1.2 million
square feet on a 7.66-acre site meant to house the literary, scientific,
and humanistic resources of a nation. Mr. Wilson's midcentury modernism now looks quite comfortably traditional, as contemporary architecture has reached for the wilder shores of postmodernism. The
French library, on the other hand, deliberately breaks with and upstages tradition in its high-style futurism. The only genuinely radical
feature in either is the computerized technology that will serve them
both. Generalizations about national character and taste are part fallacy
and part fantasy, but physically and philosophically, these two buildings
are from different worlds.

It did not matter that the French design was wrongheaded for its
purpose from the start and had to be retrodesigned at enormous effort
and expense. French architecture is all about image. If the TGB is to
be the library of the future, the French want it to look that way. It celebrates its enormous size and explicit symbolism suavely and aggressively. The overcharged imagery of the glass towers was as irresistible
as it was impractical; they have been lined with wood, and most of the
books are underground. The vast void required to construct a building
so far below grade required an act of excavation and creation of near-
biblical proportions; Mr. Perrault maintains that ground level is wherever you want to put it. It takes hubris or heady optimism to move
120 full-grown twelve-ton pines from Normandy, like the forest of

Dunsinane, to a garden below the level of the Seine. They are obviously struggling to survive.

In contrast, Mr. Wilson has done his best to make his immense building disappear, camouflaging its scale and breaking down its bulk incrementally from its highest point of 154 feet. No extravagant exterior competes with the Victorian exuberance of the neighboring St. Pancras Station; the library even uses the same hand-molded, salmon-red brick from the very brickyard that supplied the nineteenth-century landmark. The entrance is a public plaza designed as a series of intimate outdoor rooms, buffered from the noise of the street.

The approach to Mr. Perrault's building is a literally stunning, rather than reader-friendly, experience. Endless steps, stretching horizontally, lead to a 14.81-acre wooden platform of windswept or sun-baked desolation. Rigidly equidistant groups of trees are confined in gridded metal cages along the top edge. The branches will be sheared back to identical flat surfaces; no wayward leaf will escape its prison. The French have a tradition of splendidly torturing trees, which works well with the contrast of the rococo or baroque and the counterpoint of country roads and small public squares, but it reaches the end of the line with Mr. Perrault's mercilessly reductive, scaleless, minimalist style.

Having climbed to the top, you plunge down by escalator to the library far below. The conceptual bravado of this daunting reversal of normal experience and expectations supposedly cancels out its irrationality and inconvenience. (There is a growing trend toward a fashionable architecture of fear and discomfort, by which, when not threatened, I feel aesthetically challenged.) Still, there is something undeniably impressive about doing things the really hard way. On arrival, you do not go into the garden at the building's center; it is *interdit*. Another escalator takes you down (just as you thought you were safe) to the lower level of two levels of reading rooms surrounding the garden, past woven metal-mesh walls of nonstop metallic frigidity. Security locks of double sets of heavy doors would fit Prince Charles's "secret police academy." Superstylish directional signs point the way along the glass-walled corridor bordering the garden that gives access to continuous reading rooms on a podium on its other side; the regimented march to infinity is eased by red carpet and wood paneling. The steps up to the reading rooms are interrupted by boxlike wheelchair lifts in a design-forced solution to the unyielding linear plan that repeatedly emphasizes the disabled. Signs and symbols of advanced technological wizardry permeate an architecture of severe minimalist grandeur.

In Paris, the experience of getting to the library is as important as the library itself. In London, the point is simply being there. The entrance hall is a beautifully proportioned room suffused with natural light that runs the building's full height and has the reading rooms layered around and opening onto it. At the center of this superb space is a six-story glass enclosure containing the King's Library—a magnificent collection of leather- and vellum-bound volumes bequeathed by George III for the use and pleasure of the nation. Here, the face of the new technology is still the beauty, and the meaning, of the book. Contrasts of scale and use, stairs that spill into seating alcoves, oak and leather furnishings in traditional British Library blue-green, pervasive daylight with its sense of changing days and seasons—dozens of design subtleties and sensory satisfactions provide comforts and pleasures for the hand and eye. The British Library is about history and humanity. The French library is about image and power.

Wall Street Journal, August 28, 1997

Washington

The New House Office Building

IT IS MOVING TIME ON CAPITOL HILL for 169 congressmen eligible for space in the new Rayburn House Office Building. The structure's three-room suites complete with refrigerators and safes are being raffled off to applicants who may have a view of the Capitol dome or an interior court, depending on seniority. Even seniority, however, does not give any legislator a door leading from his office, or his aide's office, to his working staff without passage through a waiting room full of constituents and special pleaders. To correct this small planning error would add two hundred thousand dollars to costs already estimated at anywhere from $86 million to $122 million for the expensive and controversial building.

Some congressmen are moving in reluctantly. Representative Thomas L. Ashley, Democrat of Ohio, for one, rejected his office on sight. But he is making the move anyway this week because his present quarters are too small.

"This layout could paralyze us," he said during his inspection tour. "It's an ugly building."

Mr. Ashley is not alone. The professional architectural press has been bitterly critical as construction progressed. (The building has taken seven years and twenty-two million dollars more to complete than originally estimated largely as the result of expensive miscalculations; change orders have reached 300 percent over the government average; bid estimates on contracts have been as much as $4.5 million off.)

There have been accusations of secret planning, pork barrel commissions, and possible misuse of public funds. The fact that the general contractor was Matthew J. McCloskey, Democratic Party stalwart of Philadelphia, has not escaped notice. But the storm swirls uselessly around a behemoth that is obviously here to stay.

Architecturally, the Rayburn Building is a national disaster. Its defects range from profligate mishandling of fifty acres of space to elephantine aesthetic banality at record costs. The costs are now being investigated by the General Accounting Office.

Equal to the question of costs, however, is the question of what Congress and the capital have received for the investment. It is quite possible that this is the worst building for the most money in the history of the construction art. It stuns by sheer mass and boring bulk. Only 15 percent of its space is devoted to the offices and hearing rooms for which it was erected.

Forty-two percent of the floor area is used for parking. Endless corridors have been likened to *Last Year at Marienbad.* Stylistically, it is the apotheosis of humdrum.

It is hard to label the building, but it might be called Corrupt

Classic. Its empty aridity and degraded classical details are vulgarization without drama, and to be both dull and vulgar may be an achievement of sorts.

The structure's chief "design features" are hollow exercises in sham grandeur. A supercolossal exterior expanse of stolid, Mussolini-style pomp is embellished with sculpture that would be the apogee of art in the Soviet Union, where overscaled muscles and expressions of empty solemnity are still admired.

A monumental entrance at second-floor level is reached by pretentious steps that will never be used. The real entrance, on the ground floor just below, abandons false dignity for no dignity at all.

The formal marble front with its blank, machine-stamped look sits on a gargantuan base of informal, random-cut granite of obviously miscalculated proportions, an effect comparable to combining a top hat with blue jeans. Groups of columns meant to dress up the drab, flat façade not only fail to suggest that columns are traditionally supporting members, but they also terminate incongruously on balconies that appear to support the columns—a neat combination of structural illogic and stylistic flimflam.

Inside, a pedestrian statue of Sam Rayburn presents the seat of its pants to entering visitors. It faces a huge landscaped central court that is an artless cliché. Embracing Mr. Sam is another cliché, a two-story curved double stair fated to be not only useless but graceless.

In the hearing rooms, coarse, lifeless classical cornices and moldings are joined to stock modern acoustic ceilings and panel lighting for a state of aesthetic warfare tempered only by their matching mediocrity. This model comes in red, green, gold, and blue.

Behind the scenes, the classical false front is abandoned and working subcommittee rooms use ordinary partitions and fittings of the lowest commercial common denominator. Throughout the building, the design level is consistent: Whatever is not hack is heavy-handed.

For one hundred million dollars, give or take a few million (the cost of New York's mammoth Pan Am Building), the gentlemen of the House have got a sterile, stock plan of singularly insensitive design and detailing that was moribund more than half a century ago. Even the basic functional requirements have been insufficiently studied. The making of useful and beautiful public spaces with the power to inspire and symbolize as well as to serve—the timeless aim of architecture and one that is mandatory for Washington—is conspicuously absent.

The Rayburn Building is the third solid-gold turkey in a row to come out of the office of the architect of the Capitol, J. George Stewart, who is not an architect, but who picks them for Congress. For this one he selected Harbeson, Hough, Livingston & Larson of Philadelphia. He is also responsible for the ill-advised remodeling of the Capitol's East Front and the construction of the new Senate Office Building.

There are no controls or reviews for Mr. Stewart's work, and none for the House committee that authorized the Rayburn Building's construction and appropriations, generally behind closed doors.

An old architectural saying has it that there's no point in crying over spilled marble. Seven million pounds of it have been poured onto Capitol Hill in this latest congressional building venture, and there is nothing quite as invulnerable as a really monumental mistake. The Rayburn Building's ultimate claim to fame may well be that it is the biggest star-spangled architectural blunder of our time.

New York Times, March 30, 1965

From a Candy Box, a Tardy and Unpleasant Surprise

OFFICIAL WASHINGTON HAS JUST FOUND, to its surprise, that there is a great deal of discontent among architects, city planners, and cultural leaders with the site of the $46.4-million John F. Kennedy Center for the Performing Arts. Somebody inquired—in this case, the assistant to the chairman of the temporary Pennsylvania Avenue Commission, charged with the rebuilding of the capital's ceremonial boulevard.

Now, finally, sixty days before construction contracts are to be let for the national cultural center, an investigation was made by the commission, and the extent of the criticism uncovered was "appalling."

If somebody had asked, some time ago, it would have been clear that there has been a good deal less than professional enthusiasm for the site, a traffic island on the edge of the Potomac, and the design, a glorified candy box by Edward Durell Stone.

Ever since the Potomac site was chosen in 1958, and an even bigger candy box proposed that had to be cut down to the present large economy bonbon size when funds proved hard to raise, critics have pointed out the inconvenience of the location, its inhospitality to pedestrians, its dependence on the automobile for transportation, and its isolation by encircling thruways.

With the initiation of the Pennsylvania Avenue plan in 1962, the question was raised immediately as to whether a Pennsylvania Avenue site might not be more valid and logical in terms of total Washington planning and downtown rehabilitation.

But although far from built, the center proved to be unmovable. One of the Pennsylvania Avenue Commission's architect members, Minoru Yamasaki, resigned in protest when the possibility of locating the cultural center on the avenue faded and an unbroken line of government buildings with an FBI fortress at its center took over. He based his action on the fact that President Kennedy's directive on the avenue had been to seek liveliness and variety and specifically to avoid a solid phalanx of overbearing official structures.

The arguments, then and now, for the relocation of the center were cogent. They stressed the factor of centrality rather than isolation, the need for new vitality downtown, particularly at night, the desirability of bringing people back to the heart of the city, and the regeneration of that heart by the impetus to further building and development that a cultural center would bring.

Those arguments have been reinforced recently by the fact that urban renewal has been made available to Washington for the first time under the housing bill just passed, and by the reality of the long-discussed Washington subway which has now entered the practical planning stage.

The argument against relocating Washington's cultural center at this late date is, unfortunately, equally strong. It is a question of money, and in the American scale of values nothing is stronger than that. The

$46.4-million cost has been raised, $15.5 million by public subscription, $15.5 million by congressional appropriation, and a $15.4-million repayable loan.

To move the building now would not mean just picking up the candy box and dropping it on Pennsylvania Avenue. It is a question of total redesign for an appropriate solution for a completely different kind of site.

This means scrapping old plans and incurring large additional design costs. Site acquisition and land clearance expenses would be largely underwritten by federal urban renewal.

Obviously, redesign will not be undertaken happily by any architect who is pleased with a solution that he has brought to the point of construction, and who is then asked to start all over. Mr. Stone has done this once, when the size of the original project was drastically reduced.

Just as obviously, Congress will howl at the idea of adding new design costs to existing budgets and appropriations. The real question is whether such an expenditure would be justified by the value of the results.

This could be determined by careful professional analysis. How much would the redesign costs be? How would relocation affect the economic revitalization of downtown Washington, one of the city's serious problems? How would these effects balance against the extra costs? Would the long-term central city benefits be far-reaching enough to justify the expenditure? Does all this outweigh the simpler procedure of going ahead with present plans, on the present site, which has little to recommend it beyond a fine water view?

As it stands now, the Kennedy Center is a par-for-the-course example of what might be called the typical *arrière garde* design of cultural centers being produced like good old American hotcakes in good old American cities.

Promoted by public-spirited nonprofessionals with a warm, if not very expert, interest in the arts buttressed by economic and social power and immense goodwill, these centers have developed a curious identity never envisioned by their well-meaning sponsors. They are monuments to middle-brow culture.

With few exceptions they wrap up popular performance in a comfortable cocoon of prettily pretentious building ranging on the conventional scale from dull to pompous. They smother, rather than promote, anything that is new, creative, exciting, or experimental. They are static rehashes of old aesthetic formulas rather than proving grounds for new ideas and contributions, and in architecture, recent American contributions have been notable.

These amateur-bourgeois efforts compound many errors. Site selection is one, as in Washington. Professionals worry about the impact of a major building project on the total city and its processes of growth, change, and decay. They are concerned with the urban interaction of the social, economic, aesthetic, and functional aspects of such an undertaking. The potential renewal effects of dispersal of the arts are weighed against one-stop concentration. Amateurs do not think beyond the status value of a monument to culture.

In terms of architecture and planning, these centers generally leave the top level of the country's creative talent untouched, settling for something safe and prestigious. Attempts at progressive solutions are reduced to the acceptably familiar. The results, almost uniformly, are dazzlingly mediocre.

A small but telling bit of evidence: Denmark is contributing furnishings to the Kennedy Center by one of her leading designers, Poul Kjaerholm. This raises some intriguing speculation on how Mr. Kjaerholm's uncompromisingly sophisticated, elegant, original, and distinctly contemporary furnishings will fit into the determinedly updated schmaltz of Mr. Stone's plushy red and gold interiors as currently planned. There would be no question if the building were a parallel innovation, equally in tune with our times. The standards would match. The best that can be expected is another compromise, by Mr. Kjaerholm, or a revealing contrast that could be fetchingly unintentional high camp.

The boom in cultural centers is bringing the arts to a mass public on a scale never before possible. This is fine. Nobody argues the point. But the real point is that the same job could be done just as well by considerably better buildings and plans. In artistic terms, this design failure is the ultimate cultural irony.

New York Times, August 22, 1965

A Look at the Kennedy Center

WASHINGTON, D.C., SPECIALIZES IN ballooning monuments and endless corridors. It uses marble like cotton wool. It is the home of government of, for, and by the people, and of taste for the people—the big, the bland, and the banal. The John F. Kennedy Center for the Performing Arts, opening officially Wednesday, does not break the rule. The style of the Kennedy Center is Washington superscale, but just a little bit bigger. Albert Speer would have approved.

It has apotheosized the corridor in the six-hundred-foot-long, sixty-foot-high grand foyer (the length of three New York City blockfronts), one of the biggest rooms in the world, into which the Hall of Mirrors at Versailles could be cozily nested. It would be a supertunnel without its saving Belgian gift of mirrors.

The corridor is "dressed up," in the words of the architect, Edward Durell Stone, by eighteen of the world's biggest crystal chandeliers, with planters and furniture still to come. There is enough red carpet for a total environment.

There are two other flag-hung, polished marble–walled, red-carpeted, 250-foot-long and sixty-foot-high corridors called the Hall of States and the Hall of Nations. They are disquietingly reminiscent of the overscaled vacuity of Soviet palaces of culture. They would be great for drag racing.

The two halls separate the three theaters that are the structure's raison d'être: the Opera House, the Concert Hall, and the Eisenhower Theater. The grand foyer is the entrance to them all.

The building itself is a superbunker, 100 feet high, 630 feet long, and 300 feet wide, on the Potomac. One more like this, and the city will sink.

Because it is a national landmark, there is only one way to judge the Kennedy Center—against the established standard of progressive and innovative excellence in architectural design that this country is known and admired for internationally.

Unfortunately, the Kennedy Center not only does not achieve this standard of innovative excellence; it also did not seek it. The architect opted for something ambiguously called "timelessness" and produced meaninglessness. It is to the Washington manner born. Too bad, since there is so much of it.

The center sets still another record—for architectural default. What it has in size, it lacks in distinction. Its character is aggrandized posh. It is an embarrassment to have it stand as a symbol of American artistic achievement before the nation and the world.

The interiors aim for conventional, comfortable, gargantuan grand luxé. This is gemütlich Speer.

The Opera House, a 2.200-seat hall with superior sightliness and equipment, looks like one of those passe, red-padded drugstore candy valentines.

Its dark red fabric walls are buttoned down with rows of gold knobs, and its Austrian crystal lights suggest nothing so much as department store Christmas displays. To this observer, it is singularly depressing.

The 2,575-seat Concert Hall, its accoustic wood walls painted white, has red seats and carpet and is buttoned down with Norwegian crystal fixtures. This at least is cheerful and suggests twenties' modern.

Restaurants on the top terrace floor are in expense-account French by way of Austria. They are red.

There are two ways of defending the center's design. One, already popular, is to say that it doesn't really matter and that the only things that count are those badly needed performance halls and how they work.

But nothing justifies wrapping those halls in nearly seventy million dollars of tasteful corn and seventeen thousand tons of steel—all a conscious design decision—and ignoring it. If you could ignore it, which is hard.

To say that everything else about a landmark structure of this stupefying size is irrelevant is nonsense. The emperor, unfortunately, is wearing clothes. And the world is looking.

The second defense is simply to accept the fact that the center probably represents the norm of American taste. But it is a fallacy to equate the great middle common denomination of popular taste with the country's actual and potential level of creative achievement.

From this point of view, however, it is almost an interesting building.

If Mr. Stone has been aiming for an architecture that all America can love, he has found it. This is architectural populism. He has produced a conventional crowd pleaser. It is a genuine people's palace.

PEOPLE HAVE BEEN pouring in, before the opening, through every available crack, in T-shirts and sneakers, hotpants and bermudas, barefoot and barebellied, backpacking babies, tracking across the red carpet and under the chandeliers. The preopening charge of elitism because of all that lush decor was rubbish. They are obviously loving it and perfectly at home.

Because it so lacks the true elegance of imagination, it does not put them off at all. They are awed by the scale and admiring of the decoration, which is a safe, familiar blend of theatrical glamour and showroom Castro Convertible.

Stringent economies have made saving simplicities, but the popular style is loud and clear.

For the more architecturally sophisticated, it is hard to admire a failure of vision and art. And it did not have to be. It is not easy to commission creative courage in Washington, but it can be done, as proven by the current plans for the National Gallery extension.

It is particularly hard to know that the one creative design for a new kind of experimental theater remains an unfinished shell within the building, lacking funds.

The center was probably wrong from the start. It was conceived as a giant economy three-in-one package. If it hasn't cost more than three separate buildings, it certainly hasn't cost less, and it has had formidable construction problems as a result of the "simple" concept.

The three houses have had to be separated and insulated from each other for vibration and sound inside and jets outside, and from other floors and functions.

SUSPENSION AND SOUNDPROOFING have been achieved through incredibly complex and expensive concrete and steelwork that belies the apparent logic of the plan. Structurally, the achievement is considerable.

The giant steel trusses hidden behind the scenes are far more impressive than the truly awful, gold-epoxy-painted steel columns that run visibly through the building, which add decorative aluminum fins along the façades.

Environmentally, the center has been severely criticized for its setting and isolation from city life. But many Washingtonians like the idea of driving to a "safe" bastion of culture. Again, it's what people really want.

As completed, the center's plusses include its public amenities—its entrance plaza, riverfront promenade, eating facilities, and outdoor terraces with views. And credit as well as sympathy must go to the dedicated and hardworking sponsors who have actually brought three major performance halls to Washington.

May all the performing arts flourish. Because the building is a national tragedy. It is a cross between a concrete candy box and a marble sarcophagus in which the art of architecture lies buried.

New York Times, September 7, 1971

Full Speed Backward

IT HAS COME, AND IT IS JUST what everyone expected: The new, seventy-five-million-dollar Madison Memorial Library for Capitol Hill in Washington is to be another mammoth mock-classical cookie from the architect of the Capitol's well-known cookie cutter for gargantuan architectural disasters.

It follows, as day follows night, the notorious Rayburn Building, the new Senate Office Building, and the remodeled East Front of the Capitol, a compendium of matched errors in moribund academic clichés that Congress has been building for itself on a blockbuster scale, at extravagant expense, and with unabashed architectural know-nothingness.

The list at least has consistency. As an example of legislative establishment taste, it is as expected and American as that increasingly celebrated yardstick, cherry pie. No other country in the world produces this kind of ponderous, passé official architecture. Even the Russians gave it up ten years ago.

The design of the library was prefigured and preshadowed in a decade of political and architectural maneuvering in the halls of Congress and on Capitol Hill. It was released by the office of the architect of the Capitol on August 25.

To review the workings of that office: The architect of the Capitol, J. George Stewart, a seventy-seven-year-old engineer and political pro who is absolute aesthetic monarch of the Capitol environs, builds without review or approval from the Commission of Fine Arts, the National Capital Planning Commission, or any of the advisory bodies that function for official Washington. Their jurisdiction stops dead at the foot of Capitol Hill. His immense building schemes are developed behind closed doors and accepted in closed hearings; plans and commissions are shrouded in secrecy, known only to the committees for which he builds and from which he receives money. This is, of course, taxpayers' money, for public buildings of national importance.

For a rough idea of the bundle of congressional red tape through which such buildings must pass, with predictable design attrition, the Madison Memorial Library is a product of the Senate Office Building Committee, the House Office Building Committee, the joint Committee on the Library, and the James Madison Memorial Commission, with a coordinating committee composed of members of the three congressional bodies and the Madison Memorial Commission. Not one of these groups has been put together on the basis of professional competence in matters of architecture, construction, or design.

In addition, Public Law 89-260, passed in 1965 to authorize construction of the building, set up a series of stipulations that created an insoluble dilemma of conflicting and self-defeating directives. These included a budget, floor area, and a design philosophy, by amateur design philosophers, for a building "in keeping with the prevailing architecture of the Federal buildings on Capitol Hill," a statement guaranteed to open a Pandora's box of conflicting interpretation.

As a result of outcries against the monumental ugliness of the

Rayburn Building and in response to some concerned members of Congress, the law also set up an advisory committee of the American Institute of Architects, which was meant to be insurance against another $100 million-plus Rayburn Building debacle.

The AIA committee was duly appointed and immediately presented with another dead-end dilemma by a suave Stewart maneuver in which some of his favorite architects were commissioned for the library without the knowledge of the AIA consultants. Most of these architects have been connected in one way or another with all of the architecture of the Capitol's important buildings. They are known informally to the profession as "the Club." For the Madison Library, they are Roscoe DeWitt of Dallas, Alfred Easton Poor and Albert Homer Swanke of New York, and Jesse M. Shelton and A. Pearson Almond of Atlanta.

This left the AIA committee powerless to guide program, philosophy, or commissions, with only the sticky job of criticizing members of their own organization in what remained of their "advisory" role. They don't like the library, and they have said so in a report issued earlier this month. (Unfortunately, the Commission of Fine Arts does not like the AIA-approved addition for its own Washington headquarters, and this is being tossed back at the AIA by everyone who, in turn, does not like the criticism of the library.)

Still with me? Take a deep breath and look at the building that Congress hath wrought. The Madison Library is a badly needed extension of the handsome Victorian Library of Congress, which already has one annex and rents all over town. The Madison Memorial, originally planned as a separate, small, temple-type monument, has been combined with the library.

Inside, the building is thoughtfully programmed, packing maximum library facilities into a minimum site, plus a Memorial Hall. The plan is a tight, efficient, functional response to overdue and urgent needs.

There are three floors below grade, the full size of the site, and six floors plus mechanical equipment above grade, with varying setbacks. These interior floors are huge work areas, broken by one small, token, skyless court requested by the AIA consultants as breathing space for the unrelieved floor mass, which rises only three of the six stories and is topped by more solid work floors. Except for the Memorial Hall, there will be endless nine-and-a-half-foot ceilings. This is basically a bulk, business building.

The practical, monolithic structure, a whopping 514 feet by 414 feet and 101.5 feet high, is stuffed into a pompous marble shroud. Wrapped around the no-nonsense plan is that weary dodge, a rigidly symmetrical, so-called classical design of central, stripped-down columns and solid end walls that is supposed to be a wedding of traditional and modern modes. This is a compromise that never works; it is a redundant Washington disaster. Yet here it is again, in all of its familiar, failed, heavy-handed, stagnant lifelessness, proving once more that the formula produces nothing but hollow and meaningless results. The library is the latest misalliance.

Even the AIA committee, which was strongly critical of the library in urban planning terms, backed discreetly away from design criticism that would have been an aesthetic slap at its colleagues while murmuring something off the record about wishing that a "fresher" solution had been found.

Whether this solution represents the last gasp of what all indications point to as Mr. Stewart's almost surrealistically reactionary taste, or if it is the taste of less-than-swinging senior congressmen convinced of their Olympian omniscience, or the taste of the architects who did the job, is hard to determine. It is probably an interplay of all three. This reviewer, for one, is willing to bet that those architects' offices contain enough up-to-date talent and sensibility to produce less tragicomic results. Research has suggested that at least one progressive alternative produced during study sessions was scuttled.

One hears constant defenses from Mr. Stewart's office of the "suitability" of his buildings and how few men can produce the genre anymore. That is fortunately true. And one reads pages of debate in the *Congressional Record*, with sinking heart, in which grown men with distinguished names display the willful ignorance of stubborn children. They may not know if it's architecture, but they know what they like and they are building about half a billion dollars' worth of it.

The new library, with its abortive gestures to debased and worn-out classical formulas, is neither suitable nor compatable to its surroundings nor to the twentieth century. It is "in keeping" with nothing. In spite of its wishful aesthetic rationale, it is totally and tragically out of character with its neighbors and its times.

In fairness, the limitations forced on the architects by the legislation, the site, and the program have been instrumental in producing a design that is aesthetically, urbanistically, and environmentally unsatisfactory. But it is also unsatisfactory because the design process is wrong, the method of architect selection is wrong, the autonomy, powers, and procedures of the office of the architect of the Capitol are wrong, the lack of a master plan for Capitol Hill is wrong, and the perpetuation of such a system is wrong. The building is wrong.

But the Library of Congress needs it, and the architect of the Capitol and his congressional cronies love and have approved it, and the James Madison Memorial Library will join the Rayburn Building as another monument to the bottom end of American architecture. How sad for Mr. Madison and the nation.

New York Times, September 24, 1967

A Bureaucratic Behemoth of a Library

AFTER THIRTY-TWO YEARS OF PLANNING, twenty years of design, and nine years of construction by a consortium of three architectural firms under the direction of two librarians of Congress, two architects of the Capitol, three chairmen of the Senate Office Building Committee, four chairmen of the House Office Building Committee, and seven chairmen of the Joint Committee on the Library, and after one abortive takeover attempt by the space-hungry House of Representatives, the James Madison Memorial Building, the new addition to the Library of Congress, was finally dedicated and turned over to the cultural and informational service of the nation last week.

While the ceremony was held marking the official transfer of the completed building from the federal government to the library on the anniversary of the signing of the original Library of Congress legislation by President John Adams in 1800, workmen continued to install the interior fittings of the new structure. The massive movement of resources from the old to the new quarters will be carried out over the rest of the year. The first section to be rehoused, the Geography and Map Division, is open to the public. Although the new building will not be fully functioning until 1981, the completed structure can be assessed now.

The Madison Memorial Library is colossal; it is the second largest building on Capitol Hill, just after the elephantine Rayburn Building. This is big even for official Washington, which specializes in Brobding-nagian scale. It is less ludicrous and more efficient than the Rayburn Building, and it is the last of the solid marble bombs in the long line willed to the nation by the late architect of the Capitol, J. George Stewart. Stylistically, this one has not quite caught up with Moscow's Palace of Congresses, or the Soviet avant-garde of 1961.

Built at a cost of $130 million, it occupies the superblock bounded by Independence Avenue, C Street, and First and Second streets, just across from the main Library of Congress Building, a beaux arts monument of notable grandeur completed in 1897. The new building is 514 feet long and 414 feet deep, has nine stories, and contains 2.1 million square feet of space and enough computerized and mechanized library equipment to put Gutenberg into shock.

Among its features are a James Madison Memorial Hall with a life-size statue of Madison surrounded by marble, travertine, and teak (the memorial was incorporated into the library in 1965), a two-story exhibition gallery that one might categorize as flashily retardataire, an interior garden court which, in common with much of the staff, will never see the light of day, and 1.56 million square feet of usable working space.

Let us immediately state the best and the worst of this new building. It is both desperately needed and totally ordinary. So much ordinariness becomes almost extraordinary. The interiors that are to be devoted to the display and dissemination of the world's art and culture are pure, catalog commercial; the executive offices are unadulterated cliché corporate, from the conference rooms with sliding walls to the overcontrived lighting. The whole is clothed in enough Georgia marble to sink a ship of state.

But the building is long overdue for an institution bursting at every seam, with personnel tucked into nooks and corners of balconies and hallways and offices carved out of corridors and triple-decked under thirty-foot ceilings. The library and its staff are grateful for every undistinguished inch. The present architect of the Capitol, George White, who inherited the project, has managed to upgrade its execution with above-average supervisory care. And the space is being very well used by the library's rather awesomely named planning unit, the Environmental Resources Office, under James Trew, to put in effect a total reorganization plan that has been conceived by the present librarian of Congress, the historian Daniel Boorstin.

This reorganization involves the Main Building, the Thomas Jefferson Building (an extension largely for storage built in the thirties), and the Madison Building. Collections will be shifted to form "halls of knowledge" of related artifacts and research materials devoted to Western and Eastern civilizations, the arts and sciences, language and literature, philosophy and religion, maps and geography, manuscripts, law and bibliography, and library science. The result will create a kind of "multimedia encyclopedia" for easier access and use.

THE ADDITIONAL SPACE that makes this rational rearrangement possible is the new building's chief virtue. But there is another conspicuous and very important benefit: The spectacular Main Building will now be released from the pressure of overuse for restoration. As the index to all of the collections, this historic structure will remain the library's centerpiece.

It can be stated without reservation that the turn-of-the-century Library of Congress Building is one of the most magnificent works of its time in this country, representing a period and style, a quality of workmanship and material, a richness of color, detail, and decoration, that will never be seen again. It is the work of a Washington architectural firm, Smithmeyer and Pelz, collaborating with sculptors, muralists, and artisans. Its interiors show a masterful use of ceremonial and symbolic public space that is still inadequately understood, and in this case, almost unequaled in American architecture. This building is one of the capital's few real gems.

I am thinking, in particular, of the Great Hall with its stairs, colonnades, and balconies, of an architecture so sophisticated and skilled in its manipulation of levels, planes, and light, and so lavish in its use of decorative arts, that it recalls the Grand Foyer of the Paris Opera; this is less extravagantly baroque but no less successful. The huge, domed, circular main reading room is one of the most impressive interiors in the United States.

I am thinking also of parts of the building that cannot be seen, which are just beginning to be visible through gaps and holes as "temporary" offices start to be dismantled. Four glorious corner pavilions, connected by two-block-long vaulted and coffered corridors or galleries that completely encircle the building's perimeter, have been hidden for decades by partitions, false ceilings, screen walls, and assorted interior crimes and atrocities. One could not even guess at their existence except for the presence of floating capitals and giant column segments sandwiched between wallboard and ceiling panels.

Fortunately, little was destroyed. These changes were reasonably careful acts of spatial desperation by a growing staff dealing with burgeoning collections; such incursions can be easily removed to reveal the building's original splendor. Restoration is now a top concern and priority of both the librarian of Congress and the architect of the Capitol. Does one need to remind the Congress that this is its library as well as the national collection?

The ceremony, symbolism, and art of the older structure are the qualities most obviously lacking in the new building; there is no indication that this is a place that contains and celebrates the treasures of civilization. Nothing here suggests that architecture traditionally gives expression to such values. This is any speculative office building behind a Mussolini-modern façade.

In the Madison Memorial Hall the standard nine-foot, three-inch ceiling is pushed to two stories, and the walls and columns are buttered up with wood and travertine; the result is vacuous, not noble. The garden court behind the entrance is another exercise in punching up the space, three stories this time, in response to early protests about the building's lack of beauty and amenity. Because the court is topped, not by sky, but by six more stories, and surrounded by standard, dark glass, curtain-walled offices, a battery of artificial lights must mimic sun for ficus trees (that most durable of species) buttressed in granite. Only 6 percent of the building's surface is windowed; the set-back top floor, with a glass wall offering views from the staff dining rooms and executive offices, is like a release from limbo.

One could simply file this building under the heading of the decline and fall of public architecture, but it is more complex than that. The architects selected in a typical bureaucratic shotgun wedding—Roscoe DeWitt of Texas, Alfred Easton Poor and Homer Swanke of New York, and A. Pearson Almond and Jesse Shelton of Atlanta—were in the rear guard, rather than the vanguard, of architecture. They produced a dated and lackluster design that embodied a program which also became obsolete as the long, bureaucratic process of appropriation, approval, and construction proceeded over twenty years.

In those years, a revolution in computerized library technology took place; as recently as a year and a half ago the power capacity of the building had to be restudied and upgraded. The flexibility that was supposed to be built into the plan has proved to be more theoretical than practical in spite of modular design; the movable partitions weigh two hundred pounds. Twenty years ago libraries and museums avoided destructive natural light like the plague. But even at that time, the new filtering and reflective glass was being developed that has created a radical and agreeable change in their architecture.

Today, the windowless behemoth is dead. Two of the architects who started with the project are also dead, and most of the others are retired. The Madison Library, in fact, could be called dead on arrival.

There are no easy answers to technological revolutions or congressional tastes. But even the most superficial research indicates that other countries are building national libraries in less time that relate better to the state of architecture and science. It would be worth some studies to see how it is done. Washington is running out of room for these stillborn federal blockbusters, and it has long since run out of art.

New York Times March 4, 1980

Museums

THE SIXTIES

What Should a Museum Be?

SIX MONTHS—AND MORE THAN HALF A million paid admissions—
after the Solomon R. Guggenheim Museum opened its plate-glass
doors on Fifth Avenue to a fanfare of publicity, the controversy it set off
continues to rage. The Guggenheim, final, flamboyant gesture of the
late Frank Lloyd Wright, has been hailed as a masterpiece, attacked as
an atrocity, called the finest museum of all time, and denounced as no
museum at all. Some critics have termed its stunning circular hall "a
crime against painting and sculpture"; others have saluted it as "one of
the greatest rooms in history."

The controversy clearly is a conflict between art and architecture. Is
this extraordinary and exhilarating structure appropriate for its primary
purpose—the display of works of art? Does its eccentric design enhance
or eclipse the objects on view? Is its overwhelming strength and style
unfair competition? Serious or superficial, all discussion leads inevitably to the basic question: "What should a museum be?"

It is an insistent question, because the Guggenheim's box-office success dramatically reflects a current cultural phenomenon: the museum
building boom. The roster of museum designers reads like a who's who
of architecture. In the United States, Mies van der Rohe recently completed a large hall for the Houston Museum of Fine Arts. Philip C.
Johnson has four projects under way: the almost-finished Munson-
Williams-Proctor Institute in Utica, New York, the Carter Museum in
Fort Worth, Texas, the Sheldon Art Gallery in Lincoln, Nebraska, and
the projected new wing for New York's Museum of Modern Art.

Edward D. Stone has prepared working drawings for Huntington
Hartford's new Gallery of Modern Art on Columbus Circle. Minoru

Yamasaki has proposed an addition to the Detroit Institute of Arts. Museum facilities are part of Eero Saarinen's prize-winning Jefferson National Expansion Memorial project awaiting execution in St. Louis. Le Corbusier has completed museum buildings in Tokyo and in Ahmedabad, India. Work is soon to start on Oscar Niemeyer's new art center for Caracas.

THE CONTRAST BETWEEN these projects and the buildings that have come to mean "museum" in the popular mind is striking. The familiar fine-arts museums—Boston, New York, Philadelphia, Chicago, Cleveland, Detroit, and points west—were constructed from the 1880s to the 1930s. They followed a familiar formula of colonnaded, neoclassic façades. Their impressive shells masked a labyrinth of monumental rooms and vast flights of marble steps, haunted by the specter of museum fatigue.

These majestic monuments were the heirs of the original "museums," the palaces of European princes whose remarkable personal artistic treasuries are best preserved in collections like Madrid's Prado and Paris's Louvre. At best, such collections were massed magnificence; at worst, indescribable clutter. Whether the installations were good or had, the buildings offered advantages that are hard to equal today: impressively proportioned galleries, clearly organized plans, and unrestricted space.

With the years, however, have come basic changes in museum functions. No longer passive picture galleries, they offer today active programs of instruction, entertainment, and participation in their own and related fields. Older institutions have had to resort to massive remodeling to meet these modern needs. Among the new structures, the revolution in the museum's role has been matched by a revolution in the museum's design.

THE MODERN MUSEUMS make no obeisance to the architectural status symbols of the past—the classic columns, pediments, friezes, and embellishing academic statuary that were the universal trademarks of the public edifice. Permanent galleries have been replaced by open floors partitioned to suit the needs of changing exhibitions, or by unconventional schemes like the Guggenheim's winding spiral ramp, intended to offer entirely new answers to the old relationships of people looking at pictures.

The new buildings are startling, even shocking, in appearance. They follow no set architectural formula; each designer offers his own idea of the best way to house the museum's updated functions. The temptation to turn a structure into a personal statement occasionally has proved irresistible. The inevitable result is a conflict between the building and its contents.

This conflict is distressingly evident in most of the new museums. In the case of Wright's building, the architectural statement is so bold and so personal that only Director James Johnson Sweeney's special lighting and hanging save the collection from being blotted out. In spite of Sweeney's firm belief that "a good museum is like an iceberg, one-tenth above the surface, nine-tenths below," Wright sacrificed almost all necessary study and storage areas to his personal delight in the great concrete spiral shell. Whatever couldn't be tucked into an odd, pie-shaped corner was simply eliminated, in the name of architecture.

WHETHER WRIGHT'S UNIQUE idea of channeling the visitors past the collection along an inexorable, winding ramp is worth these functional sacrifices is debatable. The fact that he chose to call the building an "archeseum" is indication enough of his lifelong conviction that architecture is the "mother art" beyond which little else concerned him.

Mies van der Rohe's huge hall for Houston, achieved by filling in the open end of an existing U-shaped building, is one of this master architect's great rooms—designed like a jewel, painstaking in the exquisite detail of its structure, impressive in its serene monumentality. Yet it presents equally impressive installation problems because of its undivided space, thirty-foot ceiling, and outsized proportions.

Its flexible, open plan, a scheme pioneered by New York's Museum of Modern Art, is best on paper, where one can play intriguing space games with a pencil and put up or knock down walls with an eraser. Actually, temporary partitions are expensive, hard to fireproof, and seldom well finished. If walls are made movable to create spaces ranging from intimate to monumental, it follows logically that ceilings should be movable, too, to provide proper scale and lighting within changing room sizes. In addition, because the flexible plan requires a director who must double as a designer, the result can be magnificent—or a mess.

Both of Le Corbusier's museums, at Tokyo and Ahmedabad, show just as much preoccupation with the creation of dominating architectural forms as with matters of hanging and lighting. These abstract architectural exercises have been called "exhibitions of columns" by the Museum of Modern Art's Arthur Drexler; smaller works of art fight a losing battle against "sculpture" on this scale.

The upended pyramid that Niemeyer has planned for Caracas is so arresting that it will command the spectator's attention, very possibly at the expense of the art it will house. The arcades and framing filigree that are Edward Stone's increasingly insistent trademarks will make his Gallery of Modern Art an effective architectural billboard before the visitor even enters.

Museum men and architects seem to be in irreconcilable disagreement over their goals. The most outspoken directors say frankly that they don't want "architecture" at all. Firmly united against anything that will compete or achieve equal status with the objects on view, they share a common fear of overwhelming buildings.

THE MUSEUM OF MODERN ART'S director René d'Harnoncourt believes that "the first function of a museum is to make works of art understandable and available to the public." Sweeney of the Guggenheim unequivocally agrees: "The museum exists for the work of art. The architect's job is to solve the problems as clearly and pungently as possible, not to make monuments. A well-proportioned room is the best place to hang pictures." With understandable urgency from a man who has had to make his peace with Frank Lloyd Wright, Sweeney pleads for modesty, for architects who will "underdesign."

James J. Rorimer, head of New York's vast, treasure-gorged Metropolitan, says, "A museum should not be conceived as an architectural landmark. The work of art itself is the chief consideration. I have no interest in a work of art as a background. To me, it must be the foreground. The architecture should never dominate. It should be no more than a setting, creating a mood, a happy frame of mind." Is there a conflict between architect and director? "Perhaps. But I know of no compromise. It's the director's building."

"There is a very real conflict between the architect and the museum," d'Harnoncourt asserts. "The architect must soft-pedal himself as an artist. It is hard for him, because he thinks of the building as his work of art. Designing an incinerator would be easier; he then would bring beauty to a utilitarian structure. In the museum, he is competing. It is easier for him to yield to functional requirements than to aesthetics." As to the importance of architecture for museums: "'I don't even think it's a particularly interesting subject."

What do the architects reply? "The museum has become a civic necessity, a shrine for the people," says Philip Johnson. "This is a building that must be considered as important as churches or city halls in our civic schemes."

Concerning the extent of the director's control, he asks, "How much ought you to force your idiosyncratic hanging methods on the conception of the architect? You could do it, I suppose, to the point of achieving a well-functioning, but dull and stupid building. The museum must be beautiful, and its monumental aspect is the true province of the architect.

"Civilizations," Johnson adds, "are sometimes remembered only by their buildings."

Edward Stone, architect of the American Embassy at New Delhi and of the American Pavilion at the Brussels World's Fair, offers a point of view at odds with those of both designers and directors. Limiting his remarks on the desirability of creating a monument to a suggestive "I am not without ego," he argues for a setting that would afford relaxed, casual enjoyment, "as if we were living comfortably and unself-consciously with works of art."

IN AN ARGUMENT as appealing as it is dubious, Stone contends that since painting and sculpture were originally collected in a private, domestic atmosphere (the domesticity of palaces may be somewhat questionable), the museum should project an informal air.

"Why create a synthetic, laboratory environment with brilliantly lighted, austere surroundings?" he asks. "The museum should be like a club or residence, with carpeting, comfortable chairs, wood-and-fabric walls, smoking and refreshments."

Nearly forgotten in the controversy is the artist. Like the director, he favors a structure that serves rather than dominates its contents. Costantino Nivola, a sculptor well represented in contemporary collections, says, "Art doesn't need much—a good light, and space around it. But there is no reason why the building can't be a good one."

Ideally, the museum should be a fusion of art and architecture: the respectful and sympathetic installation of the art object balanced with a setting of comparable quality. The building should be handsome enough to be a recognizable landmark, important and interesting enough to attract visitors; a museum without people is no museum at all.

Is THIS IDEAL museum an unattainable dream? The answer appears to lie in the reining of the architect's ego. At present, he too often is more concerned with producing an independent artistic monument than a suitable background for art. And, in this age of intense professional competition, he is not averse to the profitable personal publicity that a striking or debatable structure will bring him. He has lost sight of the fact that the museum, by its very nature, requires a subtle, understated kind of design.

Although he provides the setting—space, light, color, scale, effects of intimacy or grandeur—he plays only a supporting role. He must play it with distinction, but he must never forget that the collection is the star.

Ironically, a return to some of the principles of the conventional museum may be indicated. Like permissive child rearing, the amorphous open plan may be on the way out. The traditional scheme, with its focal court surrounded by fixed galleries, its spaciousness, simplicity, and lack of personal architectural idiosyncrasies, suggests advantages that have been ignored or lost in current examples.

The National Gallery in Washington, for all the coldness and conventionality of its architectural details and the depressing sterility of its façade, offers impressive space and a well-organized setting for its superb collection. The welcome greenery of its courts creates restful oases and orientation points for the galleries.

Although Philip Johnson is known as a dedicated champion of the new architecture, he speaks admiringly of the "clear, concise space arrangements" of Sir John Soane's Dulwich Picture Gallery near London, of Karl Friedrich Schinkel's Altes Museum in Berlin, and Franz Karl Leo von Klenze's Alte Pinakothek in Munich, all nineteenth-century structures. Most of Johnson's latest projects are court-oriented buildings that look back toward these older models. They emphasize a spacious elegance and a delicate refinement of detail that may do less damage to their contents than more aggressively individualistic work.

THE ARCHITECT AND planner José Luis Sert has proposed a scheme for a Mediterranean locale in which galleries would be self-contained one-room buildings, united by outdoor courts and gardens. The trend is again toward a fixed plan and permanent, generously dimensioned galleries, reinterpreted in terms of contemporary materials and aesthetics and needs.

The true test of a museum is the impact of its contents on the heart and mind, and the sense of beauty or gratification enjoyed by the visitor as a private, personal experience. Whether the new buildings will improve this experience remains to be seen.

New York Times, May 8, 1960

Misalliance on the Mall

THE NEW MUSEUM OF HISTORY AND TECHNOLOGY of the Smithsonian Institution, opening to the public today, is the latest of the capital's stillborn monuments on the Mall.

Designed to house that magnificent collection of memorabilia, inventions, and cultural castoffs brought together in what is popularly known as the national attic, it could, and should have been, one of the most marvelous museums in the world.

In terms of its contents, a completely fascinating mélange of locomotives, clocks, cars, costumes, household furnishings, uniforms, flags, weapons, and unclassifiable curiosities, it is an absorbing adventure. In terms of its architecture, it is a disaster.

AN EXTREMELY LARGE building, 577 feet long and 301 feet wide with a total public area of 347,760 square feet, it occupies one of Washington's most prominent ceremonial areas on Constitution Avenue between Twelfth and Fourteenth streets, cost thirty-seven million dollars, and expects a whopping big audience of five million visitors a year. Its architects are McKim, Mead & White, a firm of great luster around the turn of the century, which has not been McK, M & W for some time, and officially became Steinmetz, Cain and White in 1961.

The building is a machine to exhibit in, to paraphrase Le Corbusier's famous dictum that a house is a machine to live in, consisting of a businesslike steel-framed enclosure with open fifty-foot spans between columns, all the latest flexible, modular lighting and wiring, and few fixed interior partitions. It is a museum-factory to be divided at will.

Outside, the factory is disguised as a monument. The steel is sheathed in stone, and an arbitrary system of projecting and receding wall planes form vertical strip windows that have driven the staff to distraction. Most have been blacked out. An awkward attempt to marry the classical and the modern, the building is legitimately neither.

Inside, escalators ascend from the basement level to the building's focus — the central flag hall scaled to the original Star-Spangled Banner that flew over Fort McHenry; fifty feet high. It could have been a superb space. But marble has been substituted for imagination.

Structure is denied and confused by busily banal bronze and steel column detailing, and instead of dignity and dramatic impact, we have the pretentious, pedestrian equivalent of a slightly passé office building lobby.

On the main cross axis is Horatio Greenough's famous, giant-size George Washington-in-a-toga statue set smack against escalators to the left, and balancing it, the solid marble access door to the machinery of the matching escalators to the right. The escalators themselves are entombed in marble. It would be pointless to continue.

The exhibits are installed expertly and pragmatically; in no case are their considerable aesthetic merits emphasized by the fortunate accident of being directly exposed under a clear light, in an A-B-C lineup based on logical chronology.

This is not all bad, because the installations are technically excellent and the exhibits stand on their own merits, with a minimum of the artificial sentimentalizing or "periodizing" currently popular. They are the real thing.

But sensitivity has come off second best to the scientific method; vistas and visual points of emphasis are nonexistent. A seventeenth-century stone carving, for example, that cries for finesse or the fine flair of the Italian exhibition designer, is dumped into a sort of varnished wood public school sandbox. The arts of design are sadly absent.

What went wrong? The obvious thing, in Washington. A joint congressional committee was set up for the museum, authorized to advise the regents of the Smithsonian on the design and construction of the building. This is not the first time that Congress has overstepped itself in the arts. It has proved once again that it is more qualified to legislate than to design, although its recent record might suggest that it has done more designing than legislating.

WHAT WOULD HAVE been a better solution? For an easy answer, see Lincoln Center for the Performing Arts. Either Philharmonic Hall or the new New York State Theater offer an architectural approach that may be a bit stodgy for New York, but would be brilliantly suitable for Washington's problem of classical continuity.

For a harder but better answer, imagine the new museum and the adjoining National Museum of Natural History and National Gallery that form the north side of the Mall as a series of enclosures, connected by gardens, arcades, and courts, inviting—rather than repelling—people, a living group of buildings rather than a row of ceremonial tombs.

New York Times, January 23, 1964

THE EIGHTIES

Museums: Lessons from the Sixties

THERE IS A MUSEUM EXPLOSION IN the eighties that is beginning to make the museum building boom of the sixties look like a practice run. In some ways this new museum wave is producing much more interesting buildings; they are far more revealing about the arts, including architecture, than most of the earlier structures. Many of today's most prestigious commissions are going to the architects of what used to be called the avant-garde—a sure indication that new styles, and new ways of thinking about the arts, are being adopted by the establishment.

The trend is international. James Stirling's Staatsgalerie building is rising now in Stuttgart while he works on extensions for the Fogg Museum in Cambridge, Massachusetts, and the Tate Gallery in London. Richard Meier has museums on the drawing board for Frankfurt and Atlanta. Arata Isozaki is designing the new Museum of Contemporary Art in Los Angeles, and Michael Graves has received the commission for the addition to the Whitney Museum in New York. All of these architects are redefining a "modern" building type that was born in classicism and the Beaux Arts in the nineteenth century.

The twenty years between these cultural building booms have made a tremendous difference. With a few notable exceptions, the museums of the sixties leaned heavily toward windowless warehousing, or more correctly, their directors did. Frustrated by older, monumental structures with enormous architectural presence requiring constant installation battles, curators demanded total control of the presentation of their collections. They asked for, and got, anonymous, all-purpose space in blind, bland boxes. The vagaries of daylight were eliminated for sophisticated artificial lighting systems. In essence, nothing was supposed to interfere with the art itself—least of all the architect, who was often a troublesome fellow.

New National Gallery, Berlin

The results, which should have been ideal, were curiously disappointing. The buildings were not just neutral; they were dispiritingly characterless. The scientifically controlled lighting lacked life. The museum was reduced to containerized art. Most surprising of all, the works of art seemed diminished, rather than liberated, by their ordinary setting. Since then, the return to day-lit galleries and specially designed spaces has been gradual, but steady, and the return of architecture as the supplier of context and measure for the other arts is quite overwhelmingly evident.

There were three particularly important exceptions to this sixties's trend: the Centre Pompidou in Paris, the East Wing of the National Gallery in Washington, and the New National Gallery in West Berlin. All three are national museums, and each was meant to establish a national cultural image. All opted consciously for architecture.

THE CENTRE POMPIDOU, popularly known as the Beaubourg, was the product of an international competition won by the firm of Piano and Rogers. The design sought to create a distinctly new kind of building for a radically conceived museum function intended to restore leadership and vitality to Paris as an artistic world capital.

The East Wing of Washington's National Gallery, by I. M. Pei & Partners, had to meet special criteria of site, status, and suitability. The New National Gallery in West Berlin, which was the last major work of Mies van der Rohe, was the summation of that master's painstaking investigations of structure, space, and style—a work of art in its own right that was to house the national collections.

How have these museums fared? The results are distinctly mixed. None has been problem-free. Each director has wrestled with his particular devil, or architect, a process complicated by changing exhibition ideas, styles, and functions in the seventies and eighties. These have ranged from the all-star supershows to increasingly didactic displays reinforced by historical and literary references.

The successes and failures of these buildings are instructive. The Beaubourg has turned out to be a winner, after a rocky and uncertain start. The New National Gallery in West Berlin is currently a loser, for reasons that have less to do with design than with unsympathetic use. The National Gallery's East Wing in Washington is an uneasy draw, depending entirely on the nature and scale of what is on display.

How much of this can be attributed to the architecture? Saying that "a building doesn't work" covers a multitude of sins and sinners. No building is flawless; its uses are too complex. Even the most careful program can be out of date by the time the structure is finished. No all-purpose space works equally well for all purposes. "Flexibility" puts even more creative strain on the abilities of those who use the spaces than on the original designer. Using any building well means working with, not against, its visions and intentions. Some buildings present more obstacles than others—turning Frank Lloyd Wright's Guggenheim spiral into a functioning museum was a formidable and exasperating job. But a Guggenheim exhibition seen from the changing perspectives of that ramp has extraordinary impact as a total aesthetic experience.

There are clear cases of overt hostility to a building by a client or user, and the result is always a disaster. Whether the hostility is conscious or not, insensitivity to the architecture can lead to sabotage. This seems to be the case with Mies's New National Gallery in West Berlin. The misunderstanding of its aesthetic and the mishandling of its space, the unfeeling destruction of this handsome structure, visually and conceptually, can make one's heart ache.

To BEGIN WITH the ludicrous, this is probably the only building in West Berlin—or perhaps even in Germany, where cleanliness counts—with dirty windows. For a Mies building, that means dirty glass walls. The crystalline quality so essential to these transparent planes is smudged by a dull, nasty film.

Mies's typical, perfectly calibrated, steel-framed enclosure stands on a stone platform in a setting as amorphous and ill-scaled as any scene of American urban renewal. By dint of its sheer design strength, however, the building makes a serene, self-contained statement.

One enters a huge, open room from the street; the land slopes sharply to the rear so that the plaza becomes a podium, with galleries for the permanent collection and a sculpture garden at the lower levels. This single, superb, unified, and unashamedly "univalent" space is the basis of the Miesian aesthetic. The making of such a grand space is a historical architectural preoccupation; the adjustment of proportions and details, of structure to openness, of materials and finishes, was Mies's main concern in the last years of his life.

All of this care is canceled out by woeful misuse and poor maintenance. In the tradition begun by Mies's 1929 Barcelona Pavilion, this room is a singular, twentieth-century setting for the selective display of the best twentieth-century art. It brooks nothing second-rate. That, admittedly, is a sublime but restrictive purpose, but for anyone truly interested in the arts of our time, this unique integration of art and architecture represents an exceptional achievement.

WHAT THE ROOM contained when I saw it were some extremely unattractive and badly related paintings documenting trends of the last two decades, all better represented elsewhere. A clumsy installation amputated the green marble columns that should soar from floor to roof. The kind of sculpture that is made of old rags and boards was dropped, as if discarded, on the far-from-clean floor. The hallmarks of the Miesian aesthetic—elegance, rigor, quality, and perfection of placement and detail—were abysmally lacking. This structure is not without problems—it is clearly short on administrative and curatorial space. But every attempted solution, from signs to coffee shop, is jarringly unsuitable. This is more of a national disgrace than a national museum.

The success of the Beaubourg, on the other hand, shows how a talented and determined staff came to terms with equally demanding architecture. This structure promised the impossible: It made futuristic claims of multipurpose space and multimedia arts. Faced with installing the same old modern art, the staff found that the stylish plumbing kept getting in the way. The building insisted on celebrating its own technology over everything else. With the Paris-New York and Paris-Moscow shows, the most serious of the installation problems were brought under control. These spectacular and scholarly exhibitions combined theme, contents, and setting to stunning effect. They were landmark events. The irony, of course, is that this building is not working the way it was supposed to—as a laboratory of the arts—but it is now working very well.

THE EAST WING of the National Gallery in Washington is still shaking down. Its monumental atrium does what the New National Gallery in Berlin was meant to do—it creates an environmental experience of the arts of this century. Mies's building would have done it better, but that, alas, is moot. The trouble comes with the transition to the smaller galleries. When the scale of the exhibits is small—like miniature impressionist paintings or royal European treasures, or when they make a discrete entity, as with the Matisse cutouts, these galleries are an intimate delight.

But the present show of Rodin sculpture is a powerhouse that writhes and twists through these rooms and can barely be contained, while the plunge down the small spiral stairs to Rodin's monumental *Gates of Hell* is an architectural absurdity. There is an incompatibility in this subject that the architecture cannot seem to handle. The problem is one that the National Gallery will continue to face.

WHEN A MUSEUM and its contents come together as an integrated aesthetic whole, something special happens. The art is enlarged and exalted, and so is the experience of the viewer. Creating that synthesis of art and setting is the challenge that still faces architects and directors. It is also the secret of a great museum.

New York Times, November 29, 1981

THE NINETIES

The Guggenheim Bilbao: Art and Architecture as One

THERE IS NO WAY TO MISS THE new Guggenheim Museum in this northern Basque city; the billowing mass of lustrous, cloudlike forms is the first thing you see against the surrounding green hills. This spectacular European outpost of New York's Guggenheim Museum will open its doors Saturday with a ceremony presided over by the king and queen of Spain and an international A-list of art, social, and business world celebrities. Designed by the American architect Frank O. Gehry, the building is more like sculpture than architecture. Its exuberantly curved and canted abstract shapes covered in softly gleaming sheets of silvery titanium are anchored to the earth by warm beige Spanish limestone, their shimmering surfaces changing color magically with the light and weather. Not since Frank Lloyd Wright completed the concrete spiral of the Guggenheim Museum in New York in 1959 has an art museum so shocked and intrigued observers or received so much preopening publicity.

A less formal dedication by Basque officials took place on a balmy evening earlier this month; the people of Bilbao streamed across the plaza, down the ceremonial stairs, and across the bridge over the Nervión River until late at night. As the crowds moved through and around the extraordinary structure, gilded by the setting sun, it came suddenly and stunningly to life, its eccentricities forgotten.

Everything about the building denies custom and tradition. Its concept and forms are as radical as the contemporary works of art they accommodate. The grand stair descends rather than rises; the broad gentle treads lead down to the entrance on the level of the river and into an immense atrium that soars the building's full 165-foot height. This stunning space is reminiscent of Wright's sky-lit spiral ramp in New York, except that here the atrium is not enclosed; it is surrounded by curving open walkways

Guggenheim Bilbao

offering constantly changing views of the vast interior and glimpses into the galleries at every level. The processional, multidimensional plan expands vision and perception dramatically. The container and the contained, the art and the architecture, are one thing, made for each other; nowhere else do all of the arts support and play off one another in a unified aesthetic that so fully expresses the twentieth century. The setting is as significant as the art; the whole is the superb sum of its parts.

The light, from the top and sides, is a luminous glow in the day that turns into a harder, theatrical brilliance at night. Sharply angled steel-and-glass enclosures for stairs and elevators recall early Russian constructivist designs like Tatlin's elaborate unbuilt platforms rising precariously into thin air. Claes Oldenburg and Coosje van Bruggen's *Soft Shuttlecock* drapes its twenty-four-foot-long painted canvas feathers over a stone wall high overhead. There are views of the river and the enclosing hills studded with ornate old buildings. Outside, a pool and pedestrian bridge interact with the river, and at night the pool erupts with blue flames as five *Fire Fountains* by Yves Klein roar into action. The scale is enormous everywhere; this is a place where Jim Dine's three twenty-foot-high *Red Spanish Venuses* can feel at home.

With no false modesty, the Guggenheim's director, Thomas Krens, declared from the beginning that the Bilbao museum was to be "the greatest building of the twentieth century." It will be a hard act to follow. But if anything could be more impressive than the building, it is the process that brought it into being. Bilbao was once the richest city in Spain; its shipping, mining, and banking businesses were prime generators of the country's prosperity until the decline of heavy industry after World War II. Faced with a failing image and economy, its officials have undertaken a series of revitalizing projects. When the vision and determination of a city bent on regeneration of its spirit and resources met the ambitions of a director with a growing collection and dreams of expansion, a bargain was struck with international reverberations.

In a shrewd gamble, the Basque government invited the Guggenheim, already involved in several European ventures, to build in Bilbao. With a background in art, academia, and business, Mr. Krens is no stranger to the art of the deal. He negotiated a $320-million package in which the Basques pledged $150 million for a new building, a $100-million subsidy toward operating costs, $50 million for the purchase of new work, and a nonrefundable $20 million up front, in case the plans fell through. In exchange, the Guggenheim would retain control, supply the works of art from its collection, and provide administrative and curatorial expertise. The completed museum, which replaces old warehouses on what was once a working waterfront, has become Bilbao's dramatic symbol of renewal and bid for an updated economic and cultural base. It is also seen as a way, after civil war, cultural repression, and separatist pressures, to reconnect with the international community. The project fulfilled Mr. Krens's desire for a global presence, something that has been sharply criticized by other members of the art world who think the Guggenheim should stay at home. Of the result, he says, "I got everything I ever wanted."

Like it or not, Mr. Krens has written a new chapter in patronage. He is a phenomenon of our time, the director-wheeler-dealer—a role that has also drawn criticism from the art world, used to more subtle, if no less Machiavellian, maneuvering. The collaboration between director and architect on this building has been unique. Most museum directors opt for negative, or "recessive," space; they favor neutrality as an aid to installation. Mr. Krens urged Mr. Gehry to take his place with the other artists; he encouraged the spatial drama of the atrium, the startling shapes and dimensions of the galleries. He has bought art on a grand scale and commissioned new, site-specific works throughout the museum: a room reconfigured by Sol LeWitt's dazzling color geometry; a Jenny Holzer installation of electronic-sign columns flashing their disturbing messages in a rush of red and blue.

Moreover, Mr. Krens is convinced that the constantly increasing size of much contemporary art makes it virtually impossible to exhibit in normal surroundings, and that to do so diminishes its impact and meaning. When works of art are so large and heavy that they must be moved by forklift truck, when walls and floors must be reinforced to install them, when canvas size is room size, display is a serious problem. He wanted, and got, the largest gallery in the world, 450 feet long by 80 feet wide, with a skylight and flying beams overhead. Richard Serra's *Snake*—three curving steel walls 104 feet in length and weighing 174 tons—was commissioned for this space. Robert Morris's walk-in *Labyrinth* and 25-by-33-foot *Aluminum I-Beams Construction* and a floor piece by Carl André also fit handily, as does Claes Oldenburg's Brobdingnagian, brilliant-red *Knife Ship*, its motorized oars rowing and its knife blades rising and lowering at the gallery's far end.

On one long wall is a series of enormous, predominantly white paintings by Robert Ryman and Andy Warhol and a mirror-finished copper work by Donald Judd, like a polished jewel among them. The passion with which Mr. Krens regards this supergallery and its contents belies his reputation as a cool, detached outsider. More conventional, but still huge galleries, roughly fifty feet square, are devoted to the Guggenheim's classic collection of modern art—Picasso, Braque, Kandinsky, Brancusi, Léger, Miró—a roll call of the names recent generations have grown up with.

Mr. Gehry's architecture is as groundbreaking as anything in the museum. With the help of advanced computer technology used to design fighter planes, he has been able to calculate structure curvature, material, and cost so accurately that forms impossible to create and build through traditional methods can now be brought in on budget and on time. But perhaps the major achievement here is an accident of history. It is possible for the first time, as the century ends, to give an overview of twentieth-century art, a period of revolutionary creativity and change. Putting a great collection in this perspective, and in this building, as an act of total aesthetic collaboration makes the Bilbao Guggenheim one of the most significant, as well as one of the most beautiful, museums in the world today.

Wall Street Journal, October 16, 1997

Hot Museums in a Cold Climate

IT IS EASY TO THINK OF THE impressive new museums in Norway, Sweden, and Finland as a good way to get out of the cold. My attempt to visit Norway's Glacier Museum high above the rugged west coast in what might nominally be called spring was foiled by a blizzard and impassable roads. Stockholm, Helsinki, and Oslo are less adventuresome destinations, but these northern capitals are still out of the main European cultural loop. Norway's connection with cultural fashion has always been tenuous, and the new Norwegian museums break both architectural and museological molds. Those designed by native son Sverre Fehn celebrate unconventional subjects in innovative structures; among the best is his reinterpretation of a medieval ruin. Finland and Sweden have opted to move ambitiously toward the continental mainstream. Their major new museums are the result of international competitions won by architectural superstars who attract press coverage and crowds elsewhere. The new Moderna Museet opened in Stockholm this February, with a sophisticated design by the distinguished Spanish architect Rafael Moneo. In Helsinki, the city of cool northern classicism and the modern Finnish master Alvar Aalto, Steven Holl's audacious, competition-winning Finnish Museum of Contemporary Art will open next week.

Inevitably, all these new museums are being measured against the spectacular new Guggenheim Museum in the Basque city of Bilbao, Spain, which is also devoted to contemporary art, or one man's vision of it, and was inaugurated spectacularly last fall with a preemptive assassination attempt just before the royal dedication attended by the A-list of the art world. The combination of an American architect at the peak of his powers, Frank Gehry, and a museum director, the Guggenheim's Thomas Krens, who thinks large and global, and knew exactly what he wanted and loved what he got, has created a unique collaborative work of art.

Kiasma, the new Finnish museum (Mr. Holl took the name from a Greek word for intersection, the X-shape of the letter *chi*, and meant it to stand for a synthesis of building and landscape), is much closer to Bilbao than Stockholm's more conservative Modern Art Museum. Mr. Holl's unconventional all-white structure glows with light in the long Finnish winter night; startling, but pleasing, it is a nonaggressive example of the kind of dynamic sculptural forms favored by some of the more romantically revolutionary of today's postpostmodernist architects. This is a style that uses advanced computer design and drafting techniques for the calculation of unusual and largely unprecedented shapes and surfaces, often achieved, ironically, through painstaking hand crafts. Boldly creative and fraught with danger in execution — eccentric shapes can create awkward and imperfect connections and details — it is full of the promise of aesthetic and poetic power.

Mr. Holl delivers both the aesthetics and the poetics in this important, large-scale building that his admirers have been waiting for, and he has probably overloaded it with ideas that he has been wanting to use. This works against lucid simplicity and ineffable logic, which may not have been the intention anyway. The jury praised the design as "mysteriously sculpturesque and sensitively innovative," and it is all that, and more. The plan, keyed to the geography and topography of the site, combines a straight series of rectangular rooms with a long, curving run of galleries of varying asymmetrical shapes and sizes; where the two intersect, a central, curved, high void is created, flanked by an ascending, sinuous ramp. This dramatic, no-holds-barred bit of pure architectural and spatial theater, seen immediately on entering, takes second place to none in our atrium-obsessed culture.

The entrance mediates between the sight and sense of the city and this overwhelming interior feature; it also leads directly to a bookstore and glass-walled café with a terrace and pools outside. Helsinki's horizontal northern light enters through an expansive glass façade at this end—the prow of the structure—to which one instinctively gravitates after touring the galleries on each floor. Mr. Holl's great skill is the way in which he builds and breaks scale, always returning to and retaining a human dimension. Like the original Museum of Modern Art in New York, which was full of the promise of sociability and adventure, there is an immediate and enviably inviting sense of place. A handsome, welcoming presence rather than a shocking intruder in the heart of Helsinki, Kiasma is an instant landmark that adds focus and enrichment to the city.

This building does what architecture is supposed to do, enlarging and expanding our response to our physical surroundings, creating an environment of sensuous, and intellectual stimulation, of discovery and wonder. Whether it will do what a museum is supposed to do—support and enhance the display of art in a way that fuses the two aesthetics— will be clear only after the collection is installed. When I visited, the structure was complete but still empty. At Bilbao, the architecture, stunning in itself, was given greater impact and meaning by these interdependent relationships.

With the Moderna Museet, Stockholm has taken a different, more traditional route. Measured by Bilbao's bombast and Kiasma's derring-do, the subtlety of Rafael Moneo's fine Spanish hand can be a disappointment. Instead of eye-boggling spaces tied together by circulation that sweeps and soars, the Stockholm museum seems grounded. What it has is logic, elegance, and beautiful details, from a master of all three: perfectly proportioned, predominantly square, high galleries, with natural light flowing from top lanterns in pyramidal ceilings that make a roofscape forest above a long, low building. The rooms are entered in sequence or from a gallery-promenade that runs their length. In some a large, windowed wall recess, with an embrasure deep enough to moderate the impact of daylight and view, is simply and effectively installed, often with sculpture. This is a particularly lovely feature. Built on the island of Skeppsholmen, the museum is respectful of adjacent historic buildings and thoughtfully oriented to its water setting. The opening show was a somewhat opaque polemic called Wounds, in which the enriching marriage of art and architecture was not in evidence. The permanent collection fares better.

Wall Street Journal, May 14, 1998

Museums: Making It New

I

ONE OF THE MOST POWERFUL AND haunting experiences of the retrospective exhibition of work of the artist Bill Viola at New York's Whitney Museum last year was a double-sided video projection showing a walking man; small and distant at first, the figure advanced slowly and deliberately, until, larger than life, it filled the whole screen on both sides. As the figure grew, flames began to lick at the bottom of the screen on one side, and water appeared to rain down from the top of the screen on the other. While the man's relentless advance continued, the hot orange flames leaped higher and higher and the cool rain became a torrential downpour. The final images were of a full screen of brilliantly flaming fire, and on the reverse, a drowning avalanche of water. Both figures had been totally consumed.

Once seen, this is impossible to dismiss. It can be read as obvious symbolism—man destroyed and regenerated by his passage through the elements of fire and water. Called *The Crossing*, the work repeats the cycle over and over. It can be taken as a morality play or a stunning piece of visual theater, a deeply disturbing use of the arts of film and sound. An unforgettable image, it transmits something intangible and profound.

That makes it incontrovertibly a work of art. The concept and the techniques push the edges of art, pursuing meanings and ways to deliver them that force the viewer to radically revise what he believes art to be. Does this extraordinary imagery make you confront mortality on the artist's disturbingly graphic terms? So do the depictions of innumerable martyred saints by Renaissance and baroque masters; even for today's secular audience the religious imagery has an inescapable impact. Images from mythology such as Titian's powerful *The Flaying of Marsyus* remain visually and emotionally forceful.

Viola filled the Whitney's galleries with remarkable images. The installation, created by the artist in collaboration with the theater director Peter Sellars, not only drastically altered normal perceptions and sensory responses, but also challenged the museum's plan, spaces, and traditional purposes. When the lights and projectors and recordings go off, the walls are blank; there is no longer anything there, no art at all. Where sound and image and motion had overwhelmed the viewer, there is only a void—empty and dark. The relationship between the building and its contents—the ongoing, difficult, and uneasy connections between art and architecture—like the art itself, no longer visibly exists. Once Viola's transitory images are gone, the space will be completely transformed.

It is in the art museum that the relationship between art and architecture is particularly sensitive and symbiotic—an interdependence further complicated by the fact that two major arts are involved and are often in conflict. The artist Donald Judd observed that art engages in a special dialogue with the space it inhabits. The thesis of Victoria Newhouse's book, *Towards a New Museum*, an unusually comprehensive and insightful exploration of today's art museum, is that the "dynamic interaction between art and architecture" is the single most important factor in the design of the art museum, ultimately responsible for its success or failure. It affects not only the nature of our communication with the art, but also our perception of the works of art themselves.

THE CONNECTION BETWEEN container and contents has been an uneasy, ambivalent, consistently controversial, and passionately debated subject since the first portrait or predella was transferred from a palace or a church to a museum built for the purpose of collection and display.

In our own time, this forced marriage has involved architects, designers, directors, and curators who have conspicuously and variously addressed, ignored, or misunderstood the importance of the alliance. The
ambience provided by the setting can diminish the art or raise the
viewer's responses to an exalted level. The relationship is the secret of a
great museum.

Perhaps because of this challenge, the art museum is among the
most coveted of architectural commissions. It provides the opportunity
for the advanced and experimental design that legitimizes architecture
as art as opposed to its more pragmatic practice. But the museum is also
an institution buffeted by unprecedented changes in art and society
and subjected to questioning about its public purposes; in the critic
Arthur Danto's words, "the manifestations of chaos in what once had
been the serenity of tempular space" is another challenge that requires
the rethinking of the museum's aims, form, and content. Danto does
not find it surprising that these new museums should be "among the
most brilliant architectures of the Post-Modern age."[1] The commission
for an art museum has brought international celebrity to more than a
few architects; the most obvious example is Frank Gehry's spectacular
Guggenheim Museum in Bilbao, Spain.

In the minds of many, the museum is the cathedral of our time. It is
a "sacred space," in Victoria Newhouse's words, that provides the serenity and splendor, the feelings of awe and reverence, the opportunity for
contemplation and enlightenment essential to the human condition.
Clare Melhuish, in her analysis of the "museum as a mirror of society,"
writes that the museum translated the sacred into the secular; established as a civic monument it has become a community center,[2] a place
peculiar to this century that uniquely combines inspiration, instruction, and entertainment.

The museum is still the sacred space defined by the classical beaux
arts imagery of the nineteenth century, with its processional route of
grand entry, great stairs, and formally aligned galleries that encouraged
the hushed, elevated ambience, the "aura" that the nineteenth century,
with its reverence for the awesome and sublime, perceived as essential
to the experience of art. The aura is still there today, in even some of
the most radical new buildings—Gehry's Guggenheim Bilbao and Kiasma, the recently opened Museum for Contemporary Art in Helsinki,
by the American architect Steven Holl, are conspicuous among those

that employ a startlingly different architectural vocabulary for essentially the same ends.

These museums, and others like them, expand the sensory and intellectual experience of being in the building as a physical and spiritual corollary to the demands of new kinds of art. At both Bilbao and Helsinki, soaring curves and angles and free-form spaces enclose us in a giant, light-filled sculpture. Space is literally reshaped, and so is our understanding of it. Stairs, walkways, and ramps are constructed with open views, combining circulation of visitors with constantly changing perspectives of the interiors and their exhibits. Moving through the building, we experience visual revelations and visceral sensations unlike any we have known before.

Somewhere at the heart of even the most unusual of these structures, there tends to be a more conventional series of grand, sky-lit galleries to accommodate a more traditional kind of art. They occupy a central space crossing the axis of the building at Bilbao, and they form one side of the Helsinki museum. James Stirling's much-visited Stuttgart Staatsgalerie features a traditional enfilade of exhibition galleries, and Rafael Moneo's Modern Art Museum in Stockholm provides superbly lit and proportioned rooms of familiar configuration. But the classic idea of an atrium and a dome, when it survives, or of recognizable rooms in a linear plan, has been stretched, warped, and twisted to relate to the new forms of art that go beyond the painted surface or the sculptured form for complex and even cinematic effects; the sets of *The Cabinet of Dr. Caligari* frequently come to mind.

No WONDER THE architecture often gets most of the attention. Writing about recent museums, the German critic Claus Käpplinger points out that it is not uncommon for the building, rather than the collection, to be the main attraction—as has been the case with the Centre Pompidou in Beaubourg, where many tourists never enter the museum, preferring to ride the dramatic exterior escalator for the spectacular view. Architecture provides the recognition factor and the publicity value that attract visitors and are useful for marketing.[3] Museum boards of directors understand this—they routinely seek "signature" buildings from celebrity architects through international competitions.

Frank Gehry's commission for Bilbao was preceded and followed by several Gehry museums in different parts of the world. Richard Meier, the architect of the new Getty Center in Los Angeles, has also built the Museum of Contemporary Art in Barcelona and a decorative arts museum in Frankfurt. A Spaniard, Rafael Moneo, won the competition for the Modern Art Museum in Stockholm, and a German, Josef Kleihues, was chosen for Chicago's Museum of Contemporary Art. Tadao Ando, with a long list of museums in his native Japan, is building a museum in Fort Worth, Texas. The Los Angeles Museum of Contemporary Art is the work of another Japanese, Arata Isozaki, and a Swiss, Mario Botta, was selected for the San Francisco Museum of Modern Art. The job of redesigning and expanding the Museum of Modern Art in New York has been given to a Tokyo architect, Yoshio Taniguchi.

Zaha Hadid, an Iraqi who favors angled planes on an aesthetic collision course in designs of abstract, prismatic beauty, was selected recently for arts buildings in Cincinnati and Rome. Hadid is more widely known among architects for her unbuilt designs than for her completed work; anything she builds is bound to raise a city's cultural visibility. Some museums are constructed before there is much of a collection to be seen—the Galician Center of Contemporary Art in Santiago de Compostela, Spain, by the Portuguese architect Alvaro Siza, has a constant stream of visitors, with very little art on its walls.

The drawing power and financial by-products of these new museums make them important for urban and economic renewal. The most spectacular example is the Guggenheim Bilbao, with its softly gleaming, titanium-clad, cloudlike shapes that provide both a dramatic new civic image and a revitalizing force for a depressed industrial city. This $320-million gamble—the Basque government paid the bill in exchange for collections and administration from New York—bet the future of the city on culture and tourism. It appears to be paying off; the first year brought crowds far beyond estimates. The building has quite literally put the Spanish city on the map.

The new museums tend to be as different as their patrons, programs, and collections. Renzo Piano's Beyeler Museum, built for a private collector of classic modern art in Basel, Switzerland, is a gentle and seductive building of extraordinary refinement and sensitivity to its setting, carried out with suave expertise in every beautiful detail. In contrast, the electrifying shock of the hard-edged minimalist geometry of Peter Zumthor's Kunsthaus for exhibitions of advanced art in Bregenz, Austria, ignores nature to create its own, enclosed identity; it is an austerely elegant building that jolts one awake to an awareness of the untried and unknown.

II

Regardless of style, the new museums depend on the money and prestige, the allegiance and support of members of an international power elite who use cultural philanthropy to testify to their social and financial success. But this kind of patronage carries less of a guarantee than when royalty was in charge; galleries in our best institutions change donors' names with alarming frequency. (The André Meyer galleries in the Metropolitan Museum, established only twenty years ago, no longer exist.) The most conspicuous architectural monument of our time, the corporate skyscraper, has turned out to be less an instrument of immortality than a real estate investment. The museum makes position and power real.

Today's museum has moved far beyond the original cabinet of curiosities to a virtually open-ended compendium of almost everything our society values or reveres or simply wants to record. The United States alone has spent four to five billion dollars on building museums in the last decade.[4] Some six hundred new museums have been constructed since 1970,[5] from the United States Holocaust Memorial Museum on the Washington Mall to a shrine in Clinton, Oklahoma, for the artifacts of Route 66, a nostalgia-driven trip down the Depression-era cross-country highway of deco diners and mom-and-pop motels. Great art competes with the limitless kitsch called collectibles. The treasure house and the theme park grow closer all the time.

In fact, the museum and the theme park are the two most visited tourist attractions in the United States today. Increasingly, the two borrow from each other and compete for tourist dollars. If anything, pervasive commercialization has only increased the museum's appeal. As home life erodes and the old city center dies, the museum is an increasingly popular destination. The temporary solitude of Acousti-guides or Artphones (technology for indoctrination keeps improving) leads to the communal lure of shops and restaurants, with concerts and "happy hour" wine tastings devised to avoid the dreaded attendance "plateau" that could suggest decreasing interest or support. New York's Museum of Modern Art has just put the contents of its several shops on the Internet for online sales.

For members there are previews and openings and restaurants that function and look like clubs. For charity galas, the museum rents itself out. The right price will buy the Egyptian Temple of Dendur at New York's Metropolitan for a night; dinners with carefully mismatched plates can be catered in the kitchen of the Tenement Museum downtown. All this is accompanied by cries of desecration and trivialization, but at the same time, as Arthur Danto and others remind us, none of it would exist without the prospect of seeing art or the artifacts of history—not as a privilege, but as a right enjoyed since the French Revolution opened private palaces and collections to the public.

With the increasing fragmentation of society, that right has been subject to debate, and museums have been dragged into the multicultural and ethnic and gender wars. Art museums are accused of perpetuating an elite ideology through an entrenched, dominant culture and of excluding the work and the participation of minorities. Subject to pressure from politicians and community activists and from their sources of public money, museums are attempting with defensive uncertainty to be "politically correct" and to cultivate diverse constituencies. Those in a position to be relatively independent make token populist concessions—New York's Morgan Library has added a restaurant, and the Frick is contemplating a buffet. Virtually all are paying more attention to educational programs for the general public and the participation of women and minorities. James Cuno, director of the Harvard University Art Museums, is concerned that scholarship is suffering as a result,[6] while others simply worry that the museum will be weakened in its primary function of collecting and exhibiting. Education and the redress of past inequities, they say, are things others can do better.

But while many museums are emphasizing head counts and outreach programs, and looking to Disney for lessons in accessibility and crowd control, a kind of museum counterculture has been growing, with artists and collectors creating small, elegant, and often hard to reach museums where personal and esoteric tastes are uniting art and architecture in a variety of radically conceived buildings. Relatively free of political or funding pressures, responsible largely to themselves and their private patrons—the Beyeler collection in Basel is a recent example—these museums are not shaped by or subjected to surveys. It is in such places that we find some of the most beautiful and adventurous modern architecture, and some of the most intriguing attempts to deepen the experience of art.

NEWHOUSE HAS PROBABLY seen more of the recently built art museums, public and private, accessible and remote, popular and recondite, than anyone else. Her book includes the obvious examples, like the Guggenheim Bilbao and the Getty, and an assortment of unpublicized buildings that are known to a much smaller number of people in the art world. She does not hesitate to criticize the results, taking account of the political and economic pressures that lead to compromise and flawed decisions. Among the largest and most prestigious institutions, she notes the successful remodelings or additions, the "wings that fly"—Louis Kahn's Yale University Art Gallery, James Stirling's Stuttgart Staatsgalerie, Venturi and Scott Brown's Sainsbury Wing of London's National Gallery—and the unsuccessful "wings that don't fly," a list that includes a series of transformations at some of the world's most revered establishments.

These renovations can be sharply distinguished from earlier directors' almost universal practice of lopping off their monumental beaux arts front stairs in an effort to modernize their architecture and popularize their institutions. But on the whole, in Newhouse's view, today's directors aren't doing much better. She calls their extravagant building programs "woefully deficient" and places the blame squarely where she thinks it belongs. "Museum trustees, directors and staffs have done things to their buildings," she declares, "that would be unthinkable if applied to their collections."

In New York, the additions to the Metropolitan, the Museum of Modern Art, the Whitney, and the Guggenheim all come in for criticism. Nor does she spare Paris's Grand Louvre. In each case, Newhouse writes, the museums have sacrificed architectural quality to expansion, making bad bargains with commercialism and abject concessions to donors. The Met's Temple of Dendur is "forlorn" in its mammoth glass-walled enclosure, designed more for social functions than for art. The Lila Acheson Wallace Wing, added for modern art, is a "confusing jumble of undistinguished spaces." She calls the Lehman

Wing, built partly to mimic the townhouse that held Robert Lehman's private collection of old masters, "a twice-fantasized reproduction" constituting "a misleading use of historical replication"—its galleries designed "in imitation of 1905 rooms that were themselves an approximation of what the appropriate background for the paintings might be."

Of Gwathmey Siegel's controversial 1992 expansion of Frank Lloyd Wright's Guggenheim Museum, Newhouse states bluntly, "Those to whom this incomparable treasure was entrusted have destroyed his concept." Michael Graves's proposed, but fortunately never executed, expansion of the Whitney would have "cannibalized" the distinctive 1966 Marcel Breuer building. The Louvre's old entrances, inadequate as they were, prepared one for a grand experience in which the viewer was immediately confronted by the art; now I. M. Pei's sleek underground entrances lead to escalators and retail stores.[7] "You don't enter a palace through its basement or via a shopping mall," she writes. So much for Pei's pyramid and French cultural authorities.

COOL AND UNCOMPROMISING, Newhouse's judgments are made with a precision and elegance that draw on the firsthand experience of each building and collection. She asks in each case how effectively decisions about style and technology serve the intent and purpose of the institution, the patron, and, above all, the works of art. She is equally skillful at conveying the emotional and sensuous responses evoked by these structures and how they work in their social setting.

She shows herself, on the whole, to be more perceptive than most other critics. The new Getty Center in Los Angeles, for example, widely criticized before it opened as elitist, exclusionary, and uncertain of its identity, has been deluged by crowds unaffected by such criticism—over one million people in its first six months.[8] Parking reservations are required. The single, subsidized fee of five dollars per vehicle includes families and groups. But the public, accustomed to ordering expensive tickets months ahead for blockbuster shows in cities like New York and Boston ($15.00 per person for the Monet show at the Boston Museum of Fine Arts, $17.50 on weekends), and to making reservations far in advance for small, private museums like the Barnes collection in Pennsylvania, or to standing for hours in long lines in hot sun at Disneyland where family admission can soar to one hundred dollars, does not, on the whole, object.

The problem of too many visitors is equally serious at the Guggenheim in Bilbao, as museum attendance in general continues to climb. Professional projections made during the planning process woefully failed to predict the number of visitors for either institution, which are easily double the estimates. In the early months after the opening, those who came to the Getty by public transportation either waited or were denied access when crowds exceeded the limits set by fire regulations, a situation that has subsequently eased.

My own impression is that those who succeed in reaching the Getty after the short, scenic tram ride from the bus stop or garage enjoy both the spectacular views of Los Angeles and the Pacific Ocean and the museum itself, which has been vastly enriched by purchases made during its construction. It now has everything from the newly acquired old masters and hugely popular pictures like van Gogh's *Irises* to superb collections of drawings, photography, and decorative arts, displayed in galleries that range in design from elegant restraint to glittering excess. The ornate French furniture that J. Paul Getty collected has been installed in elaborate period settings. Combining a great site and great art in what may be the world's most opulent art park, the Getty is a seductive day trip; visitors stay twice as long as experts projected and focus on the museum, which exacerbates crowding further. There are places to eat and to loiter in the landscape. The tram ride to the top of the hill, Newhouse points out, is in the best California theme park tradition.

Richard Meier's usual all-white façades were rejected by museum authorities with conservative taste, who were reacting to strong community concerns about the suitability of white for the exposed hilltop and the intense California light.[9] The pristine, high-modernist buildings of beige travertine and off-white porcelain enamel have been called conventional and predictable by those who would have preferred to see the foundation's considerable resources devoted to a more daring or experimental approach. For those less concerned with dramatically new architecture, the Getty offers a sophisticated populism: The architect provided a superbly executed, risk-free style for a foundation of growing, semiautonomous institutions requiring the comfort of consensus. Newhouse's reservations are shared by others; she objects to the use of period trim in the decorative arts rooms designed by the architect Thierry Despont, and she finds the garden that the Getty commissioned from the artist Robert Irwin disruptive of the landscape.

Some have compared the Getty to a high-class theme park, but New-house considers this a plus. She makes a point that many seem to have missed: The Getty has embraced art and contemporary life in a distinc-tively twentieth-century West Coast way.

III

The distance between art and life is a theme throughout Newhouse's book; she is aware of the implicit irony of the fact that the museum it-self bears much of the responsibility for separating the two. In her view the community education programs and other populist practices that distress so many others can be justified when they truly bring people and art together. Like many before her, she is convinced that the re-moval of a work of art from its original setting for the artificial isolation of the gallery is an act that deprives art of both context and meaning. The museum has established a different way of seeing art, one that em-phasizes its most abstract, aesthetic values. The intimacy associated with the historical or natural settings in which works of art were originally seen is lost and cannot be recaptured. Such displacement has usually been justified by citing dangers to the work of art: vandalism, deteriora-tion from exposure and pollution, or the possibility of disappearance from the public domain.

In the notorious and still contested case of the dispatch of the Elgin marbles to England, the British claimed they were carrying out a res-cue operation after gunpowder stored in the Parthenon exploded. But the trip from Athens to London in 1806 was made at a time when an overwhelming lust for classical art was matched by a growing desire to possess and organize art in categorical, iconographic displays meant to be universally instructive. The ultimate virtue of bringing great works of art together in one place was its professed scholarly neutrality, and the emerging model was the art museum.

BUT CAN THERE be any neutrality, any objective, disinterested presen-tation of art? Art is infinitely susceptible to manipulation and modifica-tion through the tastes and beliefs of those who own or control it and the fashions in vision and interpretation that are the cultural markers of any age. Each generation finds what it needs to fit its own sense of history and personal and philosophical concerns. If the nineteenth-century museum reduced art to didactic expositions of period and style, the twentieth-century museum stripped the crowded traditional galleries bare to make way for "the white cube" in which time and place are totally suspended. The ideas of universal values and of the timeless versus the temporal, the assumption that there is an immutable aesthetic reading, are continuing fallacies; no installation or interpretation exists that is independent of the attitudes, tastes, and concerns of its own time.

Modernism treated this isolation as appropriate for contemporary and historical work alike. Few questioned the premise of objective, abstract presentation at the time, and the exhibitions of New York's Museum of Modern Art in the twenties and thirties did much to validate and spread the practice. Alfred H. Barr Jr.'s impeccable installation of the landmarks of modern painting and sculpture in serene white rooms of appealing human scale was paralleled by René d'Harnoncourt's dramatic use of light and color for the display of the tribal arts that were closely associated with modernist theory and practice. Clutter was eliminated for an intense aesthetic and emotional experience. This is a strong legacy, growing out of a moment in history that the Modern brilliantly captured. But as Newhouse makes clear in her criticism of subsequent expansions, the Modern has been unable to meet, or deal with, reevaluations of its mission as well as its ambitious building programs ever since.

Newhouse concludes that the ideal of the neutral setting is wrongheaded. She takes particular aim at the kind of anonymous container that dethroned classicism as the preferred architectural style after World War II. "There is bland architecture that isolates and deadens art," she observes, "and there are expressive spaces that point up, elevate and animate art to make it part of our lives."

In Newhouse's view, today's postmodern, pluralistic climate can give museum directors far more freedom to display art in the ways they choose. With these wider choices, however, the risks increase; the boundaries of both art and architecture are being stretched beyond recognition. As architecture challenges the right-angled and the perpendicular, it denies everything we feel instinctively about stability and structure. It defies even the appearance of gravity with free-form shapes, such as those of Gehry's Bilbao museum, or sharply angled planes, as in Daniel Libeskind's Jewish Museum in Berlin. Such buildings were previously impossible to design or build. There was no way to calculate the

engineering requirements or the costs of complex surfaces and structures using new or unconventional materials without the help of computers. As a result of increased computer use in design, the line
between architecture and sculpture is eroding.

ARCHITECTURE HAS MOVED much closer to the other, less earthbound, arts. And as artists reject what they see as the political, economic, and even ideological controls of the museum, they are rebelling
against established institutions with new forms of art deliberately conceived to be difficult or impossible to collect and display: earthworks,
video art, environmental art, performance art, conceptual art, deconstruction and installation art, antiart. Some contemporary art self-
destructs, or it is so large or immovable that it mocks gallery limitations.
Some artists, like Donald Judd, at the Chinati Foundation in Marfa—a
twelve-building complex open to the public in southeastern Texas that
houses his own and other artists' work—have taken over the preservation and display of their art in defiance of the museum's authority and
control. What started as an act of rebellion against the academy with
the impressionists' Salon des Refusés of 1863 has led to the alternative
spaces that are defining how more and more art is seen today.

Newhouse is clearly most interested in those examples where the
new art and the new architecture come together, where collaborative
experiments take the radically new to unfamiliar and sometimes baffling ends. None leave the visitor unmoved. All are deeply absorbing
aesthetic experiences.

On entering Peter Zumthor's Kunsthaus in Bregenz, for example, it
is as if you walked, Alice-in-Wonderland-style, into a world totally un-
connected to the one outside, stripped of all disorder and ordinary references, a world of spartan essentials that express a rigidly refined and
controlling personal vision. Approaching the building, all you see is a
delicately proportioned translucent glass box. Close up, one finds that
the glass wall is actually double—a wall of individual, rectangular
etched panels attached to a steel frame, like feathers on the wing of a
bird, backed by another wall of solid glass. Inside the outer glass walls
are three asymmetrically placed concrete walls that bear the building's
weight and define but do not fully enclose the interior exhibition space;
they stop short of the exterior glass wall, allowing daylight to filter through.
The area between the glass and concrete walls contains elevators, stairs,

and ducts for heating and air conditioning, which can be seen in ghostly silhouette through the outside glass. A separate small building of strongly contrasting black concrete houses the museum's offices, library, and other services.

Immediately upon entering the Kunsthaus, the visitor is plunged into a room of breathtaking, luminous austerity—a single perfectly proportioned space almost eighty feet square and fourteen feet high, with diffused, even light coming through the translucent glass walls. The building consists of four such single-room galleries, stacked one to a floor, divisible when necessary, with two more floors underground. Between the ceiling of one level and the floor on the next is a space six feet deep that acts as a light catcher, channeling daylight from the exterior glass wall, funneling and directing it through translucent glass ceilings so that every gallery, on every level, is miraculously and mysteriously top-lit by natural light. The concrete walls are polished to a gloss, consistent with a somber palette of grays and black used throughout the building. Details of doors, handles, and installation hardware are minimal and elegantly devised. At night, the museum glows like a lantern.

In this paradoxical building with its exquisitely refined use of both concrete and glass, we see modernism reinvented as ultimate cool. In a setting of Zen-like purity, the changing exhibitions of experimental and avant-garde art—including, for example, works by the American artists James Turrell and Mike Kelley —take over completely and are invested with a heightened intensity. Newhouse writes that the "galleries' puritanical quality" can be "a liability—in its suitability to a limited number of art forms." But that is also the building's point: The architecture is tuned to art that seeks new sensory forms such as Turrell's use of floodlights to illuminate the building's "entire height with changing colors," as Newhouse writes. The extraordinary effectiveness of the Kunsthaus is in the way the architecture and the art within can speak the same language, sharing an equal sensibility, so that the whole becomes exhilaratingly more than the sum of its parts.

What we are seeing, finally, is an extraordinary leap as the various arts come together in a way that could not have been conceived or imagined before. This is what Newhouse calls the "new museum." She traces its history from Frank Lloyd Wright's Guggenheim Museum in New York, begun in 1956, with its controversial rejection of both the beaux arts tradition and the neutral modernist model in the continuous space of its dramatic sky-lit spiral, to the Centre Pompidou in Paris by Renzo Piano and Richard Rogers a little over a decade later. The Guggenheim eliminated conventional galleries and radically reordered space and form. The Pompidou was conceived as a fluid and transparent box for multimedia arts—an ideal of nonstop kinetic activity that couldn't be carried out conceptually, and more practically, failed to display art successfully, but that created a new kind of museum nonetheless.

GEHRY'S GUGGENHEIM BILBAO has completed the breakdown of the idea of the museum as either grand palace or all-purpose container. With the incorporation of site-specific works such as Jim Dine's trio of giant red Spanish Venuses in Bilbao, the art museum has entered into a new phase. Major parts of the building are the result of the active collaboration of artist and architect from the first, conceptual stage of design. They create a much more radical fusion of art and architecture than the traditional blank niches and walls reserved by architects of the classical tradition for sculptures, paintings, and frescoes. Dine's trio of Venuses in Bilbao reworks one of his familiar subjects to powerful effect. Rising twenty feet, pushing through what would be a normal ceiling plane, if one existed, the rich, red, rough-surfaced forms are seen against the sharp diagonals of a soaring metal-framed glass wall with a backdrop of river and hills. While the conventional view of the work would stop there, the architecture treats the sculpture as a changing drama revealed continuously from ascending or descending viewpoints on a Piranesian ramp.[10]

Another site-specific work at Bilbao, a brightly colored, hard-edged abstraction by Sol LeWitt, fills a three-dimensional architectural space and encloses the viewer with what might be called surround-color. The museum visitor, whose view is customarily restricted to a flat or shaped surface on the wall, is now contained and encircled by the vivid space-as-work-of-art, receiving constantly changing impressions of line, color, and form while literally walking through the LeWitt abstraction. In each case, the site-specific work and its surroundings succeed in enhancing each other's effect.

How do the new art museums, with their single-minded emphasis on the art experience, fit into a society obsessed with the accountability of institutions to a public with a variety of expectations? Do they educate or instruct, address the pluralism of our heritage, revise cultural history? Are they sending messages that are "politically correct," or any messages at all? To suggest today that an art museum need not be directly accountable to the public at large, that it is not a medium for the delivery of political or social messages, is to risk cultural excommunication. But art mirrors life, and the museum will inevitably deliver messages if it deals with the art of our time.

Artists have never relinquished the positions of outsider, protester, commentator, and visionary, even though they find it hard to fill these roles today. Irony, pornography, activism, revisionism, appropriation of the work of others, calculated and escalating outrageousness, attempts to shock or extend the boundaries of permissible experience, have been among the artist's instruments, weapons used against the conventional world in the service of the artist's ideas about it. By the seventies, when no subject was too remote or taboo, many believed this was the death of art. Arthur Danto saw it in another light; he stated, in a radio interview, that "art had turned into philosophy," with artists questioning conventions and institutions in the disturbing manner of Dada rather than continuing in Cézanne's tradition of direct visual observation. Denying the concept of beauty, they were exploring the edge between pornography and art, morality and art, and politics and art, in media beyond accepted limits, using art as a vehicle for both propaganda and intimate self-expression. Some of this work doesn't deserve space in any museum; still more is marginal, and much has already become a bore. A show called Sensation at London's Royal Academy in 1997 transgressed what many visitors thought were acceptable limits—from Damien Hirst's exhibit of butchered animals in formaldehyde, now in some well-known museum collections, to a variety of scatological and pornographic references. But in the end, sorting out the new art will be the museum's job, and always has been; the bad calls of the past are buried deep in beaux arts basements.

Filippo Marinetti's futurist manifesto of 1909 called museums "cemeteries" and demanded their destruction. Not only are we building more museums than ever; we are raising things from the dead—restoring and reconstructing fantasies and simulacra of a real or imaginary past. One museum that defies the popular trend has been built on the site of a twelfth-century fortified bishop's palace at Hamar, north of Oslo, in order to preserve and present its history. A brilliant, unconventional design by the Norwegian architect Sverre Fehn, the Hedmark Museum fuses past and present in the display of objects excavated at the site, from the twelfth through the nineteenth centuries, from religious treasures to farm machinery and ordinary articles of domestic use. The artifacts are displayed in the remains of an old stone barn built later on the same site, unrestored, but closed in with glass that covers the ragged openings in the old walls. The visitor follows a winding ramp inside the ruined barn; the path widens to create exhibition areas or narrows to become a bridge directly over the visible archaeological dig. The controlling but nonintrusive architecture underscores the continuity of history through the artfully exposed excavations and the dramatic presentation of the artifacts of centuries of art, religion, and daily life.

The irony of this beautiful and original solution that sets a new standard for museum design is that Fehn claims, like Marinetti, that he does not believe in museums, and deplores our obsession with them. He is convinced that their central role in contemporary culture is part of our denial of death, our fear of loss, the preoccupation of a materialistic society that values objects too highly and believes that they can ensure memory and immortality. He may have a point—it could be a dread of oblivion and a pharaonic desire to keep our treasures with us that has led to the museum's revered place and our worship of what it contains.

But the art museum goes beyond the preoccupation with material things. It is dedicated not only to collecting and preserving, but to the search for meaning that has always been among civilization's highest achievements. This has produced a unique building type today, based on an unprecedented kind of collaboration between artists and architects. At its most successful, it is a new art form.

NOTES

1. Arthur C. Danto, review of *The Museum Transformed: Design and Culture in the Post-Pompidou Age*, by Douglas Davis (Abbeville, 1990), in the *Print Collector's Newsletter* 22, no. 5 (November—December 1991): 183–85.

2. Clare Melhuish, "The Museum as a Mirror of Society," *Architectural Design*, November–December 1997, pp. 22–25.

3. Claus Käpplinger, "Architecture and the Marketing of the Museum," *Museum International*, October–December 1997, pp. 6–9.

4. Jacqueline Trescott, "Exhibiting a New Enthusiasm, Across US, Museum Construction, Attendance, Are on the Rise," *Washington Post*, June 21, 1998.

5. Jayne Merkel, "The Age of the Museum," *Oculus*, published by the American Institute of Architects, New York chapter, February 1998.

6. James Cuno, "Whose Money? Whose Power? Whose Art History?" *Art Bulletin* 79, no. 1 (March 1997): 6–9.

7. In the final phase of the Louvre's renovation, taking place now, an additional, street-level entrance will be opened, leading directly to the galleries.

8. Trescott, "Exhibiting a New Enthusiasm, Across US, Museum Construction, Attendance, Are on the Rise."

9. I served on the Architect Selection Committee for the Getty and on a Design Advisory Committee that functioned for the first few years of its planning and design but did not continue into the later years of the project. My responses are affected by what I learned through my closeness to the project.

10. In New York, Dine's Venuses, in green, stand in a vacuous plaza, flanking a featureless building in a standard Avenue of the Americas officescape. Drained of meaning and impact by the utter ordinariness of their surroundings, scale notwithstanding, they lose the battle against a setting that was meant to be urban and monumental but only lets out into the traffic of Sixth Avenue.

New York Review of Books, April 22, 1999

Skyscrapers

The Tall Building Artistically Reconsidered

THE SKYSCRAPER AND THE TWENTIETH century are synonymous; the tall building is the landmark of our age. As a structural marvel that breaks the traditional limits on mankind's persistent ambition to build to the heavens, the skyscraper is this century's most stunning architectural phenomenon. It is certainly its most overwhelming architectural presence. Shaper of cities and fortunes, it is the dream, past and present, acknowledged or unacknowledged, of almost every architect. From the Tower of Babel onward, the fantasies of builders have been vertical rather than horizontal. Frank Lloyd Wright, caustic critic of cities, could still project a mile-high skyscraper; when the futurists proclaimed an energetic new world, it was in the form of streamlined, soaring towers. These flamboyant visions, full of pride and prejudice, have released architectural talents and egos from the rule of reason and responsibility.

But the question of how to design the tall building has never really been resolved; it continues to plague, disconcert, and confound theorists and practitioners alike. The answers were first sought in models of the past, which were later rejected and then still later rediscovered, carrying reputations up and down with vertiginous regularity. At any point in the cycle, the arguments have an air of messianic conviction fueled by equal amounts of innocence and ignorance. In the final analysis, the results are controlled less by any calculated intent than by those subtle manipulators of art and ideas—taste, fashion, and status.

The swings of art and taste are as certain as the seasons, and men with ideas who hope to change the world tend to behave no better than those who merely suffer the consequences. But in this contentious intellectual and artistic atmosphere, the skyscraper is being discussed and dissected with more intensity than at any time since the name was coined for the multistoried office building sometime around 1890. The revisionists are busy rewriting history in terms of omission and rediscovery, which is fine, and they are also rewriting the rules of skyscraper design, which is not quite so acceptable or admirable. In the process, the right lessons are often discarded for the wrong ones.

In its most familiar and exhilarating aspect, the skyscraper has been a celebration of modern building technology. But it is just as much a product of zoning and tax law, the real estate and money markets, code and client requirements, energy and aesthetics, politics and speculation. Not least is the fact that it is the biggest investment game in town.

With all of this, and often in spite of it, the skyscraper is still an art form. The tall building has that in common with all major works of architecture consciously conceived in aesthetic terms. Every radical advance or conservative retrenchment that has been proclaimed as the latest revelation of truth and beauty has actually been devoted to a single, unchanging, unifying idea and purpose: the search for a skyscraper style. The tall building has been designed well, and even brilliantly, in many different ways, and the exotic variety that marks the best of the tall buildings is inconsistent and irreconcilable in theoretical or doctrinaire terms. There are not, and never have been, any immutable rules; there is more than one way to skin a skyscraper. Contrary to accepted opinion and the respected critical texts, there have been many appropriate and legitimate responses to the conflicting cultural forces of our time.

The architecture of the tall building has never been more on people's minds, if one judges by public and press attention to the subject. Beyond aesthetics, however, there are serious questions of cause and effect, propriety and place, structure and style, that are not being addressed. There are pivotal issues of enormous importance to the design of the tall building, both subtle and complex, from the humanitarian to the historical, that need careful scrutiny. There is an incredible default of critical appraisal where it counts, and where it hurts, in the lives of cities and people.

The most obvious blind spot comes in the failure to recognize the fact that the skyscraper—still on the rise and increasing spectacularly in number and size—may have overreached itself and may even be nearing the end of the line. There is both irony and tragedy in the realization that this is happening at the same time that the question of design has been creatively reopened by the loosening of modernist strictures, and at the moment when the exploration of the tall building's inherent power, drama, and beauty offers greater options than ever before. We are seeing some spectacular new building, but we are also seeing signs of a disturbing dead end in scale and impact, and a frivolous dead end in style. While the aesthetic debate becomes more recondite and self-serving, the effect of the tall building on our overcrowded, malfunctioning, and deteriorating cities has become demonstrably destructive and dehumanizing.

The skyscraper has totally changed the scale and appearance and concept of cities and the perceptions of people in them. The public has always loved these architectural aberrations—like freaks of all kinds. The title of the world's tallest building has a fleeting but special cachet; it is a favored setting for publicity stunts and self-celebrations, media events, and cinema mythology. But if the status and drama of the tall building, its engineering and architectural achievements, its embodiment of superlatives, are universally admired, the philosophical questions that it raises continue to be disturbing: Its symbolism is complex, its role in the life of the city and the individual is vexing, and its impact is shattering. The skyscraper is Olympian or Orwellian, depending on how you look at it.

For the skyscraper is not only the building of the century, it is also the single work of architecture that can be studied as the embodiment and expression of much that makes the century what it is. Today's tall building is a puzzling and paradoxical package. Its standardized, characterless, impersonal space creates the recognizable, charismatic monuments and the enduring image of twentieth-century cities. For better or for worse, it is measure, parameter, or apotheosis of our consumer and corporate culture. No other building type incorporates so many of the forces of the modern world or has been so expressive of changing belief systems and so responsive to changing tastes and practices. It romanticizes power and the urban condition and celebrates leverage and cash flow. Its less romantic side effects are greed and chaos writ monstrously large. The tall building probes our collective psyche as it probes the sky.

In sum, the skyscraper—in terms of size, structure, and function, scale and symbolism, and, above all, human and urban impact—remains the single most challenging design problem of our time. The other definitive architectural challenge, housing, will continue to lack patronage and priorities because it answers to social rather than to business needs. The twentieth-century architect's most telling and lasting response to his age is the topless tower of trade.

EXCEPT FOR POPULAR mythology and a totemic fascination with the skyscraper, its history has been too narrowly focused. There is general agreement on the significance of certain structures and events, such as those innovations that had their roots in many places and flowered in Chicago in the late nineteenth century. At that time, and in that place, a unique combination of industrialization, business, and real estate came together for the development of a new and distinctive building type: the American office building.

In the first, or what might be called the functional, phase of this new structural phenomenon, architecture was the servant of engineering. Rapid increases in building height were made possible by advances in fireproofing, metal framing, and the passenger elevator, as well as by less glamorous improvements in footings and foundations, plumbing, heating, lighting, and ventilation. Much larger buildings were encouraged by the rapid erection of the metal frame and curtain wall, the growth of cities and business, and the need and desire to house commercial operations that employed many people on increasingly congested and expensive urban sites. Essentially, the early skyscraper was an economic phenomenon in which business was the engine that drove innovation. The patron was the investment banker, and the muse was cost-efficiency. Design was tied to the business equation, and style was secondary to the primary factors of investment and use.

These early structures are as handsome as they are utilitarian. They possess a great strength and clarity that gives them remarkable expressive power. We are as pleased by their art as their builders were by their technology. But we can also see that it is precisely the linkage between the two—art and technology—that is the secret of their distinctive and superior style.

BUT THE DESIGN debate about the skyscraper's artistic problems grew as quickly as its size, and soon led to the invocation of traditional models. The second phase of skyscraper design sought solutions through academic sources and historical precedents. This eclectic phase, which was fueled by the ascendance of the academy and the popularity of the Beaux Arts in this country, continued well into the twentieth century, until both debate and construction were stopped by the Great Depression.

The eclectic phase produced some of the skyscraper's most remarkable monuments. The raids on the past ranged from banal to brilliant: The Gothic reached for the heavens as never before; Greek temples and Italian campaniles raised their heads repeatedly in the sky. There were stretch-Renaissance-palazzi, zoom-châteaux, and assorted versions of the Mausoleum of Halicarnassus. The size and style of these buildings made them spectacular and recognizable monuments, but their unique and unreproducible features are their sophisticated scholarship and superbly executed detail. The best examples were skilled academic exercises adapted with great ingenuity, drama, and, occasionally, real beauty to the totally new needs and aspirations of the twentieth-century city. Although the elite position has been to act as if they are, at best, pardonable eccentricities or, at worst, giant blots on the skyscape, they took their place instantly in the history of architecture.

The modernists have always read the academic victory as an architectural defeat. The characteristic of the eclectic phase that seemed like the cardinal architectural sin was not that its practitioners failed to seek new forms, which was bad enough, but that they placed such heavy emphasis on romantic recall and ornamental embellishment. After a long, austere diet of rationalism, however, younger architects are again delighting in this exotic and exuberant excess, and even an older generation is seeing these buildings with new eyes.

THE ROUT OF tradition and the acceptance of the new was neither quick nor clear; the course of true modernism did not run as smoothly as historians have chosen to relate. Until recently, it has been inadmissible in proper intellectual and artistic circles to point out that there was a "modern-modernistic" dichotomy rather than the direct revolutionary line to which all the faithful immediately adhered. The conventional and respectable architectural wisdom has treated this conflict as a split between good and bad design, between serious and frivolous art, between aesthetic enlightenment and vestigial, uncomprehending vulgarity—in short, between virtue and sin.

The modern phase of skyscraper design actually embraced this dual aesthetic in two separate but parallel strains. "Modern" was radical, reductive, and reformist; "modernistic" was richly decorative and attached to conservative and hedonistic values. "Modern" was the austere, abstract, elite, avant-garde work of the European school of Gropius, Mies, and Le Corbusier, united in its early days under the rubric of the International Style. "Modernistic" was neither pure nor revolutionary; it fused the ornamental and the exotic for what was really the last great decorative style. Derived from the luxurious, exotic combination of new and old materials and the traditional fine craftsmanship that characterized the products of the 1925 Paris Exposition, "modernistic" was despised by the avant-garde as fussy, reactionary, and, of course, bourgeois-decadent. Now called art moderne or deco, it is having a trendy revival, but "modernistic" was the name used at the time—innocently by its admirers and scathingly by its critics. The modern-modernistic split was more than style-deep, however; the reformers saw modern as both moral and beautiful; it held the promise of a better world through design. They considered the more fashionable modernistic as the betrayal of that promise and the denial of art as an instrument of social change.

Very little was built in the new International Style in the United States. There was a large body of significant work abroad dating from the period just after World War I, but only small, token structures appeared here, quite late, in the thirties. At first, modernism was a showcase style of the avant-garde. Much later, in an even greater transformation, it became the architecture of the establishment. By midcentury, the revolutionary ideal and aesthetic had been turned into slick, profitable formulas that had lost an enormous amount in the translation from the European originals to American commercial practice.

WHILE BUSINESS AND builders were busy exploiting the modern style, another more subtle kind of exploitation was being carried out by the architects themselves. Straining at the straitjacket of rigid modernist principles, while giving lip service to them, they found ways to stretch the rules. The sacred dictum that form follows function was being turned into the pursuit of form for its own sake. Structure became sculpture; sometimes the whole building was transformed into a sculptural or decorative object. Or it was conceived as a provocative, abstract play of light, planes, and reflections, a trick done with mirrors, as the glass box gave way to the mirror-glass building, a development of considerable aesthetic subtlety and intricacy. The modern skyscraper, once devoted to a Euclidian simplicity, began to display a far more complex geometry. Very quietly, the rules of rational cause and effect were reversed, and structure became a tool for creating abstract, idiosyncratic, and arbitrary results. Function followed form. Less became quite a lot more. The avenue explored ranged from macho contortions to sophisticated experiments aimed at the expansion or exploitation of the traditional relationships of function and form.

ADMITTEDLY, THE TALL building works dramatically well for business and its satellite services; to deny this fact and its corollary, that the development of the skyscraper has logically served these characteristically twentieth-century needs, is to miss the real nature of our civilization and of the most conspicuous architecture of our time. The validity of the symbolism of the tall building for its age is intrinsic to its powerful imagery. Its single historical consistency has been its predictable penchant for setting records, for rising to ever greater heights.

If the modern skyscraper has resolved any of architecture's intrinsic ambiguities, it has done so in a thoroughly unexpected and unsettling way. Today's big building is a masterpiece of economic manipulation, a monument to the marketplace and entrepreneurial skills. These are skills that command the kind of reverence and awe reserved for theological, moral, and aesthetic issues in earlier societies. They are given the respect once accorded to matters of the spirit, character, and certain shared, and even ennobling, public values. Those who deal in such financial legerdemain are aware that one of the timeless attributes of architecture is the ability to produce images of identity and status that can contribute to today's profitable package. Whether this is cynicism or realism is not important; what matters is that it puts the practitioner of the art of architecture well below the master of financial leverage in the contemporary hagiography.

In the meantime, our old cities are savage and deteriorating, and our new cities are ignoring the lessons of the past and the needs of the future. While this apocalyptic urban script is played out, the search for the ultimate skyscraper goes on. The fact that the focus and objective of the search have narrowed as the size and impact of these buildings have increased to record levels is a serious cause for unease — for cities and for architecture alike. But it is equally clear that the search for skyscraper solutions, in common with the art of architecture in general, has been released from rules and dogma and is moving on to a more complex sensibility and vocabulary that is already producing a new skyscraper age. At worst, overbuilding will make urban life unbearable. At best, we will go out in a blaze of style.

Selections from *The Tall Building Artistically Reconsidered*, 1985

Skyscraper Art Rides High

THE ART DECO AVALANCHE IS ON. THE period and its products are being flirted with by the popular press, puffed by dealers in nostalgia, and apotheosized in a series of forthcoming books. The subject is also being celebrated right now in an exhibition at Finch College called American Art Deco Architecture. The timing is just right. The show serves to put the movement into proper focus in the broad terms of American building of the twenties and thirties, with emphasis on what is increasingly called the Skyscraper Style.

No style has been more neglected, undervalued, misunderstood, or camped up. No style has been more vulnerable to the bulldozer, egregious remodeling, or the disdain of contemporary scholars. In the peculiar terms of the growing popularity of art deco (named after the Paris Exposition of Modern Decorative and Industrial Art of 1925), kitsch is being given equal standing with high art. And so the selective scholarship and qualitative standards imposed on the subject by Elayne Varian, who organized and installed the exhibition and wrote the catalog, are exactly what is needed at this moment.

It is as easy to be enchanted by this show as it is to miss its genuine substance. There is immense visual pleasure in its fantasy world of ziggurats, sunbursts, zigzags, waves, stepped triangles, stylized machines, abstract suggestions of energy and speed, and the exotic natural wonders of waterfalls, tortoises, condors, and doves. One marvels at their superb craftsmanship in marble, bronze, glass, bakelite, Monel metal, plastics, and rare woods.

The appeal of this vintage modernism—naive, romantic, and upbeat—is enormous. But I believe, with Mrs. Varian, that art deco, or style moderne, is to be taken seriously. The American work is a sizable production by men of notable talent, among them Eliel Saarinen, Paul Cret, Raymond Hood, Bertram Goodhue, and others who have not yet received their due. But what is most clearly and heartbreakingly revealed in this presentation is that the buildings shown represent the last great period of decorative art. We are struck with the poignant reality that it will never be possible to do this kind of work again. The pervasiveness of the manner is attested to by illustrations ranging from Saarinen's own house to public works such as the Hoover Dam and the Golden Gate Bridge. Even these immense utilitarian structures took forms and used applied decoration derived from the aesthetic spirit of the time.

But art deco, or style moderne, is primarily the art of the skyscraper and of the first skyscraper age. As such it is extraordinary that these structures have been systematically excluded from the modern architecture textbooks or relegated to footnotes. They are among the biggest and best buildings in a country that has earned its place in architectural history in large part through skyscraper development.

Because they failed to conform to the tenets of the International Style—a rigid "functionalism" with a "technological" aesthetic that decreed ornament a "crime"—they have been blacklisted by the official historians of the International Style, which had a valid claim and stake in the twentieth-century architectural revolution. The International Style is, in fact, correctly perceived as the prime base of modernism, but to make the point propagandistically its promoters were rigidly exclusionistic. These exclusions, particularly with hindsight, have become ludicrous.

The essential difference between the International Style skyscraper and the art deco skyscraper (and there were hybrids, such as Raymond Hood's 1931 McGraw-Hill Building in New York) is that the International Style struggled to reveal the expressive visual power of the structural frame, and art deco simply took the technology for granted and embroidered the result.

It is quite possible to read structure and function in the column and spandrel façade of the 450 Sutter Building of 1930 in San Francisco by Timothy Pflueger and James Miller. But beyond that the spandrels are decorative fantasies, and both glass and metal are angled for a richly plastic façade. One of the least recognized factors of these art deco skyscrapers is the extremely successful plasticity of the building as a whole, aside from the applied ornament; there is a great preoccupation with planes and volumes and sculptural effect. Such effects are further dramatized with light, often in the form of lit glass tubes—another element of the deco vocabulary. The Niagara Mohawk Building in Syracuse, New York, is a spectacular example.

Most of these characteristics aim at a frankly surface appeal that is highly suspect within the puritan ethic (aesthetic?) of modernism. To International Stylists, this approach, tied as it is to tradition, is original sin. Still, the ornament is often extremely beautiful. It is perhaps hard to grasp the fact that elevator lobbies can be historic interiors; art deco turned them into incredible twentieth-century art forms. They are disappearing, however, persistently destroyed by marble-slab "modernization." A radiator grille, a mailbox, or a doorknob can be, and are, collector's items. When a building is torn down or remodeled, the discarded parts are so prized that the vultures close in.

It is worth noting that art nouveau and art deco have much in common: They both emphasize the primacy of a new vocabulary of ornamental forms of a remarkable creativity and strong sensuous pleasure, bypassing structural innovation. If one style is valid, so is the other. And yet the former is accepted as part of the official twentieth-century aesthetic, and the latter is not.

These buildings are rarely designated as landmarks, and even their documentation has only begun. So far, their fate is in the hands of speculators. Los Angeles's Richfield Building of 1928 by Morgan, Walls and Clements was demolished in 1967; its bronze elevator doors are pictured on the cover of the exhibition catalog. The Cities Service Company, which moved from Wall Street to Tulsa recently, is about to tear down an assortment of its Wall Street properties in spite of New York's official pleas to save them, leaving only Clinton and Russell's 60 Wall Street tower built for Cities Service in 1932 (the one model in the show). It faces an uncertain future. In a more welcome move, Oakland, California, has converted Timothy Pflueger's Paramount Theater of 1931 into a home for the Oakland Symphony.

Those who can should not only see the show but take a few field trips as well. In New York, for example, the elevators in the Chrysler Building are a special aesthetic experience; each cab is an elaborately different marquetry and metal deco garden of delights. The best exhibitions of the art of architecture are still in the city streets. It will be tragic if these buildings end up as fragments in a museum.

New York Times, November 17, 1974

The Myth of the Invulnerable Skyscraper

MYTHS ARE IMMORTAL; THEY HAVE A LIFE of their own. You drive a stake through their hearts, and like the undead, they rise again. The one that keeps surfacing since September 11 is the myth of the invulnerable skyscraper. The belief, or hope, that the supertall building can be made resistant to catastrophe has a particular urgency after the World Trade Center attack. It is part of the need for healing and renewal, for making things whole and safe again. There is, inescapably, that hole in our hearts and the sky.

Building tall has a price. From the Tower of Babel to the World Trade Center, doing so can invite the wrath of God or other unexpected consequences. An enduring obsession, fed by vanity, hubris, and greed, it has produced something astonishingly beautiful, unlike anything ever built before.

The skyscraper is American, and so is the technology. The steel frame and curtain wall, the elevator, artificial light, and ventilation — all have made immense, multifloored structures practical and profitable. You don't need to show a builder where the money is — it's on the skyline, and to make one's mark on the skyline is to validate success. Any skyline is fair game. A recent obituary revealed that an American builder, Wylie Tuttle, was responsible for the Tour Montparnasse in Paris; its appearance in 1973 was the *coup de foudre* that alerted the city to the potential destruction of its style and grace. Legislation followed that restricted skyscrapers to the surreal, edge-city limbo of La Defense. He probably wondered what the fuss was all about.

The prize that is relentlessly pursued and constantly lost is the title of Tallest Building in the World. In the high-stakes game of development, glory and profit are equally important. Architecture helps glory along. A shrewd business investment became the Cathedral of Commerce when Cass Gilbert dressed the Woolworth tower's steel skeleton in rich Gothic raiment in 1913. It helped that it was the world's tallest building at the time. The art moderne hubcaps and stainless-steel gargoyles of the Chrysler Building immortalize the automobile company that has long since been succeeded by other owners. The Empire State Building beat it out for the title in 1931; King Kong transferred badly from its distinctive profile to the flat-topped Twin Towers when the title moved on. The Trade Center was a real estate investment that gained its beauty from atmospheric accidents; it entered history as a conspicuous target for those who saw it as a hated symbol of America's affluence and modernity. It was much too innocuous for that heavy burden; it was merely big.

We want to be assured that there are ways to balance size and safety, to create a skyscraper immune to a catastrophe of the dimensions that the Twin Towers suffered, or at least diminish the danger to an acceptable degree. We simply assume that this can and will be done, that wishing will make it so.

And yet every study of the disaster, every report so far, tells us that no tall building, no matter how constructed, can withstand that kind of terrorist attack. None of the experts will guarantee it, or even suggest that it is possible. What they do tell us is that the engineering was indeed remarkable, so good that the buildings did not immediately collapse, but that they could not resist the explosive intensity of the impact and the incredible heat of the fire, and that no building could, no matter how it is designed or engineered. They also tell us that we have learned lessons from the tragedy, that tall-building construction can be noticeably improved, that changes are essential, even mandatory.

It has long been suspected that the spray-on fireproofing used to protect structural steel in today's skyscrapers, while fast and easy to apply, flakes off under minimal stress. Earlier inspections had revealed areas in the towers where this had already occurred. With the impact and the heat, the thin coating cracked and fell away, leaving the Trade Center's formidable engineering exposed and defenseless against fire.

Older buildings in the area, like another Cass Gilbert design, his 1907 French Renaissance chateau-tower at 90 West Street (across from the World Trade Center), protected the steel frames behind their ornate façades with tile, which substantially increased their fire-resistance time. Today we value speed over style. Most firefighting equipment cannot reach high floors, and the synthetic materials and furnishings of the modern office building create a chemical hell of deadly smoke and fumes. Entire industries would have to redesign their products from scratch, at enormous cost, to eliminate this hazard. Building codes and industry practices need to be radically revised.

A study by the Construction Institute of the American Society of Civil Engineers found the Trade Center's stairwells too narrow for a mass evacuation, a consideration that has never arisen before. Nor were these escape routes in the best places for emergency use. The recommendations called for much wider stairwells or the construction of large, exterior stair towers. The report also noted that air-intake systems are accessible and unmonitored, and would be vulnerable to biological or chemical agents.

The bottom line turned out to be not engineering but economics. What became clear to the investigators, and is well understood by architects and builders, is that larger stairwells and other safety requirements would eat up so much space that 100-story buildings would no longer be feasible in purely financial terms. Not enough profitable floor area would be left in a very tall building when these features were expanded and others added. For reasons of safety and economics, the report concluded, we should not build higher than 50 or 60 stories — half the height of the 110-story World Trade Center.

Studies will continue to try to determine more specifically where the Trade Center's weaknesses were, dealing with such technical matters as the strength and connections of floor plates and columns and the relative merits of different methods of skyscraper design. There are many ways of building tall — the cagelike supporting exterior walls with inner service cores, as in the Trade Center; bundled tubes, in which clustered units reinforce each other, adding rigidity to the whole, used in Chicago's Sears Tower; or the huge, bridgelike trusses of the Hong Kong and Shanghai Bank in Hong Kong. New structural systems are constantly evolving. But none of this assures invulnerability. The skyscraper will always contain the promise of immortality and the memory of death. All of our talent and technology cannot change the equation.

Does this mean that the supertall building is doomed? Will the race for the sky stop? Only if human nature changes, and our grand, romantic impulses disappear. We move into the "earthquake proof" buildings that engineers devise after every temblor with the confidence of "lessons learned." We keep the sandbags ready for the next flood. The human capacity to forget or to minimize catastrophe, to learn to live with it, ameliorates pain and suffering and anesthetizes memory.

After September 11, some will never want to set foot in a tall building again. But most will succumb to the intoxication of living or working with exhilarating views and the magic of a distant horizon and a changing sky. Compromises will be made; the odds accepted. We will find ways to build high, as a gesture of faith, an act of defiance, an assertion of control, the refusal to acknowledge the limits of nature or the existence of an enemy, because we need to see our buildings soar as symbols of prosperity and pride. But they will be vulnerable, and we will be vulnerable, whatever we have learned, whether it is about engineering technology or the risks of being alive.

Wall Street Journal, May 28, 2002

Tall, Taller, Tallest

THE CONVENTIONAL WISDOM HAS IT that the desire to build tall received a serious setback from the World Trade Center disaster. As usual, the conventional wisdom has it wrong. The reality is that we are building higher than ever, with buildings in construction, or on the boards, that dwarf everything we know now.

Superskyscrapers are proposed or rising in London, Paris, Vienna, Tokyo, Hong Kong, Beijing, and Mexico City; they already exist in

Kuala Lumpur, Shanghai, and Taipei. While the earthbound argue about fear and safety, Asia has outstripped the West, using the most advanced structural technology and safety features for buildings already completed and occupied; Malaysia's twin Petronas Towers became the world's tallest in 1998 at 1,483 feet, and the 101-story, 1,667-foot Taipei 101 Tower broke that record when it opened in Taiwan this year. There is no turning back. This is the way it will be in the twenty-first century.

These dramatic additions to the international skyline are being designed by the familiar high-wire performers—Frank Gehry, Rem Koolhaas, Norman Foster, Richard Rogers, Renzo Piano, and Santiago Calatrava are all represented, while seasoned skyscraper pros like Henry Cobb, Cesar Pelli, and William Pederson have been quietly producing the first generation of superbuildings. They are all working with structural engineers who have so radically transformed the possibilities that the name "skyscraper" has become old-fashioned.

At least, that is the judgment of Terence Riley, the Philip Johnson chief curator of architecture and design at the Museum of Modern Art, and Guy Nordenson, a structural engineer and Princeton professor, the co-organizers of the exhibition at the Museum of Modern Art. They prefer to call it Tall Buildings, because they find the word *skyscraper* a romantic throwback to an earlier age when one considers the conceptual possibilities and structural innovations of today's enormous towers.

The twenty-five examples being shown in models, sections, and elevations are on display at MoMA's temporary outpost in Queens, where they will remain until September 27, after which the museum returns to Manhattan and its own new tall building at its old site on West Fifty-third Street. They range from a modest 187 feet for an office building in Santiago, Chile, chosen for its ingenious engineering, to a proposal for Chicago at 2,000 feet and 108 stories that would have been the world's tallest building if it had been constructed—a title as fleeting as the clouds above.

All have been designed within the past ten years, although only six have been built, with another half dozen under construction; the rest were conceived as projects or for competitions. Three were finalists for the World Trade Center site: a pair of "kissing" towers by Norman Foster that meet as they rise and are a marvel of suavely expressed technology; a forest of connected leaning towers by an international consortium of Dutch, British, and American architects that say come with me to the precipice and leap into the arms of tomorrow; and a matched set of minimalist towers joined with orthogonal precision by a prestigious New York team that included Richard Meier, Charles Gwathmey, Peter Eisenman, and Steven Holl.

It is safe to say that as long as architects are possessed by a timeless obsession to build tall—a universal ambition that can make even the most modest fancy themselves masters of the universe—and developers pursue ways to wring every ounce of profit out of expensive land, the race for height will continue, limited only by how high practicality and this alliance will take them. And that is discounting symbolism, hubris, and dreams.

There is, however, a significant difference between the tall buildings of the past and those of this new Skyscraper Age. Radical changes in architecture are the result of radical advances in technology. High-speed computer calculation and modeling of structural systems have changed the rules of the game. Surreal and sculptural shapes now rival more traditional towers of increasing decorative complexity.

The romance of great height is still there, whether in Calatrava's futuristic twisting Turning Torso or Petronas's fairy-tale fruitcakes piercing the sky. The Mobius-like strip of Rem Koolhaas's proposed headquarters for Chinese television in Beijing is monumental science fiction. The traditional curtain-walled steel skeleton functioned like a straitjacket for space and height. These buildings are freely formed within strong, trusslike exterior walls, limited only by the physical constraints of the site, the calculations of the computer, the market, and taste.

Instead of the usual stacked, flat floor plates, vertical groups of floors serviced by their own elevators and escalators can be arranged around interior atriums and gardens. Norman Foster's striking "gherkin" at 30 St. Mary Axe in London has curved exterior walls that minimize wind loads and air movement inside and out. Open, "green" space wraps around the office floors, visible as a spiral pattern on the faceted glass façade. Using new materials and techniques and sophisticated computer programs to calculate everything from airflow and thermal gain and loss to wind loads and stresses and tall building sway, these outsize structures are technologically and economically viable for the first time. Because they are far more energy and cost efficient than their predecessors, they can be promoted as sustainable architecture.

The time is past when the architect was the form giver who handed an idea to the engineer, whose job was basically to make it stand up. Today's structural engineer is a coequal designer. But names like Cecil Balmond, Guy Nordenson, and Leslie Robertson, and distinguished engineering firms like Ove Arup, are virtually unknown outside of the profession.

The exhibition argues that by acting as transportation hubs and shopping centers, superbuildings create street life instead of standing alone in offputting, isolated plazas. It has always made planning sense to include these facilities in large construction projects; the problem has been to offer the office or residential developer enough incentives. Evidently, size will do it. But New York's huge new AOL Time Warner Building kills the street and standardizes the shopping experience with a giant indoor suburban mall of monumentally homogenized upscale ennui. Mixed uses equalize financial risk more than they enrich and enliven the urban environment.

Questions as large as the buildings remain. When does bizarre become beautiful? Some of these proposals, like Mr. Eisenman's Max Reinhardt Haus for Berlin, are acrobatic exercises in computer mathematics that only an architect could love. To most of us, tall buildings are not engineering marvels as much as they are icons of power and progress and objects of consummate wonder. They carry an extraordinary emotional and aesthetic message, an experience the nineteenth century recognized and revered in nature's most awesome manifestations as the "sublime." That doesn't have much to do with engineering developments like stayed mast construction or tuned mass dampers or fashionable architectural theory's elaborately stretched metaphors.

Inherently, enormous buildings are inhumane. This has become more pronounced as the means of production and the sense of craft have been replaced by complex technologies and more formal and abstract design that emphasizes a sleek, depersonalized scalelessness. Exhilarating and alienating, promising and threatening, their ambiguity is inescapable. Right now, the sheer excitement of being able to do unprecedented things overwhelms everything else.

Admittedly, it is too soon to judge, but some of the examples in this show that are most admired by professionals for their daring innovations and startling forms are grotesques; structures that lean and loop do not give us a sense of security or suggest pleasure on a human scale. As they ascend into the vertiginous high-tech stratosphere, they leave us behind in the dust. It's big building as big brother; ambition as destiny.

It is only when they express "the means and wonder of their structural achievement," in Mr. Nordenson's words, that they succeed in visually conveying their unique power and beauty in terms that we can begin to understand, advancing timeless standards of art and symbolism as they explore the frontiers of architectural experimentation on a scale never possible before. The tall building is a gigantic instrument of market economics, but it still aspires to the sublime.

Wall Street Journal, August 17, 2004

PART III

Modernism and Its Masters

Le Corbusier

Bold Harvard Structure

CAMBRIDGE, MASSACHUSETTS, NEW ENGLAND stronghold of tradition, was the setting today for the dedication of one of the country's most unconventional new buildings. Harvard University's Carpenter Center for the Visual Arts, the latest work of the architect Le Corbusier, was officially accepted this afternoon by an academic community that, unofficially, either does not accept it at all or is sharply divided on its merits.

The new Harvard art center is the only structure in the United States by the seventy-six-year-old Swiss-born French leader of the modern movement, whose real name is Charles-Edouard Jeanneret. He directed every detail of the building's design and construction from Paris but has never seen it. Its assured, nonconformist rejection of the university's carefully nurtured colonial charm, both real and synthetic, is the source of most of the criticism. The building could not have been put down in a less sympathetic setting if it had been dropped from the moon.

Situated in Harvard's neo-Georgian heart on Quincy and Prescott streets, its concrete-and-glass hulk rudely elbows the ivy-draped brick of the faculty club and the Fogg Museum on either side. Architecturally speaking, it virtually thumbs its nose at both from its obviously inadequate site. To proper Bostonians, this is bad manners, aesthetically and otherwise. It has been said that Le Corbusier's buildings violate the street, and this one violates the street and scandalizes the neighborhood. At the same time, the new building manages to make everything around it look stolid and stale.

It does this not because it is brash, or novel, but because it is so re-markably rich in bold ideas. The building itself is an idea—the kind of creative idea that universities traditionally are supposed to deal in. The architect's commission was for an "inspirational building" that would give impetus and direction to a new, experimental program in visual arts. The objective is "the perception of quality," and the first eye opener is this extraordinary structure.

What the visitor approaching from Quincy Street sees is a curving ramp that invites him into the heart of the five-story building and car-ries him through it and out again on the Prescott Street side. To the right is a concrete-and-glass-block stairwell, to the left, the curved pro-jection of a studio workshop, behind it, a series of sunbreaks fronting the upper floors like narrow, angled balconies.

Where the open ramp rises and enters at the third floor, the whole building is suddenly revealed through glass walls that turn studios, workshops, and exhibition space into showcases—both of the visual arts and of the architecture itself. The effect is electrifying, for in one sweeping view it becomes apparent that this is indeed a new world. The many typical Corbusian devices—sunbreaks, balconies, roof gardens, bubble domes, curved walls, angled panels—contribute substantially to the design studies and progress, and provide a superb setting for them. The walk "through" Carpenter Center has become Cambridge's fa-vorite Sunday stroll.

For the stroller, much of the building's quality is, unfortunately, diffi-cult to grasp. From the street, he sees only strong shapes and raw con-crete that ivy will never hide. What he cannot sense immediately is the ingenious interplay of indoor and outdoor areas in studios and terraces. His is not aware of the remarkable manipulation of plan and space that creates the striking curved and angled elements so skillfully drama-tized, inside and out. Nor does he see the painstaking craftsmanship in the deceptively crude, but expert, use of concrete. (Shipbuilders from Nova Scotia executed some of the curved wooden forms that shape the structure.)

Le Corbusier's buildings are a curious and characteristic blend of the deliberately rugged and the artfully primitive, from a mind of un-usual subtlety and sophistication. This one is frankly a workshop; there are no slick finishes or rich materials to seduce the viewer. New

England should not object; it shares, with the French, the tradition of austerity.

But with all of its virtues, and with due credit to Harvard, the Cambridge architectural firm of Sert, Jackson & Gourley, which executed Le Corbusier's design with dedicated fidelity, and Alfred St. Vain Carpenter, who gave the $1.5 million for its construction, this is not the architect's best work.

Its weakness is in its aggressive complexity, its overbusy profusion of elements that borders dangerously on the chaotic. Barely contained by the uneasy site, it produces a kind of visual nervous indigestion. Some choices of interior finish can only be called unfortunate. At present, the ground-floor terrace looks more like a prisoner's exercise yard than an aesthetic retreat, an impression reinforced by the overuse of cheerless gray gravel in too many areas. Proper landscaping, particularly on roof terraces, is still urgently needed to complete the building's concept.

Nothing will be complete or measurable as a success or failure, however, until the courses and the building are in full operation. The center's reception, right now, is cool and cautious. But if its educational attack on "visual illiteracy" works, things may get fair and warmer.

New York Times, May 28, 1963

Architect of Today's World

A RENAISSANCE MAN WHO TURNED the twentieth century into a one-man renaissance, Charles-Edouard Jeanneret, called Le Corbusier, was one of the major shapers of today's world.

As an architect, his work shocked and influenced three generations and changed the look of cities everywhere. A painter and sculptor, his abstract compositions hang in major museums and collections. An ardent polemicist for the modern movement, his writings reached heights of poetic power that led to a cult of personality rivaled only by professional admiration for the equally poetic power of his trendsetting buildings.

These buildings, spanning half a century, are few in number compared to their far-ranging effect. Each new structure, from the coolly cubistic Villa Savoye built outside of Paris in 1931, to the rough, exposed concrete forms of the High Court Building at Chandigarh in the fifties, the Le Corbusier-designed new capital of the Punjab, has been a bomb exploded in architectural circles, with international repercussions.

Professionally he was a giant, and with two other giants of the same stature, Frank Lloyd Wright and Ludwig Mies van der Rohe, he is credited with the revolution in building known as modern architecture.

Personally, he was a contradictory combination of cool, detached Gallic intellectualism and equally Gallic fussiness over petty details. He faced a public that he always believed misunderstood and undervalued him with a brusque reserve; to his friends he displayed a quick, warm wit.

The slight, irascible architect, his gaze owlishly hypnotic behind circular, horn-rimmed glasses, became legend and prophet in his own time.

His style was intensely personal. Le Corbusier buildings stress strong, sensuous forms, very close to the shapes of abstract sculpture, and each structure is a highly individual concept.

At the same time, he sought universality. He devised a unit of measurement, which he called the Modulor, or Golden Section. It was based on the height of a man with his arm upraised, and according to Le Corbusier, any structure based on multiples of this unit of measure would be beautiful and have a human scale. His own use of the Modulor, however, proved to be as personal as everything else he did.

He defined architecture as the correct play of light and shade on the forms enclosing space, a highly intellectual and aesthetic approach to building that made the product difficult for many to appreciate or understand.

Le Corbusier's uncompromising, unconventional vision was always his own, and each building was a textbook of ideas and a wellspring of the contemporary spirit. No one ever really caught up with him. He was a modern Michelangelo, still far ahead of the field at seventy-seven, putting his inimitable stamp on a world already modeled in his own image, but only beginning to grasp his lessons.

For years, few listened. Most of his work before and after World War I consisted of paper schemes or private houses, with a few larger landmark buildings, like the Swiss Pavilion at the Cité Universitaire in Paris.

His largest commissions came in his old age, when the battle for modern architecture was won.

His only building in this country is the Carpenter Center for the Visual Arts at Harvard, completed in 1963, a building bursting with new ideas and images, on a site too restricted to hold it. It was a goodwill gesture to a country whose newness and vitality aroused his enthusiasm in the twenties, but to which he became increasingly hostile in later years.

In the United States, his legacy is especially alive. Architecture has never been more indebted to a single man. But if the movement is still young, the men who started it are old; Mies van der Rohe is seventy-nine; Walter Gropius is eighty. And two of its irreplaceable leaders, Frank Lloyd Wright and Le Corbusier, are gone.

New York Times, August 28, 1965

The Changing "Truth" of Le Corbusier

HOW DOES ONE LOOK FOR TRUTH? In art, the truth must be in what comes directly from the artist's hand, where the creative intent is most personal and direct—before other visions and interpretations garble the message from artist to viewer. That has always seemed clear enough. The meaning of the work is to be "understood" by the immediate response of eye, mind, and heart.

Or so I once thought, in more innocent days. The only thing that seems certain now is that the art object is absolute; the result of the creative act does not change. But the "truth" about it shifts with the calendar, and its coloration alters with every season of the mind. Vision depends on a moment in time. A different message is delivered for each generation.

Nothing could illustrate this dilemma with more exquisite impact than the current exhibition of Le Corbusier's architectural drawings at the Museum of Modern Art (through March 26). There are eighty-eight drawings on display, ranging from illustrated letters to sketches, elevations, and perspectives of monumental structures, almost all from the master's hand and covering fifty buildings designed between 1912 and 1962. Most are from the Fondation Le Corbusier in Paris, and many have never been exhibited before. The selection and installation are by Arthur Drexler, director of architecture and design, with the help of a grant from the New York State Council on the Arts.

The drawings are supplemented by models, but there are no photographs of the completed buildings. The intent is clearly to show the anatomy of creation, the moment at which the design idea takes form, the intensity and complexity of the search for the architectural and aesthetic ideal. It is a quiet show that staggers one's perceptions and challenges one's assumptions; it is full of stunning subtleties and moments of overwhelming impact. From the early Stein and Savoye houses of the twenties to the East Punjab capital of Chandigarh in the fifties, all of this work has had an enormous effect on the cultural and building style of our time. But most of all, these drawings offer the primary and most "pure" documentation of Le Corbusier's vision. From this conceptual moment on, both the building and the understanding of the artist's intent are compromised in a thousand ways.

A rare sequence of beautiful renderings, ten pastel elevations for the Stein House at Garches of 1927, is a revelation of invention and refinement. But what is the architectural "truth" of these elegant drawings? Certainly not the exquisite paper-thin elevation, seen as a cream-colored cutout against a sky-blue scrim, with mauve windows and russet doors that suggest not openings or transparency so much as a play of delicately recessed and tinted planes. No house could ever look like this or was ever meant to.

Is the truth in Le Corbusier's own definition of architecture, recorded in the same year as the Stein House study? He spoke then of pure structural systems expressed as a pure architectural aesthetic. Time reveals this as a seductive bit of sophistry, at best.

But it was that kind of engineering rationale, plus the Utopian promise of health and happiness through space, sun, and greenery, that sold the new architecture in the twenties and thirties. It was the rejection of the "lies" of old techniques and styles, the command to be true to one's time, to live and create in the spirit of the new age, that pervaded Le Corbusier's manifestos from 1917 to 1923.

Those "truths" of *Vers une Architecture* have become irony in fifty-five years. Le Corbusier's Voisin and other Paris plans that would have superimposed a superhuman scale and order on land ruthlessly cleared of all signs of humanity and centuries of urban culture are models of Cartesian logic and clarity in his cool correct drawings. But they are also quite mad—arrogant, wrong-headed schemes insensitive to the values of civilization and art. The messianic message got through strongly enough to sabotage the cityscape for the past thirty years, in the hands of both housing theorists and speculative developers.

As early as 1929, discussing the New Pioneers in his trailblazing book *Modern Architecture*, Henry-Russell Hitchcock called the Voisin plan "megalomaniacal" and speculated on the danger of Le Corbusier's polemical writings turning younger architects toward a false sociology. Le Corbusier's own buildings, Hitchcock pointed out, were the painstaking result of "extreme esthetic research."

In Hitchcock and Johnson's *International Style*, the book that introduced this work to the American public in 1932, that aesthetic research was formularized in a how-to-be-a-modern-architect kit: Volume was to be emphasized over mass, irregularity stressed over symmetry, and ornament outlawed. The wall became a thin, taut membrane around flexible space. These radical design rules were justified in the name of the structural revolution. It is little wonder that once this pattern of "correct" perception was set, Le Corbusier puzzled and horrified so many by a virtually traitorous change of style in the fifties that began with the rough-hewn, sculptural poetry of the Jaoul houses and culminated in the chapel at Ronchamps.

The elusive truth about his work may be much closer to a point Le Corbusier made originally in *L'Esprit Nouveau* and repeated later in life: Cubism, he said, was to be celebrated as "one of the most creative

and revolutionary movements in the history of thought . . . a radical reform in the plastic arts [that] penetrated into architecture." All of his
buildings are conscious and powerful exercises in abstract composition,
from strict geometry to free form. They are full of enough aesthetic complexities to keep several more generations busy with interpretations.

And that is exactly what is going on now. The text for this generation
is an article by Colin Rowe and Robert Slutzky with the impenetrable
title of "Transparency: Literal and Phenomenal." In this interpretation,
the transparent and overlapping planes of cubist painting, with their
many ambiguous readings of the picture plane, are transferred to the
composition of the Stein House at Garches. Almost limitless meanings
are suggested in the arrangement of clear and opaque surfaces, of physical fact and visual effect.

In the seventies, then, a Le Corbusier house is no longer viewed as
a "machine to live in" or as an instrument for revolutionary social
change. These drawings reveal houses, and other buildings, as objects
of intense aesthetic research and analysis. And thus today a sophisticated high-art game has supplanted social reform. This is the "truth" of
Le Corbusier's work for a generation concerned with a return to the art
of architecture, beyond technology, sociology, and politics. Perhaps tomorrow still another truth will emerge.

New York Times, February 19, 1978

Flexible Enough to Endure

I HAVE BEEN TO PESSAC TO SEE the future, and contrary to popular
belief and the conventional wisdom, it works. Pessac is the town near
Bordeaux, in France, where Le Corbusier designed and built a community of fifty-one houses in the twenties under the sponsorship of the
French industrialist Henry Frugès, who meant them to be a laboratory
of new domestic, structural, and aesthetic ideas.

Villa Stein

I went to Pessac prepared for the worst. Everything I had ever heard about it led to expectations of a failed experiment and an aesthetic slum, a testament to the miscarriage of modernism and the arrogance of its architects. This did not turn out to be the case. The Pessac housing, a landmark of early modernism, is now more than fifty years old. It looks, and it doesn't look, like Le Corbusier's original design.

These are not "landmark" houses in the usual sense. They were not commissioned by those who were to live in them, and they are not, like Frank Lloyd Wright houses, objects of curatorial pride, or a responsibility that has led some owners to breakdown, divorce, or flight. Pessac was built as experimental "workers" housing; there was no personal contract between occupant-patron and famous architect in which the owners' tastes, and even lives, are subordinate to the maintenance of a work of art, in which any change is a violation. With half a century of additions and remodelings, Le Corbusier's houses have been "violated" over and over. They have come a long way from his *prisme pur* or "machine to live in," and even from their concept as a social experiment. But Pessac is alive and well today and making an entirely different kind of history than intended.

The Quartiers Modernes Frugès, as the project was called, has been put down in the literature of modernism almost since it was built. In his avant-garde 1929 book, *Modern Architecture: Romanticism and Reintegration*, the historian Henry-Russell Hitchcock referred to Pessac as a "serious disappointment." He had some praise for the variety of the planning, which embraced detached, semidetached, and row houses and three-story multiple dwellings that the Bordelaise called "skyscrapers," all with individual gardens. But he scorned the interiors of the houses as "uncomfortable for the small-salaried employees for whom they were designed," and called features like roof terraces more suitable for the artists and millionaires who were usually Le Corbusier's clients.

"EFFECTIVE PESSAC ADMITTEDLY was," he wrote, "but practical not at all, even in elementary matters . . . As the first executed housing scheme of the New Pioneers in France it has actually done more harm than good to the development of modern housing there." Over the years, by way of the pilgrimage grapevine, have come vivid descriptions of how disgruntled and uncomprehending occupants have sabotaged the architecture.

With this background, Pessac has become a convenient whipping boy for those who are currently busy singling out every defect of the modern movement while declaring its demise. Pessac is the model failure. Say Pessac now, and you have said everything there is to say about all that ever went wrong with modern architecture. It is grouped ritually with that other example of modernist housing failure, Pruitt-Igoe, the public housing project in St. Louis that was dynamited after severe socioeconomic problems made it uninhabitable. Pessac was supposedly finished off by the occupants' rebellious rejection of Le Corbusier's doctrinaire modernist aesthetic and elitist ideas about how they should live.

This neat doomsday script, with the Pruitt-Igoe blast signaling the end of modern architecture, is favored over more complex realities by those rewriting history. It was the scenario presented in Robert Hughes's visually stunning program on architecture in The Shock of the New series. There is, of course, nothing more effective in the shock department than blowing it all up, even if that means compromising art and history for a tidy dramatic cliché.

And so I walked down the Avenue Frugès and Rue Le Corbusier in Pessac on a late January day expecting the shock of the old, or the future that died, but the script didn't fit. I tried blaming the springlike sunshine and the wines of Bordeaux as I found myself thinking, "If this is so bad, how can it be so good?"

The scale and relationship of the houses to each other and to the gardens was excellent; the shapes and proportions of the buildings were unusually strong and good. There was a feeling of a cohesive whole. Even with the loss of key elements of the Corbusian style—the precise repetition of open and closed geometries, the visual sense of the thin concrete, the painterly abstraction of the original colored façades—the settlement retained an impressive and recognizable integrity. Pessac was a very pleasant place to be. And these houses were clearly survivors.

It was also clear that Pessac was a survivor precisely because of its architecture. Its strong identity absorbs almost anything. Structurally, the houses are incredibly solid. One can read the original features and then read the way they have been used or assimilated. Pessac continues to give something to the eye and the spirit that only buildings shaped and informed by a superior and caring eye and spirit can. This still holds true, with all of the changes made by the occupants over the years.

Le Corbusier once said, in a statement usually turned against him, "You know, it is always life that is right and the architect who is wrong." This was not a confession of error. It was the recognition of the validity of process over the sanctity of ideology. Few architects are capable of making that observation, because it speaks not to some fixed ideal, but to the complexity and incompleteness of architecture, to how life and art accommodate each other. And that is what Pessac is really about.

The process of accommodation has been thoroughly documented in a study published in 1972 called *Lived-in Architecture, Le Corbusier's Pessac Revisited,* by a French architect, Philippe Boudon. Mr. Boudon carried out a systematic analysis of exterior and interior changes and attitudes toward the architecture through extensive occupant interviews. I have only acquired the book now, although I remember scare pictures in an architectural journal at the time. The study was almost universally misinterpreted or misunderstood—or just not read—by those who considered it proof that Pessac had been destroyed. Photographs of garage doors where there once were open entrances, small, shuttered windows replacing large expanses of glass, tile roofs and endearing touches of kitsch were cited as evidence of architectural failure.

Mr. Boudon's conclusion was exactly the opposite. "The Quartiers

Modernes Frugès were not an 'architectural failure,'" he wrote. "The modifications carried out by the occupants constitute a positive and not a negative consequence of Le Corbusier's original conception. Pessac not only allowed the occupants sufficient latitude to satisfy their needs, by doing so it also helped them to realize what those needs were."

The then-radical open plan could be reorganized and subdivided in many ways; a terrace could be roofed over for an extra room; windows of one's choice could be fitted into the large openings without knocking out a wall. There is no sense of "the architect's will imposed," or of an unyielding, authoritarian design. The houses rolled with the punches. The transition from a cool and uniform International Style to personalized, somewhat Mediterranean-look villas has led to an air of solidity, rather than openness; of individuality, rather than continuity; of enclosed volumes rather than screen walls. Because the planning is good, each owner has a sense of privacy, with no loss of a collective ensemble.

ONE ROW-HOUSE RESIDENT, who generously invited our small sightseeing group inside, discoursed knowledgeably on the strength, solidity, and longevity of Le Corbusier's reinforced concrete construction, while we stood on a roof terrace that had been resurfaced in colored tiles. Downstairs, a corridor had been created from the front door to the living room, and a formal dining space had been added by extending the living space into the garden. There was flowered wallpaper, overstuffed furniture, and the accessories of a comfortable bourgeois lifestyle.

Another owner, according to Boudon, who had never heard of Le Corbusier, was busy "restoring back" the interior of his house to the original open plan without knowing it, by removing earlier partitions; he cited Le Corbusier's own reasons of space, light, and view. Many speak with reasonable understanding of Le Corbusier, and most of the residents are aware and rather proud of the fact that the houses have been "listed" for their aesthetic and historical importance. None feel that they have attacked the architecture.

Like all of Le Corbusier's houses, these were based on five design principles that he enunciated repeatedly. The raised ground floor, wide windows, roof terraces, open façades, and open plans were all made possible by the uniquely strong and ductile new material, reinforced concrete, which freed the architecture from the traditional restrictions of thick masonry walls. Corners could be breached, openings placed almost anywhere and made much larger, spans increased and walls treated as screens, rooms opened to each other and to the light and view; the building could even be levitated to become a six-sided prism.

This unprecedented structural and design freedom was intoxicating. But if it created the challenge of a new kind of architecture that was to make the twentieth century unique, it also led to wildly overreaching ideas that went beyond making better buildings to making better cities and better people. This assumption was more innocent than arrogant, and like all utopian dreams, it was doomed.

LE CORBUSIER'S VISION of the city of the future proved exhilarating and seductive in such an atmosphere, but it never ceases to amaze me that his superblocks of slabs and towers raised above flat landscapes laced to the horizon with superhighways were ever taken seriously. Those of us who refused to take them seriously were the unconverted heathens. Those who did, and lived to see the sterile fallout in our cities, are now bumping into each other recanting.

But Pessac, even if it had been built to double its size, as intended, was no helicopter view of the world of the future; it was housing on a small, intimate scale. Its module was human, and it was both strong and flexible enough to endure. Many of its features have long since become standard. It was truly designed in the measure of man.

What everyone remembers with varying degrees of disapproval was Le Corbusier's announced wish to build "a machine to live in," based on the early twentieth-century's enchantment with the belief that only good could come from mass production. What everyone has forgotten is what he said in the next sentence. "But since men also have hearts," reads his dedication speech at Pessac in 1926, "we have also tried to insure that men with hearts would be able to live happily in our houses." They have.

New York Times, May 15, 1981

Mies van der Rohe

The Soaring Towers That
Gave Form to an Age

THE GLASSY SKYSCRAPERS AND SLEEK-WALLED BUILDINGS that are the pride of modern cities and the symbol of modern life owe more to Mies van der Rohe than to any other architect of our time. In an age of complexity and confusion, Mies knew exactly what he was doing, and what he did, essentially, was to give that age its characteristic look and style. Almost every important street of every major city today is lined with the offspring of the spare, elegant structures that were his personal contribution to the art of architecture.

Mies made the glittering, soaring, straight-lined tower of today's urban world peculiarly his own. Even more than Le Corbusier and Frank Lloyd Wright—with whom he completed the architectural triumvirate of form givers for the twentieth century—he left the stamp of his art and philosophy on much of the world's contemporary construction.

That art and philosophy were based exclusively on contemporary technology: the supporting metal skeleton frame, the non-load-bearing wall hung lightly from it, and the modern materials that made the traditional heavy masonry building obsolete. He used those materials—glass, steel, and aluminum, as well as timeless marble and bronze—with an exquisite, demanding, and even rigid sense of order, appropriateness, and beauty. There is not a cheap, vulgar, or fussy passage in anything he designed or built.

There is much that is cheap and vulgar in the legion of structures that derived from his work, however. Because he enunciated a set of rational principles that met modern building needs in terms of scale, engineering, and production, the formula was promptly reduced to its lowest common denominator by commercial builders. For every Seagram Building, there are the uncountable crudities of numberless routine adaptations of a style superficially easy to "knock off."

But more important than speculative abuses is the fact that the reduction of much large-scale utilitarian building to simple, practical "Miesian" elements has resulted in a valid and handsome, genuinely vernacular architecture for our day.

Although it is also a day when architects are increasingly preoccupied with the total environment, Mies remained an artist committed to the design of the individual building. His lifelong interest was the creation of the most perfect product that an infallibly refined taste and progressive technology could produce. His singular aim was the beautiful and efficient framing of large, all-purpose spaces; some worked superbly, and some did not. But the strong, richly austere aesthetic that he established was an unparalleled expression of new materials and engineering techniques.

He succeeded in his objectives with consummate artistry and skill. The artistry is subtle, extremely sophisticated, and not always easily discernible to the untrained eye, to which all plain, modern buildings tend to look alike. Ultimately, the excellence of these buildings rests on the same basis as that of any of the great monuments of the past: fine proportion, sensitive detail, and expressive pertinence to their times.

In recent years, when modern architecture became a stylistic free-for-all of almost baroque exuberance, he never wavered from the stripped-down, severely disciplined style that expressed his own convictions and the doctrines of the architectural revolution that he helped pioneer.

"You can't invent a new architecture every Monday morning," he commented, cutting some well-publicized Monday-wonders down to Lilliputian size.

Today it has become fashionable for young architects to call the masterworks of Mies "irrelevant" to the immediate social problems of our time. But cities endure, and Mies's "relevance" is timeless.

Mies was large — in history, as an innovator and talent of Michelangelesque stature; and personally, as a calm, massive, craggy man with the tacit monumentality of his work. His buildings are large — soaring symbols for an age. Today, however, larger buildings are being built by smaller men. And surprisingly few of the inhabitants of a Mies-shaped world know how much they have gained, and lost.

New York Times, August 19, 1969

The Making of a Master

EVEN IF THE CENTENNIAL OF THE birth of Ludwig Mies van der Rohe were not coming up next year (how quickly new worlds become old), there could be no better time for the critical and scholarly reappraisal of this seminal and influential modernist architect than right now. How tiresome and meaningless the once-revered phrase "form giver" has become to a new generation, how steady the stampede away from the master in the sixteen years since his death. The reaction was inevitable; Mies was the giant who epitomized the strongest beliefs and the most distilled practice and had the most widespread impact of the modern movement. Perhaps because the twentieth-century world continues to be so conspicuously shaped in his image, the once-Olympian and oracular Mies has become the lightning rod for postmodernist rejection—the architect who must be exorcised.

Nevertheless, or perhaps because the span of a century evokes a Pavlovian reflex in those who record and interpret such events, this centennial is about to be celebrated in no uncertain fashion. A major Mies retrospective will open at the Museum of Modern Art in February, and a number of important Mies publications are beginning to appear. *Mies van der Rohe*, by David Spaeth, with a preface by Kenneth Frampton, was issued this spring; *Mies van der Rohe: The Villas and Country Houses*, by Wolf Tegethoff, is now available, and so is *Mies van der Rohe: A Critical Biography*, the long-awaited study by Franz Schulze. To coincide with the exhibition, Garland Press will bring out the first four volumes of the Mies Archive (with three more volumes to come). Two additional Museum books will follow later in the centennial year—a definitive Mies monograph by Arthur Drexler, director of the Department of Architecture and Design at MoMA, and a volume of essays meant to further illuminate the Mies legacy.

FOR MIES ENTHUSIASTS, this is all heady stuff. Mies detractors, busy setting the record wrong (but no more so than his followers), will have to deal with significant new scholarship meant to set the record right. Each of these books adds something to the clarification of Mies's art. A fuller understanding of this enigmatic architect is emerging, and that understanding includes the obvious and sometimes disturbing connections between the man and his work. Unfortunately, not one of these books is written with the witty glitter and provocative irreverence we have come to expect from the best postmodernist literature. There is none of the smoking evangelical fervor of Vincent Scully's pronouncements from Yale and the inner circles of postmodernist gnosticism, or of the dazzling intellectual footwork of Charles Jencks, the movement's "official" historian, who concluded a passionate put-down of Mies in his *Modern Movements in Architecture* by dismissing the architect's philosophy as "farce" and his buildings as "half baked." These three early reappraisals are as solemn as Mies.

The reexamination of Mies's place in art and history can only be salutary and sobering at this transitional moment in our culture. Standards of judgment have never been shakier. Not since the height of the muzziest Victorian eclecticism has there been more widely acclaimed bad building with more foolishness written and spoken about it, foolishness directed at a confused public and an insecure profession. With a new style or personality celebrated weekly, one of the cogent infrequent Mies quotes has a particular pertinence, his answer to the accusation that he repeated his themes was that one does not invent a new architecture every Monday morning. Today, Monday-morning styles play as well in Paris as Peoria, particularly if the architect can talk and will travel. Mies did little of either, especially in later years. In this age of promo-architecture, silence and solitude are no longer the artist's lot or choice.

Franz Schulze's biography is a herculean, generally successful effort to present Mies's work in terms of both character and context. The writing style has a curious gait, from lively to plodding, but the substance is impressive and much of the material is fresh and revealing. The author is a professor of art at Lake Forest College in Lake Forest, Illinois; this book has obviously been a long labor of love and respect for which no source has been left untouched. In addition to the Mies Archive at the Modern and the letters and documents willed by Mies to the Library of Congress, his sources include publications and records here and abroad, as well as unedited tapes and transcripts and countless conversations with family, friends, and colleagues of Mies. He has carefully retraced locales and relationships. While this effort may not yield absolute truth, it is enormously helpful.

The man who emerges from Mr. Schulze's book is much as he is remembered by those who knew him: solid, slow, taciturn, devoted to the long and careful development of his ideas over many years and projects, unswerving in his standards, authoritarian and unyielding in matters of principle and design. Here is the not unfamiliar portrait of the artist as loner—a talented ambitious young man, who was born in Aachen, Germany, in 1886, rose from humble, provincial beginnings as a stonemason's son and advanced through marriage, social contacts, and a trail of broken personal and professional relationships to a position of prominence in the sophisticated art circles of post–World War I Berlin, and to world eminence in his later years in the United States.

Solitary and self-absorbed, he was unable to adjust to marriage and a family. He left his wife, Ada Bruhn, the daughter of a wealthy industrialist, a few years after their wedding in 1913; there was never a divorce, and their three daughters remained loyal to both parents. Mies's close personal relationship with the talented designer Lilly Reich, whose collaboration considerably enriched his work, ended when he came to the United States in 1938; he made no attempt to continue it, while she, for her part, attended to his affairs in Berlin and kept his papers intact. Mies's single-minded devotion to the practice of architecture always took precedence over friendship, love, and loyalty; he simply accepted attention and affection from those who could tolerate the unequal priorities on his side.

A handsome, stocky young man, Mies became heavyset and crippled with arthritis as he grew older. His tastes in his advancing years were simple and sybaritic—a few expensive dark suits of excellent cut, preferably tailored by Knize, and an endless supply of martinis and Havana cigars. He died of the complications of arthritis and alcohol at the age of eighty-three in 1969.

Mies came to the United States in response to an invitation to be the director of architecture at the Armour Institute of Technology in Chicago, later the Illinois Institute of Technology, when it became clear that his life and work in Nazi Germany had reached a dead end. He lived, practiced, and taught in Chicago for the next thirty years. Critics have accused him of being slow to oppose the policies of the Nazis. The record suggests that he was as unconcerned with politics as he was with personal relationships. He was quite capable of producing sincerely conceived designs for the imperial German state (the Bismarck monument project of 1910), the Communists (the Liebknecht and Luxemburg Memorial, 1926), and the national socialists (the Reichsbank competition of 1933). Shortly after Mies succeeded Walter Gropius as head of the Bauhaus in 1930, he moved the school from Dessau to Berlin, where the Nazis closed it. After working assiduously for permission to reopen, he realized that the school would not be able to function in its original spirit, so he and the staff closed it themselves in 1933. Mies did not ever really subscribe to the social utopianism of modernist ideology, although he headed the famous Weissenhofsiedelung in Stuttgart, the 1927 complex that remains a landmark demonstration of modernist housing design. When he could no longer work and teach according to the beliefs that shaped his style, he went. Clearly, they were the only beliefs he had.

MIES, THE MAN, is a shadowy presence in Wolf Tegethoff's book, which restricts itself to a careful analysis of documents in the Mies Archive, supplemented by dogged detective work to fill in the missing pieces. A slender volume, of which more than half is taken up by splendid illustrations, this translation of the 1981 German edition is the most important contribution to Mies scholarship to date. It is a product of that well-known scholarly attribute *Sitzfleisch*, as opposed to the more popular practice of winging it or speaking-in-architectural-tongues that is currently producing so much of what could be called, in fashionable parlance, faux history.

Mr. Tegethoff deals only with the house designs from 1923 to 1951, but he does so in the broadest terms of their spatial and structural development—explorations that had everything to do with the extension of architectural frontiers and little to do with domesticity. His research corrects long-standing errors and disposes of lingering Miesian myths. It redates the concrete and brick country house projects—two of the most revolutionary designs of the twenties and part of the group of five Mies projects on which much modern architecture admittedly rests. The implications revise our understanding of Mies's early work and have an inescapable impact on the writing of architectural history.

He also gives us a fascinating insight into Mies's working methods. The image that has prevailed—encouraged by Mies himself—is of the solitary genius cogitating silently until the perfect design springs fully developed from his hand and brow (it was quite a Jovian brow). The Mies Archive material proves that he was a constant, compulsive sketcher, forever changing and reformulating both concepts and details. Divine creative inspiration never struck; he studied and restudied every nuance of plan and façade. No architect ever drew more beautifully— from deft, lyrical sketches to precise collages with the power of much larger works of art. A perfectionist, he sought the ultimate refinement of idea and form. The buildings that seem all serene, effortless simplicity were the result of intense and endless work.

DAVID SPAETH IS an architect and associate professor at the University of Kentucky, who published an annotated Mies bibliography and chronology in 1979. Unfortunately, his new book perpetuates dating errors, such as 1919 for the 1921 glass skyscraper project and the wrong sequence for the country houses. His bibliography lists the 1981 edition of Mr. Tegethoff's study, but the contents evidently went unnoticed. (The Schulze book incorporates the new material.) As a Mies loyalist, however, Mr. Spaeth makes his case, buttressed by extended personal research.

Increasingly we see that Mies's roots were less in revolution than in tradition and the discernible past. He virtually reinvented classicism in terms of twentieth-century technology; the connection between "Berlin modernism" and "Prussian classicism" was made by the critic and historian Colin Rowe as early as 1947 in the brilliant essays of *The Mathematics of the Ideal Villa.* The precedents were close at hand—the monumental and domestic architecture of Karl Friedrich Schinkel and the open-plan villas of Schinkel and his students around Berlin. Mies admired Peter Behrens, the early advocate of the totally designed environment, and participated in the neoclassical manner of much of the protomodernist work early in the century. It was the transformation of this tradition into something new and the level of art on which he made change, rather than the advertised rejection of the past, that guarantee his place in history. For Mies, the physical and perceptual relationship between structure and space was the fulcrum of all architectural art. The respect and reverence for material learned in the stonemason's yards of Aachen never left him. He knew how the strength and measure of the brick established the module and mystique of the finished building, and the expressive and aesthetic possibilities of glass, steel, and concrete were central to his art.

His entire life's work was devoted to the search for the most magnificent and compellingly beautiful clear-span space enclosed by the most elegant structural systems made possible by modern technology—in two forms, the pavilion and the tower. The search ended with his last work, the Berlin National Gallery of 1962–65. In pursuit of this ideal, his designs became increasingly reductive, refined, and abstract. But his "skin-and-bones" buildings were never the product of a rigid, narrow functionalism. His minimalism was as lyrical as it was precise, and the result was not restriction but an extraordinary new freedom.

This was a kind of freedom never posited or made possible before: the free plan, in which spaces no longer had to be determined by bearing walls; free walls, which could be placed anywhere within an efficient and flexible support system; the dematerialization and redefinition of walls through the use of glass and translucent or transparent planes; the breakdown of barriers between interior and exterior; the ultimate romantic extension of the building into the natural landscape. There is nothing "simple" about these deceptively simple buildings. They offer unprecedented experiences, without the associations of ornament or history, and they are intended to engage the spirit in the fullest sense.

The spare, basic, Miesian vocabulary also gave the modernist architect a new freedom to succeed or fall short. The limitations of smaller talents were brutally revealed; there was no longer any way to dress up the banal and mundane. Mies's reductive theories, carried to their conceptual extreme, contained the stuff of both sublimity and failure, to which even he was not immune. His "universal" space proved elusive and troublesome; his Crown Hall at the Illinois Institute of Technology was noisy and resisted subdivision. No museum director has yet come to terms with the inescapable demands of a Mies building. The Farnsworth House (1945–51), a glass temple that celebrated the seasons, leaked and was hot; the owner sued when costs reached seventy thousand dollars.

In the end, Mies's work is a paradox. In one of history's giant creative leaps, it uses exceptional forms and solutions to enlarge the ideas and boundaries of art; it distills building to its most artful essentials.

Yet by their radical and uncompromising nature, these forms are flawed for the more conventional and complex purposes that architecture must satisfy. Obviously, he sought beauty over utility. As Kenneth Frampton reminds us in his preface to Mr. Spaeth's book, Mies attached enormous importance to the act of building as a poetic gesture. Poetry is the most difficult, demanding, and disciplined of the arts; it searches for essences and invests them with universal meanings in a way that can delight, move, or shatter us. Great architecture does all of these things. The essence of architecture is structure; Mies made poetry of it.

The postmodernist counterrevolution must continue to attack Mies; he is too central to the modern movement. To do this it is necessary to deny the knowledge that has been carried through centuries of building—at the same time that the past is being plundered for trim. We are therefore told that the presumption of structural relevance to the art of architecture is no longer valid or necessary, that there is no intrinsic integrity to the building act, that no expressive challenge is involved. Suave style-mongering, from cryptoclassicism and flash-card historicism to stage-set sophistries, is passed off as an architectural rebirth. After so many vanities, the simple logic of the despised Miesian vernacular is beginning to look good. This anonymous product may not be poetry, but it beats nonsense rhymes. Less even looks like more.

New York Times, December 1, 1985

Alvar Aalto

Alvar Aalto, Finnish Master

A New York example of the work of Alvar Aalto, a founder and leading practitioner of modern architecture, will be unveiled officially this afternoon with the dedication of the Institute of International Education Building at 809 United Nations Plaza.

The building is by Harrison, Abramovitz & Harris, but the twelfth-floor conference rooms, where the ceremonies will take place, were designed by the internationally honored Finnish architect as the gift of the Edgar J. Kaufmann Foundation.

The completion of these interiors marks a felicitous ending to what otherwise would have been a fairly routine exercise in New York's architectural economics.

In 1950, the institute bought one of the handsomest of the city's baronial houses, the Gould-Vanderbilt mansion at 1 East Sixty-seventh Street, for four hundred thousand dollars. In 1960, needing more space, it sold the building to an apartment-house developer, to whom it was worth almost three times as much — $1.1 million — to tear down. A landmark was lost.

This year the institute completed its chaste and sleek new office building, which substitutes a conscientiously businesslike taste and competence for château-style grandeur, at a cost of $4.5 million. That would be the end of an unexceptional story except for that top floor, which has been transformed for an undisclosed and probably formidable price into the most beautiful and distinguished interior that New York has seen in many years. A landmark is gained.

Here are the well-known Aalto trademarks that have been admired by two generations of architects. Pale, laminated woods are used with the plasticity of sculpture; stepped, curved walls and ceilings turn

ordinary rectangular spaces into a series of softened enclosures of seductive virtuosity, and deceptive simplicity belies a most sophisticated
style.

But even if these contributions have already taken their place in architectural histories, there is nothing dated about them. The Kaufmann
conference rooms are so far superior to corporate and institutional interior design here that they make the standardized, expensive ploys of
teak-by-the-yard, carpet-by-the-vertical-inch, and conference-table-by-
the-ton seem flashy and cheap by comparison.

This superiority rests on a large talent and small details. First, and
most important, there is Aalto's treatment of architectural space. It
might be called a sensitive and loving kind of manipulation that molds,
instead of denying, the existing architectural shell. It is creative camouflage, rather than destructive decoration. And it is frankly sensuous,
rather than severe.

Approximately 4,350 square feet of conventionally boxlike, low-
ceilinged space has been divided into a lobby, reception room, conference rooms, and a corridor. Much of the area can be opened or closed
in a variety of ways by sliding doors.

The large conference-room ceiling sweeps upward in undulating
stages to a window-wall, an effect made possible by moving the heavy
service machinery above. Side walls curve gently and unexpectedly,
giving a diagonal focus. Even the cobalt-blue Finnish tile of the elevator entrance is rounded and smooth to the hand. Inside, the colors are
white and ivory, accented by black, with the cool, elegant clarity of natural tones and materials.

Scarcely second to the resolution of space is the superb use of wood.
It is quite possible, in this country, to forget that wood is so beautiful and
that its appeal is due to its qualities as a natural material. American processes of manufacture frequently result in a mechanized and overfin-
ished product that looks as if it had never known a tree.

The rooms glow with the pale warmth of white birch. White plaster
walls are partly sheathed with white-birch panels, and slender, vertical
battens of clustered, laminated birch rods tie both surfaces together.

This wall treatment breaks into a brief abstract fantasy at one point
on the longest side of the main conference room, where a composition
of straight and bent wood forms is meant to suggest a stylized forest. It
was reduced to a small stand of "trees" by New York's fire laws.

All of these more sensitive elements, including the Aalto-designed furniture upholstered in soft black leather, an integral part of the interiors, were prefabricated or produced in Finland. The "forest" was studied at full-size in the architect's Helsinki atelier and reerected here. Large, plain sections, like the ash panels and sliding doors of the same white tone as the Finnish birch, were made in the United States.

There is no sign of the aggressive angularity or dynamic sharpness that is commonly labeled modern. Aalto might be called, to use the language of painting, a soft-edge architect. He continues to work, in increasingly subtle ways, with the free-form, a concept he virtually invented in the twenties. And he has seen it turned into the most abused of all clichés.

He himself is incapable of a cliché or a stereotype of any kind. A small, spry, sophisticated, impeccably tailored Finnish troll of sixty-six years, with a gleam in his eye and a soft barb to his wit, Alvar Aalto still leads the field of design.

New York Times, November 30, 1964

A Library in Oregon

IMPORTING THE WORK OF A FAMOUS Finnish architect known for his beautiful use of wood to the Pacific Northwest may seem like bringing coals to Newcastle. The woods here in Mount Angel, Oregon, are as full of architects as they are of Douglas fir.

But imported architecture, unlike some imported wines, can travel well. The new library of the Mount Angel Abbey, a Benedictine monastery forty miles south of Portland, being dedicated this weekend, brings a small and perfect work of the seventy-three-year-old master of the modern movement, Alvar Aalto, to the United States.

As surprising as its presence here on an Oregon hilltop is the fact that this is only the second building, and third work, of this internationally

Mount Angel Library

celebrated architect in this country. The Baker House dormitory at the
Massachusetts Institute of Technology was built in 1947, and the Kauf-
mann conference rooms were designed for the Institute of International
Education in New York in 1964.

Mr. Aalto takes only those commissions that please him. When a
letter came to Helsinki in 1963, quite out of the blue, from Father
Barnabas Reasoner, postmarked St. Benedict, Oregon, asking him "to
give us a building that will fill our needs in a beautiful and intelligent
way," Mr. Aalto agreed to do the job. It was an act of faith on both
sides.

The result is a three-story, fan-shaped structure that cost $1,272,000
and was paid for by an anonymous industrialist. It fits snugly into the
side of a hill that overlooks a vast, quilted panorama of rolling farm
country.

Right now, there are fields of red clover and bursts of orange pop-
pies. But it could just as easily be a monastic hilltop in Bavaria or the
south of France, with the cultivated land spread below, except for a
backdrop of Mounts Hood, Adams, St. Helens, and Rainier. This is

green north country, as hospitable to Alvar Aalto's architecture as his native Finland.

The whole building is from the master's hand, down to the smallest fitting. Furnishings, lamps, and movable objects were brought from Finland. All structural and trim details are on-site work. The classic Aalto-designed chairs and stools in vanilla-pale birch have a *B* brand mark on the bottom to identify them for export from Finland. The Benedictine brothers at Mount Angel raise their own beef and send their cattle brand to the factory.

Only the library's top level shows above the hill at the entrance side. It is flanked by other abbey structures built in a bland midtwenties medieval manner that might be called Lapsed Lombard. With no compromise of its own style beyond a blending buff brick, the new addition displays a kind of good environmental manners rare among name-architect "star" structures on institutional or educational campuses.

The architect could not come for the dedication, but the weekend ceremonies will be highlighted by a Duke Ellington concert in the new library, introducing the work of a resident composer, Ann Henry. There will also be performances by the Portland Junior Symphony and the Lewis and Clark College Choir and Abbey Schola.

Richard W. Southern, a medieval historian who is president of St. John's College, Oxford, and the abbot primate Rembert Weakland of Rome, head of the Benedictine Order, will speak at the dedication. The Finnish ambassador to the United States, Olavi Munkki, will attend the ceremonies.

The design was begun in Mr. Aalto's Helsinki studio from photographs and plans of the site. In 1967, before construction, he visited the abbey. He moved the location of the building ten feet to save two handsome Douglas firs and to ensure an opening between buildings for the view.

The library itself does not maximize the view; it does not focus attention on the outdoors. It is a place to work, flooded with controlled daylight, with equally controlled glimpses of the countryside.

The fan-shaped plan, with a two-story central, curving skylight, reveals the entire interior to the eye from the entrance. There is no rigid, straight-line, geometric progression of shelves or stacks; they enclose the space and the user in a gentle arc. The two floors of light-bathed stack and working areas can be seen at once, in a functionally and aesthetically inviting relationship. The whole operation can be controlled by a single librarian.

The Aalto palette of white walls, black seating, and pale, warm woods, a beauty intensified by natural light from high windows and skylights and warmed by a carefully supplementary incandescent glow, proves again that no color can be the richest color. The characteristic, lovingly used Aalto woods are birch, oak, and fir crafted here, with insistently natural finishes that make American wood products look like cheap wood imitations.

A slatted, sunburst ceiling of fir strips is repeated in slats finishing the ends of the book stacks. The free form, an Aalto innovation that suffered near-total degradation by the forties, is here in curving walls that define a small lecture hall, also fan-shaped, that seats one hundred in Aalto black-and-birch chairs facing an oak "shell." The building is superbly finished and detailed.

The structure contains about forty-three thousand square feet of space, with room for 250,000 volumes on theology, philosophy, and related educational subjects, to serve the abbey and its seminary and wider ecumenical scholarship. There are microfilm, periodical, and map rooms, a bindery, and staff offices. The associated local architects were DeMars & Wells of Berkeley, California, and Eric Vartiainen represented the Aalto office on the site.

Beyond the facts, there is a kind of architecture that is elegant, humane, and full of sophisticated skills. These skills never date. Vintage Aalto and 1970 Aalto are the same—subtle, sensuous, full of wisdom about the environment and man.

Aalto architecture continues to teach basic truths about space, light, and function. Two generations brought up on pictures of his landmark library at Viipuri, destroyed during the war when the Russians took over the Finnish province of Karelia, can find the essential lessons here. They are lessons of humanitarian sensibility and a quality of design practice that must be applied to whatever new sociological role the architect defines for himself in a troubled world.

New York Times, May 30, 1970

Where They Do It Right

ON DECEMBER 2, A MAJOR NEW CONCERT and congress hall, called Finlandia Hall, designed by the Finnish architect Alvar Aalto, opened in Helsinki. At the time, I had the pictures spread out on my desk, and a well-known dance-and-drama-critic colleague who had been through the trauma of the opening of the Kennedy Center with me happened to see and admire them. "Where's that?" he asked. "In Finland," I replied. "Oh, of course," he said, "we don't build that kind of thing here."

He was right; we don't build big civic and cultural centers in this country much above the architectural schlock level. They are rarely, if ever, great or beautiful buildings. Not because the United States has no good architects or great or beautiful buildings. But neither seems to make it to those symbolic and civic jobs that are meant to represent the country and its culture.

I have not visited Finlandia Hall, but I have seen a great deal of Aalto's superb work in Finland, where it is essential to experience it, and in other countries, including his three works in the United States, the 1947 MIT dormitory, the 1964 Kaufmann conference rooms at the Institute of International Education in New York, and the jewel-like library for the Benedictine monastery at Mount Angel, Oregon, completed two years ago.

It is necessary to know Aalto's work firsthand, because it translates poorly into pictures. So much of its excellence is its absolute rightness of conception, the three-dimensional relationships of its elements, its use of light and low-key color, the subtle sensuosity of details remarkable for consistency and restraint, and ultimately, its humanity. All this is resistant to the photographer's art.

Against the experience of Aalto's buildings, it is possible to "read" the pictures of Finlandia Hall, and the message is clear. Like all of his structures, it is a painstakingly beautiful, contemporary design in the highest creative sense. There are no gimmicks. His architecture, as he says himself, is not "coquettish." Function is translated with elegant clarity into a warm and eloquent expression of our time.

It must be pointed out that there are obvious differences between Washington's Kennedy Center and Helsinki's Finlandia Hall beyond their quality as architecture. The Kennedy Center is huge; it contains three performing arts halls for opera, concerts, and drama, joined by a foyer and corridors big enough to float several battleships, plus restaurant and executive space. The houses within the house—all, thank heavens, a resounding acoustical success or this would really be the biggest white marble elephant in the world—are larger than Helsinki's. There are differences in program, subsidy, costs, ownership, and operation.

The Helsinki building is meant for the joint purpose of concerts and congresses. A wing of large meeting rooms will extend the structure farther along the lakefront that marks the town center sometime this year. There is presently a 1,750-seat concert hall, a 350-seat chamber music hall, radio studios and executive offices, restaurant and cafeteria, some meeting rooms, and facilities for simultaneous translation in all public areas. Concert acoustics have been judged successful by a majority of critics, and some matters of debate, such as the level of the orchestra stage, are capable of adjustment.

Beyond these differences, however, there are very important, striking similarities between the two buildings. Both are avowed architectural and cultural landmarks in their respective capital cities, both entail a form of status and symbolism of national significance, and both purportedly serve their countries' highest cultural aspirations and achievements. What is of concern here is the quality level at which these comparable objectives are translated into architecture. One succeeds; the other fails.

Take, for example, the use of marble. Both buildings are marble-clad. The Kennedy Center is a gargantuanly inflated, nondescript box with marble wrapped around it like so much yardage.

The marble of Finlandia Hall both embellishes and defines the building's shapes and functions. "The finishing process does not constitute an adventitious beautification by means of coverups," says Aalto of his work generally. "It is rather an attempt to refine the already existing parts by leaving them clearly visible." Tower, stairs, and other details and the plan and scale of interior spaces are revealed through crisp exterior planes precisely proportioned and put together.

This is the artistry that distinguishes architectonic form from a large lump. The subtle, proportionate cutting of the marble, the masses broken or accented by gray granite, indicate an aesthetic sensibility, not a packaging job.

Inside, there is no red or gilt. The interior of an Aalto building is a revelation about color. There isn't any, in the conventional sense. There is pale wood, birch or beech, of silky natural tone and texture, there are natural leathers and fabrics and black leather upholstery, and sometimes a light or dark Arabia tile.

It is as if suddenly the full range of color experience, all of the warmth and subtlety possible, is released by the nuances of those blond, black-accented hues—infinite, rich, gently sensuous variations that would be killed by anything stronger. It is like rediscovering what color really is by going back to basics. Nothing could be a more definitive contrast than the visual assault and ultimate boredom of the Kennedy Center decorative scheme—any color as long as it's red.

In Finlandia Hall, every detail is from Aalto's hand. The furnishings, from chairs to lights and linens in the restaurant, have the consistency of genuine style and taste. In the Kennedy Center, the luxury restaurant has ersatz, red-upholstered, traditional French chairs made in Austria, and there is throwaway vulgarity from what are billed as the biggest crystal chandeliers in the world to the gross Miami beauty salon décor of the ladies' rooms. Finland's gift of handsomely designed Kaj Frank cups and saucers are in the cafeteria.

The Kennedy Center is also suffering from an identity crisis. It does not know whether it is a cultural center, a national monument, or a tourist feature, and it is disastrously trying to be all three. If it is a cultural center, it should be more than a booking house, because as a booking house it is a pretentious architectural overreacher. As a national monument, it is stylelessly ponderous. Something less extravagant and ambiguous in upkeep and function would make more sense as a tourist attraction. It has been neither funded nor toileted for the purpose.

Finlandia Hall knows clearly what it is. It is part of a coordinated, long-planned civic and cultural center design by Aalto for the heart of Helsinki. It is a monumental project, in the classic sense of providing formal civic space and civic buildings, and in the nature of our times it is currently being attacked by shortsighted reformers of the social condition.

They miss the point. Social conditions must, and do, change. But this is among the last major works of the last major master of the modern movement, and art outlasts change. Alvar Aalto, approaching seventy-four, is both a great artist and a great humanist. Somewhere inside this dapper little man of wry and serious wit is the key to the combination of aesthetic and environmental sensibility and appropriate social response that we seek so noisily and fruitlessly today.

New York Times, January 23, 1972

An Enduring Legacy

REVISIONISM IS THE ENDGAME OF the twentieth century, and the retrospectives and reappraisals are adding up the score. Anyone who doubts that this has been a century of spectacular architectural achievement as well as radical technological change need only visit the Alvar Aalto show that has just opened at the Museum of Modern Art here for evidence that shatters the myth that modern architecture failed. This solid, stunning, and serious exhibition of the work of the great Finnish architect Alvar Aalto: Between Humanism and Materialism (up through May 26), delivers a clear, timeless, and incontrovertible message: These are some of the most original and beautiful buildings of our time.

Directed by Peter Reed, associate curator of the museum's Department of Architecture and Design, the exhibition celebrates the centennial of Aalto's birth and encompasses a career of more than fifty years. It includes almost fifty buildings—houses, churches, commercial and industrial structures, cultural and civic centers, universities, and museums, many of them competition-winning projects—as well as his activity as a town planner and designer for industry, presented in drawings, models, photographs, and "walk-through" videos. Full-scale walls have been built of the shaped brick and deep blue or white ceramic tile that he wrapped effortlessly around columns and curved surfaces. Examples of the furniture and glassware that have become revered modern classics are from the museum's collection, but many of the pieces are still in production sixty years later.

The show begins with delicate drawings of the twenties in the romantic nationalist manner known as Nordic classicism, and ends with Helsinki's Finlandia Hall, the concert and cultural center of 1962–71, no less romantic, but in a stringently reductive, highly personal modernist style. (Throughout his career, his wives, also architects, were his collaborators: Aino, until her premature death in 1949, and Elissa, until his own death in 1979.) A handsome book that accompanies the show has excellent essays by Finnish and American scholars who explore and reassess the work and its meaning.

Farther uptown, an exhibition at the Bard Graduate Center for Studies in the Decorative Arts, Finnish Modern Design, 1930–1997 (up through June 14), is a perfect complement to the Aalto retrospective. The ceramics, glass, fabrics, and furniture on display are still unsurpassed for their continuous usefulness and seductive beauty. Tapio Wirkkala's wafer-thin laminated wood bowls and fluid, flaring glass, and the objects of art and manufacture of Timo Sarpaneva, Kaj Franck, and other Finnish architects and artisans prove once again that the intrinsic quality of materials reduced to their most basic, sensuous essence, shaped by the creative imagination of an artist, beats all the kitsch in the world. The catalog provides the socioeconomic, political, and cultural background of the Finnish contribution to the design revolution that reached a high point in Finland and Scandinavia in mid-century.

Aalto's role in the modern movement is undisputed; he has taken his place in the pantheon that includes Le Corbusier, Mies van der Rohe, and Frank Lloyd Wright. When the early modernist message crackled across Europe like an electric charge, Aalto was quick to enter the charmed circle that included Le Corbusier, the historian Siegfried Giedion, and artists like Hans Arp, Constantin Brancusi, and Fernand Léger, whose organic abstractions were soon to influence his own use of form. By the time the clarion call was sounded by the Museum of Modern Art's Modern Architecture show in 1932, he had become a master of the International Style. His Viipuri City Library of 1927–35, the Turun Sanomat Building of 1928–30, for a newspaper in Turku, and the Paimio Tuberculosis Sanatorium of 1929–33 were assured exercises in the new, white-walled, abstract aesthetic. In 1938, the Modern devoted a show exclusively to his work. Aalto became an international figure with his two World's Fair pavilions, for Paris in 1936–37 and New

York in 1938–39; his use of canted and curved wood walls and bundled wood columns for the New York Finnish pavilion, a symbolic invocation of Finland's forests, offered a warm contrast to fashionable steel, glass, and concrete that he incorporated into his imagery from then on.

The Viipuri library's suspended, undulating, acoustic wood ceiling and roof landscape of skylights not only reappeared in Aalto's own work over the next forty years, but also encouraged a concern for form and light in its purest aspects. The sinuous or angled wall, the curve, the fan that dominated his plans were not arbitrary gestures; they were responses to a particular place and program. Themes are repeated: the courtyard and the sky-lit atrium uniting indoors and outdoors; an aggregation of parts with a consistent, controlled, picturesque imagery; a human scale through the use of brick rather than more monolithic materials; references to history and the vernacular; and homage to the land.

The Säynätsalo Town Hall of 1948–52 is cut into a hillside where irregularly ascending steps of masonry and earth and grass lead to an enclosed courtyard and the building's "crown," the council chamber. At the Seinäjoki Civic Center, begun in 1958, where the land is flat, he designed both land and building together as a series of rising grassy platforms ascending to the elevated city hall. Only three of his commissions were in the United States: the Baker dormitory at MIT of 1946–49; an interior, the conference rooms of the Institute of International Education in New York, in 1963; and the Mount Angel Abbey library of 1970 near Portland, Oregon. It says something about the passage of time that they are in restoration now.

In retrospect, it is clear that he was always somewhere outside of the party line. According to the critic and historian Kenneth Frampton, Aalto's work was "continuously engaged in a critique of the modern movement." By the midthirties he had broken with doctrinaire functionalism; his initial enthusiasm had turned into a growing skepticism about the style's increasingly rigid principles. Except for his continued belief in the standardization of small things, like windows, doors, hardware, and lighting fixtures—always beautifully designed and executed—he abandoned many modernist ideas as inhuman and unworkable. His concern with physical and psychological needs that could not be accommodated by the large-scale modular prototypes advocated by the new rationalism led him to individualized, site-specific plans. He rejected tubular steel as too susceptible to glare and heat and cold and went on to experiment with the steam techniques that produced his familiar pale, satiny, bentwood birch furniture, so pleasing to the hand and eye.

His work has been enormously influential—a debt acknowledged by such distinguished practitioners as the late Louis Kahn and James Stirling and architects of such disparate styles as Richard Meier and Frank Gehry; his philosophy and practice have infiltrated countries as diverse as England, Spain, Portugal, and the United States. Contrary to the conventional wisdom that twentieth-century internationalism reduced architecture to homogenized uniformity, there has actually been an extraordinary exchange and cross-fertilization that has enriched the best contemporary practice, from Frank Lloyd Wright's incorporation of the Viennese secession and English arts and crafts three quarters of a century ago to the Portuguese master Alvaro Siza's spectacular reinterpretation of Aalto's space-modulating organic forms today.

Why, then, with this assured position, is Aalto's name so little known to a public that recognizes Le Corbusier and Frank Lloyd Wright without difficulty? For the same reason, I believe, that even the Modern's exemplary exhibition fails to convey the actuality of his buildings—there is no way to sense what they are really like until you see them or are in them. This is no one's fault; like fine wines, Aalto just doesn't travel—or reproduce. Solutions that do not rely on the strong visual impact of dramatic or eccentric innovation elude easy understanding. His deceptively simple style is a sophisticated synthesis, a reconciliation of the monumental and the popular, of the general and the particular, of the real and the mythic, of nature and art. His buildings have an emotional richness and sensuous appeal beyond their skilled, rigorous conception. Photographs flatten and extinguish this elegantly understated aesthetic; models give the bare facts of proportion and form. There is no answer, except to visit these buildings, as any architect who has done so and been transformed will tell you. In the historian Marc Treib's words, "While they can be fully experienced, they can never be completely fathomed." This is an architecture of enduring revelation and relevance that illuminates the century and its art.

Wall Street Journal, February 26, 1998

Louis Kahn

Exeter Library: Paean to Books

They're big on making movies and buildings at Phillips Exeter Academy in New Hampshire. Currently it's A *Separate Peace* and the new library.

The movie is getting mixed reviews, and the library is getting raves. A serene, distinguished structure of considerable beauty by Louis I. Kahn, the new building exemplifies much that has made Kahn the dean of American architects. Dedicated officially this weekend, the library has been shaking down for about a year. Last November, after a forty-thousand-dollar estimate for moving the volumes from the old library next door, faculty members and students drew up a battle plan and moved forty-eight thousand volumes in apple crates in two and a half days.

The building was a year and a half in design and two years in construction, and cost $3.8 million. Its handmade, wood-fired bricks (the last production of a local company going out of business) and its teak, slate, and solid white oak (milled in Maine) are quietly sumptuous and keyed to tradition. Tradition is strong at Exeter.

But the building is anything but traditional. The paradox and fascination of Kahn's work is that it seems to embody the whole history of architecture, as it proclaims how contemporary his work and thought really are.

That proclamation is strong and subtle. His buildings evoke the primal simplicity of materials used with an almost religious respect for their basic structural qualities. They also convey a keen awareness of the most sophisticated achievements of historical styles.

But none of his designs ape the mannerisms of the past. The sense of the past is just there, through the architect's remarkable, extremely personal, and very passionate love of all that is logical and beautiful in building, at all times.

Kahn's designs frequently carry this love to the point of great achieve-

Exeter Library

ment by stretching existing concepts and techniques to new frontiers. The result is the impression of a stunning symbolic synthesis of all that has gone before, and all that is still to come. Sometimes that symbiosis is imperfect, but his buildings are full of that special kind of vital inquiry called art.

The process works at Exeter. The library makes its creative statement without jarring the school's ambience, a felicitous blend of New England campus and ivied neocolonial. "Totally nice," Kahn calls it, "not really vintage, or early, but warm. I have a sympathetic response to brick, and I am taken with American history."

The library is a 108 foot square. It has traditional, exterior bearing walls of brick, with piers thickening toward the bottom. There are no "quickie" brick veneers.

Solid brick arches carry this construction seventeen feet into the building's interior, forming a kind of square outer ring. This ring contains the reading areas.

The brick arches (old technology) join concrete structure (new technology) to form an inner ring. In this inner square, the concrete provides wide-span, heavy load-bearing floors for book stacks, something brick cannot do. The two separate but equal structural systems meet consciously and interact.

Kahn explains the structural interaction in the anthropomorphic terms he favors. For him, buildings feel, think, and act.

"The brick was always talking to me, saying you're missing an opportunity," he recalls. "The weight of the brick makes it dance like a fairy above and groan below. Arcades crouch. But where brick is stingy, concrete is tremendously generous. The brick is held by the concrete restraining members. Brick likes this so much, because it becomes modern."

The two nested square doughnuts, Kahn points out, create a leftover, central interior space.

This space, soaring the equivalent of eight stories, is daylighted from above and walled by massive natural concrete with huge circular openings revealing the tiered book stacks. Unsuspected from the outside, the space breaks on the viewer with breathtaking drama.

"I just put a roof over it," says Kahn, with the ultimate understatement. But he calls the great room an "event," and, he adds, "A room is the beginning of architecture."

Light is used as skillfully as structure. The outer glass walls are rimmed by day-lit, built-in carrels with views. Book stacks are away from the windows, at right angles. All have vistas out to the reading areas and into the giant room. Light seems to flow from edge to center, and from the roof above.

After describing these exceptionally sensitive and complex structural-aesthetic relationships, Kahn says, tongue gently in cheek, "It's just a box, isn't it?"

The superior results are due in no small part to the sympathetic working relationship of the architect and client, the Exeter librarian, Rodney Armstrong, and his building committee, Elliot G. Fish and Albert C. Ganley.

Mr. Armstrong will be leaving Exeter to become the librarian of the Boston Atheneum on Walter Muir Whitehill's retirement next year, and a suitable parting gift would be completion of the still-unfinished terraces and planting. His parting gift to Exeter is one of permanent grace, in the pre-McLuhan tradition, although electronic resources are duly included.

"Book," says Mr. Armstrong, obviously not believing it, "has become a dirty four-letter word."

"No one ever really paid the price of a book," Kahn says, "only the price of printing it."

Together, they have made a beautiful box that celebrates books.

New York Times, October 23, 1972

The Meaning of a Wall

FOR LOUIS KAHN, THERE WERE TEN years of great buildings, and a lifetime of preparation. Which makes his sudden death harder to take because it was not a promising talent that was cut off, but one that flowered late, and magnificently, to create works of architecture of such enormous fullness and richness that they stand not only as masterworks of this age, but with the agelessness of great art, for all time.

Some of the best of his work, in Bangladesh and India, was still coming out of the ground; even more of it, for New Haven and Baltimore and other American cities, was still on the drawing board in his Philadelphia office. The Salk Institute at La Jolla, of the sixties, and the Exeter Library in New Hampshire and Kimbell Art Museum in Fort Worth, of the seventies, are established landmarks. He had reached this point of achievement slowly and painstakingly, and without much fanfare; it was just quietly accepted that he stood alone in creative stature at this critical phase of twentieth-century art.

THE POIGNANCY OF his death is made even more tragic by the circumstances. Alone in Pennsylvania Station on a Sunday night, returning from a working trip to Dacca and on his way back to Philadelphia for a Monday morning class, he apparently died quickly. His passport provided identification and the New York police attempted to reach his office, which was closed for the weekend. Inexplicably, they did not call his home but gave the information to the Philadelphia police, who never notified his family at all. It was Tuesday before inquiries found his body in New York. Such is sudden death in the age of alienation and anonymity; anguish aggravated by an uncaring bureaucracy.

Lou Kahn was in his prime at seventy-three; no other architect approached him. And all other architects, including some very good ones indeed, knew that the work he was doing was the catalytic kind that changes cities and culture, and the way man thinks about himself and his world.

Kahn was not a pioneer, breaking the frontiers of architecture, leading the modern movement into radical territory. He was not one of the initial form givers, offering revolutionary definition of twentieth-century aesthetics. He was a fundamentalist, seeking beginnings, and meanings, fond of saying that he consulted not volume one of civilization but volume zero.

During the early years of his career he built little, and taught and thought much, developing a personal language that combined poetry and philosophy in tantalizing and elusive intimations of deeply felt universal truths. They were truths that he sought persistently in architecture: the meaning of a wall, or a roof, or a door, the way light brought spirit to a structure, what the building "wanted to be." He pursued basic answers, in the deepest terms of art and humanism.

He tried, in a process of sophisticated purification, to "reinvent" architecture. He looked for something he called, interchangeably, Order, or Form, which he saw as a kind of self-revelatory information about building—if one looked hard enough—that forged functional and social needs and the "will" of materials and structure into a humanistic whole. He probed constantly for this "reality."

It involved intense analysis of what he called "served and servant spaces," both of which he felt deserved equal design consideration and expression. He "asked" materials what they "wished" to do. At Ahmedabad the brick answered, in Kahn's words, "I like an arch." At Exeter, the brick arches "requested" the greater support of concrete. Everywhere, he pursued the "thoughtful making of spaces."

The style he developed with much painstaking searching—if one can use a superficial word like style for something that now seems so elemental—is a fusion of past and present. It represents the rare and indescribably important moment when modernism came to terms with history. In the struggle for this stylistic resolution, his early buildings were a combination of startling strengths and unsettling failures. Sometimes they were seriously flawed. "It is better to do the right thing badly," he taught his students, "than to do a bad thing well."

He worked this way, out of the mainstream, all his life. For much of it, he was poor. He had been brought to Philadelphia from Estonia as a child, in 1905. He learned art, religion, and music at home; later he learned Beaux Arts classicism at the University of Pennsylvania School of Fine Arts, where he earned a Bachelor of Architecture degree. Paul Cret was his professor, and briefly, his employer. He never lost his sympathy for Beaux Arts style and substance.

Still later, convinced intellectually by the modernist revolution, he worked with George Howe and Oscar Stonorov. But his attempts to jettison the Beaux Arts tradition in favor of radical structural lightness and thin planes were never totally successful. Visits to Europe reinforced his love of antiquity and medievalism.

It is not surprising that for many years Kahn was a puzzle to his peers. He had no definable place on the bandwagon of modernism. He seemed out of step with his times. It was this personal phenomenon, perhaps, that slowed both his own development and general understanding and acceptance of what he tried to do.

The profession watched his "ugly" buildings grow with fascination; their probing experimentation and deliberate roughness caused continuing interest and debate. Clients were less sure. The Yale Art Gallery of 1951–53 broke the deadlock; the building was a successful, much-praised step toward his later manner. The Richards Medical Research Building of 1957–61 at the University of Pennsylvania earned a small, significant show at New York's Museum of Modern Art.

But whatever his natural bent, Kahn's fully developed work would not have been possible without the crucible of the modern movement. When he went back to the brick wall and the arch, he joined them to reinforced concrete, and he did so with the International Style. He was, at once, the interpreter of Le Corbusier and the Parthenon.

His buildings, full of strength and grace, have persuasive presence. They belong to their own age, and to all ages, with equal ease. Their almost primitive beauty, deceptively simple and yet extraordinarily sophisticated, is already an unassailable part of the progress of civilization and its arts. Louis Kahn was more than an architect; he was an elemental force.

New York Times, April 7, 1974

Seeking the Father, Finding the Architect

So here's the story line: A small, plain man, face scarred from burns as a child, a Jewish immigrant from Estonia, grows up poor in an industrial neighborhood of Philadelphia, attends the University of Pennsylvania on scholarship, and becomes one of the greatest architects of the twentieth century. He marries, works, travels, teaches, achieves gurulike status with his students and much of the architectural world, builds masterpieces in the United States, India, and Bangladesh, has a heart attack and dies alone and broke in a men's room in New York's Pennsylvania Station, lying in the city morgue for three days until his body is identified and claimed. Horatio Alger story, with a final tragic twist. The money men won't exactly fall all over it.

But wait. The family that finds him is one of three; he is living a triple life. One wife and one child are listed in the *New York Times* obituary; two other women and two illegitimate children, a boy and a girl, appear for the funeral service, seated in the rear; the widow had let them know that they would not be welcome. The three families have carefully stayed apart; they are together in the same place, for the first time. Skip to thirty years later. The illegitimate son goes on a journey to find the father he never really knew. Too over the top?

The film is *My Architect*, the architect is Louis I. Kahn, the filmmaker is Louis Kahn's out-of-wedlock son, Nathaniel Kahn, and the documentary has been nominated for an Academy Award. This is Nathaniel Kahn's first feature-length film, and it has had an astounding success. Financed with predictable difficulty, screened privately for press and professionals, its word-of-mouth popularity achieved something no one ever dreamed of: commercial distribution in multiplexes with the top Oscar-nominated movies. It was released back in November, but there are still long lines waiting to see it.

My Architect is a wonderful film, not just for its engrossing and surprisingly scandalous story, but for its remarkable personal mission. With coproducer Susan Behr, and photographer Bob Richman, Nathaniel Kahn set out to learn all he could about the father he loved and saw so seldom, the man whose clandestine visits during his childhood would be followed by long absences and loneliness. The journey took him to the places and buildings of Louis Kahn's career, and to the people who knew and worked with him.

Seated in Kahn's Assembly Building in Dacca, Bangladesh, a professor of architecture, Shamsul Wares, tells Nathaniel that his father "was no ordinary man," and gives a passionate recital of how the architect's vision conjured great buildings out of desolate, empty land. The owner of one of Kahn's more eccentric ventures, a concrete boat designed as a music barge in the sixties and still in operation, was stunned to be visited by the child he had met so long ago, and dissolved into a tearful embrace. The usual famous talking heads pay earnest homage. But it is the people Nathaniel Kahn finds, the things they say, and the sensitivity and drama of the architectural photography that make this film so richly evocative, its emotional impact matched by its visual beauty.

Did he find the father he was looking for? I think the answer is in the title, *My Architect*. The man he discovered in this intimate and intensely revealing inquiry was, first, an architect, and, incidentally and inadequately, a family man, no matter how many families he acquired. He had enough love to go around, just not nearly enough time. The professional always took precedence over the personal, and secrecy was easier than trying to resolve the unsolvable. He lived for his work, worked to excess, and went wherever his work took him. He was a nomad and often slept on the office floor. The only address on his passport was his office, and he was found dead on a Sunday, when the building was closed, so no one could be reached.

The father is always elusive; it is the architect Nathaniel Kahn finally possesses. What he learned about Louis Kahn as a person and an artist is that the two are inseparable. We learn that, too, from the unusually fine photography; the architect's soul and spirit are unmistakably present in these strong, beautiful buildings.

Louis Kahn was one of the most talented and respected architects of our time. The iconic Salk Institute in La Jolla, California, is a scientific research center with an identity of almost mystical toughness; the Kimbell Museum in Fort Worth, Texas, is admired internationally for its timeless serenity and elegance; the monumental symbolism of the educational and government buildings in India and Bangladesh suggests ancient civilizations. When he died in that men's room in Penn Station, thirty years ago, he was on his way back from Dacca.

I wonder if Nathaniel Kahn captured these buildings so perfectly—the way the water channel splits the wide, flat stone plaza of the Salk Institute in a straight, narrow line to the Pacific Ocean to engage the sea; the power and grace of the abstract geometry of the capital of Bangladesh— because he grew to understand them so well. It may have been the depth of his feelings, as much as his exploring eye, that makes the architecture so affecting and alive.

What Louis Kahn lacked in looks, he made up in charisma. He could speak like a prophet or an oracle, endowing buildings with anthropomorphic qualities. "What does the brick want to be?" he would ask, rhetorically and mysteriously. "It wants to be an arch," he would reply, making the brick's structural logic and expressive potential immediately and magically clear to anyone who heard him. He never wore clothes of his own design or adopted any of the stratagems of the Architect as Master of the Universe; he was rumpled and always on the run. He was such a bad businessman that when he died, he was several hundred thousand dollars in debt.

The film's press release tells us, in appropriate movie language, that Kahn led a life of secrets and broken promises. It would be safe to say that it was out of control. Nathaniel's mother always insisted that he had assured her that he was going to divorce his wife and come to live with them, and one of the more disturbing sequences is the son's interview with his mother, in which he questions her as she tearfully clings to her story. This must have been hard for them both.

Using pictures from his childhood, he recalls his father's secret visits and the games they played, and how both parents would put him to bed after dinner, awakening him later to take him, still in his pajamas, while they drove back to Philadelphia from Chestnut Hill. They would stop a block from his father's house and watch him walk home.

Neither affair was a passing fancy. Both women were professionals who worked in Kahn's office: Anne Tyng was an architect who had a daughter, Alexandra, and Nathaniel's mother, Harriet Pattison, was a landscape architect. There are poignant interviews with them all, and by film's end, Nathaniel has assembled them in a house designed by their father. It is not closure, that solipsism that Americans use to replace grief; there is too much remembered pain. The willingness to be together and move on is clearly restricted to the younger generation; this will never be one happy family.

There hasn't been a movie about architecture with this much popular appeal since that masterpiece of Hollywood kitsch *The Fountainhead,* in which Gary Cooper played Howard Roark, the terminally romantic, fictional architect-hero of Ayn Rand's novel. *My Architect* is reality—a moving, bittersweet, and marvelously touching film about an antihero who loved not wisely but too well, and generally made a mess of it, but left a brilliant body of magnificent work and a son who found himself, and his father, through it.

Wall Street Journal, February 26, 2004

Walter Gropius

The Future Grows Old

THE NEAR-LEGENDARY, RADICAL MODERN HOUSE that Walter Gropius built for himself in Lincoln, Massachusetts, in 1937—the revolutionary architectural shot heard across the country—is being acquired by the Society for the Preservation of New England Antiquities. The architect's widow, Ise Gropius, is giving it complete with original Bauhaus art and furnishings, views of hills and apple orchards, and an incredible complement of birds.

It is an occasion for pleasure and a few gentle reflections. There is, first, the lovely, subtle paradox of the Gropius House, that clarion call to the future, as an authenticated antiquity. How inexorably time turns the avant-garde into history! And how much delicate irony can be obtained from the fact that this house marked the conscious rejection of history in terms of emulation of past styles (indigenous tradition was the superbly rationalized substitute) and the declaration of a new aesthetic and a brave new world. Thirty-eight years later, the revolution has become commonplace, and there is revolution against the revolution. The new aesthetic is the norm, and the brave new world grows old. The landmark takes its place as part of the history that it has spurned, and the movement that rewrote history becomes history. Always, history wins.

Nor are there any clear-cut definitions of art or antiquity. All those made-in-the-Bauhaus furnishings of the twenties—a rare collection that any first-rate museum would covet jealously—were only fifty years old at the time of Walter Gropius's death and were therefore classified by the IRS, under inheritance tax laws, as "obsolete." When does obsolete become antique? In one hundred years, by true-blue, Red Queen, IRS logic. Brought out of Germany in the thirties, first to England and then to America when Gropius came to Harvard to head the Graduate School of Design, they have already run the gamut from radical to camp to classics of the minor arts.

The art history books will tell you that Gropius's arrival was the signal for change, both through example and architectural education. The school had been languishing in the beaux arts stereotype with design exercises for regal casinos and *hôtels de ville* while the vanguard of modernism was shattering the intellectual barricades in Europe. Gropius's house, designed with Marcel Breuer, who followed the same escape route from Germany, was an instant landmark when it was completed in 1938. And the generations Gropius taught at Harvard from 1937 to 1952 went out to build and teach in turn, transforming the American landscape—to an extraordinary degree—in the image and philosophy of the master. The fact that a revolution won is a revolution lost by the very nature of victory compounds both irony and history.

A trip to the Gropius House today, whether one knew it personally at the time of its greatest impact or as a standby of art history courses, is a sentimental journey. The neat, white structure sits on a hill, in a proper New England landscape of fields and woods—both timeless and a period piece. On a recent visit a reluctant spring had barely greened the grass over the stony earth; an almost invisible cloud of yellow and russet suggested buds on bare branches.

It is hard to remember that the house was built as a daring object lesson in the compatibility of twentieth-century technology and art—an ardent polemic as well as a home. To anyone expecting a doctrinaire, Teutonic, textbook exposition of functional purity and rebellious doctrine, it can only be a surprise. This is a conventional house now, familiar, lived in, *gemütlich*. The scale is intimate, the ambience informal. Plants run riot in the light rooms, there is all the impedimenta of accumulated family living, and the birds—the amazing birds—dart, fly, and feed beyond the glass window walls that frame huge tree trunks and distant views.

The famous innovations are all standard practice now; you must look closely to see them: the fireplace stripped of traditional mantel trim and frame that became a modern cliché and embattled anachronism (the argument raged for years about the romantic vestigial hearth versus "honest" mechanical heat); the wall of bracket-held bookshelves; pictures not hung but placed casually on shelves and surfaces; the lightweight, movable, casual furniture with emphasis on function; rooms that flow into each other; and of course, the glass walls with panel heating and exterior overhangs that both let in, and regulate, enormous amounts of seasonal light and sun. It is a handbook of the new rules of twentieth-century domestic architecture, grown old gracefully.

The famous Bauhaus furnishings of tubular steel, canvas, and wood are comfortably shabby now, and some of the chairs have achieved their original objective of mass production. The tables of curved tubes connected to wood surfaces with carefully visible screws no longer have the conscientiously handcrafted machine look with which they came out of the Bauhaus workshops. To the uninitiated, they would look a little like something put outside of a thrift shop as a come-on bargain. To the knowing, they are a delightful historical curiosity: aesthetic morality (the implied honesty of modern materials and machine manufacture) married to an elitist industrial art.

Is it unsuitable to say that the house is charming? The delightful guest bedroom with its toe-to-toe beds in white, black, and red, and the small master bedroom with its glass-walled dressing room, liberated forever from "bedroom suites," were startlingly different in their day but are extremely comfortable and inviting now. The downstairs and upstairs porches that united indoor and outdoor living areas with such novelty seem routine. The use of the horizontal wood siding of traditional New England construction in the inside hall is suitable, not startling. And what was most unconventional at the time—the selection of all hardware and built-in accessories from standard catalogs and frequently from industrial sources—gives a distinct nostalgic flavor, although they were among the most radical of the house's modern features.

The building not only was not custom-made, in this sense, but was constructed rapidly, from spring to fall in 1938. The cost, eighteen thousand dollars, was financed by a Lincoln sponsor, Mrs. James J. Storrow, because the Gropiuses had no funds. They paid rent until they could buy the house from Mrs. Storrow's estate after her death.

There is a strong scent of art deco and Industrial Style in such details as door and cabinet handles and lighting fixtures, including a fine torchère. An angled glass-brick wall, in spite of its pleasant logic as a light conductor and divider, cannot escape the stamp of camp. The famous outdoor industrial steel spiral stair that was almost a symbol of stark new aesthetic drama against the flat white wall plane is now a pure thirties touch.

Taken in its entirety, the house is as much a period statement as any Bulfinch treasure. It meets the same standards of style, significance, and authenticity. The rationale of its acquisition by the society is incontestable.

The Gropius House is, in a sense, a symbol of a simpler and more innocent time; it was a moment when aesthetic rebellion was seen as a social need and as "the puritanical devotion to truth which characterized everything Gropius did," according to G. Holmes Perkins, a former Harvard colleague. Truth was so much more easily perceived then; right was so clearly distinguishable from wrong. The angels were an identifiable band. If the results, with the hindsight of years, seem more complexly shaded, they are no less remarkable. This is indeed the kind of history that changed the world.

Wall Street Journal, May 18, 1975

Frank Lloyd Wright

Wright Mythology

OLD ARCHITECTS, LIKE OLD GENERALS, never die; nor, in the case of Frank Lloyd Wright, do they fade away. Almost three years after his death, Wright's image and his buildings, as vital as ever, were the subject last night of the Columbia Broadcasting System's television program *The Twentieth Century*.

The show was a smoothly sentimental production with some moving moments and an impressive number of historic film clips of above-average interest on the master and his disciples at the Taliesin Fellowship.

The program was devoted exclusively to the perpetuation of the mythology of the Wright personality (what do the Russians know about the cult of personality?) presented not in the bitter brine of his own acerbic attitudes toward art and life but in sugar syrup with mood music.

A few years ago we would probably have been deeply grateful for this reverent, slickly produced tribute, when any television program on architecture represented a pioneering breakthrough for what Wright called "the mother of the arts." Now, with the art of architecture gaining constantly in popular interest and with Wright firmly established as a public personality, we expect more. But perhaps more cannot be achieved within the limits of superficial commercial competence that television has established as its standard. It is distressingly obvious that inadequate goals have been set, and that they have been met to the industry's satisfaction.

WHAT WE WERE given was the legend of Wright's greatness, not the facts of it. Here was the god-genius, up to his hips in nature, appropriately orchestrated, a public-relations portrait he undoubtedly would have loved.

Handsome young apprentices, stripped to the waist, hauled rocks and raised timbers (Learning and Life music), trekked to Arizona to build the celebrated home and school at Taliesin West (Open Road and Blue Horizons music), stood on hills, picked flowers, gazed at trees (Man-in-Harmony-with-Nature music in crescendo).

We never met the bitingly perceptive, supremely gifted visionary, the smasher of idols, the rebel against society, to whom tributes such as this were given only in old age and death; we never understood just how he had helped to change the face of the world and the concept of beauty in our time.

THERE WAS NO mention of his prophetic ideas on the most significant and pervasive problem of our day: modern technology; we were afforded only his endless romantic evocation of the natural universe, which was never to be swallowed whole. Swallow it CBS did, and showed us shot after shot of his "natural architecture," examples in which art was far more evident than nature, where a highly sophisticated creative act achieves calculated, far-from-accidental synthesis with its setting.

This essential difference between "art" and "nature" was never explained. But it is the strength and drama of these buildings, even in the static, single-view photographs to which the film was inexplicably limited, and which seemed far less numerous than close-ups of starry-eyed acolytes, that nullified, to some extent, the intervening glossy nonsense.

Far more of the remarkable quality of Wright's brilliantly cantankerous, uniquely creative mind was revealed in the National Broadcasting Company's interview several years ago.

"For five hundred years, architecture has been phony," Wright observed early in the show, referring to his own profession's history of cumulative clichés. Television has reached that point faster.

New York Times, February 19, 1962

Fallingwater: A Marriage of Nature and Art

No MASTERPIECE ARISES UNBIDDEN and unprecedented from the mind of its creator, although popular mythology prefers this interpretation to the more complex reality. It can be a particular moment in history, exceptional patronage, or certain critical developments that make the great leap forward or great work possible. But the ultimate factor is a mind that reconceives something so brilliantly that the result creates a higher level of perception and experience, surprising and inspiring us by its unexpected art. In architecture, the building's use and setting are essential components. And there is always the matter of beauty, the most elusive and subjective measure of all.

Fallingwater, the world-famous house over a waterfall at Bear Run in the Pennsylvania woods, completed in 1935 by Frank Lloyd Wright for the Pittsburgh department store owner Edgar J. Kaufmann, meets all of the criteria. It surprises and inspires; Wright has pushed far beyond convention to rethink not only design and construction, but also the relationship of built space and the natural world, and even the nature of domestic life. The American Institute of Architects voted Fallingwater the Building of the Century in 2000; a national landmark and popular tourist destination, it is an acknowledged masterpiece.

Fallingwater is also spectacularly and unconventionally beautiful. The familiar, much published view shows a set of cascading, horizontal concrete balconies dramatically suspended over a rushing waterfall, attached to the land by a vertical stone tower that contains an anchoring chimney and interior hearth. The house is so magically married to its site that it is thrilling to experience, and even to see. Wright's sense of the land is uncanny; he has locked building and setting together in a visual and environmental embrace. The effect is not of nature violated but of nature completed—a dual enrichment.

To start, Wright discarded the conventional solution that would have placed the house somewhere on the wooded slope with a view of the rushing mountain stream. Instead, he insisted on building directly over the stream, on a large flat rock just above the falls. He liked to compare the daringly cantilevered balconies to "trays on a waiter's fingers." Their interlocked volumes appear to slide past each other in a way

Fallingwater

that suggests the stepped levels of the cascading water that continues downstream.

Wright emphasized the amazing setting with natural materials and earth colors, although his first extravagant idea was to cover the balconies in gold leaf, a suggestion quickly vetoed. He settled for painting them a warm apricot beige, with his favorite "cherokee red" for the metal trim. Unlike the European modernists of the period who would have treated the house as an isolated object of stark white volumes, and with whom he feuded theatrically over his lifetime, Wright promoted a philosophy of "organic architecture" that stressed a closer, more humanistic connection to the land. It has worn well.

It is the rare masterpiece that achieves perfection, and Wright's Fallingwater is conspicuously not one of them. The fact that the bravura concept required formidable structural ingenuity and improvised technology guaranteed problems. Difficult decisions were made by inexperienced apprentices left in charge. Kaufmann did not trust Wright's calculations and hired his own engineers, who made structural adjustments; furious when he found out, Wright secretly reversed them. Cracks and structural faults appeared and cantilevers began to deflect almost immediately. Later repairs found that supporting steel had been left out by the builder and concrete had been poorly reinforced.

Edgar Kaufmann Jr. gave Fallingwater to the Western Pennsylvania Conservancy more than two decades before his death, in order to ensure proper maintenance and presentation to the public. In the nineties, with the house near collapse, the conservancy undertook a complete restoration and retrofitting. Before handing it over in 1963, Edgar shared his last weekend with friends, and I was fortunate enough to be one of them.

Staying there surpassed any expectations. The sequence of woodland vistas, the revelations of scale and distance, light and dark, building and nature, land and water, as one approaches the entrance, were superbly orchestrated by Wright. Most unforgettably, my husband and I were given the master bedroom directly over the falls where light and sound rise from the water below. The house is on stepped levels, and the large downstairs living room has a surprisingly low ceiling, creating unexpected intimacy. Continuous casement windows lined with cushioned seats softened with hand-woven fabrics and fur throws open to the views; a sheltering stone fireplace wall is flanked by a great anchoring boulder retained from the site. An open hatch in the polished stone floor leads down to the water beneath and a small natural pool. Here are Wright's eternal themes: fire, earth, and water, in perfect equilibrium.

But what you are unprepared for is the sound. You hear water rushing softly, falling steadily, a kind of background music that stays with you as clearly as the image of the building. Designed and driven by its setting, Fallingwater fills the mind and the senses. No one has explained its magic better than the Wright historian Neil Levine. This is a house, he writes, "about stone, water, trees, leaves, mist, clouds, and sky."

Wall Street Journal, March 18, 2006

PART IV

Modernism and Its Discontents

Mutations in the Modern Movement

THE MUSEUM OF MODERN ART HAS BEGUN the celebration of its fiftieth anniversary with a major new show on a subject it introduced to the American public shortly after the museum was founded: modern architecture. The exhibition, called Transformations in Modern Architecture, will run through April 24.

The passage of half a century has turned youthful revolutionaries into elder statesmen. It has also seen modern architecture significantly transformed, as the title of the show implies. Today there is no longer one movement so strong that it can sweep everything else aside to impose a narrowly restricted aesthetic with single-minded conviction. Nor is there a universal polemic such as modernism supplied in its early years.

The purpose of this exhibition, therefore, is not to crusade or break new ground, but to show how the rules of revolutionary modernism have been bent and broken as the new architecture evolved. Probably nothing could make the transformation of the museum itself clearer than the fact that the descendants of the handful of shockingly radical buildings in the museum's 1932 Modern Architecture show have literally taken over the world. Not bad, for fifty years. And quite indicative of where the revolution, and the museum, stand now.

The exhibition, which spans the years 1960 to 1980 and presents over four hundred buildings, covers only the last two of the museum's five decades. Those twenty years coincide with the total triumph of modern architecture as the official style of our time, and with the acceleration of change.

PUBLIC ACCEPTANCE, DEVELOPING technology, and aesthetic restlessness led architects into a variety of paths that moved away from orthodox functionalism into something as deliberately expressive, and nonfunctional, as sculpture. Once out of the straitjacket of modernism, the mutations have proved endless.

How this happened, and what the results have been, is the theme of the monumental survey put together by Arthur Drexler, director of the museum's Department of Architecture and Design. The exhibition embraces no particular school, style, or development. It avoids judgments, an omission that can be extremely unsettling to those who believe, like this viewer, that the amenities of design are as important as its curiosities. But it does offer shrewd insights and telling observations, such as the obvious celebration of the brilliant "skin" aesthetic of the glass building as one of the most stunning achievements of our time, and the fact of the superiority of much "off-the-peg" technology over the "architected" version. The show unblushingly mixes good with bad in its determined documentation of trends and practices.

The approach is fiercely didactic and intellectual, based on the tradition of the art-historical listing of iconographical or aesthetic characteristics. The job of compiling, organizing, and interpreting such a sampling covering one of the most active periods of the building art, done for the first time here, is an impressive achievement in itself. I, personally, dislike many of the examples on display and find Mr. Drexler's "objectivity" almost herculean in its forebearance and avoidance of tough critical questions. But the result is still a thoroughly fascinating and extremely valuable show.

However, the exhibition inevitably raises the much larger question of what has happened to modern architecture in the fifty-year period during which the museum's existence has paralleled its development. The "transformations" actually began very early and insidiously, through the ways in which the new architecture was presented and publicized. It is quite possible that the most critical transformation, as it affected the understanding and practice of modern architecture in this country, took place in the Museum of Modern Art's Modern Architecture show of 1932.

This exhibition did more than merely introduce the pioneering new building to the United States. It presented it in terms that deviated significantly from its basic intent.

UNDER THE HEADING of "architecture," there was Hitchcock and Johnson's display and book on the International Style, probably one of the most influential events in the history of criticism and connoisseurship. This presentation reduced a complex, idealistic, revolutionary movement to a set of aesthetic exercises, or a manual on style.

But there was also a section on "housing," carefully divorced from "architecture," prepared by an equally distinguished group of enthusiastic protagonists of modernism, Catherine Bauer, Clarence Stein, and Henry Wright, with a separate catalog introduced by Lewis Mumford. That part of the presentation survives only in archives.

What became modernist practice in this country is the purified "architectural" style from which all the sociology and politics that infused the revolutionary ideology of the European modernists were removed. Those sociopolitical aspects of design were to prove, soon enough, incapable of realization. But the American taste makers didn't wait; they scuttled them immediately as uninteresting or nonessential. Philip Johnson, in his postwar years as director of architecture at the Museum of Modern Art, frankly labeled them a bore. An occasional small housing or planning show discharged a vestigial debt of conscience.

The informed historian realizes today that housing was virtually the heart of the modern movement. It was regularly featured in expositions and demonstrated in model developments. The human condition was a prime concern of European modernism, inextricably linked to radical architectural change. This was preached even when it was not practiced; surely no one could have been less sociologically oriented than Le Corbusier. But when it was practiced, as in the Frankfurt housing of Ernst May, it remains architecturally and environmentally valid to this day.

IT SOON BECAME clear, however, that there was very little housing, beyond those demonstration projects, for the museum to show. A few remarkable examples of the thirties were quickly bowdlerized by government agencies into designs for disaster. The failure of the dream was as much to blame as the lack of interest of the taste makers. Only now are scholars such as Robert Pommer, in his revealing article on American housing design in the December 1978 *Journal of the Society of Architectural Historians*, beginning to reexamine the subject of modernism on its own terms, rather than those subsequently manufactured for it.

What really doomed the most challenging aspect of modernist design was the awful reality that architecture simply could not cope with the spread and severity of the social problems that accompanied the changes of the postwar world. Least of all, could it cure them. And by trying to do so, with too large claims and too little understanding, it lost its credibility.

How easy it then became for a younger generation to announce that modernism didn't work, that modern architecture was dead. How simple to blame it all on the sanitized, stylistic version of modernism that had been so assiduously promoted by the leaders of the profession, or to turn inward to even more hermetic aesthetic concerns. The ultimate transformation of modern architecture is the total abandonment of the idealistic, overambitious, but thoroughly admirable dream that tried to define the role of architecture in modern society, for an aesthetic dandyism being practiced today. One can only fear for the art of building now.

New York Times, March 4, 1979

Rebuilding Architecture

HOW IS THE RECENT ARCHITECTURE LITERATURE dealing with the transition between modernism and postmodernism? This unusually provocative moment when the art of building is straddling orthodoxy and revolt has produced some of the most spectacular books and periodicals that the profession has ever seen. It soon becomes clear, however, that much of this outpouring will not move the art of architecture forward. Neither buildings nor the books about buildings are escaping the dead ends and enchantment with trivia of the popular culture, or the more dubious, esoteric concerns of the academic culture.

Even the best efforts to achieve some kind of balanced or historical view of the current activity, or to draw an evenhanded picture in critical terms, seem to fall into the trap of confrontation. One either joins the in-group or becomes hopelessly unfashionable, written off as a reactionary, unreconstructed thinker. For the critic to invoke a perspective requiring more than a brief attention span is an acute embarrassment.

To ask questions about meaning or validity spoils the momentum and the fun.

The denunciation and denial industry, fueled by the ex-modernist Peter Blake's early exegesis, *Form Follows Fiasco* (1977), is still going strong. Attacks continue to come from both sides, usually from those least qualified to make them. The most vociferous critics of the post-modernists are the discarded and wounded of the modern movement, the rank and file of practitioners who have failed or refused to see the postmodernist light or have not been agile enough to change course and convictions when the signals became clear. The letters columns of the professional magazines have been filled with cries of anguish and betrayal and the cancellation of subscriptions as postmodernist projects appear. Among the most vocal of the antimodernists are repentant, born-again architects renouncing their modernist sins, of whom Philip Johnson has been the nimblest and most outrageous, a position he clearly relishes. This group includes the put-down artists who have rushed in to demolish reputations while ignoring the realities of architectural history, and the large, philistine fringe that never liked modernism anyway and is no longer ashamed to say so. The audience for Tom Wolfe's gossipy idol-smashing in *From Bauhaus to Our House*[1] was already out there, waiting.

BUT MUCH OF value is being published for both the interpretation of the moment and the reconstruction of the immediate past. The range is wide, from distinguished original research to ordinary special pleading, with books divided rather neatly into revisionist history, polemical treatises, and scholarly, sometimes stunning monographs.

On the positive side, what is emerging in very piecemeal fashion and from many divergent viewpoints is a thoughtful evaluation of the modern movement in architecture, and a much more full and varied account of that movement, made possible by the passage of time and the disintegration of dogma. We are getting a new sense of the many-faceted art that modernism really was, with new insights into both accepted and forgotten figures. Ideas and trends omitted from the official accounts of modernism for reasons of polemical purity or theoretical consistency are being investigated and restored to respectability.

Neglected or actively disliked periods such as art deco, a romantic survival of the French salon arts of the twenties and the last great decorative

arts style, are now almost dismayingly chic. Until recently, the only acceptable attitude was to dismiss or patronize examples of this work as
enduringly awful bourgeois taste. Although this sybaritic, ornamental
approach to buildings and interiors actually represented one of the two
sides of the coin of modernism, all right-thinking modernists have condemned it with the same vigor that they reserved for the original sin of
academic traditionalism. Today the "modernistic" Chrysler Building is
probably the most admired of all skyscrapers.

Turn-of-the-century romantic nationalism in Scandinavia and other
transitional European styles are being explored as an authentic part of
the process of twentieth-century architectural development. The anachronism of continuing hard-core academic and classical practice in
some of the century's most important official architecture at a time of
universal radical change—a troubling, inconsistent chapter that has
been glossed over or ignored—is being resolved as part of a pluralistic
history. The architecture of the last hundred years is turning out to be
more varied and a great deal more interesting and challenging than the
official historians or taste makers have either endorsed or allowed.

THIS REVISIONISM NOT only is an enormous and necessary task, but is
what gives the current architectural publishing boom its legitimacy and
importance. Missing from such reconsiderations, however, are badly
needed studies, using rapidly disappearing documentation, of those architects and movements at the top of the postmodernists' enemies list;
Mies van der Rohe, Walter Gropius, and the Bauhaus, for example,
serve mainly as whipping boys. The climate is not yet right for the useful assessment of deposed heroes. History, unfortunately, not only repeats itself but repeats its mistakes. The chief difference between the
modernists' rejection of their predecessors and the postmodernists' denial of theirs is one of tone: Modernism was righteous and brutal, and
postmodernism tends to be witty and vicious, which is considerably
more entertaining.

The large revisionist histories are the most ambitious of the new publications, but one comes to the reluctant conclusion that they are also
the most disappointing. For all their conscientious efforts to set the
record straight, these books are far less valuable, or successful, than the
sometimes arbitrarily chosen, but frequently superb, historical studies
of people, movements, and places, based on new evidence or offering

new interpretations of existing material. We are in a golden age, or moment, of this kind of scholarly research and writing.[2]

The fact is that even with the advantage of half a century of hindsight, the history of modernism is still in flux. Gaps are being filled, and texture and variety are being added. Some early chapters, the Dutch de Stijl and Russian constructivism, are emerging in far greater detail. Defectors and dissidents, such as Bertram Grosvenor Goodhue—who worked in an eclectic range from the Gothic West Point to the "modern" Los Angeles Library—and the post-Wrightian romantic Bruce Goff, are returned to the fold in doctoral and postdoctoral studies; and even accepted pioneers of modernism like Otto Wagner and Adolf Loos are examined for the more unsettling, traditional aspects of their work that have always been played down.

But if the history of modernism is still being revised, no one has succeeded in defining postmodernism to everyone's satisfaction. A public used to being spoon-fed approved avant-garde formulas is hopelessly confused. Postmodernism has simply become a kind of umbrella label for whatever starts by rejecting the principles and practice of modernism. Beyond that, it is a license to hunt—for forms, for decoration, for meaning; its sources are the near and distant past, and its values, which turn away from society and inward to personal tastes and concerns, are primarily and almost exclusively aesthetic. Elaborate bows are made to a "search for language" that includes highly subjective expressive images.

That search received its first wide public notice in Robert Venturi's call for "complexity and contradiction" and his plea for the "inclusive" rather than the "exclusive" view of the built world that startled the profession in the sixties.[3] It was more specifically directed and defined—and therefore immediately became more controversial—by Robert A. M. Stern, one of the earlier postmodernist practitioners and the author of a number of articles and revisionist studies, of which one of the more valuable is a monograph on the American architect George Howe.[4] It was no time at all before Charles Jencks provided a more systematic outline of a postmodernist style—described as "multivalent" rather than "univalent," using "coded" design elements that conveyed double meanings about symbolism and style—gleefully reversing the "purification" process by which modernists had attempted to reduce buildings to a straight-line, functional logic. This soon solidified into a new dogma, or a set of predictable design clichés.

The roots of postmodernism go considerably farther back than these publications, however; they can be found in those brief, heretical episodes of the fifties that hardly shook the world—the "new empiricism" in Scandinavia and "neoliberty" in Italy. Although these short-lived movements were shocking aberrations to those few who knew they were occurring, they were singularly lacking as catalysts or catchy slogans for a revolution. Both were relaxations of modernist austerity that featured a creeping invasion of softened forms and a sidelong look at the decorative past.

It was not until Arthur Drexler's 1979 exhibition at the Museum of Modern Art in New York, Transformations in Modern Architecture, that the general art-loving public was informed that something might have gone wrong. Drexler's show stressed the increasing formalism of the buildings of the sixties and seventies, revealing the forced and foolish acrobatics of many "structural" and "functional" features pushed to decorative extremes. Drexler's pointed and far-from-innocent documentation—never have so many bad buildings been given so prestigious a showcase—dealt a body blow to modern architecture by showing how far it had strayed from its original premises. And because he threw in a little new work with the old, the message was received with howls of protest from the architecture profession, modernist and postmodernist alike.

IF THERE HAS been any single catalyst for the new, it has been the work of Charles Jencks, by far the most articulate and productive apostle of postmodernism from its beginnings, or from the time, one might say, when it was not much more than a gleam in his eye. His subjective rewriting of architectural history in Modern Movements in Architecture was followed by The Language of Post-Modern Architecture, Post Modern Classicism, and, most recently, Architecture Today.[5] One has the feeling that his postmodernist barrel is still largely untapped.

At a time when architectural commentary is at its most pretentious, turgid, and murky, Jencks is an intelligent, stylish, and provocative polemicist. An able manipulator of facts and opinions, a master of architectural hat tricks with styles and substyles, an expert maker of elaborate charts and graphs of cosmic, disembodied logic, he entertains at the same time that he outrages—something he does with a calculated consistency. You don't have to be a postmodernist to enjoy Jencks's books.

For sheer cleverness and wit, Jencks far surpasses Tom Wolfe's mean-spirited and tiresomely arch put-down of modern architecture, and he has the additional advantage of being able to make connections with the large context of art and history on a sound basis of professional expertise. To an acute sense of what is new, he adds that most important critical faculty, a very good eye. He rarely confuses novelty with ability. Even the most far-out examples are so judiciously selected and handsomely illustrated that you end up admiring what you dislike. The talent of the architect is always clear, no matter how perverse or difficult the building.

The formal geometries of the dining room of a house in Ticino, Switzerland, by Bruno Reichlin and Fabio Reinhart, to cite one example, are the product of exceptionally sophisticated architectural sensibilities. I am easily bowled over by the near perfection of its neorationalist aesthetic. And even while I admire its "visual language," the unrelentingly hard, cold surfaces and the punitive rigidity of the Mackintosh chairs make my head and back ache, and I know that the elegant, abstract order that makes this room memorable will be shattered the moment it is occupied. (I resist the temptation to write a commentary about the postmodernist irony of architecture as art that self-destructs in use.) Perhaps the beauty of the photography in *Architecture Today* has something to do with it. There is nothing remotely to suggest any possibility of the tacky or transient in glowing, full-page close-ups of Charles Moore's Piazza d'Italia in New Orleans, although one suspects that this presentation of clever technicolor imperial glory may be a slight exaggeration of the actual scale, reach, and setting of the design.

BEYOND THE RECOGNITION of Jencks's considerable virtues as critic and polemicist, however, there is much to disagree with in his persuasive theses. One could start, of course, by saying that "multivalence" is not achieved by sticking a lot of stuff together or assigning meanings so subjective that a glossary is needed. I, for one, have never believed that tarting up buildings with amusing bits of history or decoration, inside or out, as in Robert Stern's persistent use of fat fake columns and stick-on moldings or the "false front" collages favored by some others, either has a larger architectural significance or provides a public presence.

It is simplemindedness, not simple architecture, that is univalent—buildings that are barely two-dimensional and cannot carry more than one idea at a time. These slick ciphers abound in every American city. But the little-boy badnesses and bags-of-tricks presented by Jencks as a corrective vision have their own kind of emptiness; they suffer badly from conceptual and metaphysical overload. The line between artfulness and meaninglessness is getting very thin.

Jencks's obsession with a pejorative division between "late modern" and "postmodern," with all deficiencies and failures ascribed to the former, begs the issue of whether either meets the criteria of good architecture—or even of what those criteria should be. If, as its critics point out, late modernism is simplistic, inappropriate, brutish, and dull, postmodernism can be confusing, trivial, corny, and inconsequential; but because it is so much more sophisticated in the games it plays, it can also be extremely seductive and misleading.

Ricardo Bofill's "viaduct houses," constructed for the French new town of Saint-Quentin-en-Yvelines and used for the continuous, full-color wraparound photograph that forms the dazzling jacket for Jencks's *Architecture Today*, is obviously meant as a paradigmatic postmodernist example. The building is a showstopper—a neo-Roman aqueduct, triumphal-arch image forming multistoried dwellings of unreadable size, dramatically doubled by a lake reflection. When one visits Bofill's even newer and larger housing at Marne-la-Vallée, which is equally photogenic, one experiences aspects that escape the camera's eye. These are, indeed, novel and dramatic designs, but they are deeply disturbing buildings. The innocent dreams of impossible grandeur that gave Morris Lapidus's Miami Beach hotels their curious charm has been raised to a kind of aware and awful apotheosis. In Bofill's buildings, Lapidus's naive fantasy has become a skilled, knowledgeable manipulation carried out with infinitely more expertise, on a monstrous scale.

This artful, monumental kitsch has something for everyone; it works for both popular and educated taste on totally different levels. An exuberant haute-bourgeois pretentiousness is coupled with a Piranesian vision of space incongruously (cynically?) applied to ordinary domestic uses. The image is pop sinister. One assumes that this "double coding," this jolting marriage of the vulgar and the erudite, is another of post-modernism's calculated ironies. Otherwise it is hard to explain Bofill's colonnaded and mirrored Busby Berkeley stage set for the "theater" segment of the housing, or the "Carceri" quality of the entry courts. It is cinematic, of course; it lacks only tap dancers and swinging chains. This is a coolly, confidently, and expensively executed destruction of architectural meaning and style.

IT IS BEST not to come to postmodernism, or to Jencks's books, as an architectural innocent. This is not just a matter of missing the in-innuendoes or being an easy mark. Jencks is a brilliant and frequently infuriating critic, equally full of marvelous insights and willful misread-ings; but both need a practiced observer.

He can be scrupulously fair, as in his assessment of the talented and debatable work of James Stirling, or he can describe the elegant mod-ernist buildings of Richard Meier with keen understanding and then carefully undermine his praise with the use of an oddly belittling tone. There is no more succinct analysis of one of today's most "difficult" practitioners and cult figures, the Italian Marxist-mystic-rationalist Aldo Rossi, than appears in Jencks's *Architecture Today*, and no more wretchedly inadequate treatment of Mies van der Rohe than in Jencks's *Modern Movements in Architecture*. That Mies's buildings might have any conceptual or aesthetic significance, or any legitimacy whatever, is a possibility denied and derided in a tone that forecloses debate. They are dismissed as "empty parallelepipeds of post and lintel construction which enclose a 'universal' blank space . . . so obviously reductive as to be laughable." Jencks begins by calling Mies's work "exquisite farce" and ends by warning that those who take Mies seriously have fallen for the idea that a "half-baked, univalent architecture is better than an in-clusive one." It takes courage to risk that stigma.

On the other hand, Jencks's description in *Architecture Today* of "gridism," a Japanese "new wave" flirtation with an abstractly sinister bathhouse or mortuary style (perfect for fashion photos) is all that one could ask for in perceptive commentary.

What was a modernist principle of rationality and order, the applied grids of Viennese architects Otto Wagner and Adolf Loos, has now become both a comment on that principle and

> a subversion of it. Anonymity, neutrality and background
> order are here the content of the architecture, not a utilitarian
> device.

This says everything about the highly skilled and self-conscious creative decadence that defines where the aesthetic action is today. One cannot get closer to the nerve center of much late-twentieth-century art.

WRITING HISTORY OF any kind in a period of ideological transition is extremely difficult. In addition to the problem of perspective, there is in the arts the subjective matter of taste. Sigfried Giedion, Nikolaus Pevsner, and the early work of Henry-Russell Hitchcock read differently now; these influential modernist texts seem even more remarkable than when their apocalyptic vision burst upon a generation looking for a holy grail. This was special pleading of a very high order.

To revise these histories is no small assignment. Kenneth Frampton's *Modern Architecture: A Critical History*[6] is a major work with impressive parts that never quite seem to come together; it is difficult to discuss the book as a whole. A useful and wide-ranging work of superior architectural scholarship, this ambitious publication contains many chapters that stand on their own as perceptive essays; it is marked throughout by a consistently mature critical intelligence. Frampton gives a considerable emphasis to those subjects only lightly touched on or ignored in standard modernist histories—Terragni and Italian rationalism, for example, and the modernistic style in America (is Frampton the only one who has got the name right?). This is a pudding of a book from which one may pull any number of splendid things.

The quality of Frampton's research and analysis is high, but this is a standard we have a right to expect from architectural writing today. (He established that standard himself years ago with his article in *Perspecta* on Pierre Chareau's Maison de Verre in Paris,[7] a groundbreaking critical redefinition of both the architect and the building and their place and meaning in the modern movement.) The particular value of this kind of revisionist history is that it seeks sources and examines them thoroughly—a huge advantage if one wants to arrive at any approximation of the reality of events or a more accurate and revealing account of the influences, context, and conditions that have shaped the architect's work and beliefs. Right now, we need all the information we can get.

It is extremely unlikely that anyone is going to produce the "definitive" account of modernism at this point; such definitive accounts are usually written only as a carefully planned polemic, a form that is looked on currently with extreme suspicion. What matters most in Frampton's kind of "cultural" history is the quantity and quality of the information upon which the writer's opinions, and the opinions of others, will be based. I find myself more impressed by the depth and quality of his basic research than by any political interpretation of it he may suggest. This seems a fair test to apply to much of today's architectural writing.

Here the contrast between Frampton's and Jencks's treatment of Mies, for example, is instructive. Jencks's analysis consists of jumping on Mies with both feet after shadowboxing showily with a bit of history and philosophy; Frampton's approach has the virtue of critical exposition rather than demolition. Frampton deals directly with Mies's frequently repeated, overriding concern for "the expressive qualities of an objective building technique, logically conceived and vigorously executed." The advantages, and the limitations, of this philosophy are clear. Mies's buildings were neither universal, as claimed, nor replicable, as hoped. What Mies's followers (and critics) failed to grasp was the "delicacy of his sensibility," in Frampton's words, "that feeling for the precise proportioning of profiles that alone guaranteed his mastery over form." This superb sensibility inevitably made Mies's buildings something more than Jencks's "exquisite farce"; they were masterful, because he was a master, and, on occasion, they were great.

Frampton's discussion of Alvar Aalto greatly increases our understanding of the Finnish architect's work. Aalto's development is far more complex than the popular notion that he sprang full-blown from the brow of the International Style while adding some mysterious affinity with man and nature that has been labeled, much too glibly, "humanistic." Initially, Aalto was drawn to versions of romantic classicism and Finnish national romanticism which he admired and emulated; he was strongly influenced in his early years by the work of Gunnar Asplund and Erik Bryggman. An encounter with de Stijl at a European conference made him an ardent convert to constructivism; there was a

clear Dutch prototype for the famous Paimio Tuberculosis Sanatorium
that established him as a practitioner of the new "functionalism."

But Aalto's characteristic use of wood, which began with his furniture designs in the late twenties, and the softened and more sensuous
forms of his familiar, mature style were due less to some northern
Druidic instincts than to the patronage of the Gullichsens of the All-
ström timber interests in the thirties. The work that followed, from exposition pavilions and houses to institutions, continued to explore wood
in a marvelous way; his activity as a painter and an admirer of Arp,
Miró, and Le Corbusier, moreover, had much to do with his use of
curvilinear forms. (Frampton also tells us that the proponents of the
earlier Finnish national romanticism, wishing to promote the use of local granite, drew on the buildings of Edinburgh and the work of H. H.
Richardson for technical and aesthetic examples. The sources of style
do not have to be invented by art historians; they are usually there for
those who look for them.)

IT IS ONLY against this instructive background that one perceives why
Aalto's buildings are not cerebral, International Style abstractions, but
places of warmth and individuality. He fused his affinities for both rationalism and romanticism through a particularly gifted handling of
light, space, surface, material, and site, all strongly directed to the enhancement of personal, sensory experience. It is the extraordinary degree to which Aalto's buildings have shaped that experience that makes
his work some of the finest of this century. It is not surprising that his influence is growing while other reputations shrink. Aalto has been receiving increasing critical attention, from the detailed documentation
of his early work in Paul David Pearson's *Alvar Aalto and the International Style* of 1978 to Malcolm Quantrill's recently published *Alvar
Aalto: A Critical Study.*[8] Frampton calls Aalto's buildings "life-giving
rather than repressive." They are marked by the kind of "delicate sensibility" that Mies devoted to a diametrically opposed ideal, and for both
Aalto and Mies the end was the same: the making of a building in
which the user achieves dignity through art.

By the end of the book's discussion of Aalto we have absorbed so
much that even a rather typical Frampton sentence about Aalto's willingness to break modernist rules—"This meant that the latent tyranny
of the normative orthogonal grid should always be fractured and in-

flected where the idiosyncracies of the site or the programme demanded it"—is entirely clear, if a little overwrought. Unfortunately, he
uses a lot of that kind of language, which seems to be the identification
of a card-carrying architectural intellectual.

Frampton has two styles: He writes history as an informative and absorbing narrative that moves right along, and he writes theory in a mias-
mic prose dense with references to German philosophers. I find the
latter more of a stumbling block than a sign of critical intelligence,
something with which Frampton is singularly well endowed.

Another major effort to rewrite history, William Curtis's *Modern Architecture since 1900*,[9] is clearly meant as a revisionist textbook, and in a
field not exactly crowded with candidates it has its value. This is a book
one would love to like. Curtis has made a conscientious effort to give a
comprehensive account of the modern movement in architecture by
filling in the gaps left by modernist rhetoric and omission; he clearly
wants to tell the whole story with truth and justice for all. An able historian, he succeeds to a degree, but next to Jencks's high jinks and blithe
disregard for truth and justice for all, this is an earnest, plodding, and
pedantic work. The two books have quite different objectives, and this
makes comparison unfair. But Jencks's shrewd and accurate perceptions of contemporary culture and its intricate connections to the art of
building—as when he characterizes the various architectural responses
to the banality of the shopping center—almost always hit the mark. Unfortunately, Jencks is not immune to contemporary faddishness, which
somewhat spoils his endorsements for architectural immortality.

Curtis does not make a much more convincing case for his chosen
immortal, the Swedish architect Jörn Utzon, the designer of the Sydney
Opera House and the much more restrained church at Bagsvaerd, near
Copenhagen—the pictorial grand finale of the book. Curtis declares
the church a model of imagery supported by form, and an example of
"a genuine style, based on private, intuitive rules." I doubt this will per-
suade many that Utzon's architecture is the real thing as opposed to
postmodernism's shoddy goods. Curtis has written a serious and useful
work that contains much sound analysis, but it is no rocket across the
architectural sky. One finishes it with respect and relief.

By far the most helpful, and consistently remarkable, series of architectural publications is to be found in the books, catalogs, and journals

that have been put out by Rizzoli International Publications. Why, and how, the financially troubled and scandal-rocked Rizzoli empire has been able to publish architectural books with such professional acumen, omniscience, and omnipresence is not for this writer to understand. But Rizzoli seems to be everywhere, recording offbeat exhibitions and important competitions, and issuing student publications in addition to its constantly expanding, wonderfully eclectic book list. No other publisher has approached such excellence, diversity, and quality in such impressive quantity.

A series of monographs put out by Rizzoli for the Institute for Architecture and Urban Studies, for example, includes new material and viewpoints on such odd architectural bedfellows as the revolutionary Russian architect Ivan Leonidov and the New York establishment modernist Wallace K. Harrison. Both were the subject of institute exhibitions. All of these publications quickly became collectors' items. The books and catalogs of the Rizzoli list belong in every serious architectural library.

The best of the recent scholarly monographs, whether from trade publishers or university presses, have a common theme: They are revisionist studies bent on reviving or reinterpreting reputations. As they multiply, an impressive documentation of certain phases of early modernism is being developed. Because today's architects and commentators are intrigued by mixed messages of all kinds, studies have proliferated on maverick figures like Asplund, who was dealt with seriously and at length in Stuart Wrede's book *The Architecture of Erik Gunnar Asplund*.[10] Exactly those aspects of Asplund's work that troubled the chroniclers of the International Style—a very personal resolution of the ambiguities of new and old forms—have made him attractive to the postmodernist sensibility. The stripped classicism of his work had a subtle evocative power and a historical memory that was at odds with the emerging Functional Style. Asplund's talent was undeniable; even the modernists singled out his Stockholm Crematorium as a stylistic icon. But it was the timing of his romantic classicism, against the modernist tide, that relegated him to a minor role.

A great deal of attention is being devoted to those early modernist periods marked by a creative vacillation between past and future. The preferred subjects tend to be historically ambivalent, aesthetically offbeat, or stylishly nostalgic. The work of the Scottish art nouveau architect Charles Rennie Mackintosh with his ties to the Vienna Secession, for example, has this triple appeal. The protomodern simplicities and anti-historical references singled out by the historians of the International Style have been replaced by an examination of decorative details and praise for the expressive interpretation of tradition. Recent interest in the work of Adolf Loos stresses his links with classicism more than his notorious indictment of ornament.

The brief, star-crossed period of revolutionary Russian modernism is also receiving intense scrutiny. Frederick Starr's monograph on the architect Konstantin Melnikov,[11] based on the documentation Starr gathered in the Soviet Union during the seventies, describes the aborted relationship between Soviet politics and modernist architecture in the early years of the revolutionary state and is the definitive monograph on this important architect. Melnikov's Soviet Pavilion at the Paris Exposition of 1925 brought Russian romantic radicalism to an admiring European audience. (This was the same exposition that gave the world art deco, the least revolutionary of modernist styles.) A few years before Melnikov's death in a Moscow sanitarium, I visited the architect with Starr. We sat in a neglected, overgrown institutional garden and heard the gentle old man in hospital pajamas describe the excitement of carrying fresh drawings under his arm to the Kremlin. He spoke of the early shared political-aesthetic ideals of building a new state, and of the disillusionment of the Stalin years.[12]

An entire generation of American architects outlawed by the taste makers of the modern movement is being rehabilitated by younger historians. Practitioners banished into limbo by the rise of modernism are carefully documented in monographs such as Robert Stern's *George Howe* and Richard Oliver's *Bertram Grosvenor Goodhue*.[13] The American-born Howe has been consistently cast as subordinate to his Swiss-born partner, William Lescaze, an early advocate of the International Style, who has always received the lion's share of credit for such modernist masterworks as the 1931 skyscraper for the Philadelphia Savings Fund Society. Stern may bend over a bit to favor Howe, but the information he provides redresses any real imbalance and fills in a good deal of missing history.

Oliver's book restores Goodhue to the place in the American architectural pantheon denied him because of his eclectic work. That this eclecticism was the expression of a major original talent, ranging from a refined Gothic revivalism in his New York churches to the free romanticism of the remarkable Nebraska State Capitol of 1920, is no longer in question. Considering the size and importance of the institutional, cultural, and public building commissions in academic and eclectic styles, there is vast material for scholarly study. As an inevitable by-product, a lot of bad academic work is about to be as highly praised as bad modernist work was before it.

In a somewhat different category are those monographs that come subtly or aggressively under the heading of promotion — the glossy picture books on the work of practicing architects of many persuasions. The market has been flooded with these huge and costly publications. All are illustrated to the point of gorgeous embarrassment, although they may be written with varying degrees of intelligence or grace. For anyone interested in the state of the architectural establishment, postmodernist division, there are stunning recent books on Michael Graves, Robert A. M. Stern, and Arata Isozaki[14] that provide useful pictures of their work; the documentation such publications provide is usually valuable in inverse relationship to their size and weight.

A BOOK PUBLISHED by the MIT Press this autumn brings current publishing full circle to the who-killed-modern-architecture theme that has been a leitmotif of the architectural book boom. The initial response to Klaus Herdeg's *The Decorated Diagram*, subtitled *Harvard Architecture and the Failure of the Bauhaus Legacy*,[15] is "Oh, no, not another one on the failure-of-modern-architecture." *The Decorated Diagram* was accompanied by the publisher's information that Herdeg's book is "the thinking person's *From Bauhaus to Our House.*" If I were Herdeg I would protest. The only discernible, but deceptive, resemblance is in the presentation, which just puts more fuel on a spent fire. In some parts the book seems closer to the famous case-history method of the Harvard law and business schools than anything produced by the Harvard Graduate School of Design. But it will be too bad if the book comes across as just another example of modern architecture bashing or Bauhaus debunking, because it has far more pertinent and useful things to say. Herdeg's concerns go considerably beyond the attack he mounts on Harvard as the generator of the decorative formalism of American modernist architecture. He is interested in means, ends, and values; he sees architecture as a marriage between appearance and purpose, in which formal elements are imbued with a wide range of meanings. He believes in the kind of controlled and creative design that "challenges the imagination and offers emotional rewards, whatever its pragmatic duty."

The question of form and content Herdeg explores in his case histories of the design process will be a disappointment to anyone looking for conspiracy theories or elite plots as perpetrated at either Harvard or the Bauhaus or in any other hotbed of architectural subversion. He has no use for either the high seriousness of purpose of the modernists or the "cheap thrill eyecatchers" or "impudent irony" of the postmodernists. He is acutely aware of the gap between intent and result in both cases. His attack is concentrated on the abstract formalism of late modernism and the educational system that encouraged its development and was blind to its inadequacies. Harvard, of course, as the leader of architectural education at that time, is a sitting target. By citing the work of Harvard Graduate School of Design alumni, he aims his fire at the way this heavily rationalized decorative formalism (the "decorated diagram" of his title) was transmitted through the teaching, and the students, of Walter Gropius.

BY BLAMING HARVARD, he is killing the messenger who brought the bad news; if he did no more than that, the book would not deserve much attention. For one thing, the messenger is dead; the Graduate School of Design is under new leadership and following a different course. What remains today are a great many modern buildings, good and bad, by Harvard graduates, and a great many modern buildings, also good and bad, by non-Harvard graduates, that are essentially the same thing. They demonstrate a predictable range of sensitivities and deficiencies of the late modern style. To confuse the issue further, Herdeg has put a lot of mismatched architectural eggs into his Harvard basket. He has then proceeded to tar both modernists and postmodernists with the same Bauhaus brush, which takes considerable agility.

The real value of the book is the author's ability to analyze individual buildings with an objectivity that has been conspicuously lacking in the modernist-postmodernist debate. He deals with all pratfalls evenhandedly. The failures of both modernist and postmodernist works are dissected with equal acuity and a long view of architecture. His criticism of I. M. Pei's late modernist work, for example, is not a repetition of the currently popular judgments of "passé monumentality." The defects of these buildings are explained by showing the limitations imposed by Pei's strict adherence to modernist rules. Herdeg chooses the Johnson Museum at Cornell University for analysis, although this structure lacks Pei's usual clarity and is actually quite "schizoid," as Herdeg points out, in its spatial organization.[16] Pei's other museums are better examples of the "powerful formal devices" of modernism—the clearly ordered and unified arrangement of spaces in a smooth, totemlike container.

"The unqualified application of such powerful formal devices," Herdeg writes, "tends to inhibit spontaneous interpretation of spatial configurations for social and other purposes." These buildings are, indeed, absolute; not surprisingly, they make unequivocal modernist statements. Beyond the obvious difficulties of adaptability, they lose their essential aesthetic character if not "read" as originally designed. The East Wing of the National Gallery in Washington, for example, works superbly as public space and for an equally formal if rather limited display of compatible art. But an event with the emotional drive and shattering excesses of the Rodin show made a shambles of the building's resolute, measured image.

HERDEG IS EQUALLY effective in deflating the rhetoric and results, and some of the reputations, of postmodernist practitioners. He demolishes two luxury apartment houses in New York, one at 800 Fifth Avenue, the other at 1001 Fifth Avenue, for which two Harvard alumni, Ulrich Franzen and Philip Johnson, designed façades with much fanfare. What he does not say is that neither of these architects approached the commissions as exponents of Gropius's "total architecture" or anything in the Bauhaus tradition; both were designing as postmodernists of greater or lesser conviction. Franzen's conversion was the more recent; Johnson had not done anything Gropius told him to for a long time.

Herdeg zeroes in on the details of these two perfectly dreadful façades—Franzen's at 800 Fifth and Johnson's at 1001 Fifth— describing their formal and symbolic failures in almost clinical terms. Both façades, he says, "play out a literal heavy-handed charade" in their attempts to relate to their neighbors—a beaux arts apartment house next to 1001 Fifth and the small, Georgian Revival Knickerbocker Club next to 800 Fifth. Although each design "pays tribute to context" by taking its formal cues from the masonry, moldings, windows, or other details adjoining it, something has gone terribly wrong; both buildings are banal and busy caricatures. Johnson's vertical bay window strips, "in dark glass and metal against off-white stone, run up the façade like so many zippers," emphasizing rather than diminishing the effect of the building's excessive height. The borrowed elements "appear to dissolve into an array of unrelated and therefore confusing anecdotes."

Herdeg disposes forever of any architectural pretensions the two buildings may have. Of 800 Fifth: "The façade . . . appears as a non-façade . . . a tartan weave of glass, spandrels and wall." Of 1001 Fifth: "The question presents itself whether this display of unnerving effects amounts to a deliberate use of irony for the purpose of reconciling conflicting conditions, or whether, because of self-contradictory design actions, essential order and control have been lost."

If there is irony here, it is that both of these "decorated diagrams" are actually the product of New York's standard speculator practice of dressing up the ordinary; the fancy false front, put on for the luxury trade, covers a conventional building, tricked up, in this case, by a pretentious postmodernist rationale. There surely is no more unsavory architectural formula. It is reaching hard, as Herdeg does, to blame this on the Bauhaus.

HERDEG ALSO DEVOTES a great deal of space to dismembering an earlier Philip Johnson building of the fifties, the Sheldon Art Gallery in Lincoln, Nebraska, done when Johnson was first breaking with the International Style and flirting with history. He makes a detailed comparison with a museum that was greatly admired by Johnson's first, modernist mentor, Mies, and has since become an icon of the postmodernists: Karl Friedrich Schinkel's Altes Museum in Berlin. This is a building that has been referred to repeatedly and respectfully by Johnson in both his modernist and postmodernist periods.

The Sheldon Art Gallery is not one of Johnson's better buildings; his production, at best, is uneven, and the truly great building eludes him. There has also been a remarkable absence of critical analysis of where the failure lies. Herdeg uses this design to identify weaknesses that can be found in much of Johnson's work; they are characteristic of the architect rather than of the Harvard curriculum. In a discussion of similarities of formal structure, differences in the relationship of façade to plan, and the disposition of spaces in the two museums, Johnson comes off distinctly second best.

Herdeg writes:

> The calculated orchestration of physical, spatial, and temporal
> elements and forces into a vibrant yet serene whole in the
> Schinkel façade is reduced in Johnson's museum to a single
> chord straining to evoke a sound of grandeur . . . Where one
> façade freezes into decoration, the other opens countless op-
> portunities for human participation.

He concludes that the Johnson building is the product of

> an object-fixated, style-drunk process . . . a play of sensual agita-
> tion . . . anything but the subtly calculated interplay of architec-
> tural elements and ensembles in the service of human comfort
> and the heightening of self-esteem which we find in the façade
> and entry sequence of the Altes Museum.

The same treatment is meted out to Edward L. Barnes, a Harvard
graduate who remains a convinced and consistent modernist. Herdeg
compares Barnes's master plan for the State University campus at Purchase, New York, with Thomas Jefferson's plan for the University of Virginia. Jefferson's masterwork has always been an impossible act to follow,
and Barnes's plan, generally considered one of his least successful efforts,
highlights the modernists' persistent problems with creating an inviting
human setting. Herdeg attributes this to the modernist insistence on "the
building as object," existing independently rather than meshing with its
surroundings in more harmonious and humanistic ways. Of all the "failures" ascribed to modernism today, this, and the unfeeling and unseeing
destruction of the past, are the ones that really hit home.

But then Herdeg lumps together Barnes and Johnson, modernist and
postmodernist, against the winning team of Schinkel and Jefferson. It is
no contest. "One set of buildings," Herdeg writes, "Schinkel's and
Jefferson's—call on the eyes to lead the intellect and emotions to a richer
understanding of architecture, subtly revealing a true symbiosis between
appearance and purpose, while the other set of buildings—Johnson's and
Barnes's—permit, by less controlled and more literal appeal to the eyes,
only a discontinuous grasp of the building, as if its attributes were presented by flashcards." Flash-card architecture! The perfect postmodernism.

If what Herdeg is saying is that both examples are seriously flawed, he is right; if he is saying that both are failures of the Bauhaus legacy, it is impossible to agree. But when he broadens his criticism, he becomes irrefutable. His comment that any architecture that does no more than provide visual and tactile stimulation is a failure is right on the mark. Modernist and postmodernist buildings can all make the same bad music, only in different keys.

HERDEG'S DEFINITION OF architecture as a process that "gives formal significance to such considerations as social and functional use, structure, lighting and materials" should be a working truism, but it is largely disregarded. That all design devices should ultimately "resolve [themselves] into a deeper understanding of architecture" is indisputable, although increasingly ignored. Perhaps these words should be graven on the door of Harvard and every other school, with the remarkable observation that goes to the heart of the matter: "Architecture [is] most effective when it makes possible . . . moments of suspension between one's inner and outer world."

Architecture thus conceived is the transition point, a cleverly crafted place of space and light and thoughtful detail where we experience both worlds and that "heightened sense of self-esteem" that Schinkel and Jefferson—professional and amateur—understand as essential to the building art. Today's flash-card architecture is not good enough. When the architect succeeds in creating such a place through the aesthetic control of physical and structural reality, when he uses his art to provide "countless opportunities for human participation" and to give us a feeling of dignity and self-worth, such transcendental, civilizing moments are reached. These are the structures in which we understand architecture; they are the ones that touch society as a whole. Harvard? The Bauhaus? This goes back to the beginnings of building time.

NOTES

1. Farrar, Straus and Giroux, 1981.
2. Two outstanding examples of the genre, because of the excellence of their documentation and the focus of their viewpoint, are Carl Schorske's *Fin-de-Siècle Vienna* and John Willett's *Art and Politics in the Weimar Republic*.

3. Robert Venturi, *Complexity and Contradiction in Architecture* (Museum of Modern Art, 1966; revised ed. 1977).

4. Robert A. M. Stern, *George Howe: Toward a Modern American Architecture* (Yale University Press, 1975).

5. *Modern Movements in Architecture* (Doubleday Anchor, 1973); *The Language of Post-Modern Architecture* (Rizzoli, 1978); *Post-Modern Classicism* (Rizzoli, 1981); *Architecture Today* (Abrams, 1982).

6. Oxford University Press, 1980.

7. Kenneth Frampton, "Maison de Verre," *Perspecta* 12 (Yale Architectural Design, October 1969).

8. Paul David Pearson, *Alvar Aalto and the International Style* (Whitney Library of Design, Watson-Guptill, 1978); Malcolm Quantrill, *Alvar Aalto: A Critical Study* (Schocken, 1983).

9. William J. R. Curtis, *Modern Architecture since 1900* (Prentice-Hall, 1982).

10. Stuart Wrede, *The Architecture of Erik Gunnar Asplund* (MIT Press, 1980; 1983 paper).

11. S. Frederick Starr, *Melnikov: Solo Architect in a Mass Society* (Princeton University Press, 1978).

12. Another valuable addition to the documentation of Soviet modernism is a translation of Moisei Ginzburg's *Style and Epoch* (Anatole Senkevitch Jr., trans.; MIT Press, 1982). Ginzburg's Soviet manifesto paralleled Le Corbusier's *Vers une architecture* in France, carrying many of the same ideas. This publication restores it to history.

13. Richard Oliver, *Bertram Grosvenor Goodhue* (American Monograph Series: Architectural History Foundation/MIT Press, 1983).

14. Michael Graves, *Buildings and Projects, 1966–1981*, ed. Karen Wheeler, Peter Arnell, and Ted Bickford (Rizzoli, 1983); Robert A. M. Stern, *Buildings and Projects, 1965–1980: Toward a Modern Architecture After Modernism*, ed. Peter Arnell and Ted Bickford (Rizzoli; Academy Editions/St. Martin's Press, 1983); Philip Drew, *The Architecture of Arata Isozaki* (Harper and Row, 1982).

15. MIT Press, 1983.

16. A *New York Times* headline writer's error has come back to haunt me. My article of June 11, 1973, on the Johnson Museum called it a flawed design and expressed reservations. The headline read PEI'S BOLD GEM, which Herdeg may have accepted as my evaluation. Journalists neither write, nor see, their headlines.

New York Review of Books, December 22, 1983

Reinventing Architecture

Moving On

IF, AS A DISTINGUISHED ENGLISH CRITIC recently observed, we need more raisins in the plain dough of modern architecture, the Museum of Modern Art is currently offering us the ingredients for a fruitcake. Architecture and Imagery, to be on view through April 19, is a small, exotic exhibition consisting of models and photographs of only four buildings—the proposed TWA terminal at Idlewild Airport in New York, by Eero Saarinen and Associates; a completed church in Stamford, Connecticut, by Harrison and Abramovitz; another church in France by Guillaume Gillet; and Jorn Utzon's prize-winning design for the new Sydney Opera House in Australia—all rich, strange fare, quite unlike the austere architectural diet to which the museum has accustomed us.

Nor is the museum unaware of its departure from its customary tastes in presenting this provocative material. According to an official statement, these buildings are being shown because they represent "sane, important developments in modern architecture." They place unusual emphasis on the elaborate enrichment of the "pure" modern manner, through the use of complex structural techniques. These techniques create extraordinary new forms—decorative, sculpturesque shells and faceted prisms—that are a startling denial of the traditional straight-walled building box or cube, and of the popular design aesthetic that rests so squarely on them. In spite of their shock value, however, these "space-structures" are neither puff-pastry novelties nor the overblown abstractions of some surrealist dream. They are striking and controversial examples of a significant new direction in architectural design.

As such, they must be evaluated seriously. The small but important body of building represented by these four projects is the first meaningful addition to the limited vocabulary of the established modern style. Although there are many excellent things about this style—not the least of which are simplicity, logic, technical efficiency, and, at its best, a remarkable, bare-bones beauty—the fact remains that our buildings, regardless of purpose, look more and more alike. Thus severely restricted by a technology dependent upon the practical economics of large-scale production, the range of architecture is forced into an increasingly narrow mold.

Today, the use of an amazingly versatile material—reinforced concrete—has made it possible to break this mold. By a curious irony, the architect owes much of this freedom to his pragmatic colleague, the engineer. Reinforced concrete construction is a comparatively new technique in the history of building. Daringly developed for utilitarian needs in the late nineteenth century, its unique monolithic, free-form character has not been fully exploited until our own time. These romantic aesthetic experiments began with the roofing of factories and the spanning of rivers, in such trend-setting structural innovations as Ernest Ransome's impressive, turn-of-the-century industrial plants in America; the Swiss engineer Robert Maillart's graceful bridges of the twenties and thirties, and the noted Italian Pier Luigi Nervi's revolutionary series of stadia, hangars, factories, and warehouses which are as remarkable for their beauty as for their mathematical logic. Now, when the architect is faced with a problem for which familiar, lookalike solutions are obviously inadequate, he can devise an excitingly different form—confident that it can be engineered.

He can be sure, in fact, that he is able to transform almost any design dream into reality. Unfortunately, these flights of structural fancy can range from the sublime to the ridiculous, and for every dream there is a nightmare. A giant snail drawn by giraffes, proposed by Salvador Dalí as a nightclub for a Mexican resort, has been pronounced practicable by Felix Candela, the eminent and respected engineer. The danger is not that "it couldn't be done," as a current inescapable cigarette commercial chants repeatedly, but that it can. This is the negative aspect of freedom—its potential abuse—with which we will be forced to reckon.

On the credit side, this freedom gives us the custom-made structure in the midst of machine-made conformity; the unique design for a specific use, deliberately orientated to emotional and psychological needs. Considered by some to be the last stand of creative individuality in the face of overwhelming architectural uniformity, it is one answer to the neat, anonymous, omnipresent curtain wall. These buildings are belligerently personal in an impersonal world. They represent the revolt of the architect against standardization; the statement of the artist, in flight from the scientist and the statistician. Very well, then, they are art; but are they architecture? Is this self-conscious straining after novelty always the best solution to the problem? Does it compensate, in originality and beauty of form, for the inevitable awkward passages, the strident insistence on attention?

In the case of the few best examples, such as those in the show, the answer may very well be yes. Certainly Utzon's opera house, designed as a collection of billowing sail-like concrete shells housing an admirably utilitarian double auditorium scheme (and called everything from an architectural masterpiece to a collection of abandoned umbrellas), is an inspired solution for a civic landmark, particularly since the site is a peninsula projecting into Sydney Harbor. Such a building could be unique and memorable.

Saarinen's TWA terminal is an outstandingly sensitive exercise in the creation of a special form, physically and psychologically suited to the purpose of the building. Harrison's church, in spite of deplorably pedestrian details that jolt one unwillingly into a realization of how close to impossible it is to organize all of the elements of these unconventional structures into a harmonious whole, is still an exciting edifice. The soaring "V-piers" of Gillet's church, supporting a doubly curved "saddle" roof, evoke a medieval religiosity.

Common to all is the use of forms that are unfamiliar but strongly evocative—for these constructions are sail-like, birdlike, and cathedral-like abstractions—that suggest, as the show's title implies, that "imagery" often figures prominently in this type of design. If these buildings have a major fault, it is that they tend to be overly intellectualized solutions, so studiously and arbitrarily "aesthetic" and novel that a triumphant tour-de-force air obscures all other accomplishment.

In the hands of sincere, talented architects, such experiments can be a welcome broadening of the contemporary style, in spite of the fact that the many problems they pose are far from solved. Their effects are too easily and superficially imitated, however, and parodies of the new forms have already appeared as cheap roadside shacks, ice cream stands, and jerry-built motels. In the hands of less able men, or at the mercy of publicity-minded clients, poetry becomes prose, art becomes advertising, and genius inspires gimmicks. This spectacular "shape-architecture" is particularly vulnerable and runs the risk of being summarily reduced to absurdity.

New York Times, February 15, 1959

Don't Call It Kookie

CLOSING OUR EYES FIRMLY ONCE AGAIN to environmental crisis in New York—fountains of the absurd and equally absurd meat market sites—we present this week another aspect of the larger subject of theory and design. It is time for an interim report, on the progress of the hottest thing in the architectural field: megastructure.

The theory of megastructure, or the gathering of many components into a single unit, implying largeness or greatness, as expressed in the Greek root of the word, has been hot for five years, warming up for ten or fifteen and a source of theoretical discourse long before that. It is producing, in various modifications, some of today's most interesting work. It has been thoroughly explored by critics and intellectuals, and its flashier aspects have been reduced to a kind of kicky high-fashion novelty by the stylish magazines.

What megastructure amounts to, with considerable flexibility in interpretation, is a way of meeting the frighteningly enlarged scale and needs of today's building. It is proposed that this be done by means of huge structures that are actually made up of multiple small units that can be used over and over, serially or as accretions, in varieties of modules, through repetition and ultimately mass production. These units can be hung from or slid into or connected with some form of containing framework, but the implication always is of an ever-expanding number of smaller parts hooked into a general system of services and circulation.

Megastructure has a technological and functional rationale beyond cavil and a staggering creative and aesthetic potential. At its highest reaches it is violently antiestablishment, antiformal, open-ended, and noncentric (in the sense that classically conceived architecture is composed with a back, a front, a beginning, and an end), deliberately rejecting symmetry, balance, and focus and all of the time-honored conventions of architectural design. Bigger than any monument, it disclaims monumentality for a social and industrial image. It is "endless architecture," "action architecture," "anonymous architecture." It has "clip-on" parts for "plug-in" cities. Dig it? It's the scene.

Quite seriously, it is one of the most stimulating, promising, and problematic architectural developments of the twentieth century. Results, in practice and on paper, range from the all-purpose university structure, having a big vogue right now, to megastructure as the city of the future, a kind of erector-set environment with disposable parts. It goes all the way from a specific system of design being boldly explored here and abroad to the purest utopian vision.

Perhaps the best of the flexible, expandable, university-in-one-building experiments is Scarborough College, a branch of the University of Toronto that is now an object of architectural pilgrimage. Designed by John Andrews, it combines two of architecture's most progressive trends: megastructure and the new brutalism. This single, stunning structure of rough concrete is a continuous circulatory system embracing classroom units and student spaces. An even more ambitious megastructure by Candilis, Josic and Woods is going ahead for Berlin's Free University. A highly personal version of the principle has been constructed for the new arts center at the University of Illinois by Walter Netsch of Skidmore, Owings & Merrill. Others are under way.

The most notable exponents of megastructure in its most extreme form have been a coalition of English architects in their twenties and thirties called the Archigram Group, whose theories were brought to international attention with a London exhibition in 1963, The Living City. Interest has been whetted by occasional publication of the group's *Archigram* magazine.

Archigram's theories of a total megastructure environment of expendable, industrialized components attached to a framework of circulation and services are richly buttressed by a spectacular abstract

visualization of the kind of city that would be shaped by systems approaches, computerization, and technology. Service-and-traffic grids
fed by ducts contain rearrangeable, stacked housing and office units
swung into place by cranes; the whole thing creeps across the land on
giant metal legs. Awe-inspiring inhuman complexity has language to
match. Peter Cook's magnificent mechanistic drawings are filled with
"maximum pressure areas," "information silos," and "capsule-unit housing towers." This is Plug-In City.

Critic Reyner Banham, writing in the *Walker Arts Center Design
Quarterly*, called Archigram's "kit of interchangeable living cells and
support structures the first effective image of the architecture of technology since Buckminster Fuller's Geodesic domes captivated the
world." This is not, he warned, "a kookie teenage Pop frivolity," no
matter how many technological improbabilities it may contain.
Utopia, after all, is utopia. It deals in cosmic lessons, not instructions
for do-it-yourself.

On a less cosmic level, megastructure's more realistic versions offer
provocative answers to large-scale building. In theory, these solutions to
mass-produced housing or educational, commercial, and cultural complexes are superbly, scientifically logical. In practice, their logic runs
smack into the obscene obstacle course of tight money, artificially inflated land cost, archaic and restrictive union practices, obsolete and diverse building codes, astronomic costs of tooling for industrial
production, politics, pigheadedness, and the vicissitudes of public and
personal taste.

THE PROCESS IS being repeated, for example, for Habitat, Moshe
Safdie's brainchild and beautiful obsession that was the showpiece of
Montreal's Expo 67. What started there as serious megastructure was
completed, in a vastly reduced and compromised form, as something
less than the inexpensive, General Motors-type housing product intended. It was a handcrafted Cadillac, an enormously costly, nonstand-
ardized, custom-made model. While it offered a tentative demonstration
of a handsome and rational design principle, it was also a sad case history of production realities.

New York City and the federal Department of Housing and Urban
Development are now in the middle of Habitat studies. Attracted to
the economic and technological promise of megastructure housing,

they are coming to the same economic and technological dead ends. How curious that those dead ends should be produced by the most progressive of all scientific civilizations. We can build small, sophisticated, exotic, demonstration minimegas only. The implicit mass-scale economics and efficiencies are unobtainable. The status quo wins hands down.

There are other objections to megastructure. In the December issue of *Architectural Design*, guest-edited by Jonathan Miller on the metaphors and myths of the city, Chris Abel severely criticizes every aspect of the theory from Scarborough to Plug-In City.

Megastructure does not, he says, take into account the adaptive processes of the living community, the organic adjustments to change that must inevitably be made. It is an orderly, rigid concept. The megastructure building or city is a "closely integrated or cohesive ordering of a system of multifarious activities" that insists on a "coherent image." Life, he says, using such currently "in" words as *conurbation, homeostasis,* and *cyclic processes,* is just not like that. Megastructure ignores the "adaptive behaviour the planner cannot himself specify."

Touché. But the truth, as usual, is somewhere between the Gospel of Archigram and the Fallacy of the Aesthetic Straightjacket. Megastructure is one more important and valuable architectural tool pertinent to our times and problems. But the avant-garde moves on. Next week, the case for chaos.

New York Times, January 19, 1969

The Case for Chaos

JUST WHEN THE BANDWAGON GETS ROLLING TO neat up the environment, along comes the case for chaos. To a public learning to look at its surroundings critically and seeing the physical effects of the confusions and vulgarities of modern life, the drive for order and elegance seems an irreproachable cause. Moreover, it has been the cause of concerned architects, planners, and intellectuals representing the avant-garde of social and aesthetic thought for the past fifty years.

Okay. Turn it upside down. Like everything else today. And you have the social, aesthetic, and intellectual attitudes of the latest avant-garde: the case for chaos.

One can react in two ways. The first is to express indignation and horror at the perverseness of such an idea. Call it backsliding nihilism, part of a currently fashionable denial of existing standards and values. Or it is possible to look at it carefully and find some eye-opening observations on the urban scene. The eyes of the observers (youthful, of course) are being used with a surprising historical objectivity. At the same time, they are examining the phenomena of the present, not with the sweeping a priori attitudes of condemnation that have become pious clichés, but with a cool, analytical acuity.

In writing about this, we are not wasting your time on abstruse architectural theory. Today's theory is tomorrow's practice. With the speedup characteristic of our age, it has a way of becoming today's practice. Any thinking, feeling citizen involved with his environment in this latter part of the twentieth century (that's right—latter—with all the "projections" to the once awesomely remote year 2000 no more than comfortable middle age for the present generation) must know the wave of the future or succumb to the undertow of the past. Another generation gap.

The new theorists point out that there are sound sociological, technical, and practical explanations for the look of today's world, like it or not. We are asked to examine the mess again. They claim that we can deal with the chaotic environment in constructive and even creative ways by admitting its conflicts, analyzing its components, and recognizing the purposes they serve and the contributions they make to our way of life.

Is chaos really so chaotic? they ask. Does it not contain valuable elements of vitality and variety, complexity and contrast? Can we not learn from the organically evolving environment? What about planning by adaptive processes? Is there an aesthetic of the pop landscape? From this point on, you may have your choice of embracing chaos on any step of the scale from an instructive demonstration of contemporary realities to great art form, depending on the length of your hair.

Chaos may even contain an order of its own, we are told. It is an order of "inclusion" and "the difficult whole," rather than an order of "exclusion," or "rejection," which has been the teaching and operation of modern architecture to date. It offers a pluralistic aesthetic of "both and" rather than the selective "either-or" decisions enforced by orthodox architectural theory. This is a far more complex approach to the environment than we have been taught to take.

Rejection or exclusion has been a basic tenet of the modern movement. Its pioneers preached against the chaos of the contemporary environment with the same breath in which they called for a new architecture. If they could not eliminate the setting, they turned their backs on it. They were fighting for release from an accretion of smothering, pseudoarty Victorian clutter, and to them slob city and the landscape of the superhighway were just updated versions of the old enemy. It has now become terribly clear that they rejected too much. There are lessons of sterility wherever their reductive principles have been scrupulously carried out. That prescription for order didn't work. The present search for order calls for acceptance of the irreconcilables of our complex existences, new values, and a new vision.

This is fascinating, heady speculation, and the best of it is to be found in a slim book called *Complexity and Contradiction in Architecture*, by Robert Venturi, published in 1966 by the Museum of Modern Art in association with the Graham Foundation for Advanced Studies in the Fine Arts.

Mr. Venturi is the guru of chaos. The book is, as he calls it, a gentle manifesto. Its illustrations of great buildings of the past are rich demonstrations of ambiguity and complexity. Where the early modern architect turned to the simplicities of the anonymous and the primitive, this generation turns to the most sophisticated examples of history. In the present, Mr. Venturi finds Roadtown, USA, and the Supermarket-Supermote-Superhighway landscape, commonly inveighed against in the primers of a more beautiful America, exhilarating aesthetic experiences. He takes his Yale students to Las Vegas, much as an earlier generation made pilgrimages to Palladian villas.

He teaches a new scale created by the automobile and a new, bold architecture of communication grasped by the car in motion. The new architecture is the little building and the big sign on Route 66.

Learning from pop art, the conventional is accepted and given character by change of emphasis and context; the "valid and vivid" banalities, which are so much the reality of the American scene, are the new icons. Mr. Venturi is witty, brilliant, and challenging; for a short course read "Learning from Las Vegas," written with Denise Scott Brown, in the March 1968 *Architectural Forum.*

All right. You don't buy it. Brought up on "America the Beautiful," you find pop landscape an affront. Reyner Banham, in lively critical essays, may embrace the fluorescent plastic environment but you still suffer vertigo in motels. Everyone to his own lifestyle. No significant proportion of Yale architecture graduates has moved to Las Vegas. And even if it is doctrine that every son reject the values of his father, there are circumstances in which the elements of the pop landscape become outrage. There is always a dangerous tendency for reason and judgment to abdicate to fashionable ideas.

Still, one cannot sell this strong-stomached generation short. Quite aside from the controversial pop art aspects of the theory and the patent dangers of dogma, it is clear that a whole generation is rediscovering the umbrella. It is not just apotheosizing the Strip. It is bringing back into building and vision a challenging richness and complexity that has been lost through the ritual purification of the modernists.

At present, as in all beginnings, the new doctrine is being pushed too hard to prove the point. In practice, it shows every sign of becoming a codified set of mannerisms. Its more arcane applications must be explained to the noninitiate, and that introduces the problem of the architect, like the artist, being reduced to talking to himself. Orthodox modernism could turn into orthodox ambiguity.

The very real promise, however, is of an architecture of *adaptation* and *accommodation*, two words that have been taboo in the modern movement. It would embrace existing contradictory realities, systems, and programs, the complexities and conflicts of modern life, the growth and changes in physical form, taste, and needs. It would, in a sense, roll with the punches.

Another, even gentler cultural guru of our time than Mr. Venturi, August Heckscher, has made the telling point that the doctrine of rationalism proves inadequate in times of upheaval. "Such inner peace as men gain must represent a tension among contradictions and uncertainties." This is true, say the rebels against orthodox modernism, of outer order, as well. The revolution is dead. Long live the revolution.

New York Times, January 26, 1969

Plastic Flowers Are Almost All Right

I DON'T KNOW IF CRITICS ARE ALLOWED to be ambivalent. We're supposed to have the answers. I am about to express some personal feelings and guarded opinions about the work and theory of Venturi and Rauch that are in large part favorable, due to my conditioning as an architectural historian.

First, I really can't see the uproar the Venturis are creating. The fuss that greeted Robert Venturi's *Complexity and Contradiction in Architecture* (Museum of Modern Art and Graham Foundation, 1966), the article "Learning from Las Vegas" with Denise Scott Brown, now his wife (*Architectural Forum*, March 1968), and is currently being repeated for the Venturi and Rauch exhibition at the Whitney Museum (through October 31) is probably due to three things.

Almost everything that the Venturis have to say is heresy, if you have been brought up as a true believer in modern architectural doctrine as formulated in the early part of this century. Everything Venturi and Rauch designs is a slap in the face of the true believers. And to use irony or wit in the pursuit of either theory or design—as a tool to shock awareness or as a comment on the cultural condition—is the unforgivable sin.

Architects will tell you this is not so—that they are just appalled by the Venturi brand of design. But then why go into such a rage? There is a lot of work around that people don't like. The answer is that architects do not build the way accountants add up figures; through education and inclination they design from a set of strong philosophical and aesthetic convictions, a polemical position, that has the highest place in their scheme of essential beliefs. Attack that, and you've got a religious war.

As a historian, I don't believe in religious wars. What is despised today was enshrined yesterday or will be tomorrow. I believe not only in complexity and contradiction but also in continuity and change. I do not share a good part of the modernist dogma of the modern architects whose work I admire most, at the same time that I recognize and respect its place in the development of modern architectural history. And I think the dogma of the recent past, in the light of the problems of the present, is doing the others in.

Guild House, Philadelphia

The modern architect is a hero figure who sets his buildings in shining isolation. He sees his job as showing a benighted populace, by terribly limited example, how "rational" and "tasteful" things should be. In this antienvironmental, antihistorical stance taught by the modern movement, the architect has become the man clients often cannot get a direct answer from because he is too busy being heroic and original, or the man contractors double their estimates for to take care of the problems of unconventional construction to serve those heroic and original designs.

Now that the "environment" has been rediscovered, it seems that the architect has never been there. Its mixed bag is not his bag at all. And because its mix is exactly what society is made of, the architect is looking more and more like a mastodon than a savior.

Which brings us back to the Venturis. The Venturis tell us that "the world can't wait for the architect to build his utopia, and the architect's concern ought not to be with what it ought to be but with what it is—and with how to help improve it now. This is a humbler role for architects than the modern movement has wanted to accept."

To play this role, the Venturis suggest that the architect meet the environment on its own terms, because it is there. And because it is there we might study it, including the despised highway strip and the subdivision, to see what works and why. Their two eyebrow-raising studies in this vein, done as studio exercises with Yale architecture students, are called "Learning from Las Vegas" and "Learning from Levittown."

I will go clearly on the record by saying that I think these studies are brilliant. There are the inevitable blind spots of the totally committed; the fast buck has shaped the scene as much as real need. The big sign often means the big deal. There are false values behind the false fronts. But complexity and paradox are the stuff of which the Venturis are made.

Their insight and analysis, reasoned back through the history of style and symbolism and forward to the recognition of a new kind of building that responds directly to speed, mobility, the superhighway, and changing lifestyles, is the kind of art history and theory that is rarely produced. The rapid evolution of modern architecture from Le Corbusier to Brazil to Miami to the roadside motel in a brief forty-year span, with all of the behavioral aesthetics involved, is something neither architect nor historian has deigned to notice. All that has been offered by either are diatribes against the end product.

The Venturis see much of pop art in this pop scene, and they admire both. This admiration extends to the full range of expediency and mediocrity with which America has housed and serviced itself while the architect looked the other way or for "enlightened" clients. The Venturis vie with each other in the acceptance of the commonplace. And because these are cheap and practical answers, they suggest we use them.

They use them. But with such an educated filtering to suit their own subtle and ironic "pop" tastes that perversity and paradox are the name of the game. When one outraged architect called their work "dumb and ordinary," they said that in a way he had exactly gotten the point and adopted the phrase themselves.

They have a gift for that kind of outrage. Not content to score the "personalized essay in civic monumentality," they add the ultimate insult, "It's a bore." With more-than-candor they point out that the renunciation of decoration has led the modern architect to so manipulate his "structural" forms that the entire building becomes a decoration. Then, with less-than-innocence, they draw an analogy between the building as decoration and symbol and the building in the shape of a duck on the highway. Furious, architects reply that the Parthenon is a duck, too.

The Venturis design "ducks" and "decorated sheds." To them, Main

Street "is almost all right." So is history, and it is not surprising that mannerism suits them best. They accord the dumb and ordinary the full seventeenth-century treatment. Piling paradox on paradox, they combine the obvious and the arcane. You can peel off the layers of meaning. Call it pop mannerism.

Guild House, a perfectly dumb and ordinary, and incidentally, very satisfactory, apartment house for the elderly in Philadelphia, is a mannerist exercise that uses blatant façadism and a perverse assortment of details that sets other architects' teeth on edge. Like all Venturi and Rauch buildings, it is intensely personal, idiosyncratic, and arbitrary, done in an intelligent but totally unsettling way. It is meant to make the educated viewer look twice, to see why the ordinary is extraordinary. Because never doubt it for a moment, the Venturis are determined to make it so.

The results are undeniably extraordinary, and many qualified judges think they are perfectly awful. I have a kind of love-hate relationship with Venturi designs, more for their ideological input, their profound comments on our culture, their intense and often angry wit, their consummate one-upmanship, than for their architectural quality. Yes, I am avoiding the issue of quality.

I suspect that the conscious application of theory always produces noble experiments and abysmal failures. If theory is valid, it usually leads to something else. The ultimate irony is that the cost of building today is making the dumb and ordinary inevitable. The prophecy is self-fulfilling. But this work is eye-opening and catalytic, and if my response is complex and contradictory, so are the Venturis, and life and art.

New York Times, October 10, 1971

The Venturi Antistyle

The ALLEN MEMORIAL ART MUSEUM at Oberlin College, a Renaissance palazzo out of Brunelleschi by way of Cass Gilbert and the Beaux Arts (1915–17), is a gem of a building for a gem of a collection. It has turned a small Ohio town into an extraordinary place.

When the museum needed to expand, the architectural assignment posed a special challenge. A perfectly cut and polished Cass Gilbert building is a hard act to follow. Robert Venturi, of the firm of Venturi, Rauch and Scott Brown, which was given the job, compares it to "drawing a moustache on a madonna. A wing on a symmetrical Renaissance villa, like a bowler hat on a Venus, will never look correct." Having thus succinctly stated the problem, he proceeded to solve it.

The solution is anything but standard. The work he has done with his wife, Denise Scott Brown, on the iconography of the Las Vegas strip and Levittown has made him the apostle of complexity and contradiction and the dumb and ordinary, in one or another combination, and the conscious practitioner of plain and fancy symbolism. But the image of the architect as a pop guru is actually a cliché that serves him badly, and perhaps this building can help set the record straight. The result, in fact, is urbane, cultured, deeply responsive to history and art, and unusually understanding of existing values—a solution of sophisticated, subtle, sympathetic, and sometimes wry sensibility.

The new museum wing is only a shocker to those with predetermined ideas of how such a wing should be designed or look. To anyone who examines it carefully, a thoughtful logic unfolds. It is not a statement of dogma or doctrine, although enough of that can be dragged in by the feet to make an interesting argument. The new building has been designed, above all, with a concerned and gentle hand. The solution is unconventional enough, however, to have raised a few hackles on campus where the Allen Museum is something of an icon, and to fuel the legend of Venturian perversity.

The new wing is a stepped-back block that joins the Cass Gilbert building at the side and rear. It connects directly to it without the kind of separating link that is considered a properly respectful signal of transition from old to new. It makes no obeisances to the original structure by repeating patterns of arcades or windows in "updated" versions. It jogs back on the site unevenly. It does nothing expected or obvious.

The façade closest to the old building is a "checkerboard" of rose and cream sandstone with strip windows; the design becomes a "pure" thirties loft building as it sets back once again and changes functions from a gallery to school and laboratory. And although there are "reasons" for all of this—the kind of aesthetic and symbolic rationale for a Venturian philosophical exercise that can be both edifying and fun—everything works in purely architectural terms. The solution is successful in the justness and appropriateness of its visual, functional, and programmatic relationships, which is the test of good architecture at any time. Taste and judgment are the eternal elite verities that do the job.

Quite properly, use and a restricted site have determined the plan. This led to butting the new construction against the old and placing it toward the back of the land to gain the most space and still keep the Cass Gilbert design dominant. The transitional element is a large new exhibition space, the Ellen Johnson Gallery of Modern Art. Set slightly behind this gallery, the rest of the new wing houses the art school and library and the labs of the Intermuseum Conservation Association. The addition is crisply contemporary; its "recalls" of the older building are, at best, artfully intellectual. A deep roof overhang only suggests the Italianate original; it is equally reminiscent of indigenous midwestern modernism. The checkerboard wall is almost like a patterned fabric background for the beautiful Renaissance decoration of the Cass Gilbert design in the same rose and cream stone. Asymmetrical windows stop carefully short of the classical structure.

The new building makes a point of its respect for the old one and its conscious lack of pretentiousness. The meticulously detailed strip windows and plain buff brick of the school and lab section deliberately suggest a very classy loft building. It is exactly the kind of building that suits working artists best. Inside, the new modern art gallery is a large, almost square room, sixty-one by fifty-five feet and twenty-three feet high. But this is not the average museum director's neutral, flexible container with all-purpose modular lighting and panels. It is an extremely dramatic space flooded with daylight, which holds contemporary art beautifully. The gallery insists on being architecture at the same time that it serves as a setting, and in doing so, it enhances the total aesthetic experience.

The daylight comes from high windows that run around the top of the room, controlled by the roof overhang and translucent Plexiglas panels that also screen out harmful rays. Outside, at a point between the new gallery and the enchanting Renaissance courtyard of the old, there is a typical Venturi touch—a symbol-sculpture of a giant Ionic column at trompe l'oeil scale. It has been made by applying stylized wood forms to a structural column.

The new gallery restates the main space of the Cass Gilbert building, a superb, classical sculpture court thirty-six feet high. The firm's work in the old building includes the installations of new lighting, air-conditioning, and security systems, new graphics and paint colors, and the "rehabilitation" of spaces for print and drawing collections.

In this undertaking, as in all their work, the Venturis stress the need to follow simple and familiar models. What is not spelled out in their eclectic rule book, however, is how purpose becomes style, and that, rather than iconographic gamesmanship, is the prime lesson of the past If this kind of architecture is "antistyle," then the Venturis have made the most of it.

New York Times, January 30, 1977

Michael Graves's Personal Language

A 1979 EXHIBITION OF WORK BY MICHAEL GRAVES at the Max Protetch Gallery documented some of the most significant changes going on in the art of architecture today. A charter member of a loosely allied group of younger practitioners of quite wide diversity who have become known as postmodernists, Graves has moved from an intricately mannered modernism to a romantic historicism of equally complex artfulness.

Graves's ideas were effectively exposed in this exhibition, which consisted of fully developed schemes from intimate early sketches to detailed renderings and models, plus a selection of photographs of completed work, a sampling of sketchbooks, and the mural-size abstract paintings that he executed both for his buildings and for his own continuing exploration of color and form. Graves's painting and architecture stand on their own merits. In fact, one of the distinctive characteristics of his work is that the two arts partake of each other's nature in a way that adds a dimension to each that neither would have had without such interaction. This is, in effect, a hybrid art, exploring new architectural horizons.

Graves has built some houses and parts of houses in New Jersey and Indiana (he came from Indianapolis by way of Harvard and is currently based in Princeton) and is engaged in the design of some larger and more important buildings. One of his most interesting projects was for the Fargo-Moorhead Cultural Center, a remarkable concept that would have joined North Dakota and Minnesota in a single structure spanning the Red River. This powerful, poetic Ledoux-like design shattered a lot of ideas about what such a building, or any building, should be like. Even without that distinction, it is probably one of the most beautiful architectural drawings of recent times. The Fargo-Moorhead Center appears to have aborted before construction, but an equally controversial structure, the Portland Public Service Building of Portland, Oregon, a competition-winning project, has been completed, to the noticeable disappointment of some of its more ardent champions, who hailed the design as the postmodern beacon of the eighties. There have apparently been enough crippling economies to make the building less than a perfect exemplar of Graves's intentions.

This is the sort of work that sends the viewer away with the sense that some kind of breakthrough is being made, and that the art of architecture has been moved a step farther along its creative and historical path. A departure of this sort, arrived at gradually over the years in Graves's case, can lead to a dramatic expansion of design possibilities or to an overemphasis on surface effects. It will shock and puzzle anyone grown comfortable with the "tradition" of modernism. Radical change that readjusts vision and meaning this deeply ruptures easy understanding and carries enormous risks.

A Michael Graves façade may look like a pastiche of building parts, or a kind of jigsaw of trompe l'oeil materials and historical references. But traditional elements are never copied directly; they are filtered

through the interpretations and reinterpretations of centuries of changing vision and culture, to be recombined in an intensely personal and
abstract way. They can be wrenched out of context, like the removal of
the keystone of an arch from the entrance of a house, to have the form
reappear as another part of the structure. These buildings are like films
that use flashbacks and events seen through many eyes to tell a story of
ambiguous and multifaceted meanings. Graves speaks of his "diaries
and sketchbooks of remembered things," of sources that range from antiquity to the International Style. But the details that he records are
treated more as inspirational archetypes; he seeks the essence of walls,
doors, and rooms, the way in which style and association shape our
sense of being and place.

On the most universal level, this is an architecture that is meant to
create perceptions of special relationships between the worlds of man
and nature. In Graves's eyes, the windowed interiors of a painting by
Mantegna and the ceremonial doors and windows of a house by Palladio both reveal the "event" of the opening to the outside world in a very
special way—an event that only architecture can properly celebrate.

Graves's early designs were tortuously preoccupied with the mannerisms of twenties' international modernism. Their thin screen walls
lapped and overlapped and were embellished with a geometric fanfare
of railings, stairs, and balconies. The work was so packed with ideas and
effects that its intricacy verged on hysteria. Even so, Graves was always
in control. Unfortunately, it was just this complexity for its own sake
that younger architects chose to emulate.

But above all, Graves is a colorist. His sense of color is elegant and
subtle and an integral part of his art. Those early "white" houses that
were so well publicized were not meant to be left unpainted. Graves
uses what he calls "representational" color, keyed to nature and the environment, with base tones in dark green or terra-cotta to suggest ground
or brick, and blue tones above for sky. The polychromed wall always has
a specific set of references.

It is important that all of these references, from color to metaphor
and historical recall, serve a larger, unifying idea. Otherwise Graves's
work would be no more than disruptive surface embellishment—
something it skirts dangerously. What keeps it from being just "bits and
pieces" eclecticism is the aesthetic intelligence that digests and transforms the sources into a consistent and unified language of design.

Every age has its architectural vocabulary, based on its particular articles of faith. All architects build with such a set of principles, whether they invent them—as Graves does—or inherit them as received wisdom, such as the functional and structural determinism of modernist doctrine. That is how style evolves. Graves's architecture goes considerably beyond the borrowings from the past that are being thrown around like so much loose change today for a "historicism" that is no more than shorthand caricature. He is slowly, painstakingly, and lovingly resolving a different language of form and meaning, taking us into a realm of architecture where we have not been before.

If he has left some of the highly publicized decorative gropings of postmodernism behind, however, he must still demonstrate more than pictorial skills. The transformation of Graves's subtle and painterly collages of ideas, references, textures, and colors to important three-dimensional buildings is something one awaits with a mixture of hope and fear. The drawings are such elegant artifacts in themselves. But something happens in the translation from the picture plane to the real world, and the executed works simply do not read the same way that they do on paper; the intriguing aesthetic intelligence can turn into an architecture that is fussy, flat, obvious, or obscure. Graves's fully developed ideas have great subtlety and power, originality and elegance. Above all, they are expressed in a language of forms, colors, and details that are distinctly his own—a point of no small importance in a day when an identifiable style is the first step to recognition and reputation. How successful this stylistic language is as architecture is still an open debate; judgment can be made only on the basis of the completion of at least one major uncompromised work.

New York Times, May 17, 1979

The Austere World of Rossi

In 1976, the Italian architect Aldo Rossi created one of the most compelling images in architecture today with his competition-winning design for the Modena Cemetery. A rigidly rectangular space was surrounded by an endless, wall-like structure in which the architectural components were reduced to an elemental simplicity; repeated voids of blank, empty windows suggested a place from which all life had fled forever. Once seen, the project is unforgettable. Its spare, surreal geometry invokes a haunting and timeless symbolism of death and the eternal with an extraordinary intensity, far beyond architecture's more usual effects. In avant-garde circles, the Modena Cemetery achieved instant status as an almost legendary work of art.

This is so strong a design, in fact, that its influence has spread through architectural schools here and abroad; Rossi's work is much imitated by the young. Not only is his austerely reductive style immediately recognizable; it also seems to call forth a universal set of emotional responses. There is a distinct "Rossi world." Entering that world through his projects and drawings—there are only a few executed works—is like going through the looking glass, leaving reality behind for something that transcends it. One finds his vision incorporated into one's own experience, imposed on a landscape that will never be innocent of it again.

Whether Mr. Rossi's world is art or architecture or a purely visionary excursion into private terrain, whether it is a structural, political, philosophical, or poetic act, is the subject of much debate. But he has a way of attracting the kind of arcane critical comment that makes his work seem simple and open by contrast.

There is an unusual opportunity to judge for oneself right now, with two Rossi exhibitions running concurrently in New York through October 13. Aldo Rossi: Architectural Projects, at the Max Protetch Gallery (37 West Fifty-seventh Street), covers his built work and projects; Aldo Rossi in America: 1976–79, at the Institute for Architecture and Urban Studies (8 West Fortieth Street), is devoted to a series of drawings made on recent trips to the United States. This Rossi explosion is not surprising; he has been a much-admired figure in Europe since the sixties.

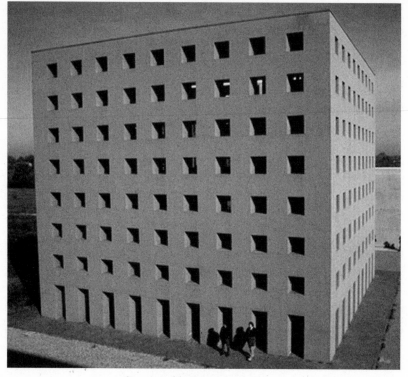

San Cataldo Cemetery, Modena

The concentrated showing reinforces the uniqueness of his product, but it does not make it any easier to categorize it within conventional definitions.

I am not sure that comprehension is aided by the two handsome catalogs that accompany the shows. One, with an essay by Peter Eisenman and a statement by Mr. Rossi, is being published by the Institute for Architecture and Urban Studies as part of its excellent Oppositions series. The other, a Centro Di catalog edited by Francesco Moschini, with an English translation from the Italian, is being distributed by Rizzoli in this country. Both are daunting flights of erudition and interpretation.

MR. ROSSI HIMSELF expresses surprise about the views of his work offered by the critics. His candid eyes widen with wonder at the theories propounded. But his work invites this kind of exercise. That wise-child

gaze suggests as much of an inward vision as an eye attuned to the
world around him. After all, how does one explain a style that combines
a concentration camp imagery of cell blocks and towers with lyrical
touches of striped cabanas and flying pennants that keep recurring in
his drawings like elements in a dream? You know that Mr. Rossi does
not see these stripped, unrelieved barracks of buildings in anything re-
sembling either human or inhuman terms; he is quite surprised at the
suggestion that this might not be an architecture of joy, or that its forms
related tenuously or arbitrarily to its programs.

For him, this insistence on what turns out to be a subtly sinister and
highly suggestive vocabulary is the elimination of "easy art" (for which,
I suppose, read "bourgeois art") for a "true art" reduced to the basic essentials of form (currently called "rationalist" architecture). What is important is that these forms then take on an overwhelming visual life of
their own.

Much has been made of Mr. Rossi's apparent preoccupation with
death, and of his connection with Marxist politics. For Marxists, architecture has lost all public meaning; its only role is a destructive or ni-
hilist one. To those practicing architects who still believe that building
is a positive, creative, and problem-solving necessity, this makes Mr.
Rossi not an architect at all.

And they are not all wrong, by conventional yardsticks of successful
design. When Mr. Rossi builds, the results are remarkably unsettling. I
cannot imagine putting children in his Elementary School of Fagnano
Olona in Lombardy. Its images are absolutely memorable, from its
crematorium-like chimney to the round, baptistry-like "common classroom and library" pierced by a few strategic openings, placed precisely
in a small, walled courtyard. Meticulously minimal, these are unbelievably eloquent forms, and they are not without echoes in some of the
bleaker Italian landscapes.

Mr. Rossi sees the design as a pleasant microcosm of the town square
in the city; to others, it looks more like a jail or gas chamber. In photographs, however, the *poverini* who are committed to it look cheerful
enough, and Mr. Rossi expresses a considerable affection for the ambience he creates. It is clear that it is totally that "life of their own" of
these forms, however, that concerns him. Such insistent minimalism,
repeated without variation, makes his housing in Milan look like a pen-
itentiary. But it also carries the impressive surreal impact of a Di

Chirico painting. Mr. Rossi's understanding and manipulation of basic geometry for its emotional content is particularly skilled. If nothing else, it is great for monuments and cemeteries.

What interests Mr. Rossi increasingly now is the series of drawings that he calls Analogues of the City. I think I know what he means, but I do not have the space, or desire, or competence to explain it here. It is safe to say that these are essentially drawn and painted collages of elements stored in Mr. Rossi's mind, all of which relate to his impressions of various cities and landscapes. An extremely thoughtful analysis of these "analogues" will be found in Peter Eisenman's essay, which is equally full of penetrating insights and impenetrable prose. In fairness, these are not easy ideas to express, but neither is it unfair to say that the life of the mind does occasionally seem to get carried away with itself. And Mr. Rossi does not make it any easier by saying that "the idea of analogy can never be fully possessed by the conscious and rational mind." If he means that these juxtapositions and relationships are made as much by instinct and unconscious memory and conditioning as by calculated intent, that seems obvious. And so is the outpouring of interpretations that this makes possible.

Without apologies, then, I offer some superficial responses that at least have the merit of comprehensibility to those who read and run. Certain objects appear in Mr. Rossi's work repeatedly—towers, chimneys, arcades, trusses, small, discrete structures like baptistries or farm buildings, the upraised arm of a saint from a baroque statue, a giant coffeepot, palm trees, long, arcaded structures, often on stilts, those boxlike bathhouses and banners—all seen as a set of special images that have burned their shapes into Mr. Rossi's mind at some point in his life. The palm trees, for example, are from Spain; the bathhouses are from Elba. Many complex explanations are offered for these choices and their meanings. Mr. Rossi's own explanation is much more direct. "These are the things that I remember, that I have seen in my travels, that have stayed with me. These are things that I like and use over and over again."

It is the way in which he uses them, however—obsessively, lyrically, evocatively—that ultimately makes it possible to define his work. Mr. Rossi is a poet who happens to be an architect. He is making poetry out of visual devices, much as a writer employs literary or aural devices. In his case, the uses of the eye parallel the uses of the ear. As words become symbols, so do objects; the architectural world is an endless source of symbols with unique ramifications in time and space. Architecture has given Mr. Rossi his poetic and artistic vocabulary. And now, to hear him tell it, he is ready to move on from architecture to another medium; he wants to work with film.

Peter Eisenman says "explaining a poet isn't simple," and of course, he is right. Particularly when architecture is a means to a nonarchitectural or supra-architectural end. It is the power of Mr. Rossi's poetic images that explains his fascination for students, and why they copy his work without understanding his sources. It is why flights of interpretive rhetoric accompany all of his drawings and projects. And it is how the boundaries of art continue to expand.

New York Times, October 7, 1979

John Hejduk—a Mystic and Poet

ARCHITECTURE EXHIBITIONS SEEM TO COME IN pairs these days. Last week saw the opening of two shows of the work of John Hejduk, at the Institute for Architecture and Urban Studies (8 West Fortieth Street) and the Max Protetch Gallery (37 West 57th Street), both to run through February 16. The institute's exhibition, called John Hejduk: Seven Houses, consists of a painstaking, abstract investigation of the elements underlying architectural form, carried out in a series of house studies made over a period of nine years, from 1954 to 1963. The show at the Protetch Gallery, The Works of John Hejduk, deals with later projects, of the sixties and seventies, in a totally different vein—these are intensely personal, visionary, and poetic schemes where architectural forms are primarily vehicles of mystery and metaphor—frightening fairy tales for the malaise of our times.

The two shows, and the two themes, could not be more appropriate; since they illustrate two sides of a very complex man. Nor are these two sides of vision mutually exclusive—any more than night and day are not part of the same quotidian cycle—a theme of contrasts that he likes and has explored, incidentally, in a scheme for a "day and night" house. There is a good deal of crossing over between these poles of expression.

Mr. Hejduk is equally concerned with vast mysteries and the most impeccably calculated structural details. He spent those nine years on the seven-house project (done with the help of a Graham Foundation grant while he was teaching at the University of Texas in Austin) working on the reduction of a basic architectural object to its most absolute elements. The houses are composed of nine squares, with infinite analysis of how columns, piers, walls, and panels create related enclosures within an ideal symmetry, carried to the point where he succeeds in demonstrating how complex the search for basics can become. It was a nine-year, one-man investigation of the architectural generators of form. This requires a mind of Euclidian curiosity and the patience of a saint; Mr. Hejduk has both.

It is clear from these meticulous drawings that he is in love with the art of architecture and filled with awe and admiration for those who have raised it to its highest level. There are echoes, in these house studies, of the villas of Palladio and Le Corbusier; there is homage to Mies.

IT IS ALSO clear that he is a mystic and a poet. There are suggestions of everything from the solemn fears learned during a Bronx Catholic childhood to the discovery of the suave beauties of the Italian landscape encountered during a Fulbright year abroad. He has become best known for his poetic fantasies—architectural metaphors and morality tales with titles like "Silent Witnesses" and "Cemetery for the Ashes of Thought," and for the lyrical drawings and paintings that express these ideas.

But what is not too well understood is that he is a fine architect, very much overpublicized as a dreamer, and underpublicized—and undercommissioned—as a builder. As head of the Cooper Union School of Architecture in New York, he remodeled, with Peter Bruder and Ed Aviles, the historic Cooper Union building, displaying great skill in the creation of new spaces within a landmark structure. It is a restoration and conversion of unusual elegance and style.

To further point up the dichotomy of his work, the house exercises at the institute are precise line drawings in black and white, or more correctly, in shades of gray, executed completely in extremely fine, hard pencils. These detailed explorations of the language of architecture are technically exquisite—it would be hard to find a roomful of more beautiful architectural renderings.

The work at the Protetch Gallery is free, fanciful, executed in a variety of media and full of color. These colors are so lovely and lighthearted that they are like candy coatings on timeless themes of infinity and dread. Picture thirteen tall, close-ranked towers on a bare Venetian plaza, containing thirteen men condemned to dwell in them for a lifetime, with one house for another dweller who will take the place of the first man who dies. And then imagine, on another solitary square, "the house of the inhabitant who refused to participate," where the functions of living are reduced to a punitive simplicity, exposed to the gaze of strangers, in an obscure symbolic world somewhere between the eye and the mind. This is a series called "The Thirteen Watchtowers of Cannaregio." A script provides the explanation, but the images have a life of their own.

The Institute for Architecture and Urban Studies has produced a handsome catalog for the Seven Houses and is also issuing a limited edition of a group of Mr. Hejduk's poems with the same name as one of his architectural parables, "Silent Witnesses." The catalog has an admirable introduction by Peter Eisenman, although the detailed discussions of the house designs will be hard going for all but the most architecturally knowlegeable.

One statement by Mr. Eisenman sums up this work superbly; he characterizes Mr. Hejduk's house studies as "a synthesis of abstraction and reality [using] a reduced vernacular of the 20th century in the 16th-century manner." He points out that this rational simplicity "contains a conceptual overload, a density and compaction of themes." It is evident that when Mr. Eisenman says that these designs "articulate an intrinsic architectural language," dealing as they do in a basic geometry of space and form, he means it as an object lesson to those who are busy today articulating such things as decorative detail or historical recall.

There are also some interesting statements by Mr. Hejduk in the catalog. One refers directly to the period of the Texas house project, and its observations and sentiments are a delightful indicator of his particular sensibilities.

"In 1954 . . . I returned from the landscape of Italy to that of the hill country of central Texas . . . The landscape of Texas is sparse; objects take on a clarity and remoteness."

"There is a magic moment in the fall after weeks of intense dry heat when the Blue Northern comes down across the northeast plains. Temperatures drop 50 degrees within minutes and the air becomes cool and crystal clear; the shadows deepen. It is also a time when you can run after armadillos."

"Now, armadillos appear to be hard, but in fact they are soft and they shed tears when you catch them by the tail; so you let them go."

"There are a lot of things you let go of in Texas. You let go of old visions and old romances, you let go of city-states and northern broodings. But, in letting go, other things and other moods are captured, such as the meaning of isolated objects, of void spaces. You capture the horizontal and you capture a flatness, a flatness which impregnates your thoughts and fills you with an anticipation—an anticipation of the solemnity of detail and of construction."

The Texas house studies are solemn, isolated objects created in precise structural detail. They have severe limitations, the result of formal restrictions that are scrupulously self-imposed. But in their response to a special time and place, and their total preoccupation with the genesis of form, they represent that part of architecture that transcends practical reality. Still, Mr. Hejduk is not a bad man with practical reality, either, as he demonstrated at Cooper Union. What he needs now are not silent witnesses but active clients, interested in the kind of vision that transforms structure into art.

New York Times, February 3, 1980

Philip Johnson: Clever Tricks or True Art?

FEW NEW YORK BUILDINGS HAVE CREATED the furor that has greeted the announcement of the new AT&T headquarters to be constructed on Madison Avenue between Thirty-fifth and Thirty-sixth streets. But the controversy about the 645-foot-high skyscraper that will join Citicorp and the soon-to-be-built neighboring IBM building as the spectacular new landmarks of the midtown skyline is not the usual outcry of the lay public protesting the mysteries of modernism, a style it has never learned to love. The consternation about the Johnson/Burgee design, with Harry Simmons as associate architect, ranges from public puzzlement to serious professional concern. Many observers are simply protesting what seems to be a monumental architectural leg-pull (that huge broken pediment at the top and the quips about the first Chippendale skyscraper), while architects and planners are in an uproar over the nature of the design and its potential urban impact.

Clearly, it is not a joke, whatever jokes are being made. A building of this importance, size, and cost—AT&T says it will cost "more than" $110 million—is serious art and business. Nothing will be spared in the quality of its execution. A new AT&T headquarters is a significant addition to New York in both corporate and architectural terms, and it is a building that the city very much needs and wants. Above all, the architect is genuinely committed to the design that has been variously described as a curiosity, an aberration, an outrage, an act of aesthetic courage or a failure of inspiration, and finally, a "postmodern" architectural breakthrough.

It is impossible to write about this building without mixed feelings. One cannot fault the impulse behind the design: to create a memorable structure that could perform the notable feat of being on the cutting edge of new architectural theories and still possess the dignity and solidity desired by a corporate client of massive means and size and monolithically conservative character.

THIS IS A high-wire act, and as usual Philip Johnson is a star performer. His instinct, a familiar one, is *épater le bourgeoisie*; he balances calculated shock value with superlative quality. He designs with brilliance, if

The AT&T Building

you equate that condition with extreme intellectual vivacity and curiosity, sophisticated historical recall, and impeccable aesthetic response.
These are remarkable qualities, by any measure. But I am not sure that
this arsenal of sensitivities quite adds up to the production of architecture. At least, not here. It has done so in the recent past, in two other
corporate towers of different approach and style. Pennzoil in Houston
and IDS in Minneapolis. But this building is a monumental demonstration of quixotic aesthetic intelligence rather than of art.

In the design for AT&T, Mr. Johnson is the first to use a major structure to demonstrate a currently fashionable attitude toward architecture. We are in a new, permissive era, in which all the strictures of modernism are being questioned and the lessons or forms of the past are no longer taboo. This exploration of forbidden sources is a course that was pursued as early as the fifties by Mr. Johnson, who has always been an admirer of his historical peers. But there is a new twist today in the deliberate distortion of historical scale and intent, which bears a curious parallel to the offbeat vision of pop art. A kind of artful scavenging approaches the capricious in the pursuit of sensory effect.

What Mr. Johnson has produced, from that pop pediment on down, is a pastiche of historical references and evocative spatial experiences drawn from his admiration of bits and pieces of earlier monuments, blown up gigantically in unconventional and unsettling relationships. This goes under the rubric of the new eclecticism—a kind of intellectual-aesthetic derring-do or game-playing with history, in which the more arcane the borrowings of design elements, and the more perverse their combination, the more provocative and progressive the result is considered to be. The outcry may well be because both the knowing and the naive suspect an architectural rabbit punch.

THIS KIND OF exotic exercise might work in the hands of the exceptionally gifted, but then, almost anything can. However, it requires a great deal more creative synthesis than is apparent here for the necessary transformation to a new level of expression that makes the result art instead of dilettantism. (That last word is used in its original sense of a knowledgable lover of the arts, without the later connotations of superficiality.)

Mr. Johnson has gone back to the classical principles of skyscraper design in its early years, dividing the tower into base, shaft, and capital, as opposed to the uniformly treated container of today. The bottom of the building is to be a 131-foot-high masonry base of rose-gray granite, opened only by ground-floor arcades. On the Madison Avenue front, this arcade will be heroic: a 110-foot-high central arch and six sixty-foot openings: on the side streets the openings will be reduced to twenty feet, with oculus apertures above. The "Palladian" return of a smaller unit on the front serves to anchor the corners. Renaissance and classical models suggest themselves from Bramante to Boullée.

The entire ground floor is to be open, except for a central glass-enclosed section that will provide access to the building's corporate entrance, placed the equivalent of five stories above. The sixty-foot-high ground-floor space is a hypostyle hall of five-foot-square columns. Behind this open, colonnaded area is a glass-roofed passage from Fifty-fifth to Fifty-sixth streets, at the back of the building, which will be flanked by a limited amount of retail space and an entrance to an AT&T multimedia exhibit on the floor above.

As designed, this "public" ground floor is austerely formal; it offers some awe-inspiring architectural vistas and diagonal shortcuts to side streets. The AT&T Building does not relate to nor recall the style or substance of its luxury shopping-street surroundings. It is clearly an architectural and corporate statement in search of a Park Avenue site. But it is just as clearly the statement that everyone connected with the building wants to make, anywhere at all.

Once constructed, the building will be far more impressive than it is on paper because of its immense size. What seems trivial in concept will become monumental in actuality. An arcade is no longer banal when it is fifty feet high; an arched entrance is imperially grand when it soars more than one hundred feet from the street. A façade that seems weak and irresolute, in spite of meticulous adjustments, at the scale of a drawing or model, will reveal handsome surface details that are not apparent now. The pedestrian will experience only the grandeur of that massive masonry base and arcade, and the large rhythms of the colonnaded ground floor. The pediment will be an identifying symbol for the company and the architect. But the building's impact will not come from the creative power or stylistic integration of its design.

Again, there is nothing really wrong with any of these design premises. But the Chrysler Building realizes the oddball top much better, with a suave, romantic form that successfully combines architecture, sculpture, and elegant ornament, rather than with quick-and-easy eclecticism or an architectural one-liner. And the classical base-shaft-capital organization of the skyscraper was defined far more creatively and convincingly by Louis Sullivan and some of his fellow members of the Chicago School.

Still other devices are demonstrably the singular aesthetic choice of the architect. Since the building consists of completely conventional floors with core and perimeter columns, the structural load could be supported in other ways than on that forest of templelike columns that appears suddenly on the ground. The desire for a massive colonnaded space has clearly been its own generator.

The remaining and overriding question is how these design choices relate to the city's zoning regulations and intent. At present, they do not, to any convincing degree.

By all zoning logic, since AT&T is on a smaller plot than IBM on the next block, regulations affecting the amounts of ground coverage and floor space in relation to the size of the site should result in a smaller structure for AT&T. But the architectural alchemy that sends AT&T shooting up to meet IBM and makes it taller than the city's planners ever intended includes starting the building's floors five stories above ground, using higher-than-average ceilings and several service floors, and adding that broken pediment top, which conceals mechanical equipment. There are only thirty-seven floors in the building's 645 feet, which would normally accommodate a sixty-story tower. AT&T has thus achieved its height without unduly increasing its permitted square footage.

NOT THAT THESE features are necessarily undesirable; high ceilings are very nice, and so are generous public spaces. But the building still has not earned its zoning "brownie points," to quote Mr. Johnson, for the bulk it proposes, by the inclusion of enough pedestrian amenities (seats, trees, shops, and services in arcaded through-block passages) to provide the "bonuses" that permit the increased size. Either AT&T will have to redesign to include more public features, or it will have to cut down on its square footage.

In any case, the building will need special legislation from the Planning Commission or permission from the Board of Standards and Appeals to waive existing height and setback regulations, in order to place the structure at the street line as proposed, instead of moving it back on its lot. In exchange for that waiver, the city can ask for design revisions. But no special legislation should be part of the negotiations that would increase the structure's legal size ratio to its lot.

The architects are already sketching movable tables and chairs where there were fewer, fixed benches, and there is discussion about lighting and shopping kiosks. Accommodations can obviously be made. None of this will transform the building into something else, but the process of adjustment may make it a great deal more agreeable from the point of view of the pedestrian and the street.

We will defend to the death Mr. Johnson's right to design whatever kind of building he chooses for the demonstration of his talent, erudition, and skill, as long as it makes appropriate connections and concessions to the city's legal requirements and urban objectives. If it turns out to be an Egyptian temple cum baroque skyscraper, or the Rolls-Royce of postmodernism, so be it. Those unpredictable odds make horse racing and architecture the sports of kings.

New York Times, April 16, 1978

The Man Who Loved Architecture

PHILIP JOHNSON USED TO SAY THAT WHAT he really wanted to be was *l'architecte du roi*, the king's architect. That was after his ideological fling with the Nazis (Hitler already had his architect, Albert Speer), and before he became the architect of choice of big business. As with so many of the outrageous statements he delighted in making, he meant it. The ancien régime would have suited him well; a man of great elegance, impeccable taste, a brilliant mind, and quick wit, fascinated by the levers of power, and delighted by intrigue, he would have played the courtly game with relish and consummate skill.

Whether the system was monarchy, fascism, or corporate capitalism was really irrelevant; neither politics nor morality was ever the issue. Kings, popes, dictators, and captains of industry made better patrons than democratic societies. He would have endorsed any regime or client that made it possible to carry out artistically ambitious projects on a monumental scale for a vision unhampered by restrictions of money, existing conditions, or social concerns. For Philip Johnson, the aesthetic was primary; art, and particularly the art of architecture, trumped everything else.

His death last month at the age of ninety-eight has been called the end of an era. How important an architect he was, and how much of a *force majeure* in the art of his time, will be subject to revision by later generations. But his passing marked the end of a singular presence, of a connoisseur and taste maker for whom the awareness, understanding, and appreciation of architecture was his central concern for almost a century of radical change that he prodded, endorsed, and often initiated.

Lacking a royal patron, he created the position and the role of *l'architecte du roi* for himself, holding court, dispensing favors, creating reputations, masterminding moves in careers and construction, building prominently and expensively for wealthy and corporate clients — and, above all, decreeing the next big thing. He devoted his mercurial intelligence to finding and promoting architecture's leading edge and its most talented practitioners; he sought the latest, the most exciting, and the most provocative styles and movements of the twentieth century. He perceived excellence instantly and had a faultless eye. The quest for the constantly new was driven by a lightning-quick mind and short attention span for anything that failed to interest him, the fear of boredom, and an insatiable need for intellectual stimulation. Ideas and people were adopted or dismissed at will — *l'architecte du roi, il s'amusait.*

When he tired of modernism in the fifties, he led the charge into postmodernism, embracing every novelty and exploring its most transient and trendy aspects, a move that took his most ardent supporters and converts to modernism by surprise. As the founder and longtime head of the Museum of Modern Art's pioneering Department of Architecture and Design, Johnson had introduced modernism to America as the International Style in the now landmark 1932 exhibition done in collaboration with the historian Henry-Russell Hitchcock. His mentor and idol for many years, the modern movement's austere and elegant master, Mies van der Rohe, once famously said that you can't invent a new architecture every Monday morning, but that would have suited Philip Johnson's restless mind perfectly. Those of us who worked for him, as I did, in my first job as his assistant curator at the Museum of Modern Art, were charged with finding a new "ism" weekly.

He collaborated with Mies on New York's finest modern skyscraper, the Seagram Building, before embarking on a series of big buildings of his own that followed the lead of the talented young architects he courted, encouraged, and commissioned in a process of patronage and exploitation that kept him creatively alive, borrowing shamelessly from their work for the hedonistic dilettantism that became his personal style. He was extremely generous with friendship, admiration, and the advancement of their careers, and they were intensely grateful.

The favored became an exclusive club, or not-so-secret society, or conspiring cabal, depending on your point of view, who met at Johnson's notorious and exclusionary Century Club dinners where they settled the future of architecture and the built world. What gave him particular pleasure was the manipulation of complex relationships and dependencies to control how the art of architecture was used where he thought it mattered most. With the right friends in high places and deep reserves of indebtedness to draw on, this was seen by some as a sinister network of trade-offs and privileges and by others as a welcome route to jobs and recognition.

Philip Johnson's legendary and persuasive charm was a prime tool in his arsenal of power. It served him well when it came time to confess his mistakes or reveal his secrets, which he did with appealing and calculated candor. His infatuation with Nazi Germany was excused publicly as youthful folly; his homosexuality was spoken of openly when it could be received sympathetically; even the fact that he couldn't draw was acknowledged and demonstrated disarmingly as he made sweeping marks on rolls of yellow tracing paper, tearing them off with panache and a brilliant running commentary.

But whatever the contradictions of a life designed to provoke and dazzle, Philip Johnson ceaselessly promoted architecture as the art that has shaped the great monuments and cities of history, and he sincerely believed that we owe the future a legacy of equal value. He led the march against the destruction of Pennsylvania Station and was quick to lend his prestige to any worthy architectural cause. He kept the subject of architecture on a front burner over a high flame, and if there was no excitement, he made it. He loved celebrity and controversy, but most of all, he loved being the center of it.

Revisionism is already offering alternative views of his achievements. Having established modern architecture as the reality of contemporary life, he also reduced it to a set of rigid aesthetic rules stripped of its revolutionary social and technological meaning. The human and social aspects of architecture never interested him. He did not believe, as modernists held, that the world could be made better by architecture.

What he believed, without apologies to populism or political correctness, was that the world was a lesser place without art.

Which leaves us with the elephant in the room, his own architecture. He was so admiring and covetous of the gifts of those who could produce the transforming miracle of space and structure that he went back to school to get his architecture degree, setting up his practice with a series of experienced and ever-changing partners. An early sequence of semiclassical museums with decorative paste-on colonnades was followed by an eclectic parade of Gothic and Renaissance skyscrapers in mirror glass and brick; varieties of modernism, some distinctly better than others, came and went with his associates.

His fame made him the "signature architect" for corporate headquarters and commercial developers. The AT&T Building's much-publicized "Chippendale" top put him on the cover of *Time* magazine, cradling the model in his arms. But his nimble intelligence and excellent eye failed to produce more than a pictorial pastiche that was flat and one-dimensional or a shallow send-up of the past. What was meant to be monumental was merely big and flaccid.

His most successful buildings were small ones, the jewel-like pavilions of the exquisite museum in the gardens at Washington's Dumbarton Oaks, and his own, iconic glass house in Connecticut built on the Miesian model, although Mies himself remarked how un-Miesian it was in its details. The beauty and tranquility of these buildings speaks to all of the senses. But none of his esoteric knowledge could substitute for the multidimensional grasp of space and form and the strength and clarity with which the tensions and relationships of structure and style are expressed that are the architect's innate, creative genius.

Whatever Philip Johnson's legacy turns out to be, it will not rest on his buildings. His dedication to the art that was central to his existence, his proselytizing zeal for new work that pushes concept and practice beyond existing limits, his driving belief in architecture as the defining art of the present and the past, did much to reestablish a sense of the importance of the way we build in an age that worships the beauty of the bottom line. In his own way, perhaps he did change the world.

Wall Street Journal, February 10, 2005

Reflections on the Glass House

I HAVE BEEN AN OBSERVER AND PARTICIPANT in the history of Philip Johnson's Glass House during its entire, well-publicized life cycle, but I was unprepared for the overwhelming sense of loss I experienced when visiting recently while the house was being readied for its opening to the public as a National Trust property on June 23. Philip Johnson died in 2005, and his partner, David Whitney, in 2006, but the house and its forty-seven-acre complex of land and buildings in New Canaan, Connecticut, had already been willed in 1986 to the National Trust for Historic Preservation—a formidable challenge for an organization with a comfort zone somewhere between the eighteenth and nineteenth centuries.

The Glass House, of course, is a house like no other, an iconic landmark of twentieth-century modernism that played a vital role in the creative culture of its day. Although it possesses a singular fame of its own, it is not an isolated artifact; it is part of an intensely personal, unique collection of art and architecture in a meticulously landscaped setting: buildings Philip Johnson designed and constructed, and artworks acquired and installed over half a century, from the forties through the nineties.

This constantly growing and changing complex was the lifework of a man of keen intelligence and insatiable curiosity who cultivated all that was new, interesting, provocative, and entertaining in the art, intellectual, and social worlds. The first two buildings, the Glass House and the Brick House, both completed in 1949, were a counterpoint to each other—transparent and solid, open and closed, with a courtyard between. Additions soon followed: painting and sculpture galleries, a library and study, a diminutive lake pavilion, and assorted follies and delights. Each reflected Philip Johnson's fascination with someone or something at the time, or a riff on the latest thing. The entrance to his underground painting gallery was inspired by the archaic Greek Lion Gate at Mycenae. The multilevel, sky-lit sculpture gallery paid homage to the early work of the brilliant twentieth-century maverick English architect James Stirling.

All expressed the elegant, discerning, and idiosyncratic tastes of a man who did much to shape and define the arts of the twentieth century

Glass House

through his creative patronage and impeccable connoisseurship. In retrospect, what he built for his own pleasure not only mirrored his continuous eclectic search for aesthetic stimulation, but helped to validate the historical license of later postmodernism, a movement he joined enthusiastically. The Glass House was incubator and salon, a place where talent was fostered and conversation dazzled, where plots and parties and pure enchantment filled magic summer afternoons. Not exactly your historic house with hoopskirts.

In spite of a sense of full stop and finality to all that, and the haunting emptiness of the silent house and its plastic-shrouded furniture the day I visited, there was an air of excitement and anticipation as the staff dealt with structural repairs and fading memorabilia, juggled dates of opening festivities and trial-run tours, and prepared schedules of programs and activities far out into the future. Nor will the opening be less than gala. An inaugural picnic on the grounds will feature the restaging of a 1967 Merce Cunningham dance performance, with gourmet basket lunches and tours of the property.

My own tour was pure nostalgia. My first job was with Philip Johnson at the Museum of Modern Art when he was building the house,
and I have visited often over the years. I have watched the glass house
become the Glass House, as it settled into modernist history. The National Trust has only recently ventured seriously into the thorny terrain
of twentieth-century modernism—with properties like this one and
Mies van der Rohe's Farnsworth House in Piano, Illinois. Earlier National Trust acquisitions of twentieth-century houses by Frank Lloyd
Wright fit more easily into the model-house mode of appropriately furnished restored rooms with a few well-chosen personal accessories.

Christy MacLear, executive director of Philip Johnson's Glass House
for the National Trust, recognizes the unprecedented nature of the
project but finds it neither sad nor daunting. Ms. MacLear has had to
face two major challenges: how to keep something that was always on
the lively edge of the new from becoming a lifeless simulacrum, and
the even more difficult problem that goes straight to the heart of the
matter—how to deal with a period and a style for which no models exist and standards are only evolving at a time when the modernist architecture of the twentieth century is being rapidly and thoughtlessly
demolished. Obviously, the Glass House could not follow the formula
of a tastefully reinvented past. You can't reinvent Philip Johnson.

The solution has been to present the Glass House as more than a historic house, using it as a catalyst for the appreciation and preservation
of twentieth-century architecture, art, and landscape, much as Messrs.
Johnson and Whitney promoted those arts while they were alive.
Events at the house will focus on other modernist buildings and causes
as a way of addressing the current crisis in preservation and modernism.
An artist-in-residence program will stress the kind of creative design intended to carry on the two men's encouragement of new talent. There
will be no "authentic reproductions"—those genteel knockoffs and cer-
tified fakes that are the staples of museum and historic-house gift shops
everywhere. Since a gift shop is as de rigueur in a visitor's center as the
restrooms, it has been decreed that only commissioned, original products will be carried.

The question of where to put the visitor's center loomed large. Philip
Johnson's last building, completed in 1995 and affectionately known as
Da Monsta for its bold eccentricity (reflective of his admiration for the

architecture of Frank Gehry or the work of the artist Frank Stella, or both—take your pick), was built with that in mind, but its small, ski-slope interior seemed less suited to the rites of tourism than to a tipsy tearoom suggested by a couple of anticipatory tables and chairs. The wise decision was made to put the building off-site, eliminating arriving and departing buses and activities not conducive to a pastoral experience. The new visitor's center is in town, next to the railroad station, and tours, also wisely, will be limited to small groups.

To say the decisions that have been made about the meaning and message of the Glass House are sensitive and enlightened does not begin to do the process justice; this is an innovative and important preservation breakthrough arrived at after rigorous thought and study. Every aspect of the presentation has received the same careful attention. The Glass House's public image, known in marketing-speak as "branding" (yes, a lot of upscale marketing is involved), depends on the right graphics for all printed and visual matter, supplied by Pentagram Studios. The "visitors guide" is a handsome set of cards, each a superb photograph of a single feature with a description on the back. I suspect there was considerable discussion about the elimination of the apostrophe in "visitors." It would have been a snap decision for Philip Johnson.

Repairs were made, including a new roof, that were skipped as the two men grew older. There were works of art and furnishings that required restoration. Access for the handicapped has been provided as invisibly as possible, the routes carefully plotted and covered with grass to be indistinguishable from the setting. But some things remain undone.

Only a miracle can restore the painting that was as iconic as the house itself—Nicolas Poussin's *Burial of Phocion*, the seventeenth-century classical landscape on a freestanding easel that was central to the life and look of the house and backdrop to every conversation. Timeless in its beauty, it affirmed the enduring compatibility of great art and echoed the embracing seasons that Mr. Johnson called his "wallpaper."

I first knew the painting when it was on the wall of the office where I worked in Mr. Johnson's Architecture Department at MoMA; he had it hanging there temporarily while he built the house. It was an unforgettable part of my coming of age. When I saw it on my visit, it had become a heartbreaking, murky ruin, paint flaking, colors vanished, and figures barely discernible, destroyed by time, sunlight, and neglect. The house will live on, as Philip Johnson intended, but some things are gone forever.

Wall Street Journal, June 19, 2007

Remembering Architecture's Dream Team

IT WAS THE SWINGING SIXTIES IN LONDON, a time of the Beatles and Carnaby Street, and of a renegade group of young architects of irrepressible spirits and awesome creativity who swung, soared, and regularly poked the establishment in the eye. Thirty-seven years ago, six thirtysomething friends—Ron Herron, Peter Cook, David Greene, Dennis Crompton, Michael Webb, and Warren Chalk—formed a group called Archigram. It was named for their broadsheets—architectural telegrams—on a witty and heady technoworld of the future characterized by the critic Michael Sorkin as a "combination of megalomania and arcadian reverie." They dealt in the common currency of the sixties: possibilities and protest. At the time, the architectural establishment was much too angry to respond with anything but outrage. I remember being amused and dismissive, considering it remarkable ephemera.

Given the chance to see it all again in a substantial retrospective exhibition, Archigram: Experimental Architecture, 1961–74, I find it still remarkable, intriguingly informative as architectural history, and quite stunning as art. The drawings, collages, models, and videos, on view until May 9 at Thread Waxing Space at 476 Broadway, in SoHo, carried the emerging postwar technology and consumer society into a utopian stratosphere of living pods, rent-a-walls, and entertainment towers, all patently unbuildable; you just have to put your head on a little differently to enjoy the idealism and irony of a version of urban life carried to zany lengths by a relentlessly inspired and surreal logic. Written off as the pipe dreams of stuntsters and visionaries, the work has had an insidious, pervasive influence and surprising trajectory to the present.

Organized by Pratt Institute, under the dedicated eye of Pratt faculty member William Menking, the exhibition opened in Europe, traveling from Vienna to the Centre Pompidou in Paris and to Manchester, England. It has been brought to this country by Thread Waxing Space in collaboration with Pratt Institute and Columbia and Cornell universities, its funding cobbled together from the sponsors and private and public sources. Neither New York nor London museums were receptive to the project, one suspects as much due to a mistaken belief that the work was dated futurist fluff as to crowded agendas or a policy of originating their own exhibitions. A supplementary display can be seen at the Storefront for Art and Architecture on Kenmare Street until Saturday; after that the show goes to Pasadena, San Francisco, and Seattle. A small, dense catalog of useful essays has been funded by the publication program of the J. M. Kaplan Fund.

In tune with the pop sensibilities of the sixties defined by Andy Warhol, Roy Lichtenstein, and others, Archigram's message was delivered in comic book style. An early manifesto shows a Doctor Strangelove type proclaiming in a balloon caption, "We have chosen to bypass the decaying Bauhaus image which is an insult to functionalism," while a busty beauty responds in a silent balloon—"(thinks) we are in pursuit of an idea, a new vernacular, something to stand alongside space capsules, computers and throw-away packages of an atomic-electronic age." So much for the task and the small talk. What follows is serious play; these were not angry young men; they were having a wonderful time. Their imagery was a pastiche of detailed technological renderings and pop culture cutouts; their gurus were Buckminster Fuller and Ornette Coleman. Their style was part Superman and Captain Marvel, part sci-fi and high-tech, part bemused social commentary. The message was that orthodox modernism was passé, that architecture was not eternal and timeless, but disposable, mutable, movable, and temporary.

What Archigram proposed was a sort of fun-fair of tech-kit Instant Cities dropped from dirigibles, complete with all the baggage of popular culture; Plug-In Cities in which capsules, pods, and clip-ons were stacked in frames with replaceable and expendable parts to accommodate

change; and, most memorable of all, Walking Cities, a kind of anthropomorphic architecture, like a giant armadillo on telescoping legs
"meant to house a large population of world traveller-workers," moving
on to wherever the economy and society dictated—a high-tech fantasy,
"part romantic glorification and part apocalyptic terror," as the *London
Observer* remarked, that looked "as though it would have stopped to eat
the rest of humanity first." Its inventor, Ron Herron, rendered it as
something absolutely unforgettable; an iconic image for our time.

The architects of Archigram thought of themselves as artists, and the
work holds up. Peter Cook's later renderings, done in the eighties, can
be phantasmagorically beautiful; the group's earlier collages have lost
none of their visual bite and wit. This is a future that has neither come
nor gone; there is no nostalgia here. What remains is a colorful, tough
poetry and the fleeting worldview of youth; in the last projects there is a
more conventional futurism that either attempts to connect with reality
or discards it totally. Archigram's one big brush with the real world, a
competition design for an entertainment center in Monte Carlo that
was not built, touches earth lightly but retains its essential pose between technowonder and pop banality.

The sixties also brought another, better-known manifesto, *Complexity and Contradiction in Architecture*, by Robert Venturi. Both
manifestos had unexpected results. Venturi's proclaimed the inclu-
siveness of past and present, initiating the philosophical and stylistic
changes of postmodernism. While it opened the door to a reexamination of history and symbolism, it also released a flood of superficial,
falsely ironic, or ineptly imitative work that is dead in the water now.
Archigram is curiously alive. One can find a diffusion of its ideas in
today's mainstream.

Archigram was probably, as Barry Curtis's catalog essay notes, "a necessary irritant" when modernism was congealing into formalism, even as
unprecedented opportunities for change were occurring. What it has actually plugged into, Plug-In Cities aside, is the continuing revision of the
modernist aesthetic that incorporates advances in structure and technology. In some ways, it was surprisingly prophetic. Archigram's "bugged"
walls, implanted with electronic controls, have become today's "smart
glass" programmed to respond to temperature and light. The "robotics"
in all of their designs anticipated the increase in electronic automation.
Their "information centers" predated the World Wide Web. They sim-

ply took off from the global village like an architectural moon shot. But they were not without their debts to the present and the past—from Buckminster Fuller's geodesic domes and Kenneth Snelson's tensegrity masts to the amorphous forms and functions of Frederick Kiesler's Endless House.

Far less predictable and quite unexpected has been Archigram's relationship to today's architecture. The idea of the megastructure—an architectural gargantua that would be all things to all people for all purposes—turned out to be futurism's biggest bomb. But the connections are obvious with the colorful, inside-out mechanics of Renzo Piano and Richard Rogers's Centre Pompidou in Paris, designed as universal, flexible space with transparent walls meant to be dematerialized by moving images—a futurism that foundered in practical application but created a twentieth-century landmark.

Mr. Rogers's later Lloyd's Building in London is a celebration of stacked service pods and dramatic structural framing. Zaha Hadid's canted shapes and spaces explore beyond the right-angled norm. Archigram's radical organizing and aesthetic features are recognizable in the industrial materials and ramps and inclined planes that control and characterize the provocative buildings of Rem Koolhaas and the work of younger Dutch architects. It is in these areas of practice, and in this sensibility, that the new architecture stakes its position.

But what infuses the best of it is Archigram's combination of the playful and the profound. Who else could have invented the Suitaloon and the Cushicle, in which clothing and furnishings morph into shelter and a lifestyle? Youthful dreams? This was world-class fantasy. We need it even more now that we've grown up.

Wall Street Journal, April 23, 1998

Going Dutch

THERE ARE NO MORE ENDURING CLICHÉS THAN the clichés about the Dutch. They are efficient engineers forever pumping out the sea and building up their land with maniacal neatness; they are the poster people for tidy traditionalism. This includes their architecture and planning—all the ruler-straight Dutch housing and even the radical modernism they pioneered in the early years of this century, with its rigidly controlled aesthetic of tightly interlocking planes, angles, and flat white and primary colored surfaces devised by such legendary figures as Gerritt Rietveld and J. J. P. Oud. Say Mondrian, and you've said it all.

And so why, in a world where the perpendicular has given way to the swooping, off-balance curves and tilted planes of Bilbao, are Dutch architects suddenly the hottest thing around, the darlings of the trend watchers, hailed as exemplars of the different, the daring, and the new? Until recently, the highest flying of these Dutchmen, Rem Koolhaas of Rotterdam, was mostly known for witty, iconoclastic writings like *Delirious New York*, but now his equally iconoclastic, and quite remarkable buildings are appearing everywhere. And there is a gathering crowd of other Dutch architects featured regularly in the professional periodicals that stress innovative and inventive design.

Even after you've conceded that architecture, like the other arts, thrives on novelty, and after you've noticed that Dutch architects have developed sophisticated media skills that help spread their words and images, it is still undeniable that something real is going on in the Netherlands. That something is a visible body of completed work by a group of like-minded but wide-ranging practitioners from their thirties to their sixties who have long since passed (lightly, if at all) through postmodernism and come out on the other side. These architects reject postmodernism's period trappings and constructivism's acutely angled discomforts; they offer no philosophical, symbolic, or literary references. Forget semantics and chaos theory—they go for the architectural gut.

In essence, the Dutch have reembraced modernism (forever rational, they never really abandoned it) in a way that respects and builds on it and blows it wide-open. Returning to the basic elements of space and enclosure, they explore and manipulate the building program for creative and unconventional plans with an immediate sensory impact. On the outside, cool, neutral containers celebrate the sleek virtuosity of advanced structural technology with exquisite, impersonal precision. Inside, it is open season on everything from the quirky to the sublime — but always with that ineffable Dutch logic, even in the most blatant send-up of the rules.

This successful combination of the playful, the sensuous, and the off-beat with a stringently austere and formal minimalism is no mean trick. Dutch architect and writer Hans Ibelings calls it supermodernism — a title he has used for a succinct small book whose significance far outstrips its size. The best of the work is recorded in a yearbook edited by Mr. Ibelings, Hans van Dijk, Bart Lootsma, and Ton Verstegen, published by the Netherlands Architecture Institute in Rotterdam.

When you visit these buildings, as I did recently, you will hardly be prepared for their striking and lighthearted departure from predictable plans and solutions. They are full of serious irreverence. I hesitate to say this, since it reveals my distance from their creators, but most are buildings by and for the young; they are full of ramps, sharply inclined planes, artful stair runs, and eccentric and vertiginous spaces. Their designers and occupants romp briskly through these cheerful obstacle courses while the older and more fainthearted hold on to anything available.

While I have always been an ardent admirer of Mr. Koolhaas's seductively subversive radicalism (who else would have suggested to New York's Museum of Modern Art that its planned expansion should express its image as MoMA Inc., identifying and exposing an institutional corporate character scrupulously avoided in polite museum circles), I have been an incomplete fan of his buildings. Brilliantly conceived but flawed in detail, they have their unsettling passages; mine have not been the only disoriented moments or barked shins, but then, attack architecture is on the rise. None of this, however, is in evidence at the Koolhaas Educatorium in Utrecht, the huge lecture and examination building that is the centerpiece of his university redevelopment plan. This is an enormously impressive, radically different, fully realized, and beautifully executed work.

There is no more potentially deadly architecture than mass education on this scale: rooms for 100 to 300 students, auditoriums seating 400 and 500, and a 1,000–seat cafeteria. We've all been there—the endless corridors, the windowless, low-ceilinged rooms with their no-time-of-day lighting and bad air. Vast, monotonous, depersonalized and depressing, they insult the idea of learning.

The educatorium changes all that; it reinvents the program in exhilarating ways. There are no blind corridors, no sealed and scaleless rooms. All of its spaces are contained within its basic, radical structure: A folded concrete slab functions as a ramp that provides access to everything in the building and also creates places to stop, meet, and lounge. This circulation device incites constant motion and puts the life of the building on display. Smooth surfaces alternate with shallow risers; changing materials, colors, and rhythms along the route provide constant pleasure and variety. The exterior glass walls that bring light and view into the vast interiors are not merely neutral transmitters, but fascinating demonstrations of the visual aesthetics made possible by today's advanced structural technology. No one has mastered this better than the Dutch; it is breathtaking here.

Where the ramp reaches a central area, a portion of the floor is glass, inviting one to walk across it for a dizzying view of what is happening below. Where the concrete slab folds, at the building's far end, it is lined with wood for a curved space as beautifully constructed as a ship. A suave, sculptural oval of the same wonderfully crafted wood gives dramatic emphasis to the focal point of this structural sleight of hand; designed as a work of art, it provides an entrance to the auditorium that has been slipped into the natural rise of the folded slab. Mr. Koolhaas plays these consistently brilliant or benignly threatening tricks superbly. It is impossible to enumerate the number of handsome details; their simplicity belies their consummate invention. Without ever resorting to gratuitous novelty, the building truly breaks new ground.

Other buildings by Wiel Arets, Ben van Berkel, MVRDV, Mecanoo, and Neutelings Riedijk are all dedicated to turning the humdrum into the adventurous. Visiting the new headquarters of the VPRO broadcast advertising and programming group in Hilversum by MVRDV is a bit like navigating a roller coaster. Formerly housed in thirteen small villas, the consolidated new offices are designed to retain some of the idiosyncrasy and separation of the various sections.

But don't expect picturesque. Behind a complex, compact glass façade are "strata" of floors and open offices linked by ramps, steps, and sloping surfaces. There is a "normal" entrance, or, if you are wearing sneakers, you can use what might be called the rollerblade, or "whoopie!" entrance, where a wood floor curves as a kind of environmental sculpture. Either way deposits you on a fine oriental carpet beneath a crystal chandelier, in a carefully staged recall of the previous traditional quarters, with a splendid view of all the supermodern fun and games beyond.

You proceed, by necessity, upward (perilously to the architecturally challenged, exhilaratingly to those released from linear, neutrally carpeted, corporate conformity) through a variety of staggered, open, day-lit spaces—each office has access to a balcony, terrace, or garden—arriving finally at a grass-topped, parklike roof, terra firma in reverse.

Another MVRDV building in Hilversum for radio and television production is set into the side of a hill (in Holland, a hill is an event in itself), showing only a cantilevered, diamond-sharp, Miesian façade. To reach the entrance you climb steps underneath the cantilever that are part of a public footpath from the top to the bottom of the hill. The trip is made through an underworld landscape of massed lava rocks lit by "glowing coals." No, I can't picture any of this at CBS.

The Dutch make the rest of us look rather dull. But then, they always did. The nearby Hilversum City Hall, built in 1926–28 by Willem Dudok, is still a marvel of surprising sensuosity, the austere geometry of its impeccable de Stijl scale and mass gorgeously accented by walls of gilded and richly colored tile. Rigidly conventional? Tidy and traditional? Not on your Dutch doubloon.

Wall Street Journal, September 18, 1998

Architecture: The Bold and the Beautiful—a Tale of Two Franks

LET IT BE SAID WITHOUT FEAR OR EQUIVOCATION: The Frank Gehry retrospective at the Guggenheim Museum in New York (up through August 26) is—and I eliminate those customary fail-safe words *arguably* and *probably*—the most important and impressive architecture exhibition I have seen in a long career. And Frank Gehry is the most staggeringly talented architect that this country has produced since Frank Lloyd Wright.

If anyone expected the two of them to duke it out in Wright's much-maligned rotunda (installation problems have driven some directors almost literally up its canted walls), they are in for a dramatic surprise. Frank I and Frank II have joined forces for the kind of visual, emotional, structural, and sensory experience that is at the heart of great architecture. You cannot stand in this space and fail to respond to the strength and beauty of the building and its contents, or not recognize that what Wright started, Mr. Gehry has continued, and that this is what architecture is in the hands of genius, to use that cheapened but still essential description of those after whom the world is never the same.

Whatever battles were fought with the notorious spiral have been stunningly resolved. Mesh sails hung from the top of the rotunda add a Gehry layer of transparency, mystery, and texture to Frank Lloyd Wright's overwhelming interior. When the setting works, as it has on occasions like the Mark Rothko retrospective that filled the rotunda with a total surround of glorious color in 1978, it is a breathtaking and memorable event.

Four decades of Frank Gehry's buildings, in twenty-four cities and five countries, including what is surely the most celebrated new structure in the world today, the Guggenheim Museum in Bilbao, Spain, wind their way up Wright's ramp. With their undulating, silvery roofs, dynamically angled walls, and sinuous shapes, they seem to float or fly rather than wind; they have all achieved iconic status. The accompanying clear, readable labels and spectacular computer diagrams are full of information that makes the work more comprehensible, but no less awesome. And although museums and institutions around the world seek the bold contours of Mr. Gehry's gleaming, cloudlike structures as a "signature" style, no two buildings are alike. Each represents a painstaking reinterpretation of the container and its uses at the same time that it establishes an intimate relationship with the site.

Pride of place is given to an enormous model of a proposed design for the Guggenheim's new headquarters on the lower Manhattan waterfront. Dramatically installed in the apselike gallery near the start of the ascent, it gets brownie points for honesty; most new developments in New York, anticipating opposition, fudge their size and impact with doctored renderings. The presentation clearly shows something approaching the height of the blockbuster downtown skyscrapers constructed on superblocks created by street closings during the urban renewal era, and takes a swath of land or water that could house a superliner. This Godzilla Guggenheim is still a study model; it will go through many changes. The architect, as is his custom, will allow that each revision is a vast improvement. My feelings are mixed; I am torn between desperately wanting a major Frank Gehry building of our very own and a nagging suspicion that this may be a baroque Brontosaurus or a waterfront barricade at its present scale.

The development of the architect's radical visual language has been as continuous as the ramp on which its evolution is displayed. A late bloomer, he was, at fifty-seven, a little-known designer of small structures of startling originality when the Walker Art Center in Minneapolis presciently gave him his first retrospective in 1986. The trip away from orthogonal geometry and conventional cladding began in the sixties with a trapezoidal studio covered in galvanized corrugated steel, designed for the artist Ron Davis. In 1977, Mr. Gehry outraged his conventional Santa Monica, California, neighborhood by wrapping his two-story bungalow in layers of sharply angled metal, plywood, and chain link, with the new windows rotated off the square. The house within a house was a domestic dream out of the cabinet of Dr. Caligari, California-style, at once wildly experimental and warmly appealing. A second remodeling, or reinvention, took place in the early nineties, less edgy but more elegant.

He continued to break down the container and reimagine its forms and uses at the Loyola Law School in Los Angeles, where he built an intimate village of small, unconventional structures in unexpected shapes, materials, and colors. Begun in 1978, the project continues today. Juxtaposed geometries were replaced by sinuous curves in the Vitra furniture museum in Weil am Rhein, Germany, in the late eighties, where he modeled space and light together for luminous effects.

As commissions and budgets increased, the Kmart look gave way to Cartier; metal, plywood, and zinc were replaced by copper, titanium, and exotic woods. But what is done is past for this architect; he left much of the execution to his partners and associates. The only project that interests him is the next one. Each new building incorporates the lessons of its predecessor, adding new twists and dimensions. Seattle's Experience Music Project, completed last year, is an explosion of warped surfaces and psychedelic color. The Ray and Maria Stata Center, in construction now at the Massachusetts Institute of Technology, will be a colliding cluster of science labs and the linguistics and philosophy departments.

If Frank Lloyd Wright famously broke open the box in his Prairie houses, Frank Gehry has ruptured the building-as-box completely—destroyed it, in fact. Whether a house or a museum, an educational, institutional, or corporate facility, these buildings are unlike anything we have encountered before. From the quality of the light to the way functions are defined and accommodated, they can affect the way you live your life.

Mr. Gehry's close personal and collaborative relationships with artists are often credited for his interest in sculptural form, but that simply avoids the obvious: He is an artist himself, and a superb one. No caveats necessary. All great architects are artists; all push the limits of the possible. All take risks.

Think of the churches of Francesco Borromini. The master of the high baroque in Rome left not a line unbent, a curve unreversed, a façade uninflected, in an extreme manipulation of form meant to change spatial experience and challenge existing classical order. Sant'Ivo alla Sapienza sweeps you into a magical denial of the Euclidean geometry on which it is based, a radical act of rejection and transformation made almost three and a half centuries ago that is still intensely moving today.

Every art makes its greatest strides at particular, fortuitous moments in history. The breakthrough for our time has been the computer.

Frank Gehry's interest in intricate sculptural shapes has coincided with the development of computer-aided drafting and modeling programs (CAD and CAM) for the calculation and production of unusual, complex forms.

Borromini had to hand-trace his curves on conventional circles; the computer uses calculus to plot points on a line with far greater ease and flexibility. Programs like CATIA, introduced to the Gehry office by partner James Glymph and originally developed for the aerospace industry, make the modeling of curved surfaces a basic design tool. The building's contours are digitized by computer, and CATIA matches the configurations as closely as possible. By providing form and construction models, as well as engineering and cost data, CATIA makes structures like the Guggenheim Bilbao achievable. Computer graphics have unlocked a digital world that makes a whole new language of forms available to the architect for the first time. Eventually, and inevitably, these processes will become mainstream.

Frank Gehry's creative partnership with radical technological advance, his bold and beautiful approach to the art of building, his sheer love of what he is doing, have brought us into a new architectural age. Without the technology, and with sheer imaginative will, Wright was straining toward the same thing in his later years. At the Guggenheim, the two Franks make a power pair.

Wall Street Journal, June 12, 2001

French Elegance Hits Midtown Manhattan

THE LVMH TOWER AT 19 EAST FIFTY-SEVENTH Street is not just another pretty face, although beauty is what you would expect from the French consortium that is the leading purveyor of luxury goods through such fashion-famous firms as Louis Vuitton, Moët Hennessy, Christian

Dior, Dom Perignon, Givenchy, Guerlain, and at least another dozen legendary names familiar to the fashionistas of the world. Beauty is what you get, however, when the corporation's new headquarters building in New York is designed by a French architect equally tuned in to the nuances of style.

But this is a building where beauty is much more than skin deep. For a variety of reasons, from its brilliantly creative interpretation of New York's notoriously restrictive zoning and building codes to a post-postmodernist aesthetic that makes everything else look definitely old chapeau, the LVMH Tower is also the best new building in New York—not by small degrees but by the equivalent of a jump-shot to the moon.

The architect, Christian de Portzamparc, is better known abroad than here; his many competition-winning designs include the Cité de la Musique, the conservatory and concert hall in Paris that was one of President Mitterrand's *grands travaux*. The New York commission, his first in this country, has been executed with the Hillier Group as the associated American architects.

After four years of construction delays complicated by a stop-and-go real estate deal and a global production process (French glass was sandblasted in Canada and assembled in Miami), the building opened officially last month with an inaugural gala of glorious Gallic excess. A light show featured a model in a Galliano gown with a sixty-foot train that unfurled down the building's façade, while 650 guests in various states of revealing overdress dined sumptuously in the IBM atrium across the way. People and champagne flowed through the Dior boutique, a superchic minimalist design by Peter Marino that occupies the new structure's ground floor.

But if the inauguration was an over-the-top crush, the building itself is the epitome of controlled, refined elegance. The slender tower sets no records for the biggest or glitziest building in New York; that distinction is relentlessly pursued by our very own Donald Trump and has nothing to do with architecture.

In fact, you may have to know a little about architecture to fully understand the design and structural savvy that has delivered so much quality and finesse, because architecture, as the most technologically and aesthetically complex of the arts, is not that instantly accessible to the passing eye. This fact has been an unremitting boon to New York's

Dior Building

developers who practice the city's perpetual property scam, the use of drop-dead lobbies and "signature" architects to market bottom-line design at prestige prices.

But you don't have to know anything at all to feel a distinct sense of pleasure if you walk by the LVMH Tower at night. The building rises from the street in two angled sections, and where they meet, a column of neon light ascends, shifting slowly from deep blue-violet to shades of green, yellow, and red, colors as dramatic in their enhancement of the building's form and style as they are rich in hue. Don't think of anything garish, or even anything you know, because this display has nothing to do with Times Square flash; it is as important a design element as the glass and metal curtain wall.

Like talented architects throughout time, Mr. Portzamparc is an artist; the aesthetics of line, proportion, light, and color rank with the challenge of turning practical programs into functional form. All of his buildings use color, and all are an accessible, sensuous delight. His watercolor studies of his projects are ravishing, suggestive, and revealing in a way that today's computer-generated renderings can never match.

The most immediately remarkable thing about this relatively small (for New York) building is the way its twenty-four stories seem to soar, making its conventional neighbors look earthbound. In the architect's words, the design "catches hold of the sky." It achieves this by breaking the building's façade into folded, faceted planes that follow a dynamic, diagonal line as they rise.

These fractured forms also evoke 1920s renderings by that poet of skyscraper drawings, Hugh Ferris. But while there are references to art deco, and suggestions of fifties details, there is no nostalgia here; grounded firmly in twentieth-century modernism and filtered through a uniquely French taste, Mr. Portzamparc's buildings are part of a radical departure in style marking much new work that is having an international impact. As usual, New York is the last to know.

The codes that have forced Manhattan buildings into a standard mold (or has it been just the easy and cheap way out embraced by developers and their zoning lawyers and captive architects?) dictated certain requirements for the site. The building must hold the street line, it has to be set back above a certain height, and it cannot exceed a specified size in terms of its bulk and interior space. These limitations are usually resolved by recessing the upper part of the structure along the building façade in a straight line at the required height. But Mr. Portzamparc's fresh reading of the zoning code revealed that the set-back does not have to be continuous; the recessed portion of the building can meet the letter of the law as long as it touches the line at two points.

He therefore chose to hollow out the building, leaving inward-facing planes that connect with the base in only two places; the angled surfaces are then carried all the way up. The space lost at the bottom is recaptured at the top to create a thirty-foot-high "magic room," a glass-walled volume of spectacular views and drama, to be used for fashion shows and special events.

But the whole building is magic. And the unconventional design solves another problem—a flat façade would have given only a reflection of the dark glass wall and multiple clocks across the street, something Mr. Portzamparc's angled planes, with their nonreflecting green and white insulated glass, avoid. For the window treatment, a special clear white glass made by St. Gobain in France has been sandblasted with thin, horizontal lines and a slanting, opaque pattern that makes the building "read" from the street, while bringing a softly luminescent white light inside.

To keep the lively, illusionistic delicacy of the exterior, the floors are shaped to a thin edge where they meet the windows, and the columns are set back from the window wall, a refinement that turned out to be the most expensive part of the job. Only the entrance lobby disappoints. A small space with honey-hued sycamore walls and gold-toned Indian stone floor was meant to appear larger through the illusionistic device of glowing white glass panels. The addition of decorative patterns to the glass, not of the architect's design, busies it up and closes it in, proving, once again, that less is really more. The elevator cabs, which repeat the sandblasted lines of the exterior glass on a mirrored back wall and the sycamore of the lobby, are the most elegant in town.

The LVMH Tower is a luxury building with a budget permitting very special details. But its lesson is not in its extravagance or stylishness; it is in its innovative solutions and the quality of its design. The building's openhanded corporate sponsorship is sure to prompt the old real estate mantra that good architecture is more expensive than bad, a comfortable canard that has been serving the city's builders too well and too long. There is no law that the cost of creativity has to be greater than that of formulaic mediocrity. There is no reason why New York construction should be abysmally ordinary or stupefyingly reactionary, while first-rate architecture recognized everywhere else goes begging here. Our developers might just try springing for the real thing.

This is a city that forgives a lot; it packs its buildings into its unrelenting grid in a powerful, irreverent, exhilarating, and constantly changing mix. The new Fifty-seventh Street is a shaky standoff between the grand luxe of the neighboring Chanel and Dior buildings and creeping Nike and Warner Brothers kitsch. The LVMH Tower tips the balance beautifully in favor of New York.

Wall Street Journal, January 10, 2000

Too Much of a Good Thing?

SANTIAGO CALATRAVA IS A MULTITALENTED practitioner of architecture, engineering, and sculpture, and that is the problem: Are his spectacular structures all or none of the above? Just how well do his awesome gifts interact? An exhibition of his work on view until March 5 at the Metropolitan Museum of Art—an institution that rarely presents a living architect and obviously endorses this one—begs the question.

Santiago Calatrava: Sculpture Into Architecture suggests a transition that is easily and reasonably made. The presentation links drawings, sculpture, and a series of exquisite models of bridges, transportation buildings, museums, and skyscrapers in a seductive narrative where natural forms are transformed through complex engineering into knockout creations of suave anthropomorphic appeal. There are repeated references to beaks, eyes, wings, and parts of the human body. His buildings stack like spines and twist like torsos. They take off like planes and soar like birds. But is he Superman?

The answer depends on whether you think that engineering—the most rational and reductive of the building arts, where achievement is measured by economy of means—has been used for a poetic break-through into the architectural stratosphere or pressed into the service of an overwrought expressionism that transcends programmatic needs. Mr. Calatrava admits that he pushes the limits—that is the trademark of his creativity. One would have to be blind to ignore the grace, ingenuity, and dramatic power of these monumental functional follies. Moreover, his buildings don't just sit there: Their dynamic forms open and shut, undulate, and perform other kinetic feats.

The modernist aesthetic applauds breaking boundaries over conventional solutions, but is there a point where one says "enough"? For those with a taste for a simpler structural logic, these dauntingly complex anatomical evocations can seem just a wee bit over the top. Euclid, alone, may have looked on beauty bare, but Mr. Calatrava never even glances in that direction. Arguably, a winglike superstructure or a whalelike exoskeleton can overstate the romantic experience of taking a train or a plane. On the other hand, one can point to Eero Saarinen's TWA terminal of 1956–62 as a respectable, even visionary precedent for the airport departure building as a bird in flight. But when the rising ribs of a cathedral suggest a pair of praying hands, one of the oldest visual clichés, doesn't that get dangerously close to kitsch?

Would the Calatrava show have been more appropriately titled Architecture Into Sculpture? That raises equally troubling questions. How much extravagant and costly engineering is needed to turn architecture into sculpture, if this, indeed, is a desirable objective, and how far can it be carried before it undermines the art of building as a direct response to a stated need? Architecture has never lacked imagination or poetry within its own parameters.

Considering how skillfully Mr. Calatrava conceives and constructs his dazzling objects, and how enormously popular they are, one feels churlish having reservations. These questions are not particular to his work, however; they are endemic to our times. The traditional interdependence of art, structure, and utility that has been the measure of architecture since antiquity has become boring to the public and to much of the profession. What drives design and patronage now is the wow effect, which has little to do with the time-tested criteria of commodity, firmness, and delight and more to do with signature styles as publicity and marketing tools. With the help of the computer, architecture as sculpture is here to stay.

Including Mr. Calatrava's sculpture in the Metropolitan show stakes its claims as art. These blandly predictable abstractions of supersmooth gold plate and highly polished stone could meet Donald Trump's standards for the glossy finishes of his upscale buildings. They prompt one more question. Was it a calculated or unconscious act for the Met to position these pieces in clearly visible juxtaposition to the revolutionary early modernist works in the next gallery? It was very unkind; they are terribly upstaged by the aesthetic richness of Brancusi's radical subtleties of line and surface and the eccentric energy of Boccioni's frozen movement. What you see in Mr. Calatrava's sculpture is what you get, alas.

It is instructive to compare Mr. Calatrava's work with that of two earlier engineers, Robert Maillart and Pier Luigi Nervi. Both had an artist's eye, but neither used engineering as a way of making sculpture. Maillart's bridges, pared down to a three-point arch, spanned the Alps with dancerlike precision from the start of the twentieth century to the thirties. A faultless synthesis of form, structure, and use, they never overplayed their hand. The structural systems of Nervi's sports, exposition, and transportation buildings display an understated mastery of means; his ribbed and reticulated domes and ceilings have the delicacy of flowers. Both stressed solutions that grew out of the most efficient and elegant expression of the structure itself.

Mr. Calatrava's romantic expressionism works best for buildings where symbolism matters. His addition to the Milwaukee Art Museum has already achieved iconic status; its importance for the city's identity and self-regard apparently overrides any difficulty its extravagant metaphors impose on installing art and the fact that attendance has not achieved anticipated levels.

Enormous publicity (not all a bad thing) accompanied the development and delays in the construction of a soaring—sorry, one cannot escape that word—*brise soleil*, or sunscreen, topping the main structure, ostensibly to control the light but guaranteed to knock your socks off. It opens and closes, yes, like the wings of a bird, after many delays and costs that also soared like a bird. Anyone who wants to know what is involved in the formidable technology needed to soar like a bird can find it in *Engineering News Record*, the publication that chronicles such things. If engineering art is defined by a lucid economy of means, this is not it.

But there are appropriate times and places in our cities and our lives when imagery and symbolism transcend function—most notably now at Ground Zero, where Mr. Calatrava's Transportation Hub, commissioned by the Port Authority, is the only structure finally beginning to rise from that desolate hole. It is also the only remaining element of the aborted plan, all other traces of life having been extinguished by the political rollover to those few families who feel that memorializing the dead should take precedence over the living and everything else.

The cultural buildings on which so much of the future depended, stigmatized by their opponents as "inappropriate," have been evicted or eviscerated for an enormous necropolis at the heart of the site. Apparently not even something as essential to the rebuilding as a transportation center can escape these maudlin pressures. The same group is threatening to stalemate construction by demanding the removal of the tracks that cross the corners of the Twin Towers' footprints where the underground trains must run. Love may be blind, but grief—you should pardon the expression—has tunnel vision.

If we ever needed something soaring, we need it here. Mr. Calatrava's talents require exceptional circumstances. Let this building fly like a bird. The design is a practical solution and a symbol of rebirth meant to bring life and people back downtown, assuming there will be a downtown to come back to. Mr. Calatrava's building is hope. With or without wings, architecture can aim no higher.

Wall Street Journal, December 8, 2005

Rewriting History

Mackintosh: A Genius to Be Reckoned With

A HUNDRED YEARS, OR EVEN FIFTY YEARS, becomes a landmark and a time for looking back, and what we look back at now are the roots of the modern movement in architecture and design. We are examining history, with the beginnings of some kind of a perspective about it, which means that we are embarking on voyages of rediscovery.

There is nothing like a retrospective exhibition to create that sense of rediscovery and reevaluation. First, the fiftieth anniversary of the Bauhaus came as a surprise to those either old enough to be shocked by the flight of a half century or young enough to think of the beginnings of the Bauhaus as shrouded in the mists of time. That show, which was inaugurated in Germany this summer, has just closed at Burlington House. Hard on its heels, an exhibition organized by the Scottish Arts Council to celebrate the centenary of the Scottish architect Charles Rennie Mackintosh (1868–1928), and shown first at the Edinburgh Festival, has opened this week at the Victoria and Albert Museum in London, to run to December 29.

To those who have simply taken Nikolaus Pevsner's word and the pictures begining to fade in the classroom art histories that Mackintosh was a genius to be reckoned with, this exhibition is indeed a revelation. It is the first retrospective of his work outside Scotland. The show consists largely of recreations of those famous interiors of 1900 to 1917 that startled turn-of-the-century professionals. These "rooms" use original furnishings and accessories, so that the effect is fresh and immediate and the impact tremendous. We are undoubtedly in for a Mackintosh revival, if in nothing more than shades of mauve floating in a sea of sculptured white.

Reevaluation is hardly necessary. This is merely stunning affirmation

Glasgow School of Art

that Mackintosh was one of the major innovative talents of modern times, with a deep and definitive influence on the forms of architecture and design that set the scene of the contemporary world.

The evidence has long been clear. Charles Rennie Mackintosh was the leader of the "Glasgow School," a small group of sensitive men and women who renounced the decorative excesses of long-entrenched Victorian taste. This movement was one of several short but significant revolts that recurred from the time of William Morris well into the twentieth century, to leave their mark on history and taste.

The contrasts could not be more splendidly revealed than they are in the permanent upstairs collection at the V and A. The Victorian room, with a huge ceramic centerpiece of unclear, elaborate function covered with roses, held by straining cupids and topped by writhing gold snakes, leads directly to the William Morris room and the ascetic works of Voysey and Mackintosh.

The moment of art nouveau paralleled the Glasgow School. There are connections—beautiful ones—between Mackintosh and those seductive forms, but he used them rarely and with exquisite sensitivity in a far stricter geometry. It is a geometry of intensely personal style and skill, brilliantly prefiguring movements as decorative as the modernistic and as basic as the Bauhaus.

Andrew McLaren Young, director of the exhibition and author of the catalog, notes that Mackintosh "did not reject the need for decoration. But for him decoration was new clothing for new ideas: new ideas on the role of function and the geometry of architectural space."

Mies van der Rohe has described Mackintosh as a "purifier." He was that, and to be in his presence in this show makes one realize that purity need not be sterility. It can be a flowering, rather than a repression of the senses. He makes one feel color more because he uses it with such supremely refined intensity: White becomes a mass of nuances; violet glows through a teardrop in a silver lamp or melts against mirror or glass in traceries of lead; red is a declamation in a black, white, and yellow wall. This is something that cannot be experienced in the scholarly journals.

His influence went directly from Glasgow to Vienna, where the architects of the Secession admired him extravagantly and invited him to participate in the Exhibition of 1900. Josef Hofmann became his friend; Olbrich and Behrens were indebted to him; the line extends to Wagner and Loos, to the Bauhaus and Groplus and Mies, to everything that we call modern today.

A lot has been lost along the way. One has gotten awfully tired of Bauhaus blue, of the tubular clichés, of the safe design formulas. Only now is a less puritanical and intellectualized sensuosity coming back into architecture and design with a younger generation involved with the full spectrum of color and dimensional experience. These are often hard and chic optical exercises, even aesthetic throwaways; Mackintosh was involved in a reformation that was also a gentle exploration of beauty and a probing analysis of architectonic surfaces and space.

He is sometimes paired, or paralleled, with Frank Lloyd Wright, but, beyond the climate of the time which led men of genius to strip beauty bare, their talents are individual and unlike. In 1896, when his Glasgow School of Art was designed, it was, in many ways, ahead of Wright.

One begins to call the art school a great protomodern building, but it was protonothing; with its expressive functional modernity enriched by the spatial definition of the remarkable decoration, and a touch of sound Scottish traditionalism, this is a great building in quite absolute terms, by any measurement of time or style. The drawings for it are in the show, with enlarged photographs and some sample furnishings, including a well-worn reading stand with a sign warning users not to take the periodicals out of the room.

There are watercolors, flower drawings, textile designs, posters, and an assortment of objects, such as the unsurpassed silver flatware that museums vie for, and other work of the Glasgow School, including that of Margaret Macdonald, Mackintosh's wife. But it would all be a ripple on the surface of art history if it were not for the strict, lyrical power of this one man. His almost equally celebrated fellow-reformer Voysey is a craftsman next to him. Mackintosh worked for an elite few, but something of the changes he inaugurated pervades every life today.

Whether it is the art school, the domestic interiors, or the series of tea-rooms for Miss Cranston, the designs are as curiously affecting now as they must have been when they first appeared. This has been expressed with particular effect by Ahlers-Hestermann, quoted by Pevsner:

"These rooms were like dreams . . . white and serious looking, as if they were young girls ready to go to their first Holy Communion. Here was mysticism and asceticism, but with much of a sense of heliotrope, with well-manicured hands and a delicate sensuousness . . . two straight chairs with backs as tall as a man stood on a white carpet and look silently and spectrally at each other across a little table."

New York Times, November 17, 1968

Peacock Feathers and Pink Plastic

IT IS HARD TO BELIEVE THAT THE first major retrospective of the work of Bruce Goff is only now being shown in this country, packed into the tight quarters of the Architectural League. (Monday through Friday, ten to five, until February 11, admission free, at 41 East Sixty-fifth Street.)

On the other hand, it isn't hard to believe, because the eastern architectural establishment doesn't really believe in Bruce Goff. He is apt to be dismissed as a figment of midwestern imagination, inspired by Frank Lloyd Wright, a designer of *outre* fantasies which elicit a polite frisson along the elite East Coast axis that has produced a generation of cool corporate splendor spawned by the "correct" International Style.

Although no one has been paying much attention in these circles, Bruce Goff is alive and well and sixty-five and practicing in Bartlesville, Oklahoma. Since he was a fast starter, at twelve, this is his sixth decade of active production. The impact of his work in this concentrated form—160 exhibition boards containing photographs, drawings, and prints, plus transparencies, of about fifty built or projected works—is mildly mind-blowing. This is one of the most provocative manifestations of the American architectural genius.

GO TO THE league, gentlemen and ladies (architects are still in that order professionally), even if those gold and silver presentation boards and houses like starfish, viking ships, and tepees give you fits. If you can shed that eugenically frightening New England—Calvinist—Harvard—Bauhaus—intellectual frigidity, if you can suppress a reaction to some obviously homegrown corn, there is an artist here. There is a consistent statement of art and purpose, a sensitivity to the land, a last-stand half-triumph of the romantic individualist in a world that is forcing the architect to conform increasingly to standardized formulas and business practices.

This is fantasy, and it is often seriously flawed. Tight budgets, cheap materials, and an ingenuous and sometimes buckeye taste make it easy work to disregard. But there is also, on occasion, poetry, and glimpses of horizons beyond brashly broken rules, rather than conventionally trained competence, as well as the inner belief of a man who follows

Bavinger House

his personal vision. For fifty-eight years Goff has done his own thing. This architecture—so out of the mainstream—proclaims a faith in the individual in every philosophical sense. The clients, touchingly and sometimes incongruously photographed in their bubbles and saucers, share the vision.

VISIONS ARE NOT part of the status quo or the silent majority or the suburban subdivision. Goff in suburbia, seen glimpsingly in slides, is

Martian aesthetics. But seen in the drawings the vision is splendid. It is worth a visit for the drawings alone (note particularly the plans), both Goff's renderings and those of his former student Herb Greene.

Greene, in particular, draws like a demon on a permanent high. His delicate colored-pencil Arabian-nights-of-the-future imagery is architectural graphics on an extraordinary level. His own fantastic shingled shambles of a prairie house in Norman, Oklahoma, has been referred to by the English *Architectural Review* as a "wounded buffalo."

Bruce Goff is a phenomenon, part of an indigenous American tradition of the unspoiled, romantic, land-loving loner that the *Review* has labeled the American grassroots mythology. This fascinates Europeans and embarrasses Americans. The architects who complete their concrete and steel bank buildings with hard-edge abstraction are made a little uneasy by a man whose tastes run to rusticity, orientalia, peacock feathers, and pink plastic. When he is published by American architectural periodicals, the tone is uncomfortable and ambiguous. Not surprisingly, his work is flashily offbeat enough to have been discovered by the full-color, popular press. Professionally, it is treated more sympathetically abroad than at home. "*L'insolite* Bruce Goff," *L'Architecture d'Aujourd'hui* called him in 1962—the unusual Bruce Goff.

What happens to his unusual designs? About half have been built. They are to be found chiefly in Oklahoma, Texas, Florida, and places where tastes are open and grassroots mythology strongest. His houses have often been do-it-yourself, with the clients constructing them lovingly over a period of years under the architect's tutelage—or they are cost-no-object jobs. The Bavinger family built its own house in Norman, Oklahoma, charging the pilgrims and the curious a dollar a head toward the construction fund. This 1950 design is an unwinding stone snail, part cave, part greenhouse, the color of late, color-drained autumn leaves.

At the other end of the scale, the house for Joe Price was a *Playboy* dream, if *Playboy* were an architect. (Price is the son of the wealthy clients who commissioned Frank Lloyd Wright's Price Tower in Bartlesville, the building in which Goff has lived and worked.) This playhouse was enlarged in 1967, after Price married, and now, as the Joe and Etsuko Price House, has such touches as a ten-thousand-dollar Japanese bath that is a kaleidoscope of mosaics topped by a glass fish pool.

One wonders if either a communication or a generation gap really exists between, say, Yale and Oklahoma; there is so much of super-graphics in Goff's uses of color, mirror, and pattern. There is also his theory of continuous composition that prefigures the popular academic antiformalism or "endless architecture" of the sixties.

Anyone who doubts Goff's serious competence need only look at the working drawings for the Price House in the show. They are an exhaustive, painstaking documentation of the resolution of the special details of dream houses. It is also clear that short of an unlimited budget, any architect could lose his shirt doing this kind of thing. Ars longa, profit brevis.

The Price House, a chef d'oeuvre of untrammeled, sybaritic fancy in gold-anodyzed aluminum, nylon-carpeted floor and walls, goose feather ceilings, and hanging plastic "rain," is super-Goff. Lesser-Goff or pure disaster can be seen in the realization of the sketch for the 1960 Gryder House in Ocean Springs, Mississippi. Here execution turns impossible flying curves into chewing gum and a precisely poised inverted cone into Dairy Queen. However, the shingled, redwood-sided cubes of the Wilson House in Pensacola, Florida, are something else again: architecture, not Mother Goose.

Except for a few bits of common vocabulary that include recurrent glass or plastic conical domes, the penchant for organic theory and things on the bias, and those colored pencil renderings, resemblance to Frank Lloyd Wright decreases after the early work. Goff is Goff, even in Las Vegas. His unexecuted sixty-story Viva Hotel and Casino, in a style that might be called Space Camp, would have raised Vegas to a creative level that its humdrum hotel caricatures have always lacked. Another unbuilt project, for the Giacomo Motor Lodge in McAlester, Oklahoma, looks like a petrified forest with balconies. Both are pure pop environment. In today's world of exploding conventions, that is a hard act to follow.

New York Times, February 8, 1970

Beaux Arts—the Latest Avant-Garde

NINETEENTH-CENTURY PARIS. *Vie de Bohème*. Artists in garrets. The beaux arts ball. The architecture students of the École des Beaux Arts in M. Gaudet's famous atelier on the Left Bank, smocks stained with *encre de Chine*, working on palatial projects for the Prix de Rome. They run careful washes behind meticulously rendered public monuments or ink in painstaking reconstructions of ancient Greek temples. A few *nouveaux* clean brushes for *les anciens*. The drawings are enormous, skillful representations of classical grandeur. Stoves at either end of the large, cluttered room barely heat the chill air. Along one wall, untidy bookshelves hold dusty copies of Vitruvius and Palladio and the prizewinning designs of students who have gone on to fame. The Ecole des Beaux Arts is more than a school. It is *la source*, the fountainhead of official architecture for Old and New Worlds.

No more. Over the past fifty years, Beaux Arts has become a bad word. For this is the large slice of architectural history (and a large part of the civilized world) which the modern movement exorcised. It is, in fact, what modern architecture rebelled against.

Now, in one of those increasingly popular, paradoxical reversals of art and taste, the discarded academic past is becoming the intriguing avant-garde. The Beaux Arts will be the subject of a large and enlightening and undoubtedly controversial exhibition starting Wednesday at that bastion of the modern movement, the Museum of Modern Art. The academy is dead. Long live the academy.

The Architecture of the École des Beaux Arts is the museum's major fall show and, in the opinion of many, one of its most important contributions to taste and art scholarship since the International Style formally introduced modern architecture to this country in 1932. It comes under the heading of that growing historical exercise called "radical revisionism," a questioning of the conventional wisdom in which reputations and movements are reexamined and reclaimed.

In truth, so arcane, so unfashionable, so discarded as proper intellectual and aesthetic baggage is the world of the Beaux Arts, that this may be the first invitation to a museum opening (tomorrow night) that includes an explanation of what the show is all about. "The exhibition ex-

Penn Station exterior

amines the dominant ideas of 19th-century French academic architecture," the invitation states. "Many of the more than 200 drawings in watercolor and ink, some as large as 18 feet wide and extraordinary in their opulent and varied detail, have not been unrolled since they were submitted by students to their professors at the École des Beaux Arts 150 years ago."

The unrolling has been done by Arthur Drexler, director of the museum's Department of Architecture and Design, over the last eight years, in the attic of the École des Beaux Arts in Paris, where he, and they, were covered with a century and a half of soot.

But a little soot has failed to dim their essential *gloire*. As drawings, they are breathtaking. The techniques of ink and wash are handled superbly; the subjects are a galaxy of monumental structures increasingly overwhelming in size and complexity as the century moved on. The subjects are unvaryingly grand and their treatment elegant, elaborate, and ornate. They deal in all the taboo words and practices—elitism, ornament, overt extravagance—of modern architectural usage.

It is a never-never world of palaces of kings, palaces of justice, and
palaces for the arts, of cathedrals, conservatories, stock exchanges,
state banks and thermal baths, emperors' pavilions, ambassadors' compounds, and mansions for rich bankers. (The last was considered a
controversially ordinary subject in 1866; if a student could design a
great state edifice, it was argued, he could toss off an establishment for
a banker.)

More pragmatic themes were public granaries and markets, barracks
for the military, and, later in the century, railroad stations. But there
was nothing small or humble. Among Prix de Rome competition subjects were an imperial residence at Nice (1860), a palace for the governor of Algeria (1862), and a casino on the sea (1889), scattered among
more or less routine orangeries, *hôtels de ville*, and royal residences. It is
a world that today seems far less accessible than the moon.

The first impact of these impressive renderings is that they represent
a dead society and lost skills. They are enjoyable as beautiful drawings
and illuminating as indicators of style and standards that go beyond art
to reveal the social structure and cultural norms of a closed chapter in
history. In this sense, they are provocative and informative documents
to a very high degree.

The point that the museum is hammering home, however, in a
rather hermetic, scholarly way, by overt demonstration and massive in-
nuendo (eighteen-foot drawings are not exactly understatement), is that
this work is not irrelevant at all. According to Arthur Drexler, whose
modernist credentials are impeccable, it offers the kind of satisfaction
of the spirit and the eye which has always been an essential component
of the art of architecture, and which is now largely lost to the modern
movement through an insistently narrow and false polemic (functionalism, purity of form, abolition of ornament).

In fact, he goes right down the line to the basic definition of architecture. The Beaux Arts defined it as the public building. Modernists
define it as the total built environment. Drexler thinks that a lot of values were lost in the trip from the monument to the environment. That
the world of the Beaux Arts depends on an exclusionary and aristocratic
concept of architecture does not bother him at all. The clear suggestion
is that the emperor, today, is wearing no clothes, and it may be that we
need the emperor after all.

That is an impossible oversimplification of a complex argument. But the far-from-buried thesis is that we have a lot to learn from the disdained academy. The museum backs and fills a bit, skirting its way around an outright declaration with layers of involved and often irritatingly abstruse scholarship. (A book will appear later this year, with essays by Drexler, David Van Zanten, Neil Levine, and Richard Chafee, who have also collaborated on the show.)

This is heresy, of course, because it clearly suggests that the modernist world for which the museum has unswervingly crusaded is not the best of all possible worlds and is even in need of critical reevaluation. It forces a reexamination of modernist doctrine—something that has actually been in process in upper intellectual strata for some time—when it has finally become the thoroughly accepted basis of establishment culture. (God may live, but the avant-garde is dead.) And it goes for the jugular by attacking the clichés, rigidities, theoretical fatigue, and excesses that have built up with time (modernism is close to a century old now and has its own academy) and that were exactly the kind of thing that led to the demise of the Beaux Arts.

But it is not the questioning that will create the greatest unease—it is the form that the questioning is taking. The deliberate revival of the discarded ideals of the Beaux Arts—the villain of the modern movement—will be pretty strong medicine for a lot of well-indoctrinated modernists to swallow.

These ideals are based on prescribed and elaborate rules of formal classical design. In beaux arts practice, the work was judged by composition—the relationship between exterior volumes and interior spaces; by *parti*—the way in which the plan was resolved; and by marche—the quality of the progression of the spaces as one imagined walking through them. Plans were usually axial and symmetrical.

For these elaborately formulated aesthetic design considerations, the modernists substituted a dogma of simple utility and technology. While form, in the basic sense, was always meant to grow out of function, and always has in the best and most rational buildings, the new architecture used a narrowly "scientific" and pragmatic measure of use and structure, while the old defined it in much broader terms of symbolism and sensuosity.

It also defined it, stylistically, in terms of the classical-renaissance tradition, a tradition in Western art that reaches to Greece and Rome. This is, in fact, the whole of the Western tradition, except for the remarkable episodes of the medieval and the modern.

The classical heritage, with its familiar orders defined by Vitruvius, Serlio, and Palladio, became more archaeological with the discoveries of the ancient world in the eighteenth century, and less restricted with the eclecticism of the nineteenth century. In both centuries, classicism was the official doctrine of the French academy and the École.

The École was an outgrowth of the academy, which was established by Colbert in the seventeenth century; its members were *les architects du roi*. The two state institutions were metamorphosed many times by revolution, politics, polemics, and French bureaucratic culture. With the separation of the École Polytechnique after the revolution, the École dex Beaux Arts was free to pursue the high art of architecture, a division of art and structure that was later a matter of much debate.

By 1830–39, the École was a stronghold of orthodoxy and conservatism. With the advent of a romantic rebellion, it reverberated with hair-splitting, hardly discernible currents of "radicalism" and "reform," led in 1860–69 by the medievalist and rationlist Viollet-le-Duc, but it remained essentially unchanged.

For two centuries, it was the headquarters of the French architectural establishment, producing France's leading practitioners of the art of building, and creating principles of design so strong that by the latter part of the nineteenth century they dominated official architecture internationally. Buildings such as Henri Labrouste's Bibliothèque St. Geneviève of 1845–50 and Charles Garnier's paris Opéra of 1861–74 were enormously influential. In fact, all the permutations of the academic classical style became known eventually as Beaux Arts.

After the mid-nineteenth century, the best-trained American architects were usually the product of the École. Among its prestigious graduates were Richard Morris Hunt, H. H. Richardson, and Louis Sullivan, although only Hunt, carried his classical education over into his working style. It was not long before the architectural elite in the United States were virtually all Beaux-Arts "boys," and with the Chicago World's Fair of 1893, the struggling strains of indigenous and innovative American design were eclipsed by the blinding white glory of the classical palaces on the lagoon conjured up under the leadership of Daniel Burnham and McKim, Mead & White.

The country's turn-of-the-century and later monuments—the great wave of museums, libraries like Carrère and Hastings's beauty at Fifth Avenue and Forty-second Street, as well as railroad stations such as Burnham's in Chicago and Warren, and Wetmore, Reed and Stem's Grand Central Terminal in New York—were all built in exemplary Beaux Arts style.

There is no disagreement about the importance and influence of the Beaux Arts in its own time. Not only was it the official style, but almost all nineteenth-century and early twentieth-century architectural education in this country was modeled on the École. The Massachusetts Institute of Technology was established in 1865 by William Ware, a Beaux Arts graduate, who later founded the Columbia School of Architecture. The Prix de Rome winners of the Beaux Arts were assiduously imported as professors, and the course of instruction attempted to re-create the French precedent as closely as possible. In 1912, there were 102 Beaux Arts ateliers throughout the country.

The state-supported Paris École des Beaux Arts consisted of schools of painting, sculpture, and architecture. The architecture school was open to students between the ages of fifteen and thirty, French or foreign, tuition free. But it was far from open enrollment. There was an exacting entrance examination that included an architectural project to be devised in twelve hours, drawing from a cast and modeling from ornament in relief, exercises in mathematics and descriptive geometry, and oral and written exams on ancient and modern European history.

Instruction combined remarkable freedom with the most rigid requirements. The courses consisted of lectures at the École and design work in the ateliers, or studios. Each student proceeded, not as part of the group, but individually, at his own pace. Every stage of the way was judged by *concours*, or competitions, in *esquisse*, or sketch form, for the lesser ones, or as *projets rendus*, completed sets of plans, elevations, and sections, for the major evaluations. A recurring assignment was the reconstruction of ancient ruins. A diploma given at the end was only instituted in 1862.

Chief among the concours was the prestigious and coveted Prix de Rome, established for architecture in 1720, which gave five years of study in Rome at state expense. It was also an almost assured stepping stone to high-level commissions and eventual election to the academy.

This signal honor was open only to unmarried, native-born or natural-ized Frenchmen: Americans had to stop short of the top award.

Perhaps the system worked so well because the emphasis was on indi-vidual instruction and independent development, measured solely by the quality of work, under the highest professional guidance. The incen-tives, however, were pure nineteenth century: competitions and prizes. What was stressed, without apology or justification because none was thought necessary, was the art of design, with all other subjects, such as mathematics, science, construction, history, and drawing, secondary to it. Structural engineering was considered a totally different métier and no one had yet invented socioaesthetics or interdisciplinary training. Much has been made since of the split between art and technology. But everyone drew sublimely.

The most interesting and widely imitated aspect of the system was the atelier. Each atelier had its professor, or *patron*, a leading French architect. He might be a revered academician or a young, "progressive" architect whom a number of students had petitioned to open an atelier. The rivalry was intense, particularly for the Prix de Rome.

The architecture student was apt to be a bit older, better educated, better dressed, and better off than the other students of the École: he was not, in the words of a nineteenth-century chronicler, "the son of a shoemaker." At the time of the *concours*, students worked around the clock, bringing their large drawings from atelier to École for the judg-ing in hand-drawn carts, or *charrettes*. During the last period of inten-sive, continuous work to make the deadline, the student was said to be *en charrette*, an expression that survives for deadline pressure in archi-tects' offices today.

But that, and a few nostalgic words such as *esquisse* and *parti*, are about all that have survived—and those drawings in the attic. Plus a great deal of building from which we have been trained to assiduously avert our eyes. For a while, in the twenties and thirties, the school straddled classicism and modernism with a stylish last flicker of art moderne—the French Beaux Arts updated with Viennese chic. Unre-pentant academicism persisted in a few late bloomers such as Washing-ton's National Gallery (1940) by John Russell Pope. World War II dealt the Beaux Arts the coup de grâce.

The École still exists, decentralized after the student riots of 1968, as

Unités Pedagogiques, for the teaching of architecture, but it has neither funds nor influence. As with so much else, real estate proved to be ultimate destiny. The rising cost of dwindling loft space on the Left Bank after the war outlawed the free and easy establishment of ateliers, and the fluid change and development that made possible. As early as the end of the nineteenth century, the École was being accused of "pedantry, despotism and a horror of progress." But it is hard to say at what point bureaucratization and ossification had set in.

Ultimately, the Beaux Arts is the casualty of a revolution in structural technology and massive changes in society and the economy. It is hard, even for would-be revivalists, to rationalize the logic and costs of the grafting of classical forms and orders intrinsic to masonry construction onto the totally different requirements of modern steel and concrete. It is equally hard to fit the straitjacket of academic classicism on the many new building forms required by the twentieth century, even if craftsmen were not extinct. The skyscraper added to its radical technology vertical composition of unprecedented scale; the public building bowed before speculative commercial construction.

The educational doctrine of the Bauhaus, brought to Harvard in the thirties by Walter Gropius and to Chicago by Mies van der Rohe a few years later, supplanted the beaux arts classical doctrine with a messianic machine aesthetic. Whatever errors and inadequacies its polemics may have perpetuated, it faced realities that the nineteenth century never knew.

Interestingly, some of the best of the older modernists were Beaux Arts trained, among them the late Louis Kahn, whose buildings are included with the finest of this century. His work clearly reflects the best aspect of the formal thinking and elegant disciplines of the academy. Side by side with the buildings of the modernists, and scored by them as sterile and passé, are the last-gasp monuments of the Beaux Arts tradition. The Jefferson Memorial in Washington, for example, completed by John Russell Pope and Eggers & Higgins as late as 1943, is commended by Drexler for its "French-Roman suavity and repose." Others persist in calling it stillborn.

The exhibition is obviously about to break a taboo. It is going to make the architectural academy respectable again, as is already happening with the academy in painting and sculpture. At its deepest level, it urges us to examine the "moral imperative" of utility and sociology, the modernist doctrine that is the basis of today's building. That is attacking a very sacred cow.

But the show has brought a lot of beautiful drawings and hidden history out of the closet, and it is certain to raise thoughtful issues about the meaning and practice of architectural design. The Museum of Modern Art is still performing its charter job of questioning the established order. This time, it is the order that it helped establish. And if it is making waves by looking backward, that is the nature of our times.

New York Times, October 26, 1975

Rediscovering Chicago Architecture

THE EXHIBITION AT COOPER UNION called Chicago Architects is full of uncelebrated, quirky, and sometimes dramatic buildings, most of which are unknown. There is only one example of a famous Chicago School "skyscraper"—D. H. Burnham and Company's curtain-walled Reliance Building, designed by Charles Atwood in 1894–95—and it is paired with the same architect's totally traditional beaux arts Hall of Fine Arts for the Columbian Exposition of 1893. Modern critics have lauded the former and ignored the latter.

This is, in fact, the point of the show. The two pictures are a deliberately loaded juxtaposition. The catalog states immediately that "the organizers of this exhibit of Chicago architecture wish to pay tribute to all those architects who were passed over by the first generation of historians of modern architecture." And the subject matter consists of the work "left out" of orthodox accounts of the Chicago School and its role in the modern movement.

What we are dealing with, then, is revisionist history. As such, the show is both an iconographic feast and an exercise in provocative scholarship. And it is important at a time when serious revisionism is on the rise in assessments of the modern movement, and official theory and history are being attacked on all sides.

The aim of the sponsoring Chicago architects—Laurence Booth, Stuart E. Cohen, Stanley Tigerman, and Benjamin Weese—reinforced by Stuart Cohen's knowledgeable catalog, is to explode and expand the doctrinaire view of the Chicago contribution. That view, canonized by Sigfried Giedion, divides Chicago architecture into two schizophrenic parts: the small-scale, personal, domestic developments of Frank Lloyd Wright and the Prairie School, and the technological development of the structural frame and the tall building, known as the Chicago skyscraper. The palm of modernism was then supposed to be handed to Europe in the early years of the twentieth century for the International Style, while Chicago languished and waited until the thirties for Mies van der Rohe to revive its progressive structural tradition.

All that happened, if not exactly as recorded. No one disputes or denies Chicago's skyscraper contribution; the confirmed achievements and monuments of modern architecture are not being rejected or downgraded. But a lot of other things apparently happened as well—particularly in those supposed doldrum years—that have either gone unrecorded or been consciously suppressed because they did not fit into accepted theories or timetables.

Chicago Architects combines rediscovery and reevaluation with irony and a bit of hubris. It is both history and polemics. There is the sound of an ax grinding quietly. But the material contains genuine implications for a broader, more objective understanding of modern architecture than the hygienically edited standard texts provide of what went on here and abroad. In fact, history and architecture may never be quite the same as this and similar rediscoveries unfold. We are finding a pluralism of ideals and styles that makes twentieth-century architecture far more intricate and dramatic than doctrinaire modernism has allowed, as well as perceiving an American contribution and continuity that may prove to be increasingly significant.

Chicago Architects was organized as a response to a larger show of more traditional skyscraper-engineering emphasis, "One Hundred Years of Chicago Architecture, which will open at the Chicago Art Institute on May 1. Most of the work in this "countershow" does not begin from engineering considerations. Mr. Cohen, in his text, charcacterizes it as romantic rather than pragmatic in approach. The buildings are

almost all intimate structures closely related to personal experience—
houses, schools, and churches rather than commercial construction, in
a galaxy of styles.

Mr. Cohen also points out that it is quite logical for society to want
different styles for its churches, museums, libraries, and civic buildings
than the style produced commercially by engineering and economic
expediency, no matter how elegant that expression may become. This
actual variety is a more accurate reflection of American culture than
those isolated examples where a structural rationale has been promoted
by modernist doctrine as the only "appropriate" solution.

But even the structural rationale can be romantic. George Fred Keck's
remarkable Crystal House—all glass with delicate metal trusses—built
for the Chicago World's Fair in 1934, and Buckminster Fuller's original
(Chicago-born) Dymaxion House of 1927 were both perfectly capable of
being produced. They were simply romantic-technological visions whose
time had not come. Immediate offshoots appeared in Bertrand Gold-
berg's mast-hung gas station and ice cream stand—precursors of Marina
City's round-towered, world-of-tomorrow look.

There are clearly traced lines presented here of International Style
and art deco in Chicago in the twenties and thirties, from Keck, Holabird and Root, Paul Schweikher, Barry Byrne, and the Bowman brothers. (I found many of these in the research files of the Museum of
Modern Art in New York in the forties, and they are probably still
there.) There are fascinating aberrations, such as the thirties work of
Andrew Rebori, which suggests both the Russian constructivism of
Konstantin Melnikov and the Parisian chic of art moderne. Early
shingle-style Frank Lloyd Wright houses are selected as forerunners of
the angular mannerisms of Harry Weese and Walter Netsch.

Specifically, what is dealt with here is ideology, as much as history.
There is an increasingly recognized, profound ideological split between the structural-functional aesthetic of the orthodox modernists
and the "formal, spatial and consciously symbolic issues" that preoc-
cupy a considerable group of young architects now. This is fueling a revival of eclecticism, not as conventional, academic borrowing, but as a
means of image making—and all is grist for the mill. This urge for style
and symbolism has been minimally addressed by the historians of the
modern movement.

That is why this kind of history so intrigues the present generation of practitioners; it is with a special eye that the past is being reexamined and, for better or worse, used in their own work. Today's eclecticism is a creative, cannibalistic combination of erudite nostalgia and extremely sophisticated aesthetics. It needs revisionist history to feed on. The results are acutely artful exercises in cultural memory and personal value projection—but these are not simple or innocent times.

Nor is this a simple or innocent show; it contains much to debate. Image makers are not going to supplant problem solvers, and technology can be as elegant as symbols. Right now, history is being revised as a polemic for style, which is where we came in. But in this case the near-past is being raided rather than discarded. In the process, a great deal is being learned, much of value is being restored to the record, and a sound and necessary input is being gained. The rewriting of history is part of the continuing historical process.

New York Times, March 14, 1976

Sir Edwin Landseer Lutyens and the Cult of the Recent Past

THE ARCHITECTURAL REVOLUTION IS GALLOPING RAPIDLY backward. The latest titillating peek at the forbidden past that the modernists have spurned with Calvinist fervor is The Architecture of Sir Edwin Landseer Lutyens (1869–1944), the exhibition that has just opened at the Museum of Modern Art as one of its major shows of the fall and winter season. Aided by a grant from the National Endowment for the Arts and cosponsored by the Philadelphia Museum of Art, the show will be on view in New York through January 7.

Of all the forbidden past, the traditional work of the twentieth century—those buildings that continued to use eclectic sources after the modernists had outlawed them for functional glass, steel, and concrete—has been the most taboo. And if there is a lower circle of

damnation reserved for architects, it has been for the ones who com-
pounded the sin by clothing modern construction in classical forms.

Sir Edwin Landseer Lutyens was guilty on both counts. If that
weren't enough, he was solid British establishment dealing in the kind
of official and monumental commissions for business and government
that ranged from bank buildings to plans for the colonial capital of New
Delhi in India. To say nothing of homes for the privileged and rich.

WHY, THEN, THIS sudden attention to his work? Actually, it is not all
that unexpected. The guest director of the show, Allan Greenberg, is an
architect who has been studying Lutyens for over a decade, and Lutyens's name has become one of the code words of the "postmodernists,"
who have been rediscovering a highly selective past.

Nor is the Museum of Modern Art displaying a perverse sense of hu-
mor in giving these traditional buildings its stamp of approval. The exhibition is in the same revisionist spirit as the big Beaux Arts drawing
show of 1975, which restored the rejected academy to respectability,
and the Gunnar Asplund show, which took that controversial eclectic-
modernist back into the fold of approved practitioners.

As your all-purpose, nonconformist architect, Asplund made an easy
transition to something even less acceptable, your all-out establishment-
eclectic architect; in this case, Lutyens. Spurred by Arthur Drexler, director of the Department of Architecture and Design, the museum is
right in the mainstream of the revisionist trend.

But beyond all the turns and twists of revisionist theory and practice today—the agony and anguish of those who profess that modern
architecture is dead and alternatives must be sought, and the fruitful
excitement of some of the more thoughtful explorations of those
alternatives—one notable fact remains. Lutyens was a superb architect.
If he had clothed his buildings in banana peels, he would have done it
with urbanity and style. He was a high-wire practitioner; one need only
look at run-of-the-mill classicism, or what passed for classicism in the
twentieth century, to see the extraordinary art and skill with which he
worked.

This is the kind of miraculous manipulation of procession and space,
of form and proportion, of visual and functional relationships, that goes
beyond style and labels. The results were achieved through erudite and
elegant devices. And this is the kind of architecture that generates

tremendous excitement among professionals—particularly among the young in the process of discovering the brilliant complexity of great building. What passes for the architectural avant-garde today is all on a Lutyens high.

But if the recognition of his work among the intellectual art elite is not perverse at this time, there is a certain irony in the relative inaccessibility of its forms and meanings to all except those with a rather recondite architectural education. (On the other hand, inaccessibility is the traditional hallmark of the avant-garde.)

Most of today's architects are ignorant of all but the most elementary knowledge of classical forms and their uses. Some are busy clambering over monuments in an orgy of making measured drawings, learning the lessons of Rome and the Renaissance firsthand. Others are trying valiantly, in a mood of reinvention, to produce moldings again, and one is unsure whether to laugh or cry at the innocently clumsy results. No wonder they are all so impressed by a master.

And if there is an interesting side effect of this reevaluation of Lutyens and other eclectic architects, it is that ignorance is rapidly going out of style. Architects will need a proper knowledge of their own art in its total stylistic and historical evolution—and that can't possibly be all bad.

Otherwise, how to really appreciate Lutyens's buildings? It is possible to walk through a Lutyens house and sense the compelling spatial organization, but it is less simple to "read" the sophisticated and subtle play of the spatial devices that depend on a learned vocabulary.

Because in every Lutyens work, from the Berkshire estates of the first decade of the century done in a "protomodern" or "new traditionalist" picturesque style, to the "high classical" of the Viceroy's House built in New Delhi, over the next two decades, there is grace and wit. Lutyens called classical architecture "the great game." It was a game that he played with an aerialist's skill.

Ambiguity and paradox are present in every example; Lutyens joined the formal and the bucolic; he liked symmetry of form with asymmetry of movement. He willfully broke the restraints of order for the accommodation of function. In his own time, the taste and polish of his classical vocabulary commanded admiration. But it is this ambiguity and paradox that intrigue another generation today.

He was wonderfully witty—his "disappearing" pilasters serve both to puzzle and delight the viewer and to transform the perception of a building's bulk. He could throw the curve of an oculus better than Ron Guidry throws a ball. No current practitioner of complexity and contradiction can improve on his treatment of the changing wall planes of the Midland Bank on Poultry Street in London.

Even the later, drier work of the thirties, such as the British Embassy in Washington or the Y.W.C.A. on Great Russell Street in London, and the buildings on which he acted as consultant, retain this consummate gamesmanship. What his project for the Liverpool Cathedral would have been like if executed is a staggering thought.

Call it classicism, or mannerism, the mastery was always there. Call it architecture, in its timeless definition.

New York Times, November 12, 1978

Discovering Ivan Leonidov

THE FIRST EXHIBITION IN THE UNITED STATES of the work of the Soviet architect Ivan Leonidov (1902–59), one of the most radical talents of the early years of the Russian Revolution, can be seen until February 21 at the Institute for Architecture and Urban Studies, 8 West Fortieth Street. This rare documentation reveals a remarkable artist whose eclipse today is equaled only by his fame within the Soviet Union in the twenties. The new material adds a previously unwritten chapter to modern architectural history and has all of the elements of genius and angst of a classic Russian novel. Leonidov's story is a personal and aesthetic tragedy of epic proportions.

It is largely a story of unbuilt buildings; of all the spectacular projects on view at the institute, ranging from cultural palaces to new towns, only an ornamental stair built into a mountainside was constructed in 1937 in the Crimea. Oddly enough, this fact diminishes neither his significance nor his position in the official assessments of modern architecture. The present display makes that position clear.

Because Leonidov's work has not been widely known and has been virtually inaccessible, the assessment is overdue. Except for a very brief initial period, Leonidov was systematically downgraded and deprived of his livelihood by the Soviet bureaucracy that controlled all architectural production. A series of portrait photos shows a young man of intense spiritual beauty reduced to a broken and eroded sadness by the end of his life.

WE OWE THIS important show and a forthcoming book to two Dutch architects, Rem Koolhaas and Gerrit Oorthuys, who have painstakingly searched out the material in the Soviet Union. The exhibition has been aided by a grant from the New York State Council on the Arts. On the basis of photographs of drawings, models, and paintings—none of the original documents could be taken out of the country—and new models made by the institute's students, Leonidov emerges as one of the towering talents of the twentieth century.

This was admittedly an idealistic and Olympian talent of vast romantic dimensions—visionary in the classic definition. The clichés of the Russian temperament are all present—intellectual passion and imaginative ardor—but the reality that comes through is of an intensely creative mind devoted to the new ideals of revolution and abstraction.

Leonidov was a leading architectural light of the related Russian movements of suprematism and constructivism, in the company of— and indebted to—such artists as Kasimir Malevich and El Lissitzky. Among the influential architects of the time were Ladovsky, Ginzburg, the Vesnin brothers, and Konstantin Melnikov. For one exhilarating decade right after the revolution, it looked as if these men might indeed remake the world, or at least a part of the Soviet Union, in their image.

Actually, the aesthetic revolution came to Russia before the political revolution. The years from 1914 to 1917 saw the innovations of Kandinsky, Malevich, Tatlin, and the other originators of the geometric abstraction that was to have such a profound influence on Western art. In the early twenties there was a sense of artists and society moving in the same direction in the Soviet Union, sharing the same radical means and goals. Architects were exhilarated by the irresistible idea of building a new state.

Building types called "social condensors" were invented—workers' clubs, palaces of health and culture, to serve new social and state needs. Workers' housing and new towns were planned. The radical designs were often beyond the economic and technological reach of the new government. But most major Soviet cities have at least one or two constructivist monuments of the twenties, such as Golossov's remarkable Zuyev Club in Moscow of 1926–27, and a wealth of documents remain from the constant competitions that became the established Soviet way of choosing public designs.

THE NEW SOVIET architecture came to outside attention through Konstantin Melnikov's much-admired Paris Exposition Building of 1925. It was greeted by the European profession as an aesthetic revelation. "They carried me on their shoulders," he recalled in 1967, a few years before his death. A book on Melnikov by S. Frederick Starr will be published later this year.

By 1930, the conservatives regained power and set out to destroy the radical art styles. The progressive architectural organizations Asnova and OSA were dissolved by Stalin in 1932 and replaced by the State Academy of Architecture. In 1937, the Congress of Soviet Architects established the familiar wedding-cake classicism as the official academic style.

The most vicious attacks of all were leveled at Leonidov. The whole range of subversive strains to be purged were lumped under the epithet "Leonidovism." He had been graduated as a star student from the Vkhutemas, the experimental school that predated the Bauhaus, in 1927; he was acclaimed and lionized for his talent from 1927 to 1929, and totally discredited by 1930. He lost both his teaching position and his apartment and became ineligible to build anything at all.

A life began for him and his family of temporary shelter in friends' apartments and offices; in later years he worked as a taxi driver and a painter of lampshades. He continued to enter the endless competitions that he had no hope of winning, and that is the body of work in the institute show.

Two projects, one near the beginning and the other at the end of Leonidov's career and life, are compelling examples of his mastery of art and symbolism. The powerful images of a 1933 competition entry for the headquarters of the Ministry of Heavy Industry, the center of all Soviet planning, are unforgettable, once seen. The plan would have cleared Red Square of such structures as the GUM Department Store to create a vast space almost twice its present width. Part was to be crowned with what Leonidov called "a sheaf of towers" on a podium base.

The towers are three symbolic skyscrapers overshadowing the Kremlin and St. Basil's Cathedral. But Leonidov saw this as the proper aesthetic culmination of the "subtle and majestic music" of the architecture of the Kremlin and Red Square—in fact, he viewed it as a historical necessity in terms of the supremacy of the Soviet state.

The three tall, clustered towers are rectangular, triangular, and circular in plan. The rectangular tower is a grid of masonry and glass, topped by a dynamic linear abstraction of stainless steel masts meant to hold platforms for "sky performances." An external elevator soars up one side. The triangular tower has stone piers and curved glass walls. The round tower tapers like a smokestack and is of black glass blocks, luminous at night, with projecting, gold-colored "viewing platforms." All are connected by aerial bridges.

Next to this overwhelming constructivist fantasy, futurism looks tame. The freehand sketches that preceded the formal drawings are very beautiful; they have an almost Renaissance calligraphy.

Leonidov's last project was "The City of the Sun," worked on from 1947 to his death in 1959. This consisted of a huge tent, for which many fanciful studies were made, with a satellite suspended over it in an intricate and delicate geometry. Whenever world peace was achieved, the satellite was meant to be released to rise and float indefinitely in the sky. It would be appropriately and darkly Russian to equate the satellite with Leonidov's spirit and to dwell on metaphors of peace and freedom. But it would be unnecessary. Leonidov's art has obviously been its own symbol and tragic necessity.

New York Times, February 12, 1978

The First Hundred Years: McKim, Mead & White

THE NAME MCKIM, MEAD & WHITE is to architecture what J. P. Morgan is to banking and Dom Perignon is to champagne. To the public, it means monuments, mansions, and millionaires, and the glamour of high society and high life. It also means Evelyn Nesbit and Harry K. Thaw and a crime of passion on the roof of the former Madison Square Garden—a McKim, Mead & White building, of course.

The victim, the architect Stanford White, is remembered as a celebrity, bon vivant, man about town, creative genius, and fashionable arbiter of taste—a *Fountainhead*-like image (establishment rather than maverick division) of the sort that occasionally propels architecture into the popular imagination. So great is the power of the legend that local mythology credits any opulent and elegant turn-of-the-century house to Stanford White, who could not possibly have designed them all, while every sufficiently grand public building is assigned to Charles McKim.

Scholars are busy sorting it all out. The early monographs have been reissued, and in 1979 a major show at the Brooklyn Museum, called The American Renaissance, dealt with all of the arts and many of the artists of the period from 1876 to 1917; the Brooklyn Museum, appropriately, is a grandly colonnaded McKim, Mead & White building. Previously unexhibited documents from the collection of Columbia University's Avery Architectural Library offered fascinating sidelights on the principals' work and personalities. They were displayed in Low Library, a Pantheon-like space with massive columns and marbles, and also a McKim, Mead & White building.

The firm of McKim, Mead & White was founded in 1879, when the young Stanford White joined Charles Follen McKim and William Rutherford Mead in a practice that would soon become the most important and influential of its time. Domestically, it ranged from the large shingle "cottages" of the New England aristocracy to the marble châteaux of the Newport overachievers; institutionally, it included the civic centers, state capitols, universities, libraries, and museums that represented the political power, cultural ambitions, and philanthropic ideals of the day. The period of the firm's ascendancy was called by most of its art world participants—few of whom could be faulted for modesty—the American Renaissance. It involved a collaborative effort in all of the arts, based on what was fondly believed to be the Italian Renaissance model. Instead of noble and papal palaces, McKim, Mead & White built mansions for the new millionaires. Ambitious projects were initiated over lavish meals, fine wines, and Havana cigars in exclusive clubs, naturally, by McKim, Mead & White.

The architecture built in this spirit still looms large on the landscape. But the taste for it has had its ups and downs. From a high point around the turn of the century, it reached its low point during the modernist revolution, when its eclectic classical design stood for all the things that modern architecture was rebelling against. Everything this work represented—the borrowings from the past, the trappings of the conservative power structure—had to be destroyed if the revolution was to succeed. Although much that was rejected was tiresome and pretentious, the good, unfortunately, was jettisoned with the bad.

Today's young "radicals," in revolt against orthodox modernism, are looking for some of the lost symbols and skills that were grounded in so many centuries of a highly developed tradition. What they have found are the academy, the Beaux Arts, and the American Renaissance. Only something that has been so completely out could now be so far in. In fact, celebrations of the work of McKim, Mead & White would have been virtually impossible not too long ago. Or it would have been a very small party. Admirers of the American Renaissance, like Henry Hope Reed Jr. and John Bayley, the founders of Classical America, a group devoted to the appreciation, study, and revival of the classical style, have been trying for many years to roll the firm's reputation back uphill with Sisyphean determination. Their major vindication came with the Museum of Modern Art's large Beaux-Arts exhibition in 1975, which gave academic architecture the stamp of the establishment again. And now the unthinkable has happened; some young architects are actually designing in the "new classicism."

No one would have been more surprised at the changes in their fortunes than McKim, Mead & White. Certainly humility was not part of the imperial manner. There is the story about the planning session of artists and architects for the Columbian Exposition of 1893, for which McKim, Mead & White set the image that was to turn the Chicago fairgrounds into a great white City Beautiful. In a fit of aesthetic euphoria,

Augustus St. Gaudens turned to Daniel Burnham to sum up the feelings in the room. "Look here, old fellow," he said, "do you realize that this is the greatest meeting of artists since the fifteenth century?" It is not recorded that anyone demurred.

A far less sanguine observer at the time was Louis Sullivan, who, almost alone, did not espouse the classical revival that was to sweep all else before it after the phenomenal success of the fair. The golden arches of his Transportation Building were neither snow-white nor indebted to Greece or Rome; their bold forms and interlaced ornament were meant to be a creative contribution to a native American development. The fair helped break Sullivan's cantankerous heart. His often-repeated observation was that its reactionary design would set back the course of American architecture fifty years or more.

He was right, of course, and he was also wrong. We eventually got the best of the academy and the best of the brave new world, and the worst of both. We are standing at the point where we no longer have to choose sides. This is the moment when the two faces of art—the academic and the innovative—are finally being put back together, and we are once again looking at history whole. Now, if we can just look at it straight. The range, in nineteenth- and twentieth-century academic work, is from the magnificent to the perfectly dreadful. That which lacked content or meaning filled the void with lifeless pomposity. The craftsmanship and materials were often superb, which can do a lot for mediocrity, but some of the embellishing art definitely makes one queasy.

The work of McKim, Mead & White maintained a superior standard and has provided buildings that are among the chief ornaments and richest adornments of our cities. The norm was a cultivated competence, however, rather than greatness, and many of the later buildings were as cold and spiritless as they were maddeningly nonfunctional. It is now up to the scholars to call the hits, the misses, and the errors.

New York Times, December 2, 1979

Holabird and Root

It probably shouldn't, but it still comes as something of a surprise to find American architectural firms celebrating their hundredth anniversaries. Last year it was the centennial of the founding of the firm of McKim, Mead & White, which coincided nicely with what might be called the rediscovery of their work. Rediscovery is probably the wrong word, since McKim, Mead & White buildings have continued to be an important part of the public consciousness—consisting, as they do, of a large number of monumental public and institutional structures of the late nineteenth and early twentieth century. What made the occasion special was a kind of McKim, Mead & White revival for a younger generation, a reevaluation that recognized the firm's sophisticated and skillful use of the academic, classical tradition that was consigned to the dust heap by the modernists and remained generally untouchable for the last fifty years. That renewed and generous appreciation made a very nice birthday party.

The most recent centennial celebrant is the Chicago firm of Holabird and Root, which, as Holabird and Roche, was central to the development of the skyscraper in the thirty years from 1880 to 1910, and to what is known, internationally, as the Chicago School.

Probably no single firm reflects more accurately the complete span of American architectural practice over the last hundred years, which includes a varied and quite valid sequence of styles. It has had its aesthetic ups and downs. The office began with the pragmatic and innovative emphasis on engineering and aesthetic clarity that characterized the early Chicago skyscrapers, which changed to the fashionable and sometimes tortured eclectic conceits with which tall buildings were clothed just before and after World War I. This was followed by the original and elegant "modernistic," or art deco, designs of the thirties, and then a return to something akin to the early structural pragmatism in the "modernism" that followed World War II.

As appreciative as I am of the grand achievements of McKim, Mead & White, give or take a fair number of impressive potboilers, I find myself more interested in the vicissitudes of the Holabird and Root story. It lacks the lordly masterworks of the eastern establishment firm, but it tells us a good deal more about invention, adaptability, changing taste, and the struggle to survive as part of the American architectural mainstream.

I LIKE THE kind of tradition in which two and three generations of distinguished architectural names like Holabird (father, and son, and grandson in the one Chicago firm) and Root (father and son, anchoring two Chicago firms) continued to practice in the same city—particularly a city that has claimed to deal primarily in progress and change. I like it better than the instant, academic tradition in which a firm like McKim, Mead & White wrapped itself so splendidly and successfully for a borrowed style of life and design, which descended into spiritless aridity in the work of its later members.

Holabird and Root produced sound rather than spectacular buildings. Even at its time of greatest strength, from 1880 to 1910, there were other firms and individuals in Chicago, from William Le Baron Jenney to Louis Sullivan, who made the great leaps forward in structure and style. But if other architects built greater buildings, few built consistently better ones. The office's claim to fame is based on that most interesting and important chapter in American architectural history, the development of the skyscraper, a field of design and construction in which it held a leadership position for a surprisingly long time. There were changes in partners and philosophy over the years, but it continued to produce top-rank tall buildings right through the twenties and thirties.

Chicago's great contributions in 1880–99 were the technological achievements of steel-frame construction and related engineering, and the handsome visual expression of that new technology. The Chicago Style became one of the strongest and handsomest aesthetics of modern times. (Revisionists are adding many styles and schools to the Chicago story that have been overlooked in the critical preoccupation with the tall building, but that does not change its significance or supremacy; there is really no point in trying to stand history on its head.)

Holabird and Roche specialized in the careful, logical adaptation of structural means to functional ends—which resulted in the creation of a distinct design formula for the new, large business buildings whose rise skyward was made possible by the metal frame and the elevator.

THE HISTORIAN CARL W. Condit has characterized that formula as "a basic norm or type exactly developed to fit a particular set of conditions." The historian and critic William H. Jordy calls it an architectural type virtually beyond "design," something so well suited to its use that it led inevitably and properly to mass duplication. He makes it clear that it was "a superb type."

The formula became the skyscraper style. To a stroller of Chicago's streets today, these early buildings still have an extraordinary impact. The visible scale and pattern of their structural frames, filled with the generous expanses of bayed or plain glass known as "Chicago windows," have an architectonic clarity and force that is only achieved through a sensuous and rational reference to structure. Architecturally, this is a hard act to follow.

It was exactly suited to the needs of business and builders. Boldly stated in Holabird and Roche's Tacoma Building of 1886–89, the formula was carried further in the Marquette Building of 1894, which definitively established the supremacy of the structural frame. The solution was at its most refined in the Republic Building of 1904–9. (The Tacoma and the Republic were both demolished in the sixties, and the architectural vandalism is continuing in the seventies. What remains of the Chicago School owes a great deal to the pioneering efforts of the Chicago Heritage Committee, and much of what is gone was beautifully recorded by Richard Nickel, who lost his life in the collapse of an Adler and Sullivan building that he was photographing in the process of demolition.)

WITH A BOSTON builder named Peter Brooks, Holabird and Roche laid out the fundamental principles of the new commercial construction. They stressed the provision of light and air, and the importance of the quality of public facilities, like lobbies, elevators, and corridors. Above all, there was to be no second-class space, because it cost as much to build and operate as first-class space. Proper materials and good details were to simplify operation and maintenance.

Like so many others, Holabird and Roche succumbed to the

avalanche of eclecticism after 1910, but the firm never had a sure hand
for academic revivalism. In 1928, after a change of partners, the office
emerged as Holabird and Root, and in the thirties it produced a brilliant succession of "modernistic" skyscrapers of a radical, streamlined
elegance that included the Chicago Board of Trade, the Palmolive,
now Playboy Building, and the Chrysler Building at the Chicago
World's Fair.

The forties brought the war, and the fifties saw a lot of uneven and
pedestrian work. In the twenties, some of the senior partners retired; today the principals are Eugene A. Cook, John A. Holabird Jr., Gerrard S.
Pook, Gerald Horn, and Roy D. Solfisbury III. The firm is now em-
barked on a search for quality and style that is yet without a name; it reflects the newer, younger partners and the aesthetic pluralism of
current architectural trends.

Meanwhile, the old Chicago—their Old Chicago—is tumbling down
around them. The city has been shamefully delinquent in protecting its
early skyscraper heritage. Building codes and economics militate against
preservation, and new projects constantly call for landmark demolition.
The British magazine the *Economist,* in a recent feature on Chicago's
historic architecture—which is more admired abroad than at home—
deplored "the loss of many of the buildings that have inspired reverence
for the city." The second hundred years are the hardest.

New York Times, March 2, 1980

Resurrecting a Prophetic Nineteenth-century Practitioner

In any survey of out-of-favor architects least likely to be revived, the easy winner, until very recently, would have been Eugène
Emmanuel Viollet-le-Duc. Probably no architect has been more consistently put down in this century; it is hard to look at a medieval mon-

ument in France, from the Cathedral of Notre Dame in Paris to the walled town of Carcassonne, without hearing imprecations against Viollet-le-Spoiler. He is the nineteenth-century French architect (1814–79) who spent his life elaborately reconstructing the buildings of the Middle Ages and who represents everything the twentieth century has disdained: the overrestoration of monuments, the popularization of quasi-historical styles, and, perhaps most unforgivable of all, the preeminence of the traditionalist in official art and culture. From 1830 to 1879, Viollet-le-Duc was one of the most active, influential, and respected architects in the Western world.

On second thought, that would probably make him a prime candidate for revival. In today's spirit of revisionism, scholars seem bent on standing history on its head, with the rediscovery prize going to the most unexpected choices. Last year was the centenary of Viollet-le-Duc's death, a moment when reputations have a way of beginning to rise. There has been talk of reassessment studies in progress. All this has come together now—the rumors, the research, the serious reappraisal— in a major exhibition at the Grand Palais in Paris, Viollet-le-Duc, which will be on view through May 5.

This exhibition, which is attended by the same kind of long lines waiting to see the Monet show, also at the Grand Palais, is one of the year's notable cultural events. It is the first one-man show ever given to an architect in this prestigious setting, under the auspices of the French National Museums. The display takes up three floors and includes drawings, paintings, models, photographs, furniture, and objects of decorative art, material gathered from archives and collections all over France. The comprehensive documentation covers every facet of Viollet-le-Duc's extraordinary career—as restorer of monuments, builder and theoretician, artist and painter, champion of innovative technologies, master of decorative arts, guardian of the past, and prophet of the future. An excellent catalog provides useful essays.

The viewpoint is neither the customary condemnation of Viollet-le-Duc as the dead and destructive hand of convention and violator of the past, nor the one-sided reading of his progressive tendencies in such things as his vision of metal construction as the key to a new architecture.

THIS EXTENSIVE AND evenhanded presentation gives a picture of a whole, quintessentially nineteenth-century man. If a little special pleading makes him come off more heroically than necessary—he is still a far better theoretician than designer—we are finally able not only to see the true dimensions of his work but also to understand it in the appropriate context and framework of his own time. It was a complex time, with established traditions being shattered by political, social, and industrial revolutions, and it was not an easy time for architecture, which was caught between the poles of technological advance and cultivated practice. In France, under the Beaux Arts, that schism between architecture and engineering was particularly troublesome.

But aside from the contributions that the exhibition makes to an understanding of the man and his period, there is a great deal of pleasure in the viewing; the drawings and paintings on display have a skilled and ravishing delicacy. In everything from the controlled curve of a carved acanthus leaf and the details of a stone grotesque peering from the foliage of a crumbling capital, to serene views of nature, these are refined and beautiful renderings by a man whose acute visual perceptions were accompanied by a freshly sharpened pencil wherever he went. He drew like a dream.

In his travels through France, all during his life, he recorded mountains and monuments, landscapes and ruins, in meltingly lovely watercolors. And whether it was a design for sculpture or stained glass (an art he largely revived), a minutely detailed church steeple, a piece of furniture for his major antiquarian invention, the Château at Pierrefonds, the decorative woodwork and ironwork for the imperial train, or a sketch of a bat in flight, there is the ease and enchantment of a fine eye and great technical expertise.

The controversial restorations form a long and impressive list; among them are the monuments of Vézelay, Sens, Amiens, Beaune, Avignon, and Toulouse; there are churches, cathedrals, châteaus, and *hôtels de ville*. This work was based on the best archaeological knowledge at that time, but the art and science of archaeology have advanced immeasurably since then. Viollet-le-Duc overreached, undeniably, and his confidence in his ability to recreate the past, to recapture the irretrievable, was boundless. But his concerns, as recorded in his writings, were often surprisingly sound and sensitive.

One must remember that the preservation philosophies of the nineteenth and twentieth centuries could not be more unlike. Viollet-le-Duc's world wanted things put together the way they were, Humpty

Dumpty fashion; he played the delicate and dangerous game of "restoring back." The twentieth century stresses the value of whatever is left of the original fabric over everything else.

THE IMPORTANT POINT is not how much of what we see today was put there by Viollet-le-Duc and his sculptors and artisans, but that without them, there would be little or nothing to see at all. France's superb medieval heritage was literally crumbling away, and sheer structural survival often made considerable rebuilding necessary.

The recent rediscovery of the statues of the kings from the portal of Notre Dame in Paris reveals both how amazingly close to the originals Viollet-le-Duc and his sculptors were, and yet how critical the difference is in the tilt of an eye or the turn of a lip. The softer modeling and insidious nineteenth-century sweetness of the reproductions replace the greater strength and sharpness and subtly exotic character of the earlier vision and style. That kind of thing has given him his bad name.

But he has a good name among modernist historians. Sigfried Giedion, in his account of skyscraper development in Chicago in 1880–89, quotes LeRoy Buffington's claim to the "invention" of the steel-framed tall buildings based on the inspiration of Viollet-le-Duc's widely published and translated *Entretiens sur l'Architecture*. The French architect's earlier endorsement of the radical possibilities of the structural ironwork that was being actively pursued, and his emphasis on the visible, rational structure and truth-to-materials of medieval architecture and design, had a strong appeal for the aesthetic reformers of the nineteenth century. Viollet-le-Duc himself considered medievalism the most "modern" of all styles.

It is not surprising that the historian and critic Henry-Russell Hitchcock has characterized Viollet-le-Duc's work as "curiously ambiguous." He praises the iron projects but calls them paper boldness. He condemns the restorations as "no contribution to 19th-century architecture; rather they represent a furious diminution of authenticity in the monuments of the past." Even in the sympathetic display at the Grand Palais, Viollet-le-Duc's new buildings do not come off well. They remain correct and spiritless exercises in revivalist styles. It is not surprising that he lost out to Charles Garnier's flamboyant planning and theatrical sense of circulation in the competition for the new Paris Opéra in 1860–1.

Good show won over good form, to Viollet-le-Duc's considerable and lasting distress.

Still, the man who emerges from this exhibition is tremendously impressive. He was the architect-born, who never wanted to be anything else from the time he was a child. At sixteen, when revolutionary barricades were being erected in the streets of Paris, he gave advice on their construction. He bypassed formal education at the École des Beaux Arts to work in architects' offices as soon as possible, and his travels in France and Italy established his taste for the past as a very young man.

A DAGUERREOTYPE AT the age of thirty shows him as vibrantly attractive and assured, with a dark beard and remarkably clear and observant eyes. His cross-legged position is debonair; there is a bit of stylish Scotch plaid on his vest, and a gold chain and fob hang below a well-cut coat. Only his carefully combed hair displays any signs of youthful unruliness. This is already a confident and elegant man.

Photographed at sixty-five the year before he died, the elegant air and clear gaze are undimmed, but the beard and hair are white and everything is impeccably under control. Perhaps controlled is the key word to Viollet-le-Duc. His art was one of precedent, rules, and measure. It did not aspire to break out of tradition or to transcend expectations. He practiced architecture as the controlling art to which other arts were subordinate, and he practiced all of them exceptionally well. But he could neither control nor resolve the ambiguities of the nineteenth century, the split between the world of art and the world of technology that the twentieth century has devoted so much of its aesthetic energy to try to heal. What he left us is a superb record of his delights and dilemmas, and the work of that rare kind of artist—the universal man.

New York Times, April 6, 1980

Born-Again Modernism

FOR THOSE WHO THOUGHT THEY HAD DRIVEN a stake through the heart of modernism, the news is bad; for unrepentant modernists who persisted in believing that it had never been buried or otherwise disposed of, the news is good. Redemption, if not repentance, is at hand. Modernism has risen again, but with a twist. Depending on your take, it is the last word in nostalgic revivals and cool, retro chic, or the latest and most radical chapter in a continuing revolution in building and seeing. Call it modernism redux, or born-again modernism, but anyone still in postmodernist denial has a problem.

The best news is that the popular sport of modern-bashing is over. Not many postmodernists had the wit and hubris of Stanley Tigerman's immortal montage of Mies van der Rohe's Crown Hall tilting into the ocean like the *Titanic*. You had to love it, whether you agreed that the end had come or not; it was the ultimate postmodernist image and statement, the consummate nose-thumbing at the modernist establishment. But Mies never sank. Today's most radical practitioners are quick to acknowledge their debt to the modern masters. Twentieth-century modernism is the basis of all their innovative work.

As someone who was there during modernism's period of ascendancy, I am both fascinated and bemused by the rebirth of something that never really died, and intrigued by the anomalies that beset its recognition and revival. Ironies abound. The revolution is not only old, it is falling apart. The International Style is an endangered species. Some of the buildings that were unloved and unwanted at the time are being designated as landmarks. Tree huggers have become building huggers, which is good, in spite of their quixotic and arbitrary choices. (How many gas stations and hamburger stands do we need preserved when Irving Gill's Los Angeles houses and other International Style survivals are being destroyed or disfigured daily?) The British, recognizing the problem with responsibility and a dogged lack of judgment, are busy protecting brutalist housing flats and office blocks that look as if they had been run up on giant knitting needles, and that's bad.

A few legendary icons of the fifties and sixties, such as Gordon Bunshaft's Lever House in New York, Alvar Aalto's dormitory at MIT, and

Paul Rudolph's Art and Architecture Building at Yale—possibly the period's most conspicuously reviled modernist structure, trashed by students and damaged by a mysterious fire—are being thoughtfully restored, after going through the full historical cycle of admiration, denigration, abuse, and respectful rediscovery. California's minimalist Case Study houses—beacons of the future in the fifties—are being snapped up by movie stars. According to promotional material, "Gucci's Tom Ford and actress Kelly Lynch have them and Leonardo Di Caprio wants one too."

The most reliable indicators of which way the fashionable architectural wind is blowing are the commercial developers, who are abandoning their faux-classical office towers and terrible good taste for a racier, high-tech signature look. The *Los Angeles Times* reports that many West Coast firms want to project an image of the high-energy, hip world of technology and the Internet. Builders and clients favor something "lean and spare and industrial, more like an Armani suit than a Versace." Stone is out. Glass and aluminum are in. The knockoff of the knockoffs has begun.

At a time when the accelerating crossover between architecture and fashion has reached the speed of light, trivialization, or the reduction of modernism to a "look," has become a major art form. For the fashionistas and trendy cognoscenti, midcentury modernism is the latest version of retro cool. Not for them the classic beauties of the high period of Italian and Scandinavian design, the spiraling patterns of Tapio Wirkkala's woods, the perfect curve of a Finn Juhl chair. The objects of choice are the heartwarming superclichés that so beautifully express where it all went off the tracks to expire in the pop heaven of mangy motels—the shag rugs, the boomerang tables, the Shiva-armed lamps, the chartreuse, aqua, and salmon pink tchotchkes that would have had Mies and his brethren hurling themselves from Morris Lapidus's serpentine Miami balconies.

The objects of desire range from the rare and astronomically priced ponyskin-covered Eames plywood chairs endorsed by the Museum of Modern Art in its early years, to the cartoon modern and attack colors of low-end furniture stores. It was the only period during which Venini made awesomely ugly glass. Bright young people are lusting after conversation pits (no one ever went into them, because the steps down seemed to be as much of an off-putting barrier as a wall).

There is a lot of attitude here, and material for serious study. The privileging of absolute awfulness and its amusements signals a freedom from the pious solemnities of the modernist establishment. Received standards and values are upended for a revisionist reading of the period that embraces the marginal and the rejected and delights in the excesses of the absurd. It is a kind of eye-opening or consciousness-raising exercise in reverse, in which everyone shares a nostalgia for things sentimentally remembered or never known. This is taste with an edge, beyond simple kitsch and pink flamingos, slightly perverse and just outrageous enough to be fun.

I'll confess to a fascination with and even an occasional will to possess a piece of emblematic awfulness; I'm as amused as anyone by its cockeyed presumption. It lightens things up; a pitch-perfect reflection of the popular culture, it deserves a place in cultural and materials history. But I'll get mine at yard sales, thank you, not from pricey dealers (isn't that what gives it a lot of its cachet?) because this is where you find the survival of the worst for the least. A dollar, tops. And it's unbelievably cool.

My concern is that the preoccupation with mannerism rather than substance misrepresents and downgrades some of modernism's most valuable and lasting work. Future revisionists, of course, will dig it all up again. Harvard hated its High Victorian Memorial Hall for decades; it has now been conscientiously restored. Miami deco was retrieved from oblivion and certain demolition to become a landmark district and the temple of hyperchic. High art and pop art are equally vulnerable to neglect and overkill. Fifties fallout will remain the in-thing for the in-crowd until the next in-thing comes along and all the overpriced trophies are dumped again. Following an absolutely predictable time-taste cycle, the best of the fifties and sixties is suffering its own oblivion, so unknown and underappreciated that you can find it in yard sales, too. If you see any in the trash heap, grab it.

These shifting standards make the preservation of twentieth-century modernism a difficult and unprecedented problem. We have come to the sudden, startling realization that the product of the modernist revolution is a style that has taken its place in the succession of past styles, even as it endures and is transformed in the practice of the present. There are enormous questions of inclusion and exclusion, criteria and methods, standards and values, restoration and reuse. The modernists themselves threw the whole past in the trash can, and there are those who would like to forget that modernism ever happened. Preservation groups like Docomomo—Documentation and Conservation of Buildings, Sites and Neighborhoods of the Modern Movement—have begun to call for action in the face of a disappearing and mutilated heritage, once we have decided what it is.

Someday, for example, we are going to realize that the glass boxes critics have been bad-mouthing for so long are the breathtaking essence of New York; their soaring, faceted, reflective mass gives the city both its hard-edged brilliance and powerful poetry. This is the great modern urban vernacular. These buildings will survive or be replaced by others that will up the ante of technology and profit. The new modernism—a computer-aided breakthrough in ideas about space, time, and form—will be added to the mix. I can think of no beauty greater, at any time in history, than this glittering mirror of a city in changing light, or in the phosphorescent darkness of night, when it lights up the sky.

Nostalgia has its place; pop has its place; the typical and the exceptional, the monuments and the vernacular, the doctrinaire and the offbeat, all have their place. We are writing our history now.

Wall Street Journal, March 1, 2001

Modernism, in Perspective

REVISITING MODERNISM TODAY is like visiting a foreign country—a place where attitudes and beliefs are so alien and incomprehensible that the gap between the present's harsh realities and the past's vision of a utopian world can hardly be grasped or understood. For many, modernism was something visited upon them, unasked, unloved, and unmourned when its demise was prematurely announced in the seventies. But there was no way to undo the twentieth century. The modern movement and modern times are joined at the hip in the most radical

and lasting transformation of every aspect of art and life since the Renaissance.

No one has resisted modernism as stubbornly as the British. Proudly
insular, devoted to tradition, they viewed it as left-leaning, cosmopoli-
tan, and international—in a word, foreign, which they detested. Even
now, young architects indebted to modernist precedent can dismiss the
modern movement as something associated with "bad regimes"—didn't
Soviet suprematism, Italian futurism, and the German Bauhaus, those
hotbeds of early modernist theory and practice, become the handmaid-
ens of communism and fascism? (Not really. Modernism was briefly
embraced and quickly denounced in favor of a colossally vacuous, de-
rivative classicism, with the most revolutionary talents sent packing.)

For the English, modernism is an unpleasant aberration that gave
them some grimly inhospitable public buildings and the dismal housing now called point blocks that brutalized their cities with an excess of
raw concrete in the sixties. It should also be noted that the British practiced a particularly stolid, neutering form of modernism that could be
achingly well-meaning and dull. They tend to overlook things like the
Russian émigré Berthold Lubetkin's enduringly desirable council flats
of the forties and his 1936 Highpoint apartments in London's Highgate,
a meticulously maintained, jealously guarded landmark that probably
requires a pass from heaven to get in if anyone ever leaves.

It has therefore taken someone with a profound sense of the significance and impact of the modern movement to mount the ambitious
show currently at the Victoria and Albert Museum, Modernism, Designing a New World, 1914–1939. It has probably helped that the show's
curator, Christopher Wilk, keeper of furniture, textiles, and fashion at
the Victoria and Albert, is an American with fewer hang-ups about the
subject. He is clearly a believer. And this is a landmark show. It offers a
revelatory, in-depth examination of international modernism in terms
of its times, context, and sources. Handsomely installed by the London-
based Czech architect Eva Jiricna, it can be seen in London until July
23, but a substantial version will travel to the Corcoran in Washington
next spring. There is an extensive and weighty catalog with essays that
further illuminate the subject.

The modern movement is a story of high hopes, boundless optimism,
innocent social idealism, and considerable hubris in which the artists,

architects, and artisans of the world would make it a better place through a radical new kind of design. Change was necessary to reinvigorate a corrupt, exhausted, and war-weary society. "Architecture or revolution!" Le Corbusier proclaimed, not surprisingly settling for architecture to improve people's lives. The machine was to be the symbol and instrument of salvation; mechanization and standardization would serve humanity through progressive political systems. Everything would be stripped down to its functional essence and reinvented, and this would lead to an aesthetic as modern as the message was messianic. Clear out the mess. Banish the past. Design for the future. Modernism was the original extreme makeover.

If the flawed rationale of the dream is obvious, the magnitude of what followed is equally clear. There are three parts to the show: Searching for Utopia, Building Utopia, and Rethinking Utopia. The first treats the centrality of the machine and the art produced in its image, and includes painting, sculpture, and performance art. The second presents architecture, interiors, and articles of domestic life. The once-startling cantilevered chairs in a section called Sitting on Air are now contemporary classics in continuous production. Two less familiar segments deal with healthy body culture and the relationship to nature. But the ultimate and inescapable point is that if the modernists' goals were touchingly unrealistic, the movement they set in motion did indeed change the world, permanently and irrevocably.

Painting, sculpture, architecture, furniture, tableware, interiors, graphics, photography and film, theater, costumes, and clothing are all here to prove it. There are familiar icons and the unexpected from Paris, Berlin, Moscow, the Netherlands, the United States, and eastern Europe. These are the masterworks of modernism by Piet Mondrian, Fernand Léger, Kasimir Malevich, Laszlo Moholy-Nagy, Marcel Duchamp, Wassily Kandinsky, Naum Gabo, and Hans Arp, with buildings and furniture by Le Corbusier, Mies van der Rohe, Walter Gropius, Marcel Breuer, Alvar Aalto, Erich Mendelsohn, and Gerritt Rietvelt, and photography and film by El Lissitzky, Alexander Rodchenko, and Man Ray.

Russian "mechanical ballet" costumes are displayed in front of film clips of actual performances; models of Le Corbusier's white-walled, ribbon-windowed villas coexist with a silver Czech automobile. Photos show artists as dashing young men in futuristic coveralls, "workers' clothing" infused with style and revolutionary politics. Wool swimsuits have bright geometric patterns designed by artists Sonia Delaunay and Giacamo Balla; one was worn by the famous Channel swimmer, Gertrude Ederle.

A surprise of the show is the emphasis on health and fitness and the start of a cult of the body; modernism promoted sport, exercise, and dance. These were years with a high toll of death and disease—the losses of World War I and the influenza epidemic, the prevalence of tuberculosis for which there was no known cure. There are stunning pictures of leaping gymnasts perpetually in midair in front of the Bauhaus buildings. Alvar Aalto's Paimio chair was designed in the early thirties for the open-air balconies of his TB sanitarium in Finland.

A kitchen, one of a mass-produced line created for a twenties housing development in Frankfurt, Germany, has been installed with an accompanying film clip describing its modern hygienic food preparation and utensils, the efficiency of its modern plan and design, and the clean, uncluttered look that established its modern credentials. Many are still used; others have been removed only because the counter depth does not accommodate today's appliances. The transfer of modern design to popular culture and consumer goods began early in the United States with the production of Sears radios in the thirties.

This is a show that delights the eye and clears the mind. Its timeless designs have traveled across class and taste—Breuer chairs at every price level, stacks of handsome housewares in home furnishings stores. The union of art and utility as a moral imperative may seem quaintly obsolete, but it produced little that was superficial, much that was rational, and a great deal that was beautiful. Everything here still looks very, very good. It has a lot to teach design fashionistas.

The real surprise is in the small, symbolic drawings, known from all the basic texts but seldom exhibited because of their fragility. Heartbreakingly lovely and breathtakingly prescient, they still convey the excitement and daring of a creative sea change after which nothing was ever the same again. Erich Mendelsohn's unexpectedly tiny 1917 sketch of the Einstein Tower is a vision of fluid motion only recently made a practical reality by the latest computer technology. Mies van der Rohe's prophetic glass skyscraper of 1921, the transparent elegance of its sharp prow rendered in bold crayon strokes, has turned brown with age. Unbuildable then, it stands for all the glass towers lining our city streets.

Tempered by time and hindsight, these drawings restore a kind of wonder that we have lost or denied.

It was revolution then, but it is art now. Without the full story, it has been reduced to style. It is time to stop using modernism as a convenient punching bag or turning it into trendy kitsch; this was one of the most powerful movements in history. We need to put its successes and failures in perspective, to suspend judgmental cynicism long enough to restore its proper meaning and context. Like it or not, we cannot reject or repeal history, particularly when it's our own.

Wall Street Journal, July 12, 2006

The Man Who Remade New York

Robert Moses, the man who remade twentieth-century New York on a scale equaled only by Sixtus V's transformation of sixteenth-century Rome and Baron Hausmann's radical reshaping of nineteenth-century Paris, is a hot topic again. He is the subject of three exhibitions, two lectures, two symposiums, and a continuing stream of press coverage that today's architectural superstars can only envy.

He stands on a bright orange steel beam suspended over water, a dwarfed Manhattan skyline behind him, supremely confident, blueprints in hand, in a life-size photomural that opens one of the three shows under the title Robert Moses and the Modern City: The Transformation of New York. Remaking the Metropolis presents his major public works at the Museum of the City of New York through May 28; The Road to Recreation focuses on his beaches, pools, parks, and the parkways that tie them together at the Queens Museum through May 27; Slum Clearance and the Superblock Solution covers housing and urban design at the Wallach Gallery of Columbia University through April 14. The curator of all three shows is Hilary Ballon, professor of art history and archaeology at Columbia University. She has also edited the excellent book of essays that serves as the catalog, in collaboration with Kenneth T. Jackson, professor of history and the social sciences at Columbia.

As historical revisionism goes, this reassessment is probably overdue, but the rehabilitation of Robert Moses is not an easy walk down memory lane. The reconsideration of a long career of wildly contradictory highs and lows has also had the unsurprising effect of awakening—or, rather, reawakening—the kind of passionate debate not heard since Jane Jacobs dealt the Lower Manhattan Expressway its final, fatal blow more than forty years ago.

Revisionist scholarship questions received opinions and reassesses accepted points of view. The acknowledged purpose here is to add balance to a story in which the brilliant restructuring of the public realm has been obscured by projects that rode roughshod over history and neighborhoods with an unfeeling arrogance of epic proportions that lingers in the collective mind. Dramatic photographs are used to reveal the scope, significance, and beauty of Moses's great public works: the elaborate network of roads, bridges, parks, and parkways; the superb, accessible Long Island beaches; the astounding number of local parks, playgrounds, and public pools; the cultural and international institutions that included Lincoln Center and the United Nations. The dominant theme is the magnitude of Moses's accomplishments and his remarkably prescient visualization of the needs of New York in the twenty-first century.

The argument is also made that an understanding of the ideology, practices, and resources within which Moses operated explains both his extraordinary achievements and his most controversial behavior. According to this thesis his activities were part of a general consensus; he was doing what was being done at the time. The fact that the gross misjudgments of his later years became apparent to many others, but not to him, as ideas about cities and planning changed, makes this a troubling rationale.

What it all comes down to, still, and probably always will, is the "good" Moses versus the "bad" Moses, the "early" Moses versus the "late" Moses, and how the "good" Moses could create the glorious public works of the twenties and thirties and the "bad" Moses became the symbol of the worst aspects of slum clearance and urban renewal in the forties and fifties.

The evolution can be seen in the architecture he embraced over the four decades of his career. Moses was a traditionalist who believed that nothing should be built that was above public taste, and yet his initial projects were designed in a contemporary manner enriched with handsome classical and deco details, solutions highly praised by Lewis Mumford. There is a stubbornly stunted architectural sensibility evident later, when he moved from architects of reputation to big commercial firms and buildings of obdurate mediocrity. Pseudocolonial-with-cupola became standard issue for recreational facilities; little brick outhouses in Howard Johnson style were all-purpose replacements for Calvert Vaux's authentic Victoriana in Central Park. What Moses understood was engineering; what he really loved were his suspension bridges.

IF WE ACCEPT that he was a man of his times, he obviously didn't get the message when times changed. In the words of one of the contributors to *Robert Moses and the Modern City*, Owen Gutfreund, from being the right person in the right place at the right time, Moses became the wrong person in the wrong place at the wrong time. Planning in the early twentieth century was broad and paternalistic. Its philosophy and practice grew out of the radical ideals of modernism and a belief in social reform that focused on public health and well-being. Moses's agenda was a perfect match.

The more intimate, humanistic view of planning as a small-scale, socially sensitive awareness of the street, the neighborhood, and individual lives had its catalyst in Jacobs's 1961 book, *The Death and Life of Great American Cities*, which became the bible of the planning revolution. This approach would have had no appeal for Moses even if he understood it. When asked by his biographer, Robert Caro, if there was a difference between building parkways on open land and expressways in the inner city, he replied, "Only that there were more people in the way."

Mr. Caro's take on Moses in his definitive work, *The Power Broker: Robert Moses and the Fall of New York*, published in 1974 when New York faced bankruptcy after a decades-long downward spiral, is considerably darker than the revisionist reassessment. There was an embarrassing moment and a whiff of scholarly scandal when it became apparent that he had not been invited to participate in any of the well-publicized events. The subliminal suggestion, intended or not, was that it was Mr. Caro who was being revised. A discreet announcement followed a special lecture set up by one of the show's sponsors. An overflow crowd gave Mr. Caro a standing ovation, adding a little edge to the proceedings.

It was obvious that those who remembered the midnight bulldozers sent into Central Park to rip up a playground for more parking for the Tavern on the Green, or the road that would have bisected Washington Square Park with high-speed traffic—both opposed by "a bunch of mothers"—were still clinging to Moses's image of audacious evil. Some (there are still a few of us) who manned the ramparts against his most damaging interventions and were submitted to his most creative vilifications were resisting his canonization. The fight to kill the infamous Lower Manhattan Expressway that would have destroyed SoHo, much of the Cast-Iron District, and parts of Chinatown, Little Italy, and the West Village (Moses insisted there was nothing to save) is a subject that defies detachment. The parade of gorgeous images of bridges and beaches, newly photographed for the exhibitions by Andrew Moore, upstages the mute testimony of old letters and news clips protesting wholesale demolition of homes and businesses or the threat of an enormous, elevated, ten-lane superhighway across Thirtieth Street that would have permanently dismembered Manhattan. The carefully inclusive narrative tells it all in safely worded labels that neutralize outrage. The presentation achieves its purpose of comprehensive objectivity, but its very evenhandedness is disturbing. It is almost too cool; there was nothing evenhanded about Moses.

TODAY, THERE IS great prosperity and renewed interest in thinking and building big. As city and state officials wrap themselves in Moses's mantle and try on his shoes for size, we hear upbeat talk about "breaking eggs to make omelets" and the way Moses "got things done." Many eggs were broken for his Cross Bronx Expressway—about five hundred thousand, if you count eggs as the dispossessed—when he demolished the East Tremont neighborhood, rejecting an alternative route that would have done less damage.

New York suffers from planning amnesia, a memory black hole between Moses and the present. In the late sixties and seventies, the Lindsay administration established local planning offices in all the boroughs that answered directly to the mayor and were staffed by the best and the brightest young professionals, who vied for the jobs. Edward J. Logue, a planner of vision as committed to social objectives as to economic development, who revived Boston in the sixties, changed Roosevelt Island from a weedy wasteland with a derelict smallpox hospital into a mixed-use, mixed-income community built around a Philip Johnson plan with Main Street as its spine when he headed the New York State Urban Development Corporation in the seventies.

He returned to New York in the eighties to put up the little houses in the rubble on Charlotte Street that symbolized hope and renewal when the South Bronx had become the poster child for terminal urban decay. You could say they were the right thing in the right place at the right time. If Logue had lived to be in charge of Ground Zero, the commitment to a cultural-commercial mix instead of a surplus of trophy towers would have been carried out and construction well started, because he knew what mattered and he also knew how to get things done.

With all due credit to Moses's achievements, he is not the man to emulate. I do not believe that this is the message we are meant to take away. He built in his own image, larger than life, on an unprecedented scale, and he was the force majeure responsible for much of the beauty and efficiency of the city we know now. Fortunately, he was stopped before he tore it apart.

Wall Street Journal, March 14, 2007

PART V

New York

Adding Up the Score

WITH THE OPENING OF THE METROPOLITAN OPERA House, Lincoln Center's four theaters and major open spaces are substantially complete. It is time to ask the $165.4-million question. What hath money, hopes, dreams, and talent wrought?

Although architecture and design must be broken in, like new shoes, until they have settled normally into the city's pattern of use, some assessments can be made. It may seem churlish to make them at all, in view of the fact that on any busy evening Lincoln Center is an agreeable place, full of light and movement and the tangible promise of varied entertainments.

What we have, architecturally, are four buildings designed to accommodate opera, drama, dance, musical theater, concerts, and film festivals—no small cultural package. Three played it safe: Philharmonic Hall, the New York State Theater, and the Metropolitan Opera are lushly decorated, conservative structures that the public finds pleasing and most professionals consider a failure of nerve, imagination, and talent.

With a totally new aesthetic and technology, the twentieth century is making dramatic contributions to the history of the art of building. But not here. The only place one senses the possibilities is standing in front of the Vivian Beaumont Theater, a design of strong, structural good looks that offers, with its fronting pool and Henry Moore sculpture, the only honestly contemporary vista in the place. This is the sole moment that lifts the spirits of those to whom the twentieth century is a very exciting time to be alive, and for whom the fleeting sensuosity of lighting effects and matching travertine is not enough. Even the Beaumont Theater formula was done better by Mies at Barcelona in 1929.

By contrast, however, the *retardataire* fussiness and aesthetic indecision of the rest becomes painfully clear: a gift wrap job of travertine trim and passepartout colonnades applied to basic boxes, in a spatial composition new with the Renaissance and reworked six decades ago by the Beaux Arts. In the most depressing sense, the Lincoln Center complex has defaulted as contemporary architecture and design.

Fortunately, the scale and relationship of the plazas are good, and they can be enjoyed as pedestrian open spaces, a value that may well increase with use and age. This, and the massive amounts of entertainment that will be provided, are its major successes.

There are other successful features. In real estate terms, it's a smash. Values of Lincoln Center and adjoining land have risen dramatically and will continue to increase. According to certain renewal standards that have wide currency in metropolitan circles, a lot of nice, shiny new buildings are replacing a lot of shabby, substandard old buildings, and that, in simplistic terms, looks good.

But there is serious question as to whether this is successful urban renewal. A bulldozer operation cleared the way for the cultural center and the new private office buildings, motels, and luxury apartments that it has sparked. The most serious accusation leveled at federally aided renewal, that it has failed to replace the stock of low-and middle-income housing that it destroys, holds true here.

Some renewal specialists and planners offer the alternative of scattered cultural facilities combined with new housing and urban services for the necessary social and physical rehabilitation of neighborhoods, rather than the creation of bloodless but profitable commercial-cultural complexes. The idea that the cultural facility is a tool, rather than an end in itself, deserves thoughtful attention, even if it offers less immediate monumental gratification of the current cultural megalomania gripping most communities.

In further terms of urban planning, Lincoln Center has been created on a traffic island of converging avenues, and the situation worsens constantly as new buildings open. The underground parking that repeats the tangle above ground is neither the corrective nor the supporting circulation design that should have been part of the original scheme. Murmurings by the city of remedial traffic measures have thus far failed to make any substantial improvement.

There is, finally, the question of culture, around which the whole complex revolves. If we define culture as average to expertly executed established and familiar fare, available to many people in maximum comfort, Lincoln Center is providing an impressive amount of it.

But there is no culture without creativity, and there is no meaningful culture of any period without that vital spark of fresh ideas and new forms that, fanned into brilliance by the greater epochs, becomes the enduring expression of an age. This is art, and culture, whether it appears in a cellar, a slum, or the back room of a bar. It has not appeared in Lincoln Center.

It is, after all, by the standards of art that all art must be judged. As entertainment, Lincoln Center promises to be an operational success. By creative measurement, much of its product and most of its plant are an artistic failure. And that is why its expensively suave, extravagantly commonplace presence is making a great many people in the fine and performing arts profoundly uneasy.

New York Times, September 24, 1966

King of Checkerboards

A FUNNY THING HAPPENED ON THE WAY to a Civic Center. While New York backed and filled and studied and restudied plans for the environs of City Hall, the federal government went ahead and built a forty-one-story office building and connected courthouse in City Hall's backyard that dominates and destroys the entire Civic Center area. The new blockbuster can scarcely be called a surprise. It has been rising in solemn, outsize nonsplendor for about three years and is quite impossible to miss from anywhere around. Just look for the biggest checkerboard in the world. The office tower is attached to the smaller building with structural paranoia; hung by trusses, supported by columns, and cantilevered at the edges behind a standard glass skin. Is it a suspended structure or isn't it? Only its architects know for sure.

Together, they are about as funny as a bad Joe Miller joke. Architecturally, the federal government has laid a colossal egg.

What has been going on in planning and design terms for at least the last four years, however, is not so much funny as it is pure farce. As a case study of how New York got one of the most monumentally mediocre federal buildings in history, it is edifying. It could be called a classic performance in bureaucratic inflexibility.

In the fall of 1963, New York City released the results of a Civic Center study that attempted to pull together the chaos around Foley Square, including bridge approaches, highway spaghetti, fragmented open space, and new building needs. The design of the federal building and courthouse, by Kahn & Jacobs, Alfred Easton Poor, and Eggers & Higgins, was complete, but construction had not yet begun.

In the interests of sense and symmetry, the city asked Washington (the General Services Administration, which builds federal structures throughout the country) to move the building toward Broadway to conform with New York's plan. The answer, apparently based on the fact that while the wheels of government grind slowly, they cannot reverse or change direction, was no. End of Act One.

Act Two: During excavation for an office tower, foundations of several older office buildings on the Broadway side gave way. The federal government was forced to demolish them. This extended the site to exactly the location that had been requested by the city. Asked again by the city for relocation and redesign, Washington again said no.

Act Three: The buildings went up as planned, with an immense, blank, featureless concrete wall facing Broadway. This civic embellishment will remain, as well as the vacant Broadway frontage, until more space is needed, and then the federal building will double its size.

Considering its size now, and what can only be called its belligerent banality, this might be called Washington's gift to New York of double disaster.

Just across Broadway are two matching Victorian buildings fronted in cast iron on the corner of Thomas Street, framing the vista of the huge, blank wall and mammoth checkerboard beyond.

Called the Thomas Twins by the Landmarks Preservation Commission, their "Renaissance palace" façades of cast columns and repeated arches, rich in plasticity, style, and scale, point a mute, visual moral. They are the nineteenth century city; the federal building is the twentieth century city. It is automation versus architecture.

New York Times, December 9, 1967

Manhattan's Landmark Buildings Today

In New York City, architectural preservation is real estate driven—but so is everything else. Old buildings must earn their way. And that goes even for the fabled skyscrapers that are the legendary stuff of its celebrated skyline. The icons of our modernity, the timeless symbols of the city's spirit, are showing their age; they, too, are subject to obsolescence and decay and the cycles of real estate boom and bust. The Empire State Building, the Chrysler Building, the Woolworth Building, the 1930 McGraw-Hill Building, and Rockefeller Center either have been radically upgraded or are now receiving a major overhaul.

And while you can't exactly kick these wonders of the building art around, most have suffered vicissitudes of ownership and management over the years, with treatment ranging from Rockefeller Center's careful stewardship to the outright neglect, ballyhooed Band-Aids, and uninspired remodeling of some of the others. It takes consortiums (real estate also makes strange bedfellows) to buy and sell them, in a process involving the financial and legal mechanisms of leveraged investment and complex tax advantages that are the club rules of New York's property market. Some are kept briefly, like trophies; the Chrysler Building, for example, has had numerous owners since its 1930 completion and a bumpy existence until its recent purchase by Tishman Speyer after what was reported as a fierce bidding war. In today's explosive economy you don't pick these things up for a song; the purchase was from another consortium, of Japanese lenders, for something in excess of two hundred million dollars. The Japanese acquired many of New York's landmark skyscrapers like status souvenirs during the go-go eighties and have been unloading them ever since.

Maintenance of this art deco treasure has been sporadic, with periods of conspicuous neglect. Its last owner, Jack Kent Cooke, whose trophies included the Washington Redskins, restored the building's extraordinary crown to its original luster. The historian Christopher Gray has found that the striking metal top was made of a special chrome-nickel steel developed to resist corrosion by the German steel manufacturer Krupp—a revolutionary feature quite equal to the romantic beauty of the design by William Van Alen that has been a beloved beacon to New Yorkers for the past seventy years.

Other buildings did not change hands; the Woolworth Building remained the flagship of the company's corporate real estate portfolio until the demise of the five-and-ten. The sixty-story Gothic tower built in 1913 by the architect Cass Gilbert at a cost of thirteen million dollars was paid for in cash—legend has it, in nickels and dimes. Sold last year to the Witkoff Group for a reported $155 million, the building is now undergoing a total technological upgrading.

The McGraw-Hill Building was the only one of these landmark skyscrapers admired by early modernist critics, although Lewis Mumford had reservations. It has been struggling along on its isolated far west site on Forty-second Street since its construction for the publishing company. The architect, Raymond Hood, a skyscraper designer of notable bravado, was also responsible for the Daily News Building and served as a member of the Rockefeller Center design team. McGraw-Hill's ribbon-style factory windows and blue-green metal panels with Indian-red terra-cotta trim were considered shocking at the time; today its color and style lift the spirit and delight the eye. After the company moved to its humdrum pinstripe tower on Sixth Avenue in 1972, the building went through a series of owners until Deco Towers Associates bought it in 1994. The new owner has already invested seven million dollars in restoration and advanced technology.

It would be nice to believe that investor interest in these properties has been motivated by their architectural excellence or some sentimental regard. To put it more realistically, art and sentiment are understood and used as marketing tools. They give a competitive edge at a time of high demand. These are the original status or signature buildings. That advantage makes it worth putting money into upgraded preservation. The appeal of the Chrysler Building's lusciously ornate art deco details of bronze and rare inlaid woods, or the Byzantine splendor of the Woolworth Building's mosaics, translates into top market dollar. Nor could liberties really be taken, since most of these buildings have been protected as designated landmarks since the seventies. But underlying all these calculations is that prime rule and real estate mantra: location, location, location. When choice development sites are scarce or require lengthy Machiavellian negotiations, the value of these desirably located landmark skyscrapers soars.

Upgrading these buildings not only means routine repairs but on a massive scale—the Empire State Building has replaced more than six thousand windows—but also requires the skillful insertion of state-of-the-art service systems. In the case of Rockefeller Center—sold to the Japanese and repurchased by a Tishman Speyer consortium—architectural restoration and the replacement of aging technology has been tied to maximizing the income from store and office rentals. Some changes have been contested—cutting double-height shop windows into the Fifth Avenue masonry façades was quite properly vetoed by the Landmarks Preservation Commission. One major revision, meant to bring increased activity to the underground shopping concourse—the latest of many failed attempts to do so—will replace the thirties black glass walls with lighter stone surfaces, a bit of conventional design wisdom that will be a serious stylistic loss. Improved access and circulation, also proposed in the plan, will do much more to achieve the desired result.

In today's profitable market, everything from skyscrapers to tenements attracts developers. The idea that the same tenements that provided the entry point for a generation of immigrants living in poverty and squalor can now be the entry point for young professionals at rents that would make the original tenants blanch is not without irony. But these buildings are also landmarks reentering the city's life stream. The renovated apartments are small, and the plumbing is indoors, and the latest appliances are included. And while no one would question the ardent sincerity of the sponsors and supporters of the popular Tenement Museum, I find equal irony in its attempts to preserve history and memory by simulating those original conditions with archaeologically researched wallpaper and lacquered bagels in a kind of freeze-frame unreality. History is a continuum, and stop-time denies it. Reused as low-rent artist's studios and starter apartments for the young and upwardly mobile, these buildings become part of the city's support system again. It's not always a socially sensitive process, but it feeds New York's creativity and keeps its past alive.

For the same reason, I prefer the casual vitality and continuing utility of the old buildings just beyond Fraunces Tavern in Lower Manhattan to the ones so carefully restored on that landmark block. The signs, fast-food shops, and laundromats of these virtually identical early nineteenth-century survivals have a lively legitimacy that makes the genteel restoration across the street seem moribund. Although the alternative at the time was demolition and the real Georgian buildings flanking the fake Fraunces Tavern, a twentieth-century reconstruction, were saved — another irony—something dies when the old denies or excludes the new.

That is why I also deplore the turn-back-the-clock mentality of those brownstone owners in the East Sixties who are "correctly" replacing the stoops removed from the buildings when earlier owners adapted them to the taste and functions of their time. These changes have authenticity, interest, and charm, and are part of a neighborhood's history and style. Reasonable accommodation is far less destructive than the fantasy of "restoring back" to a past that no longer exists.

Change and continuity, a synthesis of past and present, are the lifeblood of New York. The serendipitous reuse that continually regenerates historic stock is the only kind of preservation that works, but it requires a combination of vision, appreciation, enabling economics, and eternal vigilance to keep landmark buildings in the mainstream. Preservation battles are won and lost; there are triumphs and terrible losses; but essentially, the system pays off. Old buildings survive because it rarely makes sense in bad times to demolish, while in good times there is every incentive to invest. The city renews and enriches itself when it reuses its landmarks in an economically sound way. In New York, the art of architecture is inseparable from the art of the deal.

Wall Street Journal, May 6, 1999

Huntington Hartford's Palatial Midtown Museum

ON COLUMBUS CIRCLE, WHICH SOME PEOPLE HAVE long remembered as a sordid and dismembered open space on West Fifty-ninth Street watched over by Christopher Columbus on a column, a small white palace is approaching completion.

Columbus now points a hortatory finger at a tenth-story arcaded and screened marble building that is causing more talk and speculation among New Yorkers than anything since the Guggenheim Museum.

The new Gallery of Modern Art, including the collection of Huntington Hartford, will open in mid-March. Its costs are undisclosed, but good guesses put it at seven million dollars, including land. This month, a steady stream of curious and privileged visitors has been entering its bronze-framed glass doors to be confronted with a discreetly chiseled quotation from Kipling on the marble elevator wall:

> *But each for the joy of the working,*
> *And each in his separate star,*
> *Shall draw the thing as he sees it*
> *For the God of things as they are.*

Kipling has been out of style in cultural circles for some time. So has the exclusively realistic and representational art of the Hartford collection, for which this is the teaser.

But with that curious reversal of chic in which the chic New York world specializes, where "out" becomes "in" for the avant-garde, the Huntington Hartford gallery promises to make the unfashionable extremely fashionable from now on. By purely fortuitous timing, the professionals are "rediscovering" the neglected work of the nineteenth and early twentieth century that Mr. Hartford has loved tenaciously all along.

In spite of its name, the Gallery of Modern Art is primarily a museum for a collector who does not admire modern art, if modern art is understood as including a hard core of progressive, experimental abstraction.

The building is by Edward Durell Stone, an architect who rejects the provocative, puzzling, and sometimes brutal aspects of today's architecture in much the same way. No traditionalist, he simply prefers a less controversial idiom, avoids the more provoking and stimulating experiments, smooths off the rugged edges, and pads well with wall-to-wall luxury.

Outside, the new museum resembles a die-cut Venetian palazzo on lollypops. It begs for a canal or garden setting, rather than the dusty disorder of a New York traffic circle. Its effect, which now borders on poetic grotesquerie, will be vastly improved if the architect's sympathetic redesign of the circle is carried out by the city.

Inside the new museum there is much more than meets the passing eye. The irregular-shaped building is only about ninety-six feet on its longest side, but its plan is an accomplished demonstration of one of the basic principles of architectural design—the expert manipulation of space by an expert hand.

Fire stairs and tower required by the building code, plus public stairs and elevators, made the small structure virtually all service core and no galleries. The architect solved the problem by putting the main galleries at the front of the building, wrapping smaller galleries around the service core, and widening the stair landings to provide high-ceilinged supplementary galleries at half levels between floors. On alternate floors the main galleries are entered from these side stairs.

The theme is dignity and formality, rather than the exhilarating spatial fireworks.

This interior planning is the building's conspicuous success, an achievement to command considerable admiration. What will be admired by the public, however, are the building's cosmetics—many running feet of rich macassar ebony, walnut, bronze, grasscloth, thick red and gold carpets, parquet floors, the celebrated Stone grilles—all applied with lavish generosity and occasionally smothering overtones of domestic luxury. Mr. Stone believes that art should be shown in an atmosphere suggesting the visitor's own home or a club.

The Hartford Gallery will provide a sybaritic setting for some interesting, offbeat shows that New York might otherwise not see. The building works well, poses no challenges, asks no hard questions, and gives no controversial answers. (The questions raised by the collection are considerably tougher.)

There will be Polynesian luau lunches in the ninth-floor penthouse, an espresso bar in the eighth-floor lounge, and the soothing strains of a twenty-three-foot-high Aeolian-Skinner organ accommodated between the second and third floors.

A small auditorium in the basement seats 154 persons. Four floors will be devoted to exhibitions. It is a costly, comfortable building that breaks no architectural frontiers but seems perfectly suited to its functions, purposes, and patron.

New York Times, February 25, 1964

Columbus Circle: A Project Without a Plan

AFTER THE PRESENTS HAVE BEEN RETURNED and the New Year's hangovers dealt with and the record crowds and congestion recede, one memory of the holiday season lingers on: the absolute, festive beauty and flawless functioning of Rockefeller Center under siege by wall-to-wall people having a wonderful time. It had it all, of course, the tree, the music, the ice skating and whipping silver flags, the dramatically illuminated skyscraper and the moving light projections of snowflakes caressing the lower building walls. But it had something more: an idea, a vision, a plan, now more than fifty years old, which turned a massive real estate investment into an urban masterpiece.

As New Yorkers, we simply take it for granted. Several generations have grown up thinking that Rockefeller Center was always there, like Manhattan schist, brought into being by some forgotten magic, a place sprinkled with fairy dust and Rockefeller money. Perhaps it is worth remembering, at the start of a new year in which the city seems to be proceeding on a dismally planless course, that Rockefeller Center was neither accident nor miracle, nor some softheaded exercise in selfless philanthropy. Its sponsors and investors in the thirties were just as bent on getting maximum bang for the real estate buck as any of today's megadevelopers. But it is only in our own time that planning has dropped out of the lexicon. Politicians and bureaucrats, visions of profits dancing like sugarplums in their heads, are busy with the piecemeal selling off of public property in a process euphemistically called privatization that permanently disposes of the city's irreplaceable assets and its future options.

I am not exactly sneaking up to a point here; I am about to make a depressing comparison between then and now, between Rockefeller Center and what is happening at Columbus Circle, New York's current and most conspicuous planning disaster, as an example of how far our vision, reach, and standards have fallen architecturally, urbanistically, and politically in the past half century.

There are obvious differences: Columbus Circle is a centralized disperser of traffic, and Rockefeller Center is a largely pedestrian precinct. Rockefeller Center land has always been in private ownership, while most of the sites surrounding Columbus Circle have been in public hands, a fact that would seem to mandate some coherent public action in the public interest. At least, that was the case and the possibility until the Port Authority sold the Coliseum site, which occupies the west side of the Circle, to a private developer, after a competitive charade that brought in variations on the same old office-cum-entertainment formulas, as an antidote to an earlier, grossly oversized proposal defeated by popular protest. Until that sale, the only properties in private ownership around Columbus Circle were the former Gulf & Western Building on the far north end, now converted into Donald Trump's supersleek hotel and condominium complex, and the postwar apartment house on the slightly offset southeast corner. All the rest of the sites surrounding the Circle belonged to public agencies.

The little seraglio built as Huntington Hartford's Gallery of Modern Art by Edward Durell Stone in 1965 forms the south side of the Circle. It has been city-owned since shortly after the museum closed and occupied by the Department of Cultural Affairs until last year. This is the only recognizable building in a sea of banality that gives any indication of where you are or relates in any way to the geography of the place. It is also for sale. A pointless debate is now taking place over whether it would be better for it to go to a private museum or be sacrificed to Donald Trump in his continuing quest to create Trump Circle. Central Park flanks the remaining, east side. Filling in this nearly continuous lineup of public-owned parcels are subway exits, one of which pops up as a suicidal traffic island somewhere behind the Columbus statue. There are a few other odd, shipwrecked, death-defying bits and pieces dismembering the Circle itself that include traffic dividers and a forlorn strip of dislocated grass and a few disoriented trees. Everything is enclosed by iron railings and one of the most hideous devices ever devised by man or engineer, the concrete Jersey barrier.

One assumes that these adornments are meant to facilitate the current experiment in changing traffic patterns, although it would be foolish to believe that anything as beloved by traffic departments as the Jersey barrier will eventually disappear. A sign announces that a "reconfiguration test" is under way, with a phone number, 422-0506, for questions or comments about the proposed new route. It would not be advisable to make the call while driving through Columbus Circle.

Other aesthetic touches are a clutch of red Wrong Way signs and, to further emphasize the point, a bevy of black directional arrows on bright yellow panels topping a hemicycle of more Jersey barriers. Abandoned in the middle of all this beauty, a cowed Christopher Columbus stands on his column irresolutely facing south. He keeps his back, advisedly, to the glitzily discordant world's fair–type globe, fronting the Trump International Hotel and Tower that marks the beginning of Donaldland. On the Central Park side, the sculptural allegories of the Maine Memorial of 1913, beautifully restored by the Central Park Conservancy, which also reopened the important southwest entrance to the park that had been progressively disfigured by the city, adds its pigeon-bedecked, high-minded beaux arts grandeur to the surreal mix.

The public agencies involved in this planning mayhem are the Port Authority of New York, the New York State Economic Development Corporation, the New York City Economic Development Corporation and the Department of Real Estate, the New York City Traffic Department, Planning Department, Parks Department, and probably some I have missed, for truly stupefying cross-jurisdictional chaos. It is not irrelevant to note that traffic swirls around the Place de la Concorde in Paris at a dizzying rate, but it does not finesse unity, majesty, or splendor for a traffic tangle. The trashing of Columbus Circle goes beyond greed or bureaucratic confusion; it is an abdication of public responsibility and an education in municipal default.

Going to Rockefeller Center from Columbus Circle involves more than a trip across town. This is another world. Movement through the Center is a processional and pleasurable experience all year round, against a backdrop of architectural excellence. The Channel walk and gardens created as part of the overall scheme in 1930 opened a new

public space from west to east, from Fifth Avenue at one end to the
sunken plaza on the other, where the route divides and follows the plaza's
edge. Changes in level provide spatial and functional variety, and the use
of strategic planting separates the inner streets from the outer sidewalks,
in a double pedestrian ring. Movement is as much social as directional.
Rockefeller Center accommodates an amazing democratic and demo-
graphic mix in a place without populist pretensions; this is a setting of
outstanding aesthetic and architectural quality based on superb urban
design.

After a proposal for a new Metropolitan Opera fell through in 1929 at
the start of the Great Depression, the Center's amenities were carefully
configured for their market appeal at a time when the bottom had
fallen out of the commercial market. The height and position of the
RCA, now GE, Building were calculated for prestigious offices; to improve access and circulation a new north-south approach was cut
through from Forty-ninth to Fifty-first streets. But the concern with profit
margins is the only similarity between what built Rockefeller Center in
the thirties and what is driving the city today. Those who conceived it as
real estate also viewed it, in their own words, "as an example of urban
planning for the future."

Obviously, this pedestrian model cannot be transferred to Columbus
Circle. But the basic thinking behind it is timelessly relevant and woefully lacking today. Rockefeller Center is the brilliant, enduring result
of a creative, coordinated vision for an area unified by design. There are
other kinds of deals that can be made in a public-private partnership
than the Columbus Circle selloff; professional expertise can still offer
constructive solutions. Lacking a plan, however, or even sensing that
there should be one, or, one suspects, not really knowing what one is,
New York's public officials are throwing away their leverage and foreclosing the future. This is city planning by the Marx brothers. You've
got to really love short-term profit to sabotage the long-term city this
way. You've got to like Jersey barriers a lot.

Wall Street Journal, January 14, 1999

The Best Way to Preserve 2 Columbus Circle

I HAVE BEEN WATCHING, WITH WONDER and disbelief, the beatification of 2 Columbus Circle, né Huntington Hartford's Gallery of Modern Art, aka the lollipop building (so-named, for better or worse, by me). This small oddity of dubious architectural distinction, designed by Edward Durell Stone, has been elevated to masterpiece status and cosmic significance by a campaign to save its marginally important, mildly eccentric, and badly deteriorated façade—a campaign that has escalated into a win-at-any-cost-and-by-any-means vendetta in the name of preservation.

Never has that term been so taken in vain. The opposition to the renovation of this derelict little building with an uncertain future as the new home of the Museum of Arts and Design (formerly the American Crafts Museum) seems to be operating by tunnel vision and a blind resistance to change. What is conspicuously missing from the orchestrated hysteria that has replaced rational debate about 2 Columbus Circle is any desire to see or understand the plans for the building's conversion before going into attack mode. For those fixated on saving the existing façade, that is simply not an option.

The architect of the conversion, Brad Cloepfil, of Allied Works Architecture, reports that he has not received a single call or inquiry from anyone writing the impassioned pieces that have flooded the press, which appears to have abandoned the idea of fact checking or a balanced point of view. There is enough irresponsibility to go around. Few have seen the version of the evolving design now receiving city review. Any civic or architectural virtues it may possess are irrelevant. The facts would only spoil a good fight.

The most basic preservation question is not being asked at all. What will be lost, and what will be gained? The proposal being rejected out of hand is a promising solution by a talented young American practitioner that will reclaim an abandoned building of debatable merit for a desirable cultural facility. We do not lose the building; everything that is good about it will be retained: its size, its scale, and its intimate relationship to the street. Although three stories could be added legally, the decision was made to change nothing about its iconic form and presence.

What is bad about the building—the dark, cramped, and virtually useless interior and those faux harem walls that close off spectacular views—will be changed. Yes, we will lose the façade, and the new one will not offer the instant appeal of exotic kitsch; it is a restrained, expressive reflection of an unusual way of using the concrete frame to open the building visually, inside and out. It is hard not to see this as a trade-off worth making.

I have studied the design carefully, and I have also visited Columbus Circle, which is in the process of a long-delayed rebuilding and revitalization. The city's most notorious traffic circle, a survival challenge of Jersey barriers, is coming into focus, and the surprise is that it is going to be wonderful. The immense, nearly complete AOL Time Warner Center on its west side, by David Childs, of Skidmore, Owings & Merrill, totally eclipses Donald Trump's hotel and residential tower on the north, an alienated Central Park has been refurbished and reembraced to the east, and a landscaped surround for the traffic-impacted Columbus statue in the middle is under way. Columbus finally stands tall, and even the Maine Memorial looks grand. Think—sort of—Trafalgar Square.

The AOL Time Warner Center is exactly what a New York skyscraper should be—a soaring, shining, glamorous affirmation of the city's reach and power—and its best real architecture in a long time. Its two tall towers rise from symmetrical lower sections rotated in a bow to the Circle, where the huge building morphs into pedestrian shops and restaurants at ground level. But the wonder is the delicacy, the elegance, of these perfectly calibrated, glittering glass façades, the suave, sharp-edged precision that is amazingly subtle and refined for a structure of this enormous size.

Seen against AOL Time Warner's astonishing and unexpected beauty, the shabby little punchboard façade of 2 Columbus Circle sticks out like a small, sore thumb. It didn't seem so bad before, but the sophisticated finesse of Mr. Childs's first-rate building makes it look like the second-rate building that it really is. Its retro mannerisms are suddenly crude caricatures.

Because Brad Cloepfil is also an architect who designs with a precise delicacy, the new look for 2 Columbus Circle works in this setting. The building's enrichment will be its façade of terra-cotta panels, the texture and tone of the tiles to be developed in collaboration with an artist, in

keeping with the museum's crafts tradition. But the exterior is only part
of the story; it is integral to a far more radical, three-dimensional concept that is virtually impossible to understand from pictures—a system
of cuts into the concrete structure starting on the outside walls and carried inside on the floors and ceilings to the building's core that create a
continuous sense of space.

Exterior vertical and horizontal bands in a linear pattern provide
daylight for the galleries and outside views. They connect to interior
slits that open ceilings and floors to slotted glimpses of other spaces and
galleries above and below. As one approaches, the building's solidity
will give way to layered transparencies, from terra-cotta screens to large
areas of fritted, or patterned, glass at the top, with glimpses of galleries
near street level.

But let us assume for argument's sake that none of this matters; that
the façade should be saved even if everything else about the building
remains unresolved. Structural studies made in the heat of battle are
suspect; I've been through too many cooked reports to believe them.
However, some facts, although unwelcome, are incontrovertible. Inspection has found the façade so badly deteriorated that it can't be
saved; it would have to be rebuilt—a copy or reproduction would have
to replace it.

The metal shims—pieces of metal attached behind each piece of
marble to level the stones—have rusted as water got into the joints, and
the damage has spread to the marble, which has cracked and spalled.
Because the entire façade is affected, all of the rusted shims would have
to be replaced and new marble cut and installed. There is no way it can
be repaired. Nothing less than a Sansovino survival would justify an expensive replica, and only as a last resort for a rare artifact of the Venetian Renaissance, but a Sansovino façade this is not.

The necessity of constructing a vapor barrier for humidity control
around the building—all museums require them—complicates things
further. This is done on the exterior, although landmark buildings
have been retrofitted inside at great cost and with extreme difficulty.
We begin to get into a Catch-22 dilemma when a vapor barrier cannot
be installed under a damaged façade, the preservation of which is debatable in the first place, and cost and space restrictions foreclose doing it inside.

What I find most personally disturbing, however, is the manipulated and manufactured history that has accompanied the demand for land-mark status for a building already denied designation—and let's forget those paranoid ideas about political plots and underhanded deals that always surface when things get hot. I marvel at the spin that is being put on both the building and its architect, Ed Stone, to reposition them in a mythical past. I don't have to invent history; I was there.

Actually, there were two Ed Stones, the good one and the bad one, architecturally speaking. The first was Edward D. Stone, a talented practitioner of the International Style, and the architect, with Philip Goodwin, of the landmark building for the Museum of Modern Art, a charming man who frequented the better clubs and watering holes to the eventual disruption of his career. For a while, his life fell apart. Then it came together again with the help of a new wife and helpmeet, who informed me that he was to be referred to, henceforth, in anything I wrote, as Edward Durell Stone. Thus began the new persona and sec-ond career of Edward Durell Stone.

This second phase was his better-known seraglio period, which coin-cided with the start of a State Department program for new U.S. em-bassies abroad. The program stressed the hiring of architects for reasons other than their political connections and specified that these buildings should not be brash interlopers, but that each should be designed to re-flect or respect the particular country's culture. This well-meant but somewhat shallow and patronizing idea led to curious architectural ac-robatics; the buildings strained to incorporate something "native" in their forms, and the strain shows. The significance of the program in Mr. Stone's work has been explained by Laurie Kerr on this page—it is the only real history we have been given.

There was one outstanding success—Edward Durell Stone's Ameri-can Embassy in New Delhi, an enchanted place of fountains, arcades, and screens that achieved immediate fame. He was besieged with com-missions and he obliged—with screens. His clients couldn't get enough of them, and they conveniently covered everything he built. What they covered was often not very good, but it was very popular, culminating in Washington's most vacuous marble monument, the Kennedy Center. Mr. Stone's pierced and arcaded façades became his signature gim-mick, a crowd pleaser that never rose much above mediocrity; to those who knew his earlier work, this was all downhill. Along the way he built 2 Columbus Circle, which had a certain toylike charm.

Some profess to see its palazzo pretensions as a forerunner of post-modernism. I find that a stretch. You could say that anything like the State Department's Foreign Buildings program was a step on the way to the liberation of architecture from the shackles of the functionalism and antihistoricism of the modern movement. But the Overseas Embassy program soon succumbed to the government's pendulum swing between patronage and periodic attempts to upgrade, and significant change occurred only after the silly season of postmodernism had passed. At best, 2 Columbus Circle is memorably idiosyncratic.

One wonders at what point New York's civic groups lost their vision, just when they decided nostalgia and trendy revisionism overrode a positive contribution to the city's cultural and architectural quality. In St. Louis, Brad Cloepfil has just completed a fine small museum that successfully shares a plaza with Tadao Ando's Pulitzer Foundation for the Arts in the revitalization of an older area. The news does not seem to have traveled as far as New York.

There is a great deal more at stake than this one building. When preservation distorts history and reality in a campaign of surprising savagery, it signals an absence of standards and an abdication of judgment and responsibility. It has lost its meaning when we prefer a stagnant status quo.

Wall Street Journal, January 7, 2004

MoMA's Big, New, Elegantly Understated Home

MY RELATIONSHIP WITH NEW YORK'S MUSEUM of Modern Art began in the forties, in the intimacy of the original 1939 Goodwin and
Stone building. A student-friendly twenty-five-cent admission made it
headquarters for young New Yorkers drawn to its exciting modernist
message. It was the cool place to be. We dated beneath the undulating
cheesehole canopy of the roof terrace restaurant, and my first job was in
the Department of Architecture and Design, with Philip Johnson as
boss and Alfred H. Barr Jr., the museum's founding director, as mentor;
you don't get any luckier than that. We preached truth, reason, the
gospel of art in our time, and the rational beauty of everyday things.

I do not believe in nostalgia; that was then, and this is now. Even modernism moves on. Today's visitors cluster around van Gogh's *Starry Night*
in the same way tourists flock to the Louvre's *Mona Lisa*. MoMA—the
acronym known all over the world—expanded incrementally until a
perennial shortage of space led to an invited international competition
for a comprehensive solution. The proposal submitted by the Japanese
architect Yoshio Taniguchi was selected in 1997.

Which brings us to the new MoMA sixty-five years after it began its
march down West Fifty-third Street: a suavely sophisticated, exquisitely
executed, elegantly understated building that doubles the museum's
size. Mr. Taniguchi's style—where less is so much more than trendy
minimalism, with every carefully reasoned detail honed as close to perfection as possible—is the right architecture for the Modern. It is also
the right building for New York.

The design is driven by the rationality of its plan and its response to its
surroundings, essential factors that have taken a backseat to today's obsession with drop-dead forms. It makes sense of the museum's ad hoc development by unifying old and new elements into a harmonious, smoothly
functioning whole. The reconfigured complex employs an uncompromisingly contemporary vocabulary, a lesson to those who confuse nostalgia with compatibility. This is genuine contextualism.

Mr. Taniguchi's architecture celebrates the city rather than itself. It
embraces heart-stopping views through glass walls that court immateri-
ality with the precision and delicacy of their framing and the thinness

of the floor plates. The new lobby runs from Fifty-third to Fifty-fourth streets as an open, through-block passage. New Yorkers have always been very possessive of the Modern, unlike their formal relationship with the more off-putting, magisterial Met; these gestures have given MoMA back to them, and to the city, in a very public way.

Two new structures flank the garden: the building that is now the heart of the museum, with the entrance, galleries, and offices, and a huge central atrium, and a smaller addition for educational activities. The nearly block-long, Fifty-third Street frontage incorporates the rebuilt façades of the Goodwin and Stone building and a later one by Philip Johnson, skillfully maintaining the lower, side-street scale. This reconstruction is a symbolic act of homage rather than preservation, since the originals are gone. The architect has obliged sentiment further with a copy of the legendary stair to the second-floor galleries, now a ghostly connector between the new second and third floors.

The income-producing tower of Cesar Pelli's earlier renovation, which the museum did its best to pretend wasn't there, has been brought down to the ground to take its proper part in the urban composition. Philip Johnson's immensely popular garden, restored, is entered from the new building so the long lines of pools and paths are seen end-on instead of facing one as serene horizontals; that view is now reserved for the restaurant terrace.

The vastly enlarged institution is saved from oppressive monumentality by its simplicity, lightness, and the elegance and ingenuity of its technological detailing, which has been innovatively engineered in collaboration with the New York firm of Kohn Pedersen Fox Associates and structural engineering firms Guy Nordenson Associates and Severud Associates.

The most dramatic and debated feature is the building's 110-foot-high atrium, a soaring central space that starts one floor above the entrance lobby and is ringed with exhibition galleries that give us more of the permanent collection than we have ever experienced, including a treasury of drawings, photographs, and prints.

The displays around the atrium can be seen from the garden, where a glass wall that flirts with invisibility projects impeccable proportions and a subdued palette of black granite, aluminum panels, and white and gray glass, its transparency sparked by the museum's classic red 1946 Cisitalia automobile inside. The atrium is so vast that the figures seen across it, in stairways and at railings, are minuscule, and the view from top to bottom, vertiginous or not, depending on your susceptibility, is of miniatures in motion.

Circulation and the handling of crowds seem to be the point of this design as much as its visual drama. Vast numbers of visitors have already proved that it works. But the art in the atrium is upstaged by the continuous motion and diminished by the scalelessness of the immense walls. Paintings are flattened to postage stamps or posters, barely relevant to the passing activity. Woe to the poor *Waterlilies*—Monet's masterpiece, deprived of the quiet isolation and intimate serenity that it needs, is wallpaper. Circulation trumps everything.

In the galleries, circulation displaces contemplation. With openings in three walls out of four in almost every room for a relentlessly revolving path, Rothkos and Matisses are cornered beside doorways; there is always something else insistently entering your peripheral vision. This arrangement may present a broader, more inclusive view of modernism as it is currently understood (that, too, will change), but it is more disruptive than helpful, with artists seeming fragmented or lost in the cross references. Exterior glass walls are covered for hanging space and light protection, but one longs for more of the transparency and daylight the architecture could provide to relieve a sense of monolithic uniformity. What is missing is the quiet place where one can communicate directly and deeply with a single work or artist. At the new MoMA there is no repose.

Buildings accommodate needs and provide opportunities; they do not transform institutions. This is an updated MoMA, not a reinvented MoMA, if that ever was necessary. What Mr. Taniguchi has done is to apply the skills evident in his many beautiful museums in Japan to a distinctly American phenomenon—the modern megamuseum as cultural icon, social center, status symbol, tourist attraction, art mall, and high-end shopping opportunity, and what some still consider its primary purpose, the art experience as spiritual retreat.

The new MoMA is a model of modernism and urban sensibility and a showcase for a magnificent collection of twentieth-century art. The building is true to MoMA's philosophy, which has always been highly selective and strongly aesthetic no matter how radical its thesis, a process that is a careful validation rather than a bold gamble or risky prophecy. The museum is forever a product of its brilliant beginnings. No one has surpassed or replaced Alfred Barr's founding vision, lucid prose, and impeccable eye. If his modern art history was overly neat, it had room for the revisionism that has since enriched it. Neatness counted at MoMA, and it still does.

But we yearn for more than a cloakroom and gift shop in the cavernous entrance; the atrium cries for the really big gesture—even Barnett Newman's *Broken Obelisk* becomes a decorous gesture that ceases to alarm. This requires a powerful, perception-altering work, a site-specific creation that deals fearlessly with the scale—something new, provocative, and outrageous—a naughty newcomer that must wait to be judged worthy enough to be invited in. MoMA has never looked so uptight as in this stupendous new space. Something needs to turn that void into a connection between past and future, something that takes a chance on the transformational experience only art can provide. MegaMoMA is fail-safe and risk-free.

Wall Street Journal, December 7, 2004

The Morgan Library's Cool New Building

THE NEW MORGAN LIBRARY, NOW CALLED the Morgan Library and Museum—reconceived, reorganized, and reopened at the end of April after a three-year, $106-million makeover—is cool, in every sense of the word. There is not a false step in this aesthetically sensitive and admirably rational expansion. It is cool in its understated excellence, its laid-back drama, the refinement of its details. It manages to speak of money and magnificence in the coolly understated way that has become the hallmark of the upscale institutions of our time.

The old Morgan Library was hot—unashamed of its extravagance, its ostentation, its lush velvets, marbles, and bronzes, its overt display of wealth and personal taste. Discretion was not the issue. For generations, New Yorkers have remained respectfully behind the velvet rope of the famous financier's red damask-walled office with its priceless paintings and objets d'art, transfixed by the notoriously penetrating gaze of J. P. Morgan, Pierpont Morgan's son and successor, dominating the room from the portrait above the ornate fireplace, behind the massive desk. A short trip across the elaborate Roman entrance rotunda took one to the equally impressive book-walled library and reading room. On bad days, the Morgan's somber splendor was a magical escape into a powerful and privileged world, providing refuge, restorative, and a refreshing cup of tea.

In the new Morgan Library and Museum the velvet rope is down. You can enter the room now, but the temperature has dropped several degrees. With the emphasis on the superb collection of rare books, manuscripts, and works of art, and more extensive exhibitions in an expanded and reconstituted institution, the balance has shifted from the powerful Morgan personality to the sleek elegance and smooth efficiencies of the twenty-first-century museum. Gone are the peculiarities and quirkiness that drove directors and curators mad.

In 1902, when Pierpont Morgan sought an architect for his library, the place to go was the firm of McKim, Mead & White. If you were fashionably inclined, you hired Stanford White; if you were solidly old

Morgan Library

guard, you used the überestablishment Charles Follen McKim. McKim's building for Morgan, completed in 1906, on Thirty-sixth Street between Madison and Park avenues, was as classically correct and richly Roman as money could make it.

By 1928, a second structure ("the Annex"), a somewhat dry and denatured classical building by Benjamin Wistar Morris—the establishment architect of choice by then—was added at the corner of Madison and Thirty-sixth Street. With the Morgan residence, a brownstone on the corner of Thirty-seventh Street, built in 1852 and enlarged in 1888, this construction completed the Madison Avenue frontage of the block. Ad hoc additions were made over the following decades that did little to solve increasing problems of space and function.

Today, the designer of choice for many in the museum and cultural worlds is the Italian architect Renzo Piano; he has been setting the standard for the contemporary museum ever since his serenely beautiful Menil Museum in Houston in 1987 showed the way to put art and light together. Mr. Piano has mastered the museum's aesthetic and public roles at a time when elevated attention and attendance are crucial to its existence and success.

The Morgan is Mr. Piano's first completed museum in New York; the Whitney will follow. His extremely skillful solution for the Morgan is based on the retention and restoration of the three original buildings, all of markedly different times and styles, and their unification through the addition of three new glass and metal-walled connecting structures, with everything held together by a four-story, fifty-foot-high clear glass court, or "piazza," as Mr. Piano likes to call it. This central court creates a completely new focus; long before reaching the original library, one encounters a new, defining gallery, a classic twenty-by-twenty-foot cube of the purest elegance that features the Morgan's rarest treasures.

A concept that placed so much emphasis on the expert preservation of the original buildings and their successful integration into a radically revised plan required an exceptional team. The Renzo Piano Design Workshop collaborated closely with the New York firm of Beyer, Blinder Belle, known for its preservation of notable historic buildings, in the restoration and reuse of the landmark structures.

To accommodate the ambitious redesign, all previous additions were demolished. This made it possible to move the main entrance from its makeshift position on a side street to Madison Avenue. The new entrance replaces the appealing, tree-filled garden room added in 1990 by Voorsanger and Mills, where one could get that restful cup of tea. Now it will be available in the court café, upgraded to current standards of museum chic.

More than half of the new space, seventy-five thousand square feet, has been added below ground to avoid going higher than the existing rooflines. This required the removal of almost fifty thousand tons of famously solid Manhattan schist to create an underground level for an exquisite small concert hall and facilities for educational and public programs. The restored Morgan residence contains offices, administration, a ground-floor restaurant, and an expanded gift shop, now as neatly and efficiently organized as it was previously delightfully serendipitous. A bookstore occupies the handsomely paneled former music room.

All this, obviously, is a good thing. So is the elimination of cramped, dark staff offices for light, airy accommodations, the replacement of grossly inadequate storage by a huge, climate-controlled underground vault, and vastly improved quarters for conservation and research. A fine new reading room that recalls the original with its surrounding balconies enjoys filtered natural light from above.

The new construction makes no gesture to faux contextualism by replicating anything already on the site. By putting so much underground, the design respects current building heights; breaking the construction down into smaller parts, repeating the same modestly scaled building unit throughout, and refining the proportions of the additions ensure compatibility. For solidity, Mr. Piano substitutes transparency; for classical clothing, the direct expression of modern glass and steel. His contemporary aesthetic of visible technology coexists comfortably with the historical recall of the older styles. And while I do not buy the clichéd idea that transparency is the new morality, or the hackneyed notion that all this glass and openness suggests an equal openness in art and life, in architecture, at least, exposed steel framing the clearest white glass has a stripped-down and subtly articulated beauty that works. It sends its own message while accepting the past. Painting the steel the rosy white of the older, Tennessee pink marble buildings is the only obvious bow to precedent.

The Madison Avenue entry, flanked by the inevitable coatroom and the essential donors' wall, is, perhaps, too cool. After this blankly impersonal start, the full-height glass-walled court is suddenly revealed just beyond, with its views of sky and surrounding buildings, the exhilarating multileveled interior alive with natural light. This stunning central space provides access and visibility for all parts of the complex; even the links between new and old buildings have views through to the side streets. In a bit of unexpected spatial magic, a glass elevator becomes a visual extension of each floor level as it travels up and down, constantly changing the perception of the interior as it keeps recomposing static space. Majestic permanence is a peripheral value now.

This Morgan is all about architecture; it takes a while to even know where you are. In the past, there was a pleasant ambiguity about the Morgan; you felt that you were being allowed to participate, briefly and for a modest fee, in the personal experience of an intimate, rarified world of arcane research and costly connoisseurship. You really didn't belong there, but you enjoyed the privilege of visiting. Not anymore. The Morgan has gone public, with a new mission, in a dazzling new setting. As the director, Charles E. Pierce Jr., has noted with some satisfaction, you can't keep one of the city's cultural crown jewels a secret forever.

Wall Street Journal, June 8, 2006

The World Trade Center

Who's Afraid of the Big Bad Buildings?

ANY DISCUSSION OF THE WORLD TRADE CENTER at this point may be in the nature of locking the barn after the horse is gone, but, to mix a couple of barnyard metaphors, there is no reason why New Yorkers should be getting a pig in a poke. They have had very little objective information or evaluation of this huge and highly controversial project unless they have read a report on the subject by the City Planning Commission, including between the lines, or have had access to a commission-ordered study of Lower Manhattan which will not be released until next month.

What has come out of public hearings and protest is: 1. establishment-baiting, in this case the Port Authority; 2. Yamasaki-baiting, particularly popular among architects; 3. emotional arguments, usually aimed at the project's size; 4. fears of the real estate interests; 5. concern for the destruction of a small but irreplaceable business community.

On balance, the World Trade Center is not the city destroyer that it has been popularly represented to be; its pluses outweigh its minuses in the complex evaluation that must be made, and its potential is greater than its threat. The issues are far from black and white. The proper basic question may well be whether any agency should have the right to indulge in city-building on this scale and with this freedom, without obligations to the city and beyond city review. Since the Port Authority has that legal right, the pertinent issues are those of the plan. Certainly its impact will be so great that it is a matter of legitimate public concern.

The focus of the argument is a $525-million, sixteen-acre complex bounded on the north and south by Vesey and Liberty streets and on the east and west by Church and West streets. It will be the largest commercial superblock in Manhattan, closing all internal streets of fifteen

World Trade Center under construction

small blocks, with a perimeter coverage on each side equal to the distance between Fifth and Park avenues. The twin 110-story towers, each
two hundred feet square or about the size of a city blockfront, are
flanked by four seven-story structures around a five-acre plaza. The architects are Minoru Yamasaki and Associates and Emery Roth & Sons.

The greatest storm has centered on the size of the towers, which, as
everyone knows by now, will break the skyline and be the tallest buildings in the world. The argument goes that the flat-topped behemoths
will destroy the beauty of the romantically spired Lower Manhattan
skyline. The hue and cry equals that raised at the time those spires were
built. They were attacked then as barbaric, oversized wreckers of scale
and sunlight, and with the building of the (now modest) twin towers of
the Equitable Building in 1914, the outcry became so great that the

city's first restrictive zoning law was passed. Wall Street was a symbol of architectural transgression. The responsible intellectual community refused to forgive the design sins of those early skyscraper builders with their decorative curtain-wall classicism, fancy-dress Gothic, "senseless" spires, and Halicarnassus water towers for another forty years. This is the skyline that the same intellectual community now wants to protect.

With today's engineering advances, it was only a matter of time when the skyline would be broken again. The inevitable may or may not be desirable, but it must be dealt with as a fact of life. Barring war or depression, the impact will be ameliorated by buildings of intermediate scale as history, technology, megalomania, the skyscraper, and the skyline pursue their natural course.

We do not believe in embalming or Williamsburging the New York skyline. This valid and dramatic testament of the city's brutally competitive grandeur and vitality has produced an incomparable twentieth-century aesthetic. What we do believe in is the absolute necessity of relating these corporate and speculative status symbols to the needs, functions, and uses of the city at ground level. The rationale of planning goes far deeper than a picture of the skyline, which is not static, and which changes its composition and alignment from every viewpoint.

The World Trade Center is no Pan Am Building, muscling into an overcrowded neighborhood of maximum big-building concentration. It is closer to Rockefeller Center as a city-shaping group of structures (another example of buildings rejected by the architectural community for many years and now hailed as successful urban design). The area is of minimum interest to preservationists. Separate studies by the Regional Plan Association, the City Planning Commission, and the consultants preparing the new Lower Manhattan plan, Whittlesey and Conklin, Wallace-McHarg Associates, and Alan M. Voorhees and Associates, Inc., confirm the planning logic of the location.

Rapid transit (three subway lines and Path) and street capacity are judged to be more than adequate for the fifty thousand employees and one hundred thousand visitors expected daily. The Regional Plan Association, which is conscientiously concerned with long-range planning goals and particularly with better public transportation, feels that the downtown location encourages more transit than car use, and that it has the right kind and number of jobs in the right places.

The city's consultants for the Lower Manhattan plan are not exactly bankers' boys in their view of what is best for downtown New York, which includes people-oriented waterfront reclamation, parks, and pedestrian streets. They nevertheless have concluded that the economic realities of Lower Manhattan are a critical issue, and that without the revitalizing emphasis of the Chase Manhattan Building, the World Trade Center, and some coherent solution of the muddled Civic Center plan, the continued vitality of the area is in doubt.

Regional Plan and Planning Commission studies indicate that the eight million square feet of rentable space in the Trade Center will be properly absorbed. It will be spread over six years of staged construction in a city that builds an average of five million square feet of new office space annually. The commission would prefer to see more than a year between the completion of the two towers to ease the effect of the release of the major spaces.

The serious issue that remains, then, is the disruption of the present business community. One of the worst unsolved problems in the renewal of cities is the loss of those healthy small enterprises of a kind and character that large-scale projects increasingly and tragically destroy. The situation is particularly bad in New York, and the Port Authority has done even worse with it than the average municipality. Untouched by local laws, endowed with the right of eminent domain and a sovereign state position from which it negotiates at an absurdly one-sided advantage with the city, the Port Authority offers only a bonus as inducement to the tenant to move, which is less liberal than the liquidation or small business displacement grants under Title I urban renewal.

If skill, imagination, and even enlightened philanthropy were required to keep this business community as an economically and humanly viable part of downtown, they should all have been employed. At this point, the default is clear and inexcusable. The public finds it less easy to excuse and the mammoth project less easy to accept because the Port Authority has not, in the opinion of many, used the power and prosperity gained from the ceding of municipal rights for the greatest municipal good. It has acted more as a private investor than as a public agency.

The Regional Plan Association points out that foreign trade is projected as a growth industry in New York, and that the scale of the World

Trade Center is consistent with its prospects. However, without modern port facilities for New York, which are now going to New Jersey in the Port Authority's balancing act of largesse dispensation, the coordination of modern office facilities in Manhattan makes limited sense. The World Trade Center will actually function as an arm of the financial community, permitting its expansion and tie-in with trade. Its use for government offices outside of Customs (1.9 million square feet of the 10.165 million total have been taken by New York State) is questionable in the extreme. It could be one more blow to the reeling Civic Center.

If we come to aesthetics last, there is good reason for putting this at the bottom of the list. Buildings of this substantial an effect on the life patterns of the city are a great deal more than art objects. Unless they represent design irresponsibility, which means raising the cheap and ordinary solutions of the speculative builder to monument status, their relationship to those life patterns must be the primary consideration.

No one would suggest, however, that aesthetics are not important in big buildings. Nor is Detroit architect Minoru Yamasaki's work to everyone's aesthetic taste. He has developed a curiously unsettling style which involves decorative traceries of exotic extraction applied over structure or worked into it. His choice of delicate detail on massive construction as a means of reconciling modern structural scale to the human scale of the viewer is often more disturbing than reassuring. It makes many competent architects go to pieces. Here we have the world's daintiest architecture for the world's biggest buildings. But no review board could refuse to pass his buildings, even if it pined for a Corbusian or Miesian masterwork.

The design has been revised significantly in the two years since it was announced. The towers' aluminum facing on incredible three-foot-four-inch modules will still shimmer at a distance like windowless metal grilles. The four low buildings, originally to be finished in the same aluminum, are now in a brownish concrete, tied to the towers by the use of aluminum spandrels. At model scale, the relationship is undefined and disquieting.

These buildings, which were joined to provide an enclosing arcade for the plaza, have been separated to give access to views of the river and to the waterfront in future development when the West Side Highway will hopefully be depressed. They give the appearance of having been merely broken apart. As a result, the immense formal plaza now has subsidiary open spaces. It is to be hoped that they will enrich rather than distrupt this awesome area. The danger is that they could leak limp and uncoordinated out of the five-acre vastness, as in the smaller Holford plan for the rebuilt St. Paul's precinct in London, rather than give the intimate relief intended.

The plaza has now been reduced to an ornamental role, or a kind of paved promenade for fine weather, with most circulatory and access functions relegated to the concourse level below ground. All elevators start on this lower level, which also connects to rapid transit. There is a serious need now to improve pedestrian use and circulation at street level. With Church Street doubled in width, the Trade Center becomes traffic-isolated. A tunnel to be built deep under the street will lead again to the underground concourse. A bridge over the street would bring pedestrians more easily to the plaza and make it a more physical, functioning part of the neighborhood.

The final, inescapable fact remains that architecture is now breaking scale, and style, everywhere. (In his secret heart there is hardly an architect who doesn't want to do so.) The objective historian realizes that the twentieth century is in transition to a remarkable new technology and a formidable new environment, before we have learned how to handle the old one. Who's afraid of the big bad buildings? Everyone, because there are so many things about gigantism that we just don't know. The gamble of triumph or tragedy at this scale—and ultimately it is a gamble—demands an extraordinary payoff. The Trade Center towers could be the start of a new skyscraper age or the biggest tombstones in the world.

New York Times, May 29, 1966

"The New York Process"—
the World Trade Center Site

THE TWIN TOWERS NO LONGER STAND AS a symbol of New York. The skyline, and the city, are changed forever. When the site is cleared, and the lost lives are counted, there will be a huge hole in the heart of New York and of every New Yorker. The city, proven vulnerable to hate and horror, will return to a kind of normal—aggressive, ambitious, chaotic, and creative, still the center of money and power that made its tallest buildings the target of terrorists bent on carrying themselves and thousands of others to a pointless and terrible death.

New York's hubris will return; its prime indicator, Donald Trump, is already talking about building bigger than ever on the World Trade Center site. The skyscraper as symbol refuses to die. There is nothing healing, however, about the usual process of reaping record profits from the most expensive land in the world; rebuilding seems less an act of proud defiance than something inappropriate and obscene. If real estate is our religion, we should find another. This is not about renewal or regeneration—concepts that will be widely championed—it is about memory, and the need to think in terms of solutions of the kind that have determined the splendor and meaning of cities throughout the ages. Development is not destiny.

The Trade Center towers were never beautiful buildings; they achieved landmark status only because of their size. There is nothing compelling about replacing them for their architectural distinction; they had none. The architect, Minoru Yamasaki, a Japanese American, was a talented and gentle man best known for introducing an innovative kind of concrete construction, who did far better buildings elsewhere. His delicate, expressive style was essentially defeated by the enormous scale of the towers—perhaps there was a lesson about monumental civic architecture in their aesthetic failure, one that we failed to understand or acknowledge.

There will be, and should be, passionate disagreement about replacing them at all. Rebuilding on this site requires serious consideration. There will be, and should be, calls for a memorial park, a public open space to serve as a permanent reminder of one of the city's, and history's, worst catastrophes—a detestably man-made, as opposed to natural, disaster—and for a tribute to those who died needlessly and tragically in an act of unredeemed horror.

And yet, one can almost predict what the New York process will be. This city can show its compassion, and its resolve, as it is doing now, but it is also a city incapable of the large, appropriate gesture in the public interest if it costs too much. That, too, is something that can be debated. What are our values? How do we count the cost of those lives? Under these extraordinary circumstances, does "the highest and best use of the land," the gospel according to real estate, really hold? Traditionally, that has meant filling the land to the maximum permitted by law, for the greatest return, while ignoring every social or human factor.

If the usual scenario is followed, the debate will lead to a "solution" in which principle is lost and an epic opportunity squandered. With the best intentions the Municipal Art Society, a conscientious watchdog of the city's urban quality, will announce a competition to determine what should be done with the site. The results will make a nice little exhibition, and discussions and lectures will be held. All this will be ignored by the movers and shakers making big building plans under the expedient banner of physical and symbolic reconstruction. There will be a fuss in the press, with letters to the editor, pro and con. City Hall in a split political decision between greed and glory, will come out for the builders and a memorial—a monument or a small park, something financially inoffensive in the larger scheme of things. This is the Compromise. Or the trade-off, to put it more bluntly. A properly pious, meaningless gesture that everyone can buy without loss of face or obvious shame.

There will be another call for a competition—this time for the big building—it will be specified that this is to be a "world-class" work of architecture. The most conservative design will be chosen by a consortium of potential investors. No one will pay much attention to the token park, which will be a blank spot on the plans, eventually done in a faux retro style for brown-bag lunchers. There will be world-class nothing.

What should be done? Discussion is inevitable, but it should start with the premise that this is going to be the most significant and beautiful memorial public space since Rome or the Renaissance, designed in response to an eternal need, in the nature and style of our own time. That is, if we still know how to do it. We should call on our best talents, perhaps by an international competition, run to the highest standards, and enlisting the greatest expertise. And until the answer is found and built, the site should be a ruin, a place to gather, and mourn, to think about how great, or trivial, our values are, perhaps even to know each other, and our city, better. Ruins are the repositories of memory; construction erases them. A city's greatness is not measured by square footage or pricey views. We need a different kind of symbolism now.

Wall Street Journal, September 17, 2001

The Art of the Deal: Six Dreadful Proposals Devoid of Artistry

THE SIX PROPOSALS—I AVOID DIGNIFYING these retarded exercises in crushing commercial square footage and meaningless memorial voids with the term concept plans—that the Lower Manhattan Development Corporation and the Port Authority have provided for the rebuilding of the tragically maimed World Trade Center site are six cookie-cutter losers. We do not need a necropolis of the urban-renewal mistakes of the sixties. The titles only dimly disguise the fact that the phalanxes of massed office buildings are the revealed reality of official intentions. Called Memorial This and That as a gesture to the universal desire for commemoration, they are dedicated to maximum return on the land, while obviously begging the future.

Professionals, the press, and about four thousand New Yorkers attending an unprecedented public forum have agreed. They expressed their opinions loudly, in true New York fashion. There was too much office space, too little noncommercial use, and the site was too densely built. But what they perceived, and the Lower Manhattan Development Corporation apparently did not, was the absence of the creativity that turns a complex set of requirements into a vitalizing solution that adds to a city's presence and power through the arts of architecture and urban design.

What they said was that the plans weren't ambitious enough. Actually, they are dreadful. It would have taken Panglossian optimism to expect anything better when the profession's major talents were shut out of the process from the start. This is not how a world-class city gets world-class design.

If the public was smart enough to know this, why didn't the LMDC know it? The kindest conclusion is that they haven't a clue. Out of ignorance, convenience, or co-option by the only system its members evidently know and understand, they chose to do it the way it has always been done in New York, using a process that neither encourages nor accommodates excellence in design.

Because they drew a blank doesn't make them blameless. There are other, better ways to go that have been well established by cities and institutions with large new building programs. But in New York, development is not planning; it is bluffing, power brokering, and well-honed legal skills. It is the art of the deal, not the art of the city. It has nothing to do with that elusive thing called vision.

The starting point for these plans was not the thoughtful resolution of complex conditions, but the bargaining position of those with a vested financial interest in the site: the Port Authority, the owner of the World Trade Center, and Larry Silverstein, the developer who had acquired the lease. They insisted that all eleven thousand square feet of lost commercial space be restored. Scrooge could not have done better. The buildings are monsters.

As the game is played, the developer sets demands beyond what he knows he will settle for, negotiations ensue, and a compromise is found and called a triumph by both parties to the deal. If the developer and his lawyers have played their hand well, he ends up with perhaps more than he had set as his real bottom line, but almost certainly with as much as he needed (not wanted—that has no limit). Amenities are trade-offs in the process, often goaded by civic protest, not part of a creative, comprehensive, or community-based concept. That's how it works, and how it has been set up here.

What will now be negotiated for rebuilding Ground Zero—and the ritual negotiations have already begun—is totally unrelated to the conceptual poverty of the plans. There is talk of buyouts and other economic escape hatches, and rumors that the Port Authority may even cancel that onerous lease, at considerable cost, freeing Larry Silverstein to act like a hero. Although it would be naive to think that the process is being rescripted in response to public opinion, the protests may indeed be awakening dormant instincts of civic responsibility in the face of unspeakable tragedy and the political shadow of an election year. The city has suffered a tremendous loss. Profit-as-usual hardly seems appropriate. What Mr. Silverstein had in mind when he swore to rebuild is too awful to contemplate, now that we have contemplated it.

Gestures by the LMDC meant to broaden the process included the really heroic and largely successful attempt to hear the voices of many concerned groups—and the mistake of appointing as adviser a single architect with a single point of view, who, in turn, selected a design coordinator with a fine reputation for historic preservation but not known for vaultingly original ideas. The job was then given to less-than-earthshakingly innovative firms that became the captive planners of the financially involved parties, a guarantee that the results would be limited in a disastrous way.

One senses that all of the agencies with a controlling interest in the rebuilding of Ground Zero—the LMDC, the Port Authority, the New York State Economic Development Corporation, right up to the governor's office—are also clueless. Not one of them has demonstrated the ability or desire to conceive of development beyond the most conventional, deadly design, and real estate criteria. Planning agencies (remember them?) have simply shriveled away in the face of the state agencies' coordinated power. Only New York's mayor seems to be quietly unenthusiastic.

The LMDC calls the proposals "a starting point" for discussion and modification. That will provide a convenient distraction from the real issue—that there's nothing to discuss. These plans can't be tweaked; they have got to go. You have to begin with ideas, not clichés. They do serve a purpose, however. It is easier for most people to understand pictures than descriptions, so it is easier to grasp how awful they are. They also show what has been dropped from the guidelines: the mixed uses, the social and cultural life. The memorial, upstaged by the massive commercial development, is pushed from place to place.

It is fashionable to say that greed at a grand scale has made New York great. That's a dismal outlook. Our buildings are great to the degree that their architecture is great; where the city is great, as at Rockefeller Center, it is because there are subtleties of scale and relationships that elevate the urban experience. If size and square footage is where all office buildings begin, they do not end there with landmarks like the Woolworth, Chrysler, or Empire State buildings; they are not memorable for their visibility (like the Twin Towers, which were neither architecturally distinguished nor a trade center), but for their quality and character. This is not the same thing as building big with trim.

Successful, city-enriching plans are achieved by those trained and talented specialists who have surprised us ever since Michelangelo miraculously transformed the impossibly mismatched grades and buildings of Rome's Capitoline Hill into the superbly synthesized Campidoglio. The rest of us were born without the ability to conceptualize such things or the skills to execute them.

A campaign has begun to convince us that the rejection of the six proposals will mean the loss of time and money, delays in transportation facilities, and further pain for small businesses. But who lost all these months doing the hopelessly wrong thing? Who shut out the gifted individuals who could take the commercial, public, and private needs, and the memorial, and give them a form that honors the site rather than exploiting it? What is not negotiable is the history, symbolism, and emotion on an epic scale that marks Ground Zero as a special place. We have only one chance to rebuild with glory, to memorialize with honor, to add beauty and humanity, as well as profit and prestige, to the city we love.

Wall Street Journal, July 25, 2002

Rebuilding Lower Manhattan

THE CROWDS VIEWING THE SECOND ROUND of designs for the World Trade Center site on display in the Winter Garden of the World Financial Center are as international as the seven teams of architects who have produced them. The interest is global, and the spotlight is on how this extraordinary coalition of the world's most celebrated and innovative talents, commissioned by the Lower Manhattan Development Corporation after the earlier design debacle, proposes to heal the shattering wounds to New York's fabric and psyche suffered on 9/11.

The conceptual daring and advanced technology of these schemes—the sheer drama of their bold images—brings cutting-edge creativity to New York, where it is long overdue. Buildings like these have already changed skylines from London to Hong Kong. This is the architecture of the twenty-first century, and about as good as it gets.

That's the good news. The bad news is that these provocative and beautiful presentations have also given us a stunning demonstration of how to do the wrong thing right. With no proper program—a wish list from the public, elicited through opinion polls, is not a program—they have shown us how skillfully and elegantly the wrong thing can be done.

Under the adventurous forms and the transparent purity of glowing plexiglass models of Lilliputian skylines, the priorities remain the same—with a little juggling, virtually all of the eleven million square feet of preexisting commercial space has been replaced, either directly on the site or immediately adjacent to it. That concentrated bulk is still with us; it just looks a lot better.

In response to loudly voiced public displeasure, the eleven million square feet were reduced to ten million square feet, with the little-noticed proviso that if less than ten million is built at Ground Zero, the remainder must be on contiguous sites. Retail space has been increased to six hundred thousand square feet from the four hundred thousand that existed before 9/11, with a possible top of one million square feet. Retail is more profitable than offices, which accounts for this shell game with numbers.

The objective is still the reinstatement of real estate, not the revitalization of Lower Manhattan, with the memorial an afterthought to be plugged in later. There is no guiding blueprint for the future of downtown, nothing to which these examples of the new, the beautiful, and the cool can relate in any useful or rational way, although you can see how the architects have struggled to get out of that straitjacket, eagerly projecting tentative lines of connection beyond Ground Zero. The rebuilding is still being driven by Port Authority leases and the recovery of cash flow lost with the Twin Towers.

Don't blame the architects; they followed the rules they were given. They have done their best to transcend this obstinate programmatic and planning vacuum that the official agencies seem determined to maintain in the face of all reason, logic, and the public interest. Some of the most popular demands have been incorporated: the restoration of the street grid, a promenade to the river, and a marker on the skyline. There are handsome transportation hubs that might, or might not, work with the transit reconstruction under way. All their proposals share concerns for safety and sustainability. All are environmentally friendly, often through amazing new technology. Most exploit new materials and innovative techniques. They stress escape routes. The use of computers from design to display is dazzling.

If density is the soul of the city, this is its spiritual or, better, commercial apotheosis. How else could all that square footage be accommodated? It is achieved in some marvelously creative ways. The British architect Norman Foster's triangulated twin towers meet and "kiss" as they rise; the group called Think uses Rafael Viñoly's steel and glass geometry for latticed towers or a vast public room; United Architects' massed, canted buildings create a computerized, cathedral-like image. Four of the participants project the tallest building in the world. Height is an aphrodisiac to architects; they lust after it. That soaring something on the skyline, a problematic feature at best, set off an orgy of megalithic excess.

What looks like the world of the future is the world of the past in steel and glass space frames and soaring sky cities, where all but architects might fear to dwell. Will we really go up sixty stories for coffee or relax in a vertiginous park raised high over West Street when we avoid a plaza even slightly above or below grade like the plague? New York's vitality is on the street. The World Trade Center notoriously destroyed it.

Building enormously high as a gesture of revenge and affirmation raises serious questions of wisdom and practicality. The construction of the World Trade Center by the Port Authority in the seventies depressed the real estate market for decades downtown. However impressive the Twin Towers were in sunlight and moonlight, whatever symbolism is now falsely ascribed to them through a catastrophic act, do we really need to make the same mistake again?

An expert on the subject, the architect David Childs of Skidmore Owings & Merrill, is quoted as saying that above sixty-five or seventy stories a building is increasingly expensive and inefficient and must be heavily subsidized. It becomes an act of vanity, or greed, or both. When that gives us a Woolworth or Chrysler Building, we can be nonjudgmentally grateful. But should those subsidies go into the emotional rush of flinging something defiantly into the sky, or should they go to the parks and housing and cultural institutions that will make downtown a viable and desirable community? New York's skyline changes naturally and spectacularly over time.

The true quality of these designs is evident in their response to the ever-present question posed in his presentation by John Whitehead, chairman of the Lower Manhattan Development Corporation, "What does September 11 represent?" Every one of the proposals incorporates the answer. Each delivers a timeless sense of the terror and tragedy, tied to a unique regeneration of place. All have indicated memorial sites for a future competition, as required, but each, in itself, in its concept and imagery, is already a memorial. This has been understood as integral to the site, and to any construction on it.

How could these talented, responsive artists, in the very nature of the charge, resist? Who could have expected them to do otherwise? Remember, we are talking about memorials after Vietnam, when the heroic figure gave way to the solemn space and somber wall, when memory was held in names inscribed on black granite, grief expressed by the haunting, enduring nature of an evocative place. Anyone familiar with the process of design knows that memory and signification are inseparable from conceptualization.

There is no realism, no traditional sculpture group of heroes or victims that can satisfy all of the bereaved or reveal the magnitude of the loss. The isolation and postponement of the memorial has been wrong from the start; instead of making it more important, this marginalizes it.

One design breaks the rules and sets the priorities straight. Daniel Libeskind's powerful concept does not beg the issue of the memorial; it is the centerpiece of his proposal. Mr. Libeskind has done what he does superbly, like no one else, as anyone who has visited his Jewish Museum in Berlin knows; he has perfected an intensely individual, profoundly moving architecture of memory and loss of unsurpassed impact and meaning. The design struck a common nerve; one had the sense, at the presentation, of an end to an undefined yearning and search. You could tell by the sustained applause and tears that this is what people really wanted, and what New York needs.

Mr. Libeskind takes you down seventy feet to bedrock, the real Ground Zero, where the slurry wall holding back the Hudson River looms like some overwhelming, archaic survival. In the void, he builds a museum out of the jagged shards and symbolic spaces that characterize his architecture, and that pierce the soul as much as any memorabilia. There are two public places: a Park of Heroes and a Wedge of Light. In an annual commemorative ritual tied to sun and sky, a shaft of light will illuminate the void between the time of the first and second attacks. An elevated walkway circles the site. The area is served by a transportation center that forms a nexus of commercial and cultural activities. Buildings at its borders could be designed and phased according to market demand. A fractured tower rises 1,776 feet with a spine containing "gardens of the world." But Mr. Libeskind proves that depth, rather than height, has a supernaturally commanding presence.

Forget the additional time and expense of a competition; nothing will ever be better than this. Build Mr. Libeskind's memorial, and it will become a world magnet for the hotels, restaurants, shops, and theaters that will make Ground Zero a center of life downtown. It will be a source and incubator of renewal.

We are promised a plan by the LMDC at the end of this month—although what kind, by whom, and according to what criteria are unclear. All that we have been told is that it is to be a land-use plan; it will not be any of these designs. With the kind of thinking demonstrated so far, this will probably be an assortment of real estate parcels that take priority over a vaguely indicated public realm. Why the rush? With a surplus of commercial space downtown and a soft economy, no one is going to build now. It would take at least ten years for the market to absorb the construction. Why this insistence on a replacement before a framework has been established as context and support for the future?

Just before the unveiling of the LMDC's designs, Mayor Bloomberg weighed in with New York City's Vision for Lower Manhattan. Developed by Peterson/Littenberg, whose Ground Zero designs are as retro as the other solutions are visionary, its emphasis on urban design principles is both inviting and sound. It specifies public investments in transit, streets, parks and open space, housing, schools, cultural institutions, and waterfront uses. The focus is on neighborhoods. It provides costs, and calculates private market response to public investment in improvements and amenities, the proven way to attract capital and construction. This is a plan, not a lock-hold on real estate or a dream dropped from outer space.

Generously, you can say that the Port Authority and the incestuous chain of New York State Authorities leading from the LMDC to the governor's office have no idea what planning is, or don't want to know. More realistically, they would see no political advantage in a procedure that violates their dedicated alliance with the development community and its limited objectives. It sounds like a bad joke, but the development mantra in New York has always been that "the highest and best use of the land is its most profitable use"—an actual quote, repeated often, and believed devoutly. The public realm is nebulous and unprofitable.

The land swap must be pursued that would exchange the city-owned land under the airports, now rented by the Port Authority, for the Authority-owned land of the World Trade Center. The Trade Center leases can, and should, be bought out; Larry Silverstein cannot replace the Twin Towers, and a massively increased mall must not dictate street and land uses. A negotiated buyout is possible for all concerned that will leave insurance money for future construction. Everything has changed so radically that no return to preexisting conditions is possible.

The skyscraper is not dead; these marvels of our time will be built as long as egos, demand, art, and greed, and the sheer, vertical exhilaration of the city, exist. But depending on your level of cynicism, this whole design exercise can be seen as the politics of accommodation or as a detour leading inevitably, after pious analysis and appropriate lip service, to business as usual as practiced by the political-development establishment in New York. What a waste, what a loss, of talent and potential; what a betrayal of the past and future that would be.

Wall Street Journal, January 7, 2003

The Next Great City Center?

MIRACLES HAPPEN. EVEN IN NEW YORK. Now that we have stumbled through a nonprogram and a dyslexic process (everything backward) that made all the mistakes in the plan book and invented a few, we have a competition-winning design for Ground Zero that promises that most elusive prize of all—a concept of character and style that will address the symbolic needs of the past and the physical needs of the future.

The design by Daniel Libeskind is not about death and destruction, as some have feared; it is an original and eventful reconstruction of the World Trade Center site that brings the architecture of the twenty-first century to New York, where it has been sadly and shamefully lacking. Even as we preserve that tragic pit and its sustaining wall, they will become the source of new life. But this will happen only if the spotlight stays relentlessly on the rebuilding process, and if we do not lose the urgent sense of necessity and inevitability that has brought us this far.

No one can write this plan off by saying it can't be done. It is no secret that there are builders and bureaucrats dedicated to the status quo who believe, and hope, that a long drawn-out memorial design process will be all that survives of progressively debilitating compromises. That would be a default of epic proportions that would send 9/11 to the trash heap of history.

Reality was addressed during the tense period before the choice was made between the two finalists, Daniel Libeskind and Rafael Viñoly; both worked to turn their visionary proposals of the first presentation last December into practical solutions. The updated versions dealt with construction and costs—what to build, for what purpose and on what schedule, and how to keep the integrity of the memorial district while encouraging a variety of uses to support renewal and rebirth downtown. Both plans placed their highest priority on the public and cultural features at their center. Because reality in New York is a function of market forces, the large office towers will be built as demand requires.

Until now, attention has focused almost exclusively on the desire to restore a soaring presence on the skyline and create a memorial and garden on the site. The Libeskind plan includes a symbolic skyscraper, a memorial park, and the element that has profoundly affected so many, the exposed slurry wall, the barrier that surrounded the World Trade Center site to keep back the river and held fast the day of the attacks. To understand the promise and the reality of Mr. Libeskind's vision, however, it is essential to know what happens on the ground, as well as below it, or in the sky.

THE PLANS ARE not easy to read; they avoid right angles and include many intersecting spaces and changing levels, and little attention has been paid to anything except the most visible and dramatic features. Some see a superficial resemblance between this and earlier proposals, but that totally misses the point. There is much more to urban design than a plot plan. Diagrams do not resolve the integration of culture and commerce, the relationship of the public realm and private enterprise, the balance of new building and open space; they do not create the kind of places that combine memory with a vital and active urbanity. All this determines the experience people will have on the ground.

   I think we should look closely at what we had before 9/11, and what we are about to get in its place. Realism will serve us well here, too. The World Trade Center was the poster project for the worst kind of urban renewal imposed on American cities in the sixties and seventies—nothing changes that fact. The land was acquired by eminent domain and stripped of small businesses; the huge buildings were made possible by the Port Authority's right, as an independent government body, to bypass the city's laws and codes, as well as to take the city's land.

   The project amputated and eliminated Lower Manhattan's historic streets, putting in their place a vast, cold, dead plaza with a pair of grossly overscaled, architecturally undistinguished towers that instantly ruptured the magic of an intricate and evocative skyline. Some of that magic was transferred to the Twin Towers when light gilded and colored their bland façades, and there are those—most young enough never to have known another skyline—for whom the towers still hold a nostalgic appeal. I, for one, am unable to romanticize them. They were big. Inevitably, their size made them beacons, and then targets, and tragic emblems, in the curious and sometimes terrible way history confers immortality.

   Some of those lost streets will be restored. Greenwich Street, a major thoroughfare that runs north-south paralleling West Street and was brutally dismembered, will be reopened, and a reinstated Fulton Street will eventually continue across a West Street park to connect directly to the World Financial Center's Winter Garden and the river. West Street will tunnel under the park from Liberty to Vesey streets.

The memorial area was originally placed in the void opened by the catastrophe, seventy feet below ground at bedrock. It has been raised to thirty feet below ground to accommodate underground transportation, and to provide the bracing needed for the slurry wall. This change makes the park more accessible, while still buffered from street noise and activity above. A void down to bedrock from the park will parallel the slurry wall. The memorial will rise vertically from bedrock to the park above, to be seen at all levels. The park, the slurry wall, and the memorial will be accessible by escalator and stairs. The museum and cultural buildings will flank the memorial park.

The intersection of the restored Fulton and Greenwich streets will become a new hub of activity. The performing arts building, an office and hotel, the new transportation center, and continuous street retail are located here. Small symbolic parks slice through the area diagonally, between buildings, providing relief and counterpoint.

The Wedge of Light, where the sun will strike through on each September 11 for the exact time and duration of the attack, forms a triangular plaza along Fulton Street. This subtle memorial gesture, and the symbolic skyscraper's height of 1,776 feet, have been called kitsch; I feel more strongly that the insistence on the tallest building in the world is less an act of patriotic defiance than one of the more enduring conceits and evanescent follies of our time.

Another wedge-shaped plaza, the September 11 Place, leads from this focal corner to the entrance of the Ground Zero park and memorial. The Heroes Park, an irregular open space across Fulton Street, is a protective transition from the memorial site to the future office towers. A new south wall and one more small park complete the Liberty Street side. The intimacy and humanity of these serendipitously encountered green areas in what will again become a densely populated place is one of the great pleasures of this plan.

THE FIRST PHASE of construction will be the initial public investment in streets and transportation. Phase two will build the symbolic skyscraper, the Ground Zero park, and the cultural buildings. Phase three will be the commercial construction, when it becomes economically viable.

The brilliance of this plan is its recognition of the fact that cultural facilities are the magnet for investment and regeneration; they are the engine of economic renewal. The process starts with the public space and services and the amenities that draw people and enterprise; this brings the private capital for hotels, offices, shops, and housing. It does not matter which of the buildings are used for theaters, museums, or even unanticipated purposes; they form a nexus of attraction and revival. They will speed up commercial construction, once the economy improves.

There will be no problem finding occupants for these buildings. The New York City Opera, orphaned by Lincoln Center's unsettled plans, and looking for its own theater, has already begun enthusiastic negotiations for Mr. Libeskind's performing arts building and is contacting him about designing to their specifications. There could be a home here for the Museum of the City of New York, frustrated in its aborted move to the restored Tweed Courthouse behind City Hall. Other dance and theater groups are eyeing the downtown cultural spaces hungrily. They see this, correctly, as the next great center of the city.

By building parks and restoring the waterfront, the mayor of Barcelona began the process of revitalization that has made Barcelona one of Europe's most popular and desirable cities. Tacoma, Washington, less than a hotbed of aesthetic involvement, is completing a major investment in cultural facilities, not for the sake of art, but with the prime purpose of activating downtown. This is sound, proven planning procedure.

The large office buildings, arranged in a spiraling cluster around the memorial sector, will be a far more proportionate and elegant addition to the skyline than the Twin Towers' bruising banality. These towers will vary in height, but none will exceed seventy stories. The question has never been how much square footage should be provided, but whether it should be allowed to dominate or trivialize the memorial sector. There is no need to be disturbed by the transformation of the prismatic shapes of the towers in the first proposal into the more conventional and rentable floorplates of accepted commercial models; this is real estate reality. The center will still hold.

There is serious cause for alarm, however, in the treatment of the slurry wall in the revised version of the plan. For all of its miraculous strength in keeping the river at bay, the wall has been weakened and, once exposed, it is vulnerable. Two engineering proposals are being made to brace it. Neither will affect the wall's visual impact; the bracing adds a kind of Piranesian drama. But that, apparently, is not enough. The intent now is to enclose the slurry wall with a glass wall placed about six feet in front of it, closed across the top; this will create a covered space reaching down to bedrock that can be temperature and humidity controlled.

Behind glass, the wall's raw power will be lost; the direct confrontation with its enormous presence will be gone. It will become a display object, removed from reality, its terrible message tamed and transformed—just another museum-style, climate-controlled artifact. The emotional charge it delivers, the overpowering evidence of destruction it represents, the heart of the Libeskind concept, is compromised. To save the wall by providing a solution for its continued existence that effectively destroys it is an ironic twist. It turns 9/11 into catch-22.

Ancient Roman walls, eloquent in their survival, stand everywhere without elaborate protection. This is a ruin, and it is meant to be. If we take away so much of its meaning, then we must add something else— other layers of meaning that deliver a deeper and more complex message. Etch that glass wall with all the names of the dead; treat it as part of the memorial. Make concealment and revelation work together symbolically, with the slurry wall as witness. This should be included in the challenge of the memorial design.

IN AN APOCALYPTIC way, the land has been given back to us, regardless of who owns or controls it, all of which is under intense and intricate negotiation right now. Constant architectural oversight will be necessary as the plan evolves. This is something Daniel Libeskind knows all about, after ten years on the job in Berlin guiding his competition-winning Jewish Museum to completion. He is both an able collaborator and a seasoned fighter—a realist, in other words.

That handshake at the announcement ceremony between Mr. Libeskind and Larry Silverstein, the developer who holds the Twin Tower leases and is being dragged kicking and screaming into enlightenment, was a historic New York first. Whether it turns into arm wrestling remains to be seen. New Yorkers are not about to let the future go. And the rest of the world is watching.

Wall Street Journal, March 19, 2003

Death of the Dream

THE FINAL BETRAYAL OF THE PLAN for the rebuilding of the World Trade Center site—the news two weeks ago that the performing arts center has been dropped from the five-hundred-million-dollar fund-raising campaign for the memorial and museum—was consigned to an inner arts page of a Saturday edition of the newspaper of record, where weekend stories go to die. Picked up by an astute reporter, Robin Pogrebin, the latest development in the downward slide of the ideals and aspirations embraced for Ground Zero was buried in the hoopla of the announcement of the fund-raising committee.

The death of the dream has come slowly, in bits and pieces, not as a sudden cataclysmic event. It has not been a casualty of the more obvious debate over whether the replacement of the lost ten million square feet of commercial space demanded by the developer is an economic necessity or the defilement of the land where so many died. This has been a subtler, more insidious sabotage, through the progressive downgrading and evisceration of the cultural components of Daniel Libeskind's competition-winning design.

The plan, by nature and necessity, was schematic, a framework within which the objectives could be realized in a number of ways. New Yorkers are realists, and we expected a long period of adjustments and accommodations, political and otherwise, a process in which hope springs eternal and serendipity is often an ameliorating factor. As our architectural expectations plunged, they were revived again in 2003 by the Port Authority's surprising commission of Santiago Calatrava for its Transportation Hub, a stunning, spirit-lifting building that spectacularly refocused the site.

But whatever the compromises, four essential components needed to be maintained. There was the iconic image to replace the Twin Towers, achieved by a spiraling ring of skyscrapers increasing in height until they reached their tallest point in a building called the Freedom Tower, for a strong visual and emotional impact on the skyline. The importance of memory was stressed by a single powerful element that was the design's basic theme: the retention of the rough concrete slurry wall that held back the river from the Trade Center's foundations, to be preserved and exposed as a reminder of the tragic event, a symbol of destruction and salvation.

The area's creative renewal was symbolized by the central position of the arts and cultural buildings, which included a performing arts center and a museum. Clearly designated social space at ground level provided parks, promenades, and street life to vitalize the new construction and tie the community together.

Legitimate factors soon presented serious obstacles to the design and contributed to the disintegration of its physical and symbolic aspects. The inevitable difficulties of translating a schematic idea, taken much too literally by many, while respecting and retaining its most significant features, took their toll. The sixteen acres of Ground Zero are a jungle of jurisdictional and infrastructural conflicts. The restoration of working transportation was an immediate priority, forcing irreversible decisions. Mind-bending complexities of grade changes, utilities, circulation, traffic routes and transportation lines, public and private use and access had to be resolved, as well as the incompatible needs and desires of local communities with those dedicated to a single, overriding purpose: memorializing the dead.

There have been demonstrations of graceless greed and ambition. In a New York–scale catch-22 dilemma, the developer, Larry Silverstein, must make enormous payments to the Port Authority for a rental contract on the Twin Towers executed shortly before the attack or risk forfeiting the contract and the right to rebuild, which he cites as one of the document's obligations. He also claims that he must rebuild at the same size (a combination of height and density equal to the previous construction) to meet those financial obligations or default and lose all. Violins, please. Obviously, the size of the gamble and the potential payoff do not encourage selfless or public-spirited behavior, but then, New York real estate has never been a humanitarian calling.

And there was the unedifying sight of an architectural marriage made in hell—a shotgun arrangement between Mr. Silverstein's architect, David Childs, and Daniel Libeskind, the architect of the plan, over the design of the Freedom Tower. Alas, poor Libeskind; both he and his tower were aggressively co-opted by the more powerful duo, and the unfortunate result of the architectural arm-wrestling—an awkwardly torqued hybrid of the original offset, prismatic form—speaks more of ego and arrogance than art.

Something has been terribly wrong with the approach to the cultural components from the start. A selection process that was to bring a significant representation of New York's creative institutions downtown ended as an exercise in bland cultural tokenism. What except fear of elitism and the determination to be incongruously evenhanded could have eliminated the New York City Opera, desperately in need of its own home and willing to devote energy and commitment to its funding and construction? Not that any of those chosen are unworthy or undeserving, but none is the strong cultural anchor required. This was such a conscious leveling of art to the most acceptable common denominator that it is impossible to divine any effort except the terminal safety of political correctness.

The lovely little Drawing Center was shoehorned into a museum meant to commemorate freedom, an odd couple at best. Called the International Freedom Center, but still largely undefined in its program or purposes, this building, with the memorial, is marked for immediate fund-raising; the Drawing Center appears to be barely hanging in there.

A match was made between the Joyce Dance Theater and the Signature Theatre Company for the promised performing arts center to be designed by Frank Gehry, whose name has given more cachet than immediacy to the project; he is waiting for an unscheduled go ahead and nebulous funding, perhaps due in part to the fact that no one knows yet where to put it. We are told that a program for the arts must come before construction plans, something not yet discernible for the apparently more fundworthy Freedom Center, but where, in this dilatory and evasive chaos, can one exist? When officials were questioned about the elimination of the arts center from the fund-raising effort, their explanation was a vaguely pious disclaimer about a "second phase," when, of course, there will be little if any money available for a building estimated at four hundred million dollars after the completion of a half-billion-dollar campaign. Or as any true New Yorker would put it, succinctly and without hesitation, you should live so long.

The Lower Manhattan Development Corporation has just issued a detailed report on how carefully it has listened to the public in the disposition of its funds. Clearly, some voices have been louder than others. The most vocal and best represented are those calling for restricting the fund-raising to "9/11–related" elements of the plan. That is an abdica-

tion of the need to temper an unrelenting drive for commercial maxi-
mization of the site with something more than an aching emptiness at
its heart. The slurry wall is now a relic, its relevance as history and
metaphor replaced by an enormous competition-winning void within
the Twin Towers' footprints, a memorial so vast few accurately understand its size.

Because the entitlements of loss and grief are the third rail of the rebuilding effort, no one has challenged the subversion of the aims and
intent of the plan. The parts that speak of hope and the future have not
been able to survive the pressure for a single-minded commitment to
the tragic past. Even at Ground Zero, not all the bereaved share the
sentiments of the most politically active survivors. Some quietly want to
get on with their lives, and there are those who would like to see a more
constructive renewal as an antidote to grief.

The poet Wallace Stevens reminded us that art helps us live our lives.
Yet no one has had the courage, or conviction, to demand that the arts
be restored to their proper place as one of the city's greatest strengths and
a source of its spiritual continuity. We have lost what we hoped to gain: a
creative rebirth downtown. At Ground Zero, what should be first is last.
An affirmation of life is being reduced to a culture of death.

Wall Street Journal, April 20, 2005

The Disaster That Has Followed the Tragedy

A NEWSPAPER CARTOON SOME YEARS AGO showed a very large building in the shape of a massive dollar sign, Power Towers, being contemplated by two smiling, portly men, one saying to the other, "I find it
charming and you find it charming and all the others just like us will
find it charming."

It would be a stretch to call the three enormous towers proposed for
the World Trade Center site charming, but many in New York's

development community will undoubtedly feel satisfied that the highest aspirations of art and profit have been met by these "signature" buildings by three internationally famous architects, Norman Foster and Richard Rogers of London and Fumihiko Maki of Tokyo. The designs were released for the fifth anniversary of 9/11 by the Port Authority, which owns the land, and developer Larry Silverstein, who holds the leases for the World Trade Center towers and is committed to rebuilding.

Given the notoriety of the site, a passionately observant and deeply involved public, and the proven financial advantage of what goes by the dreadful name "starchitecture," Mr. Silverstein's move from standard commercial construction to high-end high style required no great sacrifice or philanthropic awakening. Good design makes excess palatable. Marquee names command higher rents. These are all virtuoso performances—architecture as spectacular window dressing and shrewd marketing tool for the grossly maximized commercial square footage that has remained the one constant through the perversion and destruction of Daniel Libeskind's master plan, a process in which vision succumbed early to pressure groups and political agendas. Call it irony or destiny, the architecture once rejected as a costly "frill" is now embraced for its dollar value.

The first and most obvious comment to be made about these buildings is that whatever the pious rhetoric, their proximity to sacred ground, and the care with which the reality is skirted, they are machines for making money, just as the Twin Towers were, with only some rearrangement of the square footage. Wringing every possible dollar from a piece of property is a traditional New York practice celebrated in the oft-repeated real estate mantra, offered with a straight face and impressive hubris, as "the highest and best use of the land." Say it often enough, and no one will question the absence of any need or purpose other than profit in the calculations.

The second observation is that these buildings don't talk to each other or to the site. They do not so much reach for the sky as drop down from it on a designated parcel. There is no suggestion of interaction except Mr. Foster's claim (is he serious?) that his building is tipping its slanted hat to the memorial far below. If these architects were really working together in the same room, as we have been told, what were they thinking? Did they have any concept in common except building big? How in the world did they define collaboration? Or is there a new mantra, the highest and best use of the land is to establish the architect's unmistakable trademark style, above all other symbolic or urban considerations?

Only Mr. Maki's solution has a refinement and urbanity that suggests the possibility of compatibility rather than competition. This is not the place for the dramatic chaos of unrelated development that defines so much of New York; Ground Zero begs for something more. The original concept of spiraling, crystalline towers was stunning and magical. It identified the site and made a unified impact on the skyline. There is no meaning or magic left in the token rise in building heights to a much-compromised Freedom Tower.

The balance of commercial and cultural facilities meant to be the basis of the area's rebirth and regeneration is also gone, sabotaged by the supine political response to the escalating demands of those bereaved families whose inconsolable grief required the elimination of the plan's cultural components on the disturbing and specious grounds that the arts and liberties that mark a free society equaled disrespect, or less honor to the dead. They became Ground Zero's censors and de facto designers, eliminating buildings and dictating content to a commission that seemed to have no clue about appropriateness or professional expertise.

The intensely moving image of the surviving slurry wall that saved Lower Manhattan from the waters of the Hudson River was buried under the weight of an expanding memorial that preempted the site, discarding guidelines and voiding the commitment to renewal and the need to build creatively for future generations. Official pandering and political waffling tortured the master plan to death. Piecemeal dismemberment and an unfulfilled mandate have gone hand in hand.

For some of us there has been a persistent sense of déjà vu. A generation that never knew the city without the Twin Towers has placed them high in skyscraper hagiography because of their terrible fate. But the New York skyline has changed many times, and will again. An earlier skyline, dominated by earlier icons, the Empire State and Chrysler buildings, had a richness and variety not yet diminished by the brutal breaking of scale and loss of architectural detail when the Port Authority built not one but two of the tallest buildings in the world. Whether the move from bridges and tunnels to gargantuan real estate was vanity, greed, or the deal of the century, the Twin Towers could be built only by using the authority's independent powers to override all of New York's height, building, and zoning codes and restrictions. The same excessive bulk is being reproduced today.

Power has shifted from the Port Authority to Mr. Silverstein, who holds the leases and the insurance payments as bargaining chips in a spectacular demonstration of negotiation as spectator sport, turning the screws to his advantage in every conceivable way while foreclosing the possibility of a more publicly responsive development.

After 9/11 it was easy to forget that the Twin Towers were an economic disaster that depressed the New York rental market for years. As a palliative, Governor Nelson Rockefeller packed the near-empty buildings with New York State offices. Learning, or not learning, from the past, Governor George Pataki is once again dragooning government agencies to avoid the same problem in the tenantless Freedom Tower, while protests rise against the unseemly public subsidy of Mr. Silverstein's creatively calculated fifty-nine-dollar-a-square-foot rent, and captive workers revolt at occupying a high-rise symbol of terrorism.

New York has been no stranger to controversial projects of this scale. What began as a search for a new home for the Metropolitan Opera became Rockefeller Center when the Met withdrew as the Depression deepened in the thirties and John D. Rockefeller Jr. found himself holding a huge, money-losing tract of midtown land. A businessman who always insisted on his 6 percent of any philanthropic undertaking, he turned the project into a hard-nosed real estate development. The bottom line, and there always is one in New York, is that these sites involve some of the highest land values in the world, which inevitably influences the outcome.

But Rockefeller Center was built with a master plan. When millions of square feet were thrown onto a market that could not absorb them—déjà vu all over again—this distinctive complex of commercial and cultural facilities with its attractive public spaces was able to survive as a prestigious international business venue and a popular entertainment center. Not least, its coherent style was the work of a group of architects as prominent in their own day as those currently involved downtown. Raymond Hood had designed the Daily News Building and Wallace Harrison would become the lead architect of the United Nations, but both were part of a consortium of top practitioners known simply as the

Associated Architects. No one did his own thing. Together, they achieved a lasting level of coordinated excellence.

Rockefeller Center is not a model to be followed literally—every age has its own style and sensibility. Today's aesthetic and technological resources are enormous; they can support a wide variety of solutions. I do not believe for a moment that we are no longer capable of building great cities of symbolic beauty and enduring public amenity. What Ground Zero tells us is that we have lost the faith and the nerve, the knowledge and the leadership, to make it happen now.

Wall Street Journal, September 28, 2006

PART VI

Failures and Follies

A Vision of Rome Dies

PENNSYLVANIA STATION SUCCUMBED TO PROGRESS this week at the age of fifty-six after a lingering decline. The building's one remaining façade was shorn of eagles and ornament yesterday, preparatory to leveling the last wall. It went not with a bang, or a whimper, but to the rustle of real estate stock shares.

The passing of Penn Station is more than the end of a landmark. It makes the priority of real estate values over preservation conclusively clear. It confirms the demise of an age of opulent elegance, of conspicuous, magnificent spaces, rich and enduring materials, the monumental civic gesture, and extravagant expenditure for aesthetic ends. Obsolescence is not limited to land use and building function in New York.

It was still the Gilded Age in 1910 when the building was completed by Charles Follen McKim of McKim, Mead & White, one of the turn-of-the-century's most gilt-edged architectural firms. There was plush in the Pullmans, crisp damask in the diners, silver bud vases on tables, and the New York–bound traveler debouched into a Roman tepidarium.

Modeled after the warm room of the Baths of Caracalla, the station's concourse was longer than the nave of St. Peter's in Rome. Its vaulted ceilings were 138 feet high, and its grand staircase was forty feet wide.

The soot-stained travertine of the interiors, reputed to be the first used in this country, was from quarries in Tivoli employed in building the Eternal City. Its mellow, golden-cream was used in the Coliseum in the first century A.D. and St. Peter's fifteen centuries later. New York could be called the Mortal Metropolis.

Six murals by Jules Guérin, huge topographical maps of Pennsy territory in sky blues, pale browns, and yellow, high in the reaches of the massive walls, gradually disappeared under layers of the same soot. Generous deposits turned the exterior Massachusetts granite from warm pink to dingy gray. Now marble pomp has been reduced to rubble; stone to dust.

Today, there are new symbols for a new age. The modern traveler, fed on frozen flight dinners, enters the city, not in Roman splendor, but through the bowels of a streamlined concrete bird, as at Trans World

Penn Station interior

Airlines' Kennedy International airport terminal. Classic columns are replaced by catenary curves.

Architects' conceits may change, but businessmen remain the same. Alexander Cassatt, an extremely astute businessman and head of the Pennsylvania Railroad when the station was designed, wanted to build a hotel on the valuable air rights over the terminal.

His architect dissuaded him, arguing that the railroad owed the city a "thoroughly and distinctly monumental gateway."

As Lewis Mumford has observed, "Professional and civic pride won out over cupidity."

It was a shaky victory that lasted only fifty years. A soiled symbolic gateway has been carted to the scrap heap, and its replacement will be the Madison Square Garden sport and entertainment center connected to a twenty-nine-story office building. Land values and air rights will push the main concourse completely underground. The style will be not Roman Imperial, but Investment Modern.

The station's decline began long before demolition. As time passed and grime gathered, life and architecture became noticeably less grand.

The Great Depression made the once-elegant terminal a home for the homeless, its increasing shabbiness and sense of inert time and the stale chill of hopeless winter nights immortalized by William Faulkner, when he wrote:

> In the rotunda, where the people appeared as small and intent as ants, the smell and sense of snow still lingered, though high now among the steel girders, spent and vitiated and filled with a weary and ceaseless murmuring, like the voices of pilgrims upon the infinite plain, like the voices of all the travelers who have ever passed through.

With the return of prosperity, and the traveler, demolition by commercialization began. Colored ads appeared like blasphemous utterances in the marbled halls; automobiles revolved on turntables; shops and stands were added in jazzy cacophony.

In 1958, a huge, lighted plastic clamshell was hung on wires from the Corinthian columns, hovering over a sawtooth arrangement of new ticket booths The result, according to Mr. Mumford, was sabotage, a "masterpiece of architectural and visual incongruity."

By 1963, when a group of prominent architects and citizens picketed the building to protest the announcement of the decision to demolish, it was hard to realize, with Philip Johnson, "that man can build nobly," in the light of the aesthetic debris.

Functionally, the station was considerably less than noble. The complexity and ambiguity of its train levels and entrances and exits were a constant frustration. Except for its great glass and iron waiting room, it was a better expression of ancient Rome than of twentieth-century America.

But its great spaces and superb materials were genuinely noble, in a sense that architecture can no longer afford, in cubage costs alone. The new terminal will have 9-to-22-foot ceilings, against the original 138, all below grade. And the concept was noble, in a sense that society now tragically undervalues.

In 1906, when the $25-million hole was dug in the old Tenderloin district for the $112-million terminal and landmark, the city's and the railroad's sights were high. Now dreams of urban glory and broken Doric columns lie shattered in the Secaucus meadows.

New York Times, July 14, 1966

How We Lost Lower Manhattan

AFTER ALMOST TEN STOP-AND-GO YEARS, during which plans have been drawn, scrapped, and revised, work on one of the first and most controversial of New York's urban-renewal areas, Brooklyn Bridge Southwest, is finally going ahead.

Demolition is under way in the fifteen-acre site bounded by Beekman, Fulton, Frankfort, Pearl, and Nassau streets, just below the bridge and east of City Hall and the Civic Center.

When this eighty-million-dollar project is complete in 1970, it will provide expanded facilities for the Beekman-Downtown Hospital, an enlarged Pace College, new commercial construction, and housing for sixteen hundred middle-income families.

In the process, it will erase all traces of the past in one of the most historic sections of the city. From site selection to final design, every aspect of the renewal process in Brooklyn Bridge Southwest has been viewed with serious reservations by experts in the planning and redevelopment fields. Many consider it a casebook of urban-renewal errors.

Initiated in the late fifties under the Slum Clearance Committee, which was headed by Robert Moses and was the city's first renewal agency, the project was inherited by the present administration. A total bulldozer plan, as were all of New York's early renewal efforts, Brooklyn Bridge Southwest is materializing just at the time when the city has officially renounced the bulldozer approach.

At present the area is a half-razed ghost town below the bridge. This week the last of the solid granite columns and lintels of the classic brick buildings of 1830–49 are going down like tenpins on Ferry Street. They will be followed by the destruction of a curved-corner Greek Revival structure of a rare type described by Talbot Hamlin, the historian, in *The Greek Revival in America*. Also listed in the book is a companion structure in the area, the Lorillard Building of 1837, demolished earlier by the city.

Jacob Street, for which the curved façade formed an entrance, was part of the city's early street pattern, evocative of New York's ship and sailing days. Already closed off by wooden horses, its narrow outline blurred by rubble, Jacob Street will disappear into a modern superblock of skyscraper apartments.

This superblock, to be bounded by Gold, Fulton, Pearl, and Frankfort streets, will eliminate Ferry, Beekman, and Cliff streets as well as Jacob Street. The names and buildings were redolent of New York history, and the scale was the human one of the nineteenth century.

This new seven-block, thirty-four-million-dollar development, to be carried out by the Tishman Construction Company, will feature three sets of twin apartment towers twenty-five to thirty stories high, with a kindergarten-through-second-grade school in the ground floor of one tower, four six-story residential buildings, two block-size, eight-story commercial buildings, and shops.

Some of the new six-story buildings will stand almost where the five-story historic rows were demolished. There is no rehabilitation or preservation in this plan.

Between buildings, there will be two open plazas and landscaped terraces over covered parking. Public walkways will permit passage through. The architects are Kelly & Gruzen, a New York firm responsible for some of the city's more progressive middle-income housing.

Compared with an earlier scheme of massed tower blocks, the present design represents the addition of a number of amenities intended to ameliorate the vastness and impersonality of new construction on this scale. The changes have been brought about by constant review by the Housing and Redevelopment Board, with responsive revisions by the architects and sponsor.

At the Tishman superblock's upper, or western, boundary, Gold Street will be bridged by an overpass to the new $13.2-million Pace College superblock, bounded by Gold, Spruce, Nassau streets and the Brooklyn Bridge.

A continuous five-level structure will cover the entire two-block site, topped by an office and dormitory tower. The architects are Eggers & Higgins. This, like the Tishman scheme, is also a second, radically reworked version by the architects, which followed earlier studies by another firm.

Parallelling the Pace superblock will be the $4.25-million Beekman Hospital superblock, between Spruce and Beekman streets. William Street will be eliminated from both projects.

Here the bulldozers are having a harder time. On the Pace site, the Tribune Tower with its massive additions to the original Richard Morris Hunt building is in the process of demolition.

There will be difficulties also at the corner of Gold and Ferry streets, where the Tishman project begins, and where one of the city's sturdier examples of the protoskyscraper style, the 1890 Healy Building, stands. Its ten stories of tightly laid intricate, rounded corner brickwork with terra-cotta inlays, much admired by historians and connoisseurs of the building art, will not give way as easily as the earlier, handcrafted Greek Revival product.

Before the bulldozers moved in, Brooklyn Bridge Southwest was a shabby, but far from unsound, area of small businesses in low-rent, nineteenth-century commercial structures that ranged from the historically important and aesthetically satisfying vernacular Greek Revival style to pleasant and serviceable Victorian.

Some buildings were in poor condition; others were well preserved. Land uses were a mixture of business and residential. New York's artists' colony, priced out of fashionable Greenwich Village, was finding its lofts and atmosphere hospitable. It was never a hard-core slum.

City officials are rueful, but they believe that they have had no alternative to letting the wrecking ball swing.

The Housing and Redevelopment Board points to long-standing verbal commitments of land to the sponsors from the initiation of the project, all of whom have paid out substantial architectural development fees on the city's promises. The board's staff has invested substantial time and effort in the development of the proposals, since it took over from the Slum Clearance Committee in 1950. The lengthy relocation of tenants is complete. Off the record, the city admits to trying to make the best of a bad thing.

Critics of Brooklyn Bridge Southwest call it a compendium of just about everything that can go wrong in the renewal process. They consider it a negative object lesson for the large renewal programs now planned or in process in New York.

Differences of opinion begin with the selection of the site. The district was the typical "fringe" area that was favored by the city's early urban-renewal schemes . . . not really blighted enough to make the commercial developer shy away, but "gray" enough so that improvements could be quickly profitable. These sites were often arbitrarily chosen, according to the preferences of the real estate developers who offered to take on the job.

Second, critics site sponsor selection. Developers were awarded the sites of their choice on which they carried out their own plans, not the city's.

The Logue Report on Housing and Neighborhood Improvement in New York has summed up the procedure. It observes that this city's urban renewal in the fifties was handled by the Slum Clearance Committee as a real estate operation. There was no attack on the problems of the hard-core slums and the deteriorating stock of lower- and middle-income housing. Economic not social, criteria were employed.

In addition Brooklyn Bridge Southwest had two institutional tenants sorely pressed for space. Under urban renewal the land write-down made possible by federal grants made expansion very much more attractive than if expensive land were purchased at commercial rates.

Given three willing sponsors, verbal agreements were made that have been considered binding by later administrations and agencies, even though urban-renewal polices have since been drastically overhauled.

These commitments were formalized in 1960 and later when the Housing and Redevelopment Board succeeded the Slum Clearance Committee after a series of scandals broke about its operation. Questions were raised about methods of sponsor selection, delays in initiating projects, and the prevalence of new luxury housing on renewal sites.

Only in Board of Estimate action this year, however, is title to the land and streets being transferred to the sponsors, over serious protests by some of the city's renewal watchers, including the Architects Council of New York City.

Professional protest revolves around a larger issue: the lack of an overall plan. The project has no relation to any of the surrounding downtown developments directly on its borders.

It has been contended by Nathan Ginsberg, the architect-watchdog of the Civic Center, in stormy Board of Estimate hearings, that the commitments in Brooklyn Bridge Southwest have become a peculiar instrument of urban paralysis.

Critics agree on these points:

- Any flexible growth of the adjoining Civic Center, now under development, has been cut off completely by the renewal area's boundaries.
- Any logical choice of possible solutions to Brooklyn Bridge traffic problems have been choked off. Bridge approaches are hamstrung, traffic is forced back into the Civic Center, and Civic Center decisions are being made of permanent functional and design inadequacy.

Within the area of the project, experts fault the planning process further. In terms of urban design, the project never touched base with the history and character of the old city streets.

The streets themselves will disappear under skyscrapers and superblocks. There were no celebrated monuments to save, but there were scattered stands of homogeneous brick and stone street architecture of the early nineteenth century that knowledgeable observers prize for pleasant proportions, a disappearing vernacular Georgian style, and historic associations. This was punctuated by some notable Victoriana.

According to Jordan Gruzen of the architectural firm of Kelly & Gruzen, "We felt ambivalent about the nice old brick buildings."

"The thing had gone so far," he said. "We had worked through a dozen versions since 1957. It was just always understood that it was to be total site clearance."

No architectural historian was consulted by the Housing and Redevelopment Board during the planning process: the Landmarks Preservation Commission had not yet come into existence.

The best urban renewal today is defined by urban-renewal adminis-
trators such as Edward J. Logue of Boston and Edmund Bacon of
Philadelphia as the sensitive, efficient combination of new and old.

Preservation and rehabilitation retain the city's historic fabric and
neighborhood character. It also keeps older housing and commercial
spaces operative. New construction provides improvements and modern facilities. Together, the two create the elusive synthesis known as
urban character.

With the urgent problems of the hard-core slums and the limited
funds currently available for renewal in New York, many noncritical renewal area plans have been dropped. In city circles, Brooklyn Bridge
Southwest is looked on as a kind of inherited bureaucratic juggernaut. It
moves ahead with the ponderous relentlessness of the bulldozer itself.

New York Times, October 21, 1966

Where Did We Go Wrong?

THE FOLLOWING ITEM WAS NOT INVENTED by some gifted pixie
mentality; it is from *Preservation News*, published by the National Trust
for Historic Preservation. The National Trust would not put you on. We
quote:

> Babe Ruth's birthplace and a few neighboring properties were
> recently purchased by the city of Baltimore for $1,850. The
> home of one of baseball's immortals is located on Emory
> Street, a narrow alley of humble row houses. The Mayor's
> Committee for the Preservation of Babe Ruth's Birthplace is
> now debating whether to leave the house at its present location
> or to move it and the neighboring houses to a site adjoining
> Memorial Stadium, to be part of the Babe Ruth Plaza. Vandal-
> ism in the present neighborhood has prompted the committee

to resolve "to restore the house at its present location only if environmental amenities are found to be reasonable." The inaccessibility of Emory Street is also cited as a reason to move the house elsewhere. However, Emory Street is too narrow to move the house intact and dismantling would be the only solution.

It reads exactly as if Lewis Carroll wrote it.

"Leave the house where it is," said the Red Queen. "I can't," said Alice. "It's inaccessible and there's vandalism." "Then get some environmental amenities," said the Red Queen, "and be quick about it." "What are environmental amenities?" asked Alice. "Don't ask foolish questions; just move the house," said the Red Queen. "But the street is too narrow," said Alice. "Nonsense," said the Red Queen, "don't you know anything? Take the house apart and put it back together again. And move the rest of the houses with it." "Poor things," said Alice. "Where to?" "To the Memorial Stadium, naturally," said the Red Queen, "and call it Babe Ruth Plaza." "Couldn't we just leave it?" asked Alice. "If you do," said the queen, "you will have to take out the other houses and put up a sign, NO BALL PLAYING ALLOWED." "Mightn't BALLPLAYERS WELCOME be better?" said Alice.

Alas, it is not straight out of *Through the Looking Glass*; it is straight out of life. And if it sounds like parody, that is exactly what much of the preservation movement has become. It is game-playing. The game as it is played—by a strict set of rules—is to seal off historic buildings from the contemporary environment in a vacuum of assiduous make-believe.

The process ranges from babes in Babe Ruth–land to the phenomenon of Williamsburg, where the art of scholarly self-delusion reaches the extravagantly (seventy-nine-million-dollar) sublime. It deals in "cut-off dates," which means ruthlessly destroying anything later than a certain arbitrarily selected year that interferes with the illusion desired, and "restoring back," a horrendous process of faking the chosen period by removing all subsequent accumulations of time and history. The final perversion is "reconstruction," or rebuilding things that no longer exist, and that, if you take the blinders off for a moment, merely means putting up brand-new "old" buildings, which, no matter how carefully researched, are a contradiction in terms and values that shows how sick the whole thing has become.

"I say the moon is made of green cheese and this is the eighteenth century," the sponsors of these historical "enclaves" (a favorite euphemism) of the studiously unreal tell us. No matter how you slice it, it is still green cheese, and you can slice it many ways, from Strawberry Banke to Old Sacramento. The point is that the whole idea and purpose of preservation—saving the past because it is part of the living heritage of the present, so that the process of history enriches the city and the environment—has been lost.

The result is a cross between playacting in the name of history (and the lesson being taught is curiously subversive if one still equates education with traditional values of truth and, by extension, morality, or knowing what is true or false) and a museum of period arts. The inevitable conflict set up between the forms of the past and the uses of the present—a conflict denied overtly but carefully and often comically disguised to accommodate the tourist trade—is an abrasive anachronism. It all dead-ends in a head-on clash of new, old, and new-made-to-seem-old for which there is no solution except playing the game harder, increasing the make-believe and the confusions of real and reproduction, not for a living lie, but for something that is a dead lie, at best.

THE TRAGEDY IS that this concept has become so popular that it has almost totally aborted the proper approach to the conservation of our urban heritage. The purpose of preservation is not to "recreate" the past, a laughable impossibility filled with booby traps like the lady in saddle shoes, harlequin glasses, and hoop skirt who shattered this observer's first schoolgirl visit to Williamsburg. (No, changing the shoes and glasses wouldn't fix up anything at all; you really couldn't restore the lady back.)

More shattering, on a much later visit, was the lack of information from guides as to what was authentic and what was not, since obviously no distinction was made between copies and genuine survivals in their own minds. Even the survivals have been so smoothed up that the line gets fuzzy. To them, it was all real. Actually, nothing is real except those buildings that have lasted a couple of centuries, gathering a significant patina of changing American culture (stripped, naturally) and the collections of furnishings that are curatorial triumphs, deliciously arranged to simulate someone's personal possessions by a well-researched extension of wishful-think.

It is all art and artifice and the finest green cheese. It is a beautifully hollow stage-set shell, totally removed from the life force of the society that gave it form and meaning. A little fudging for effect hardly matters. (Please don't write, oh superpatriots, to tell me that I am simultaneously sullying both Williamsburg and the American flag; I have your letters from the last time. It is not treason to look art and history in the eye. I value both beyond the call of tourism.)

WHAT PRESERVATION IS really all about is the retention and active relationship of the buildings of the past to the community's functioning present. You don't erase history to get history; a city's character and quality are a product of continuity. You don't get any of it with "enclaves" in quarantine. What a cutoff date cuts off is any contact with the present at all. In urban terms preservation is the saving of the essence and style of other eras, through their architecture and urban forms, so that the meaning and flavor of those other times and tastes are incorporated into the mainstream of the city's life. The accumulation is called culture.

In New York, the sentiment for preservation is a relatively new thing. The city has never preserved anything. Its nature is to destroy, build, and change. New Yorkers are not antiquarians, and that is part of their pride and strength. To be successful in New York, preservation must strike a singular balance with this spirit; even the past must face the future.

A CASE IN point is the South Street Seaport project in Lower Manhattan, centered on the early nineteenth-century Schermerhorn Row on Fulton Street between South and Front streets. This is the first really promising preservation venture that the city has undertaken in environmental terms. Credit is due to all connected with it for vision, courage, and the desire to do the job right. But this very important undertaking is teetering on the brink of falling into the popular preservation bag.

As the thinking has gone, and it could, hopefully, change, a "representative" nineteenth-century date would be picked for the area. The date in New York is 1968, not 1851, and to pretend otherwise would be the first false step. The model shows the long-gone Fulton Street market reconstructed. Here we go, playing preservation parlor games, on the way to the standard picturesque baloney of gas lamps and horse-drawn cars. One little step leads to another. Next, Williamsburg-by-the-river, and we don't mean Williamsburg, Brooklyn.

It all hangs in the balance now. If it follows the established route of stage-set archaeology firmly closed to the twentieth century, it will go very, very wrong. With the best talent in the world, the most imaginative architects, the sophisticated sensibility to bridge old and new with creative, contemporary links to make a landmark for the future, why make false copies of the past? The challenge is to make the city's heritage a working part of the dynamic vitality and brutal beauty of this strange and wonderful town. And above all, to make it New York.

New York Times, July 14, 1968

A Conference on Cities

WHEN THE INVITATION CAME TO BE "CREDENTIALED" for Boston's "Great Cities of the World" conference—the grand windup event of the city's 350th birthday celebration—I knew that I could not go. I frankly did not want to be credentialed—by anyone for anything; beyond my dismay at the word, I was intimidated. I might not earn my badge. And if I did, the idea of being tagged and slotted was depressing. The affront was double—to one's professional personhood and to the language of Emerson and Lowell that was being replaced by communispeak.

Things got no better with the "media advisory" that arrived from City Hall. The press was promised a clambake and a boat ride, the chance to photograph visiting mayors from around the world against the Boston skyline, human interest features such as barbecues in Boston backyards, and ample opportunity to listen to and take pictures of Boston's mayor Kevin White. One preferred plum was the unique experience of seeing guests dine on the stage of Symphony Hall while Boston Symphony musicians serenaded them from a box, a feature advertised as a novelty, which the fourth estate, uninvited for dinner, was offered the first few minutes of the meal to record. All these were unabashed media events—a term that seems to have lost its original pejorative sense, in Boston at least, as a nonevent created purely for publicity purposes.

As for the working sessions of the conference, press attendance was not guaranteed because of restricted space; only the promotional hoopla was as big as all outdoors. Although the meeting was billed as "the first major urban affairs conference ever sponsored by an American city," it seemed surprisingly short on urban affairs and long on political hurrah. Whatever was missing in serious content was apparently to be made up for by the latest in "computer conferencing"—also known as "teleconferencing"—which eventually will substitute communication by computer terminal for old-fashioned speeches and panel discussions. The medium is the message, and it does not truck with the niceties of nouns and verbs.

Boston was referred to in the releases as a "world-class" city (put that one on the verbal hit list with credentialing and conferencing), but official tours of the world-class city were minimal. There was a boat trip around the harbor, which offers a spectacular example of impressive waterfront renewal. Boston's mix of the marvelous old and the striking new, the richness of its restored and recycled landmarks of solid eighteenth- and nineteenth-century brick and granite and the dramatic twentieth-century development of the adjacent Government Center and business community, sets a high level of civilized continuity. It is unlikely, however, that anyone pointed out how close this exemplary and delicate balance is to destruction by success and a formularized gloss.

A walk was planned for the rather unexceptional downtown retail district and its predictable pedestrian paraphernalia. The clambake took place in the historic Charlestown Navy Yard, which is the site of a redevelopment program. But in a city so blessed with architectural and urban history and sophisticated students of its style, the accent was overwhelmingly Chamber-of-Commerce. Maybe that is what world-class means.

Instead of seeing Boston as an urban and cultural whole, mayors and planning officials from abroad were taken to visit appropriate ethnic neighborhoods—wind up a politician, and he runs to ethnic neighborhoods. However, neighborhoods, as such, were not on the agenda. "They don't have them in other parts of the world," a spokesperson explained.

What may have saved the week, and the conference, were the programs contributed by the educational institutions across the river in Cambridge: the Massachusetts Institute of Technology, Harvard's Kennedy School of Government, and a joint conference held by the Institute of Urban Design and the Graduate School of Design at Harvard. Where City Hall's idea of serious sessions consisted of those weary, cosmic subjects that no one can come to grips with and that can always be relied on to produce platitudinous generalities, like "The City in the Year 2000," the Harvard program took up the hard issues—the role of public investment in development and change, for example, and specific guidelines for relating the historic city to new needs.

That everything is not necessarily peachy in Boston was acknowledged in Mayor White's opening address, which referred to "the challenge of pavement and pollution, of ambition and angst" and confirmed the presence of "suffering humanity." It was a stunning rhetorical performance that touched all bases. But the opportunity was lost for a genuine international forum in which the problems and programs of cities could have been usefully addressed. Boston was the ideal setting for such a dialogue; the city's physical rebirth is remarkable in both economic and aesthetic terms. Its successes and failures provide valuable lessons, from the bulldozer destruction of the West End, which taught cities what not to do with their neighborhoods, to the overwhelmingly popular Faneuil Hall Marketplace, which taught cities what to do with their landmarks.

But how a revitalized downtown can be plugged into the larger social and economic welfare is something no one has begun to solve, in Boston or anywhere else. Many of the visiting dignitaries offered little more than glamorous travelogues and upbeat statistics. Everyone was shortchanged by this exercise in mutual boosterism.

For those who did not attend, the *Boston Globe* carried generous reports of the week's activities. To its credit, the paper passed up most of the "media opportunities," although it did go in rather heavily for visiting celebrity interviews with canned background material.

There was one lively exchange between Jane Jacobs, author of *The Death and Life of Great American Cities* and champion of neighborhoods and incremental growth, and James Rouse, the developer responsible for the Faneuil Hall Marketplace and its burgeoning offspring in other cities.

Arguing the virtues of big plans versus little plans, Mr. Rouse recalled Daniel Burnham's famous exhortation to make no little plans
that fail to stir men's minds, and came out for big plans as the "new,
compelling, rational images of what a city could be." Mrs. Jacobs didn't
find the image particularly compelling. She thought that piecemeal
should be made a respectable word again. "Life is an ad hoc affair," she
said, "and has to be improvised all the time."

The only point on which all apparently agreed was that plans should
be "humanized." Mrs. Jacobs's observation that "cities would never be
humanized by conceiving urban models at Harvard" got her the conference's standing ovation.

The warnings of Ian Menzies, the *Globe*'s urban affairs columnist,
against "cosmetic recitations" went unheeded, along with his urgently
expressed hope that Boston would be a pacesetter in the discussion of
"gut issues" of violence, racism, and the quality of urban life. Great
cities, he wrote, "are the conscience of mankind." It takes more than
hype from City Hall to make great cities great.

New York Times, October 12, 1980

The Great American Flag Scheme

THE GREAT AMERICAN DREAM MACHINE is about to produce the
Great American Flag, and if you haven't heard about it, you will.
The Great American Flag will measure 210 feet 12 inches by 411 feet,
which translates into an Old Glory roughly one Park Avenue block
high and two blocks long, or about two and a half acres in size. It is
currently being woven, dyed, assembled, or however you fabricate a
two-and-a-half-acre flag, in Evansville, Indiana. It is a far cry from
Betsy Ross's little handmade number.

The Great American Flag is supposed to be installed on the
Verrazano-Narrows Bridge, near the Brooklyn end of the span, where it

will be "unfurled" on all flag holidays and national occasions. But one just does not "hang" a two-and-a-half-acre flag, any more than one "unfurls" it. This flag requires thirty tons of support steel and nine synchronized motors. The Great American Flag is clearly a lot of flag; its sponsors refer to it as a "symbolic monument" and a "catalyst for America." It is also an environmental event; an architecturally scaled addition to a major example of construction art. The target date for its installation and display is July 4 of this year.

The cost of this Great American Boondoggle is estimated at $850,000, and its life expectancy is ten years. Of this amount, $250,000 is being raised privately, and $600,000 is to come from the public, or you and me.

The concept, as if you couldn't guess, is something run up by the advertising and public relations business, which sees this as a really Big Idea. It's got absolutely everything: plenty of patriotic hoopla with quotations from Carl Sandburg and Abraham Lincoln for starters; glorious, motherhood-type publicity for big corporate names supplying material, money, or expertise, and terrific promotional gimmicks like Star Sponsors, "one for each of the Stars of the Flag" (their capital letters) who pledge gifts of ten thousand dollars or loans of twenty-five thousand dollars as an advance on construction to be repaid when the public money comes in. The sponsors include the advertising and public relations firms of Interpublic; Doyle, Dane, Bernbach; and Hill and Knowlton. Corporate support is coming from Pfizer, Milliken, and *Time* magazine, among others. Materials and services are being donated by such firms as Allied Chemical, Celanese, and DuPont. The publicity releases will be studded with their names.

With that star-spangled—you should pardon the expression—roster, one would wonder why the nickels and dimes of the public would be sought at all. We are informed that the flag (oops, Flag) is to be "a gift from the people to the people," to provide "a source of continued inspiration to us all."

For so monumental a project, for something so enormously big and so inescapably visible, for an object that will become an important part of the city scene and of a public structure, there has been a surprising absence of public information. It seems incredible that this undertaking should have proceeded to the actual manufacture of the flag, with completion expected next month, while its involved and costly engineering is being actively pursued, totally without description or debate. It is even more curious that the city has played no role whatever in this public endeavor. There is a point where location, size, and conspicuous display become questions within the public domain. Waving the flag won't make those questions go away.

The waving is about to begin in earnest with a fund-raising media blitz, even as construction proceeds. Everyone will soon be hearing a great deal about the Great American Flag, in television commercials and through other promotional channels. The public drive, we are told, will consist of "a mass media campaign, fund-raising projects from supporting non-profit organizations, and special promotions by supporting businesses." Wrapping themselves in the flag, of course, won't do anyone any harm. And if there should be some legitimate doubts about the suitability or necessity of this bit of patriotic oversell, no one is prepared to be the only rotten kid on the block who doesn't love his country. Those who refuse to contribute to this campaign, for any reason, run the risk of being branded as churlish pinkos.

I am willing to be the first rotten kid by saying that I have run the idea up the flagpole, and it doesn't fly. There are a number of things seriously wrong with it. There is, for one, the inexplicable absence of municipal or other official responsibility for such a major installation. And for another, there is evidence that badly needed corporate funds will be diverted by this project from business support of the city's cultural affairs.

IN VIEW OF the fact that the present city budget, among other painful cuts, has had to drastically reduce funding for the Department of Cultural Affairs, this can only be a threatening development. Grants from the National Endowment in Washington and the State Arts Council have also been declining. The only good news is that corporate contributions have been taking up the slack. This fact—the one ray of sunshine in a bleak forecast for the arts—has been identified as the critical factor for the future by the report on New York's cultural affairs just issued by the private, not-for-profit Cultural Assistance Center.

To have any of that corporate support siphoned off in this fashion endangers activities that are far more vital to New York than this silly scheme. Some businesses have begun to respond to requests for the kind of aid they normally give to urban and cultural causes—help that is more urgently needed than ever—by saying sorry, we've contributed to the Great American Flag. Surely the opportunities afforded by a dance group in Harlem, or the community efforts of a block association in the Bronx, speak more appropriately of the real American spirit. The availability to all of New York's great collections of literature, history, and art is a far better demonstration of the democratic ideal. Creative activities enrich and revitalize a city; they raise both its spirit and its economic base. The arts are New York's best growth industry, but you can't salute them.

The unanswered question is who has allowed this simpleminded, vainglorious proposal to go ahead? Has it been done through default or tacit consent? The Triborough Bridge and Tunnel Authority, which constructed and operates the Verrazano-Narrows Bridge, has approved. But the bridge was built with a public bond issue; it is not TBTA's personal property. Is this action really in the city's larger interests?

Where is the City Art Commission? Only recently, it had to make the public announcement that it was responsible for the aesthetic review of New York's bridges. That fact was being ignored while every politician and his brother were busy picking colors for them. Where are the city's cultural watchdogs, the Municipal Art Society and the various architectural associations?

Finally, there is the matter of the project's unassailable inspirational and patriotic intent—the factor that has made it so hard for anyone to say no to its sponsors. This is the saddest and funniest aspect of the whole affair. Within clear sight of the Verrazano-Narrows Bridge stands the greatest monument to freedom in our history, the symbol of this nation as an open and compassionate society with the highest democratic ideals—an image that dominates New York Harbor and the American dream. Does anyone really want to spend $850,000 to upstage the Statue of Liberty?

New York Times, February 10, 1980

The Way It Never Was

I DO NOT KNOW JUST WHEN WE lost our sense of reality or interest in it, but at some point it was decided that reality was not the only option; that it was possible, permissible, and even desirable to improve on it; that one could substitute a more agreeable product. It followed that reality was, first, mutable and then expendable; its substance was abdicated for what could be revised and manipulated. Downgrading the evidence of the built world—its cities and its structures—has profoundly affected architecture and urbanism. One would think that these hard physical facts would present a reality so absolute, so irrefutable, that it would be difficult to distort, deny, or trivialize it. These places that are the containers of life and experience—the mother lode of societies and cultures—have always provided an amazing account of the human condition in all of its uncommon, unpredictable, and unexpected diversity. The built record, which holds most of the lessons of art and history, is there for anyone to see; but, increasingly, we have not wanted to see it. Or we have preferred to pretty it up, to reconfigure it for other purposes. Denial has spread like a virus, invading, infecting, and changing architectural and urban standards in the most basic sense.

The replacement of reality with selective fantasy is a phenomenon of that most successful and staggeringly profitable American phenomenon, the reinvention of the environment as themed entertainment. The definition of place as a chosen image probably started in a serious way in the late twenties at Colonial Williamsburg, predating and paving the way for the new world order of Walt Disney Enterprises. Certainly it was in the restoration of Colonial Williamsburg that the studious fudging of facts received its scholarly imprimatur, and that history and place as themed artifact hit the big time. Williamsburg is seen by the cognoscenti as a kind of period piece now, its shortsightedness a product of the limitations of the early preservation movement. Within a conscientious range of those deliberately and artfully set limitations, a careful construct was created: a place where one could learn a little romanticized history, confuse the real and unreal, and have— then and now—a very nice time. Knowledge, techniques, and standards have become increasingly sophisticated in the intervening years, and there have been escalating efforts to keep up. But it is the Williamsburg image and example as originally conceived that has spread and multiplied, that continues to be universally admired and emulated.

HISTORY IS QUICKSILVER that runs at the touch; it refers to events that derived their life, breath, color, and meaning from some elusive shaping moment in the irretrievable past. It is both charged and changed by the prism of passing time. The essential, defining clues of a particular moment may not even survive. By its very definition, history is something that is gone forever. Do the passage of time and the irreversible effects of that inexorable process, seen through our shifting, conditioned responses, make preservation an erudite, often misleading game, with artificially embalmed remains and suspiciously elegant artifacts? Does it not follow that inventions and simulacra, of things that existed and things that did not, will be given equal value and credibility? Is it tempting to value them more than the shabby, incomplete survivals? Must one always exorcise the ghosts for costumed extras?

What the perfect fake or impeccable restoration lacks are the hallmarks of time and place. They deny imperfections, alterations, and accomodations; they wipe out all the incidents of life and change. The worn stone, the chafed corner, the threshold low and uneven from many feet, the marks on walls and windows that carry the presence and message of remembered hands and eyes—all of those accumulated, accidental, suggestive, and genuine imprints that imbue the artifact with its history and continuity, that have stayed with it in its conditioning passage through time—are absent or erased. There is nothing left of the journey from there to here, nothing that palpably joins the past to the present, that makes direct physical and emotional contact with the viewer, the bittersweet link with those who have been there before. What are gone are the cumulative clues, the patina of age and use, the sense of "others"—that essential, irreplaceable quality that Stephen Greenblatt has so insightfully called "resonance." It is this resonance that gives an object "the power . . . to reach out beyond its formal boundaries to a larger world, to invoke in the viewer the complex, dynamic cultural forces from which it has emerged." Significantly, it is precisely this central, intrinsic quality that has been eliminated from the reproduction, that no longer exists in the restoration. These objects and places simply do not resonate. They are mute. They are hollow history.

I AM NOT ARGUING FOR an end to preservation; I have fought too long and too hard for heritage consciousness and preservation legislation, for stylistic survival, for the recognition of the beauty and necessity of older and undervalued buildings. The cherishing of the aesthetic and urban achievements of the past is critical to the quality of our environment and our lives. To lose history is to lose place, identity, and meaning. But continuity can be achieved only if the past is integrated into the contemporary context in a way that works and matters. Our awareness and appreciation of historic buildings and neighborhoods must be coupled with a sensitivity to and desire for their continued relevance and use, for their "connectedness," for the way they bridge the years and the continuum of social, cultural, urban, and architectural history. It is their recycling and adaptation that will keep them as a living part of today's cities and communities. Their uses may be unconventional; they may even become marginal; they may offer a casual palimpsest rather than textbook history; they will certainly be impure rather than pure—if there is really anything admirable about that kind of pedantic reduction to irrelevance.

I am devoted to the principle that every age produces its greatest buildings in its own image. I believe that the art and act of contemporary design must be rooted in, and cannot avoid, the conditions and references of its own time. Ultimately, it is the addition and absorption of this continuous record of changing art, technology, ideas, and uses that make cities unique repositories of the whole range of human endeavor. Within this understanding and context, there is a preservation principle that can, and should, apply. There are viable criteria: the manner in which the historical setting accommodates change, the degree to which style and identity support authentic functions, and the frequency with which destruction is avoided by legitimate continuity through an appropriate role in contemporary life and use. All this determines whether, and how, and in what manner we keep our heritage—and the meaning and worth and success of the effort. The past lives only as part of the present. The results will never be perfect, but they will be real.

Real architecture has little place in the unreal America. A public increasingly addicted to fakes and fantasies is unprepared and unwilling to understand the unfamiliar and, often, admittedly difficult new work, although its complexities answer to the contemporary condition. Instead of a public architecture, or an architecture integrated into life and use, we have "trophy" buildings by "signature" architects, like designer clothes. Our cities, shattered by change, victimized by economics, are still the rich containers of our collective culture, the record of our continuity, the repository of the best we have produced. But themed parodies pass for places now, serving as the new planning and design models even as real places with their full freight of art and memories are devalued and destroyed.

IT HAS BEEN A SHORT DISTANCE down the yellow brick road from Williamsburg to Disneyland. Both are quintessentially American inventions. Both deal in a doctored reality. What they have in common is their suspension of disbelief, the expertise of their illusion, and their promotion of a skillfully edited, engineered, and marketed version of a chosen place, or theme.

The possibilities are limitless. Each subject is designed as an appealing visual narrative, presented, as its creators would say, as a "themed" package. The result, which covers a wide range of variations, is the theme park, a singular product of our time and a distinctly American contribution to world culture and human experience. The theme can be geographical or historical, fiction or fantasy; it can invent worlds of the past, present, or future.

The "theming" of America is not limited to such tourist enterprises; it includes restaurants, shopping centers, hotels, and housing developments, whether it is just a "look" or a complete concept carried out to the last "authentic" touch.

It follows naturally that the great American pastime of shopping figures prominently in all of these enterprises. From credentialed restorations carried out by trained professionals to the most blatant pit stop on marginal historic tours, from the Colonial craft-and-candle shop and the general store in the rebuilt western ghost town to the roadside rest and souvenir stand, behind the reconstructed or imaginary façades, there are always goods for sale. In still another related and uniquely American invention, buildings of genuine antiquity are used to create a "festival marketplace," as in Boston's historic Faneuil Hall Market, or "themed" new construction serves the same purpose, as on Baltimore's waterfront. All are designed according to a preset commercial formula based on the essential number of continuous shopping feet considered necessary for merchandising success. The standards for the shops are set and maintained by restrictive clauses in leases. When the historical setting is fragile or discontinuous, as at New York's South Street Seaport, most of the eccentric and believable fabric of the past is lost—distorted by and subordinated to the commercial calculation.

The themed shopping environment that uses style as a distinguishing marketing factor is the ultimate extension of the shopping mall as purveyor of entertainment and social activity; it is the heart of modern consumer culture. Potemkin villages offer postmodernist façades with false dormers, towers, arches, and trim in shades of mauve, pumpkin, and pistachio, while the chains and franchises behind them are predictably the same. They are not meant to convince; these are stage sets supplying a background architectural theme. Tucked artfully behind Los Angeles's glittering Rodeo Drive is a new, cunningly curved street, a pseudo-Continental mix of small period-revival buildings devoted to luxury shops. History is a marketing ploy; shopping is the end of the preservation rainbow. More serious is the carryover of the same pretense to other buildings and places where what remains of an indigenous urban life is being replaced by these "lessons" in merchandising and make-believe.

The Unreal America: Architecture and Illusion, The New Press, 1997, and *New York Review of Books*, December 3, 1992

The Hudson Yards: Plenty of Glitz, Little Vision

IF ANYTHING EVER PROVED THE OLD SAW about committees and camels, it is the schemes for the extremely large and extremely lucrative redevelopment of New York's Hudson Yards, the twenty-eight acres on Manhattan's far West Side currently up for sale by the Metropolitan Transportation Authority to the bidder with the most financial allure and the best camel—oops, plan.

Anyone who has watched this ritual real estate dance in New York before knows what to expect: After the display and the discussion and a tortuous path of catch-22 obstacles and Machiavellian deal-making, we will get a lot of very, very big buildings that will make someone very, very rich. There will be a great many of these very large buildings because the site is enormous. The twenty-eight acres that span the rail yards from Thirtieth to Thirty-third streets and Tenth Avenue to the Hudson River, dwarfing Ground Zero's sixteen acres, have already been rezoned in part for the biggest buildings possible.

The only other thing we can count on is that whatever is eventually built there will bear very little resemblance to what we are being shown now. For which we should be tremendously thankful. Because it is hard to believe that teams with this much financial heft and assembled star power could come up with something so awesomely bad. Only two of them appear to have thought about it beyond the standard investment model blown up to gargantuan scale.

The scenario is right on schedule. The decision by the public agency, the cash-strapped MTA, to sell the land to private developers was followed by a request for proposals that included guidelines for commercial and residential construction, landscaped open space, and a cultural building and school. (Historically, the amenities have a way of fading away or being relegated to reduced, fringe status later on; see, for example, the case of the disappearing cultural buildings at Ground Zero.)

Once the bids and presentations are in and the show is over, the real negotiating will get under way. So why the charade—the expensively executed and seductively lit models, the earnest presentations by the architects, the request for public reactions? Why do we discuss the proposals at all?

Hope springs eternal, of course, because the chance to create something of lasting value on this incredible site begs to be honored; other world cities are making it clear in projects of similar magnitude that more than money matters as they embrace standards of architecture and planning that leave New York in the dust. We continue to find the spectacle of developers' promotional and political savvy riveting, knowing that success will depend on the deal and not the design.

Only two of the five proposals being considered are worth talking about. Extell Development's submission, by the architect Steven Holl, could have the unity, character, and potential beauty of a Rockefeller

Center, and it is unique in this respect. The scheme flies in the face of the current cant about pluralism and diversity and proves once again that architecture is about vision and ideas. While the other proposals include a massive truss over the yards that is meant to support the new construction, Mr. Holl substitutes a suspension deck. (The trains will continue to run underneath.) This bridgelike deck carries the lesser weight (and expense) of a park, while the structures surrounding it, handsomely grouped for views of the Empire State Building and the Hudson River, can be built on solid ground. You have to admire Extell's courage in going with a single gifted architect and putting all its chips on design.

The plan offered by Brookfield Properties is the work of Skidmore, Owings & Merrill and the landscape firm Field Operations. (Brookfield-owned property in Lower Manhattan includes the *Wall Street Journal* offices at 200 Liberty Street.) The fine environmental hand of Field Operations is easy to discern. The planning process starts with the nature of the site, addressing the huge variations in elevation from street to platform to waterfront, changes in grade that create a formidable barrier to the city around it. This is not easy to read in the models or in the other proposals with their emphasis on hype and heavyweight names.

Continuing the local streets through the site establishes the connective tissue. Instead of treating landscape as leftover space between buildings, Field Operations makes it the unifying factor, softening transitions and tying everything together. Recognizing Chelsea to the south, the plan connects the Thirtieth Street frontage to existing neighborhood fabric and scale, with the High Line, the elevated park-in-progress on the abandoned train bed that skirts the area, incorporated as part of the action. This section of the High Line was considered expendable by a number of the developers until public opinion made them think otherwise; it appears in all of the schemes, usually as a kind of peripheral trim. Or worse, a device for enhancing commercial properties by allowing direct exits onto the elevated park, a terrible idea. Skidmore, Owings & Merrill's most conspicuous contribution is a pair of skyscrapers that look, in profile, alarmingly like sex toys. A reasonable selection of innovative architects completes the proposal.

Both the Extell and Brookfield schemes suffer from the lack of a major tenant. Tishman Speyer has the promise of Morgan Stanley, the Durst Vornado team has brought along Condé Nast, apparently already out of room in its relatively new Times Square headquarters, and the Related Companies comes with News Corporation, which recently added the *Wall Street Journal* to its publications with the purchase of Dow Jones. The fact that such deals frequently fall apart in the changing economic climate of the intervening years of construction doesn't seem to diminish their value.

The Related Companies, with a drop-dead list of consultants, contributors, collaborators, and anyone else who could be thrown into the mix (design teams can be camels, too), has covered all possible bases with something dreadful for everybody. This is not planning; it's pandering. They are either cynical or clueless; how else to explain the grossly opportunistic architectural zoo of Arquitectonica's jazzy modern and Robert A. M. Stern's ersatz traditional and the high-powered skyscraper-style of the lead firm, Kohn Pedersen Fox? Related is rumored to be the front-runner because of a shrewd combination of financial backing, political connections, and establishment names. It is quite clear that they know what they are doing and why they are doing it—and it is perfectly awful.

I seem to have blocked out the Durst Vornado team; possibly there were too many abstract planning clichés fished out of the past to absorb. I am resisting the inexplicable revival of the discredited elevated walkways of the sixties that were a notorious failure in places like London's Barbican and South Bank, presented under the trendy archispeak of "biomimetic concepts," "microclimates," and "layering." Even worse, they slither across parkland, where they do not belong, and will stand vacant and unused because it is already a matter of record that people avoid them. The rest is standard city-of-the-future.

Finally, there is the elephantine dead-on-arrival proposal by Helmut Jahn and Peter Walker for Tishman Speyer. What in the world were they thinking? This oppressive arrangement of immense matched towers (I will not mention the diagonal stripes) relates to nothing; it is a throwback to the most insensitive urban-renewal projects of the past century. The landscaped platform and its concentric steps evokes all those abandoned outdoor amphitheaters that looked so great in bird's-eye views but never worked. You have the feeling that if you gave the whole thing a good push it would slide right down to the bottom of the Hudson River.

The most disturbing aspect of this high-stakes game is the default of the city and the public agencies involved: their failure to create—or is it simply disinterest?—a coordinated plan for a West Side bursting with development from Penn Station and Madison Square Garden to the Javits Center, allowing these cobbled-up investment schemes to substitute for any appropriate, larger solutions.

The city thinks like a developer; that vision thing, the long-term overview, the balance of private investment and public utility and amenity, is just not there. The disposition of public land is expedited on the developers' terms even though the land is the most powerful negotiating tool of all—something so valuable in New York that builders would kill for it—and the Hudson Yards are an estimated seven-billion-dollar prize. It is accepted that whatever the plans are for these vast tracts of squandered opportunity, they will ultimately be controlled, compromised, or scuttled by the winner of the financial contest that is at the heart of the matter. New York will continue to sell itself short all the way to the bank.

Wall Street Journal, January 2, 2008

PART VII

Taste and Style

The Melancholy Fate of Danish Modern

WHATEVER HAPPENED TO DANISH MODERN? Where has all the furniture gone that was such a tidal wave of good taste and good design in the fifties? Danish dominated every prestigious design exhibition and profitable furniture promotion; it was in all the best model rooms, as an important part of the Scandinavian design supremacy of the years just after the Second World War. Danish products were the cachet of the homes of the artistic and intellectual elite, the darlings of museums and markets everywhere. Handsome and utilitarian, they stressed simplicity, logic, and truth to life, structure, and materials. Danish Modern was the war-delayed promise of a better and more beautiful world.

What happened, of course, is what happens to all home furnishings and consumer products—they went out of style. Or more accurately, they were supplanted by other styles, because the best Danish Modern is beyond style in its unassertive timelessness. After being widely acclaimed and acquired, it was copied and cheapened and then replaced by those whose business is marketable novelty and change.

Something with a familiar resemblance is still around in endlessly bowdlerized versions that seem to have been spawned spontaneously in dentists' waiting rooms, in the rear sections of suburban furniture stores, and in standardized motels. The best descendants have filtered down to mass-produced furnishings for the middle class, sold through design-conscious retail outlets that stress natural woods and the healthful life. The original, superbly crafted Hans Wegner and Finn Juhl pieces are certain to last a lifetime, wherever they are.

BUT THE DOUBLE kick of rejection was finally given by the counter-culture, which would have none of the earnest establishment image of Scandinavian design, and the new culture, for which only the shocking is chic. That plunged Danish Modern into the indisputable category of the passé.

Not surprisingly, the Danes are less than happy about this turn of taste, particularly those who deal in the design, marketing, or national image business. Their concern has led to a special event this summer, held under official government auspices, called the Danish Design Cavalcade, a series of seminars, trips, and informational briefings intended to make it clear that design is alive and well in Denmark today and Danish designers are still producing beautiful and useful things.

Part of the problem is undoubtedly the fact that there is a lot more design competition in the home furnishings field in the eighties than there was in the fifties. At that time, Scandinavia and Italy were the source of the most interesting new ideas. But those standards are being met almost everywhere now. And with the general rise in design sophistication, there is also a tendency to wear out styles quickly.

Some of those who experienced the fifties firsthand are convinced that the Danish design dominance of that time owed as much to the spirit of one man as to the excellence of the product. Just Lunning, who headed George Jensen in New York with a fine-tuned combination of taste and daring, made the famous Fifth Avenue corner store synonymous with the new and the beautiful. (Even the building is hard to find now; after the famous silver Jensen plaque was removed, the structure was stripped of its limestone facing for an anonymous, all-purpose "modernization.")

THE BEST APPEARED first at Jensen's, to become the wedding gifts of choice and most coveted possessions of several generations of purchasers. The Jensen silver box rivaled Tiffany's blue box in status and surpassed it in the design distinction of its contents. Just Lunning was the not-very-grisée éminence, the patron and promoter who commissioned and supported the finest Danish work. When he died in 1965, Danish design lost its most quietly charming and persuasive and consummately knowledgeable spokesman.

But the story of Danish Modern begins long before the fifties, when it reached its high point of international recognition and astute promotion. Danish design was part of the modern movement, although its development was less of a revolution in style and structure than a slow, careful evolution devoted to matching traditional furniture-making skills to the needs and tastes of modern life. The Danish avant-garde started as part of the European functionalist movement of the twenties.

Released from historic references, Danish designers sought simple forms directly expressive of purpose. They aimed at a "natural" vocabulary of form that would retain the "intrinsic" value of materials—notably wood. Ethical considerations became as important as aesthetic standards; this furniture was supposed to bring a useful beauty and higher standard of living to a modern democratic society. Unlike the products of the Bauhaus, which were far more radically oriented toward a machine aesthetic, Danish furniture never renounced its handcraft tradition. In fact, craft remained the anchor that provided suitable standards of design when other considerations were rejected. Art was always synonymous with craft and skill.

In 1924, the architect Kaare Klint was appointed to head a new class in furniture design at the Royal Academy of Fine Arts in Copenhagen. His systematic reduction of furniture structure to its most basic and elementary parts, achieved through a thoughtful analysis of use, influenced an entire generation of Danish architects and designers through the thirties. The simple pieces he produced, which seemed so revolutionary fifty years ago, are the direct antecedents of everything that followed.

In 1930, a series of annual competitions for new furniture designs was begun by the Danish Cabinetmakers Guild. This encouraged the development of experimental prototypes that were to be put into more general production later, in the forties. The collaboration of architect and cabinetmaker, of design and craft, remained characteristic of the Danish product, and because relatively small quantities were made, the line between handcraft and industry was never very sharply drawn. The transition from hand production to assembly line production took place after World War II, as the market for Danish design grew.

The furniture of the architect Finn Juhl that was so highly prized in the fifties—and is still so handsome now—was actually developed a decade earlier. By 1945, working with the cabinetmaker Niels Vodder, Juhl had established the suavely sculptured wooden frames, with elegantly shaped leather on upholstered seats and backs treated as separately articulated parts, that are so characteristic of his work.

This style became more elegantly extreme in the fifties. One piece by Hans Wegner, which was known internationally simply as "the chair," was a stripped-down version of traditional forms brought gracefully up to date; it was first produced in 1949 for the cabinetmaker

Johannes Hansen. The tactile elegance of these pieces is still unsurpassed.

It was not until the fifties that a machine aesthetic based on industrial materials flowered in Denmark, most notably in the work of the architect Arne Jacobsen. Characteristically, however, he stayed with curved and flowing shapes. The first models of his steel and plywood chairs were made in 1952, and the famous "egg" and "swan" chairs of 1957, with upholstered shells of synthetic materials, represented a breakthrough in factory techniques.

Poul Kjaerholm's steel and woven reed chairs were no less appealing for their straight lines; they bridged the gap between the warmth of craft and the cool elegance of the machine—in a typically Danish product.

The sixties saw more laminated woods, plastic, and technologically advanced assembly techniques. But the furniture always had the look of something meant to please the eye and hand. Only one notable exception—a chair of runny blobs of sprayed urethane foam that was not the work of an architect but of a painter, Gunnar Aagaard Andersen—managed to be fashionably revolting and to join the Juhl, Wegner, Jacobsen, and Kjaerholm examples in the design collection of the Museum of Modern Art.

The resistance to transient aesthetic kicks, to departing from all traditional norms, was probably the real reason for the decline of Danish Modern among the style setters; those carefully crafted or machined classics just don't say "now." Or even a definite enough "then." The furniture that says now is inflatable or industrial, made of cardboard or carpeting. It is admired to the degree that it shocks or outrages, is trendy, trivial, or nostalgic. Novelty and camp are the preferred values.

Since Danish Modern is none of the above, it is currently nowhere. Its elegantly understated aesthetic is based on inadmissable elitist values. It is totally old hat—or old chair.

Today, who wants timeless form or craft in the manner of Chippendale or Hepplewhite? Good taste is for suburban squares. Since this kind of design is neither eccentric nor ephemeral enough to be revived, neither fun nor fashion, the Danish second coming has not yet come. But give it time. Like the Victoriana in the attic, it will all be rediscovered again.

New York Times, August 21, 1980

Conquering Clutter

THERE ARE TWO KINDS OF PEOPLE in the world: those who have a horror of a vacuum and those with a horror of the things that fill it. Translated into domestic interiors, this means people who live with, and without, clutter. (Dictionary definition: jumble, confusion, disorder.) The reasons for clutter, the need to be surrounded by things, go deep, from security to status. The reasons for banning objects, or living in as selective and austere an environment as possible, range from the aesthetic to the neurotic. This is a phenomenon of choice that relates as much to the psychiatrist as to the taste maker.

Some people clutter compulsively, and others just as compulsively throw things away. Clutter in its highest and most organized form is called collecting. Collecting can be done as the Collyer brothers did it, or it can be done with art and flair. The range is from old newspapers to Fabergé.

This provides a third category, or what might be called calculated clutter, in which the objets d'art, the memorabilia that mark one's milestones and travels, the irresistible and ornamental things that speak to pride, pleasure, and temptation, are constrained by decorating devices and hierarchal principles of value. This gives the illusion that one is in control.

Most of us are not in control. My own life is an unending battle against clutter. By that I do not mean to suggest that I am dedicated to any clean-sweep asceticism or arrangements of high art; I am only struggling to keep from drowning in the detritus of everyday existence, or at least to keep it separate from the possessions that are meant to be part of what I choose to believe is a functional-aesthetic scheme.

Really living without clutter takes an iron will, plus a certain stoicism about the little comforts of life. I have neither. But my eye requires a modest amount of beauty and serenity that clutter destroys. This involves eternal watchfulness and that oldest and most relentless of the housewife's occupations, picking up. I have a feeling that picking up will go on long after ways have been found to circumvent death and taxes.

I once saw a home in which nothing had ever been picked up. Daily vigilance had been abandoned a long time ago. Although disorder descends on the unwary with the speed of light, this chaos must have taken years to achieve; it was almost a new decorating art form. The result was not, as one might suppose, the idiosyncratic disorder of a George Price drawing, where things are hung from pipes and hooks in a permanent chaos of awesome convenience. This was an expensive, thoughtful, architect-designed house where everything had simply been left where it landed. Pots and pans, linens and clothing, toys and utensils were tangled and piled everywhere, as well as all of those miscellaneous items that go in, and usually out, of most homes. No bare spot remained on furniture or floor. And no one who lived there found it at all strange, or seemed to require any other kind of domestic landscape. They had no *hang-ups*, in any sense of the word.

I know another house that is just as full of things, but the difference is instructive. This is a rambling old house lived in for many years by a distinguished scholar and his wife, whose love of the life of the mind and its better products has been equaled only by their love of life. In this very personal and knowledgeable eclecticism, every shared intellectual and cultural experience led to the accumulation of discoveries, mementos, and *objets de vertu*, kept casually at hand or in unstudied places. Tabletops and floors are thickets of books and overflow treasures. There is enormous, overwhelming, profligate clutter. And everything has meaning, memory, and style.

At the opposite extreme is the stripped, instant, homogeneous style, created whole and new. These houses and apartments, always well published, either start with nothing, which is rare, or clear everything out that the owners have acquired, which must take courage, desperation, or both. This means jettisoning the personal baggage, and clutter, of a lifetime.

I confess to very mixed reactions when I see these sleek and shining couples in their sleek and shining rooms, with every perfect thing in its perfect place. Not the least of my feelings is envy. Do these fashionable people, elegantly garbed and posed in front of the lacquered built-ins with just the right primitive pot and piece of sculpture and the approved plant or tree, feel a tremendous sense of freedom and release? Have they been liberated by their seamless new look?

More to the point, what have they done with their household Lares and Penates, the sentimental possessions of their past? Did they give them away? Send them to auction galleries and thrift shops? Go on a trip while the decorator cleared them all out? Take a deduction for their memories? Were they tempted to keep nothing? Do they ever have any regrets?

This, of course, is radical surgery. The rest of us resort to more conventional forms of clutter combat. Houses have, or had, attics and cellars. Old apartments provide generous closets, which one fills with things that are permanently inaccessible and unneeded. In the city there is stolen space in elevator and service halls. And there is the ultimate catchall: the house in the country.

Historically, clutter is a modern phenomenon, born of the industrial revolution. There was a time when goods were limited; and the rich and fashionable were few in number, and objects were precious and hard to come by. Clutter is a nineteenth-century aesthetic; it came with the abundance of manufactured products combined with the rise of purchasing power, and the shifts in society that required manifestations of status and style. Victorian parlors were a jungle of elaborate furnishings and ornamental overkill. The reforms of the arts and crafts movement in the later nineteenth century only substituted a more "refined" kind of clutter: art pottery, embroidered hangings and mottoes, hand-painted tiles and porcelains, vases of bulrushes and peacock feathers. There were bewildering "artful" effects borrowed from the studio or atelier.

Clutter became a bad word only in the twentieth century. The modern movement decreed a new simplicity: white walls, bare floors, and the most ascetic of furnishings in the most purified of settings. If ornament was crime, clutter was taboo. Architects built houses, and decorators filled them. Antiques were discovered, and every kind of collecting boomed. There were even architects of impeccable modernist credentials—Charles Eames and Alexander Girard—who acquired and arranged vast numbers of toys and treasures. They did so with a discerning eye for the colorful and the primitive that added interest—and clutter—to modern rooms.

Today clutter is oozing in at a record rate. Architect-collectors like Charles Moore are freewheeling and quixotic in their tastes; high seriousness has been replaced by eclectic whimsy. Nostalgia and flea markets coexist on a par with scholarship and accredited antiques. Turning the century on its head, the artifacts of early modernism are being collected by the postmodernist avant-garde. At the commercial level, sophisticated merchandising sells the endless new fashions and products embraced by an affluent consumer society. The vacuum must be filled. And the truth must be told. Our possessions possess us.

New York Times, May 14, 1981

Battling the Bulge

WHAT GOES AROUND COMES AROUND, as the cliché puts it, and those of us who lived through Chiclets, amoebas, and tailfins are hoping to outlive the latest design aberration, the "power bulge." Called streamlining sixty years ago, what seemed ultrachic and futuristic (a word as delightfully dated as the style) has become retro-fashion, forgivably silly and lovable with the passage of time. But what comes around is never the same the second time. That is why those who save old clothes look as if they're wearing old clothes when the styles are revived; only the very young have the right revisionist panache. There is always that telling difference that reflects a radical change. So if the first streamlining was all about speed and the exciting promise of things to come, this time it is about, yes, power—a kind of visual machismo, the biceps and abs of inanimate objects; an image determined by marketing gurus and fashion stylists who have progressively replaced those early practitioners of aesthetic engineering in the unchecked downward slide of product design in this country.

The newspaper of record tells us that the power bulge is the invention of Mercedes-Benz, an updating of the legendary 300 SL of the fifties, only that car had one bulge and the new model has two. The *New York Times* has described this feature as "two long swellings on the hood" meant to "suggest that the power and potency of its supercharged engine can barely be contained." Also called "power domes," they are the "signature design motif" of a wide range of Mercedes spinoff items dedicated to something called "lifestyle merchandising" that Mercedes tells us will "make a clear statement about your taste and your sense of style." For wannabees, there's always the signature T-shirt with the power bulge logo.

Barnum was right about the inexhaustible supply of willing victims, but that's not the point. The point is best made by an exhibition at the Museum of Modern Art on the work of the Italian designer Achille Castiglioni, who has been demonstrating with style, clarity, and wit for fifty-two years what design should and can be all about. Assembled and installed by Paola Antonelli, associate curator of the Department of Architecture and Design, the show is worth a visit before it closes on January 6; there is more on view here than a wonderful collection of exhilarating, timeless, and still-desirable objects. Each solution is an elegant expression of an ingenious analysis of function, from a vacuum cleaner of the fifties to cutlery produced this year. Many are familiar — the Arco lamp of 1962 that offered an alternative to the omnipresent over-table light with the dramatic arc of its graceful polished chrome arm and shade swinging wide from a white marble base is a classic design. There is intelligence, imagination, and a sophisticated understanding of how to join use to pleasure, combined with what we have come to think of as the taste and playfulness of a uniquely Italian sensibility.

The roughly 150 objects on display, designed by Mr. Castiglioni with his brother Pier Giacomo, or by him alone, after Pier Giacomo's death, range from a gorgeous constellation of very large clear bulbs that brilliantly updates everything you ever thought about chandeliers to the famous found object red tractor seat. Among the recreated rooms is a restaurant for a Japanese client that uses folding tables, seats meant for kneeling, and the delicate drama of small, blue-shaded standing lamps as table lights, backed by an airy ring of plant stands, for a minimalist beauty that is anything but austere; this is the magical ambience of a Mackintosh tearoom stripped down, but just as evocative of a special place and time.

Outside of the museum, the power bulge is taking over. If the original sin is Mercedes's, Detroit has been quick to bite the apple. The new cars are bombe-shaped from tail to snout, with an inflated, aerodynamic look that owes less to Pinin Farina than to Looney Toons. But the trend really hit home when I ordered a new fax machine and it arrived with an inflated, rounded top and a set of graphics in pink and aqua ovals that appeared to be Disney-inspired. There was no technical, electronic, practical, or aesthetic reason for that top to be pumped up. A trip to Staples suggested that this was only the beginning. Here was a printer shaped like the Pillsbury dough boy. I have nothing against curves, but there is no redeeming logic here. There are those who still cherish Olivetti's typewriters designed by Marcello Nizzoli in the forties, not because they are old or quaint but because they were beautiful to look at and to use. *Liscio*, smooth to the eye and hand, gently rounded, not in defiance of the inner mechanism, but in harmony with it.

And that is the crux of the problem. What the designer does, essentially, is to house a mechanism, creating a skin. Strictly speaking, of course, form has never followed function. Shapes can be sharp or smooth. There is nothing wrong with design with an attitude, or an edge. But the form that results must express both the idea and the actuality of what makes the product what it is. When possible, the aim should be to reinvent or reconfigure or reengineer the product to devise a better and more desirable solution. There is a lot of leeway here; no two architects, for example, given the same program, would design the same house. But "appearance design," or "styling" for transient promotional purpose, produces dumbed-down objects that eliminate the possibility of anything genuinely new and appealing because the truly innovative or unprecedented cannot be visualized through marketing surveys or by focus groups. Outstanding products are a creative integration of technology, art, and fantasy, carried out by a trained professional with an industrial intelligence and an artist's eye. No second-class, second-guessing art form, design is a potent sales tool and persuasive vehicle for our dreams and aspirations. Until now, the new electronic equipment has been housed rationally and handsomely, luring us with a look of sleek efficiency and the visual promise of a smoothly competent, if somewhat illusory, futurism. Even the computer clods among us were flattered and beguiled.

I am not suggesting that we go back to the kind of earnest "good design" enshrined and promoted by the Museum of Modern Art in its early years. Or that we try to legislate or dictate "good taste"; what a deadly dull effort in design elitism that turned out to be. But we should at least have a choice, or a chance, based on some understanding and practice of the abused, misused, and misunderstood arts of design, so central to our lives and so dishonored in the breach. Meanwhile, I am putting off all purchases until the muscle-madness passes.

Wall Street Journal, December 30, 1997

Send in the Clowns

MAYBE IT'S RETRIBUTION for the now-well-documented excesses of Stanford White. But you'd have to believe in guilt by association, since it was actually Joseph Wells of White's firm, McKim, Mead & White, who designed the Villard Houses on Madison Avenue in 1884, which were then engulfed by the addition of Emery Roth & Sons' Helmsley Palace Hotel in 1980. Or maybe it was one of those ideas that seem wonderful late at night after the right amount of wine (very good wine, in this case) and that look a lot worse in the light of day.

The idea, of course, was to turn the elite Manhattan restaurant Le Cirque into a circus, when it moved to the landmark Villard rooms that were saved and incorporated into the Helmsley Palace (with Harry Helmsley, the unlikely preservationist, carried—in his own words— "kicking and screaming" all the way). Under his wife, Leona's preincarceration curatorship, the elaborate salons with their rich marbles and murals by a galaxy of Gilded Age artists were done up in the grand manner as part of the hotel restaurant; tea was served in the Gold Room, with its musicians' gallery.

Into this profligate period example of glorious overstatement, in the midst of a damp and reluctant spring, came the canny and, when he wants to be, ingratiating owner of Le Cirque, Sirio Maccioni (and his interior designer Adam Tihany), having vacated Le Cirque's old haunt at the Mayfair Hotel, that crowded cynosure of the Reagan era all set about with painted *settecento* monkeys. When faced with the overwhelming panache of these ornate interiors, one can either fight them or join them, and Messrs. Maccioni and Tihany have chosen, as has been noted all too accurately, to punch them in the nose.

Many observers have considered this aggression a creative act, one requiring daring of an uncommon sort—the kind of courage that produces uncommon results like the French architect Philippe Starck's conversion of the tunnel-like, block-through ground-floor space of the Royalton Hotel on Forty-fourth Street into a people-place of enduring delight through the sheer magic of design. No way. There is no magic here. Though attacked and disguised by an overlay of hokey shapes, patterns, and strident colors, one-armed chairs, and winged settees with Martian lights springing from the backs of those not treated to clown buttons, the Villard rooms win, hands down. Not without a struggle, though. They are nearly dealt a knockout blow.

It takes more than courage to make this sort of thing fly. It requires serious wit, in addition to a high order of talent and taste. Mr. Tihany is the architect of choice for any new restaurant that aspires to fashion in New York, and he has a string of glamorous successes in a suave, hard-surfaced, modern style. He has not repeated the formula here. He has attempted instead a high-wire act that never gets off the ground.

The tented entrance gives no warning of things to come—unless you look down at the floor. This could make you cry like Caruso in *Pagliacci*. It's hard to know what to say about the nonstop clashing motifs and colors of this carpet act, which has no shame; there is no way you could insult it. There is only the silent rebuke of an occasionally visible bit of magnificent marquetry floor. In the main dining room, rococo damsels hide on wall panels behind garish backlit screens. Yet there are almost as many original crystal chandeliers as in the dining room of the Hôtel de Crillon, a Parisian institution that has yet to show interest in tricking up its image. Would that have been such a bad image to go for, given the unique character and quality of the Villard Houses' interiors? Is classic beauty so hopelessly out of date?

Comparison with Mr. Starck and the Royalton is unavoidable, in part because Mr. Starck is the other ranking high-stylist for hotel-or-restaurant-as-theater, and also because one cannot escape the impression of a certain indebtedness to the Royalton's cozy radical chic. Surely there is a smidgen of knockoff—or tribute—to Mr. Starck's winged chairs and sofas in Le Cirque's overwrought winged settees, but at the Royalton they wing off with grace and a sense of flirtatious enclosure, edgy and protective at the same time. Le Cirque's settees go beyond edgy to uncomfortable. The Royalton's "untailored" white slipcovers say "this superchic place is really like home"—a look that has since slipcovered the fashionable world. Mr. Starck's colors are so subtle you have to look twice; Le Cirque's screaming mix constantly fights for attention. Assault is not seduction.

Part of Mr. Starck's magic is that he deals subtly in symbols— everything he designs is almost a symbol of itself. The "chairness" of his chairs makes one eager to sit in them; a handrail is so alluringly directional that it must be used; a pouf is so pouffy that it must be sat on. But best of all at the Royalton is the "barness" of the bar, where Mr. Starck defines, by design, the deep, contradictory appeal of bars: retreat and gregariousness. A small, round space near the hotel entrance has an offset, hard-to-find door; the womblike enclosure, intimacy itself, soothes and sedates. In the open lobby outside is a long table with seats on all sides; unlike standard bar seats against a wall, this offers a new model of boozy sociability.

At Le Cirque, the bar is in the Gold Room. Although by law nothing can be permanently attached to the walls of these interiors because they have been designated as a New York City landmark, the Gold Room has been ambushed. The restaurant's much-publicized design gimmick, a traveling clock, moves constantly about the room on its elliptical neon track. Clearly meant to fracture the enormous height and classical proportions of the space, it does so with terrifying success. As a signature piece, it is curiously miscast. Who needs a clock, much less a peripatetic, inescapable clock, in a bar? A bar is nepenthe, forgetfulness, a place to turn time off. A bar is escape, for the solitude or companionship that briefly stops time and shuts out the world. But here a large television set cannot be heard over recorded music. The musicians' gallery is barely visible above.

One remembers (with nostalgia) the brilliant bustle of the old no-style Le Cirque as a class act. The new Le Cirque 2000 is already a tourist trap at lunch. The large dining room is a kind of super-Siberia where the provincials are shielded from view by the high-backed seating that breaks the cardinal rule of any great restaurant as a place to see and be seen. The elite—who include the ladies who lunch, but don't— eat in a smaller, less vertiginous space.

There is nothing wrong with the idea of creating contemporary contrast rather than a traditional setting. I remember being blown away by the sophistication and style with which Italian architects did this in the fifties and sixties. They took on palaces and castles of awesome grandeur, refitting them with fearless innovation and exquisite taste. They made the past and the present partners in a wonderful aesthetic game—something we then considered vaguely immoral. Franco Albini's stripped-down museum installations at Genoa's Palazzo Bianco dramatized the old building's bared beauties con brio. Ignazio Gardella painted out all but one female figure with flowing draperies on a frescoed ceiling, leaving her floating in an all-white room where old paintings wearing thin gold-leaf frames were set on slender black-metal easels that made delicate geometric traceries in the opulent space. Carlo Scarpa's minimalist interventions are legendary and much admired still. What these architects did was to set up a dialogue and tension between different styles and periods, in which the airy and temporal played elegantly and exhilaratingly against the solid and ornate.

What has really happened at Le Cirque 2000 is that it has succumbed to the dread disease of theming. This kind of thing not only perverts design but sends serious chefs over the edge to kiddie desserts like Jugglers' Balls. It breaks the timeless principle that the décor should never upstage the food and the people. It should be avoided like kiwi and resisted like sin.

Wall Street Journal, July 1, 1997

When the Outrageous Became Mainstream

SERIOUS STUDIES HOLD THAT DEVELOPMENTS in the arts are due to cosmic shifts in the culture of a time or place. But they're really about the irreverence of the young and the irrepressible instinct with which each generation disowns the vision and values of established practice for a style and credo of its own. Change is actively pursued for the excitement of the new and the importance of doing your own thing, for which read, anything your parents will hate.

If the art is incomprehensible, the music unbearable, the clothes unwearable, and the furniture uncomfortable for all but the very young, then raise the volume and the shock value—it's an exhilarating and liberating trip. The more disturbing the results, the higher the rejection rate, the more certain you can be that these are the developments that will become the art and cultural indicators of their time.

That this kind of creativity was notably present at a specific moment in New York's recent past is the intriguing theme of a small but ambitious design show, Anarchy to Affluence, New York City, 1974–1984, on view until April 2 at the Parsons School of Design of the New School University, now somewhat awkwardly renamed for obscure semantic or institutional reasons, Parsons The New School for Design.

The displays include the fashions, graphics, furniture, and interiors of a challenging decade that started in free-style chaos and ended with the outrageous embraced as mainstream. A companion exhibition that expands the theme, The Downtown Show: The New York Art Scene, 1974–1984, is at the Grey Art Gallery of New York University.

The Parsons show, conceived and carried out by Christopher Mount, director of exhibitions and public programs, is an evocative exercise in nostalgia and revisionism, with a bit of affectionate proselytizing thrown in. The backstory is the sixties, as the text acknowledges. Bookended by Allen Ginsberg's "Howl," that decade's anthem, and Tom Wolfe's "Masters of the Universe," the exhibition is a fast ride from the dropout generation to the material age. Sixties granny gowns and love beads were followed by seventies punk and designer grunge and eighties over-the-top consumerism.

The seventies began with a fiscal crisis. By the midseventies, New York's desperate plea for federal help to avoid bankruptcy brought the epic *Daily News* headline FORD TO CITY: DROP DEAD. The crime rate soared, a notorious twenty-five-hour blackout spurred riots and looting, and the first reports appeared of a rare cancer in homosexuals, the beginning of AIDS. Artists seeking cheap rents moved to unfashionable industrial areas where they illegally occupied abandoned old buildings, soon perceived by less hard-pressed New Yorkers as chic and desirable. By the end of the decade those loft dwellings had been legalized and gentrified as SoHo and Tribeca and reoccupied by prosperous young professionals in the trendy trek downtown.

Social protest of the sixties was redirected into punk rock and a subversive design radicalism to match. Groups like the Ramones and the Voidoids, following the design lead of the Sex Pistols in England, embraced a graphics style of rough hand lettering or cut-and-pasted collages, abandoning expensive typesetting for a random, "amateur" look. A "ransom note" style used the unmatched "appropriated" letters supposedly favored by kidnappers to hide their identity; this gave a desirable outlaw tinge. Photocopied instead of printed, posters and flyers for clubs and discos were cheap and easy to produce. Album covers and publications like *Punk* magazine replicated the effects. This crude, spontaneous style shattered existing design conventions for a lasting break with tradition, although the free spirit was lost to the even greater computer-graphics revolution of the eighties.

What you will see in the show are the things you probably disposed of (who thought the seventies were anything?), and now you will regret it. Much was trashed; a few of the Stephen Sprouse fashion sketches on exhibition were literally rescued from the rubbish; more prescient owners saved Sprouse's clothes. Pieces on display include his barbed-wire and graffiti-printed fabrics used in fresh and stylish ways.

Outfits by Norma Kamali and Parachute show off Kamali's broad shoulders and sleek draping and Parachute's signature use of nylon. These were clothes with attitude—the jumpsuits, the embrace of androgyny, the snaps, zippers, and Velcro all had their message of revolt. But as wealth returned it brought the desire for a more conservative and ostentatious lifestyle. Ralph Lauren's uncanny faux-aristocratic knockoffs fueled knockoffs of the knockoffs, and now an international knockoff industry rivals the profits of the drug trade. Never underestimate the power of design.

Interiors were characterized by the economical and innovative use of standard industrial products like aluminum pipe, factory lighting, and warehouse shelving with chemical and pharmaceutical glass and ceramic accessories. (You wouldn't want what your parents liked anyway.) The machine aesthetic of modernism was remade into an industrial *arte povera* of "found" components for the look that became known and celebrated as high tech. A typical high-tech room has been re-created in the show with pipe-constructed loft bed, moving-pad quilts, factory flooring, beakers, and retorts; for some it will be a memory trip as poignant as any museum model room of tasteful period correctness. Oh, to be young and carefree in New York!

This is a cyclical city, and its relentless engine, real estate, soon drove it toward prosperity again. Artists priced out of their lofts by the conversion of their no-longer-shabby spaces into costly condominiums moved still farther toward the city's fringe as the downtown scene took off. By the end of the affluent eighties, a fringe culture was no longer possible. But Mr. Mount reminds us how profoundly influential the decade's vision proved to be. "A great deal of what happened in New York thirty years ago," he writes in the accompanying broadside that serves as a catalog, "has become a significant part of our popular culture. The anti-Establishment has become the Established."

That is true, although this has sometimes happened in a peculiarly perverse way. As high tech migrated to high culture, off-the-shelf interiors have been replaced by a custom-designed, techno-style with a superchromed, supercool look so far from inspired make-do that it speaks as clearly of cost as of an industrial aesthetic. The suave discomfort of this masochistic minimalism is something that only the superrich can afford.

Architecture is conspicuous by its absence from the show. Parsons's dean, Paul Goldberger, points out in a catalog essay that it was also being transformed, but in a different way. The undying image of dissent was Stanley Tigerman's wickedly revisionist collage of Mies van der Rohe's iconic modernist Crown Hall upended as it slides down into the ocean to a watery grave. The most significant changes had occurred in the sixties, when the English group Archigram took perfect aim at the permanence and predictability of accepted architectural norms. Archigram's witty and iconoclastic proposals included "Walking Cities" that moved, armadillo-like, with insouciance and self-sufficiency. Designs for sci-fi "Suitaloons" offered inflated service-providing shelters; "Cushicles" added functional comforts. Movements like "Ant Farm" combined art, architecture, and graphics in cultural send-ups that included half-buried old Cadillacs, rear ends protruding jauntily from a parking lot.

Robert Venturi's "gentle manifesto," published as *Complexity and Contradiction in Architecture* in 1966, called for a reconsideration of the lessons of history and the subtleties of spatial relationships and enriching ornament of the past.

That led to seventies postmodernism, less a period of creative vitality than of confusing signals and flawed buildings, a half-understood historical recall supposedly leavened with irony in the way past and present were combined. This, too, succeeded in rupturing old pieties, opening architecture to a paroxysm of experimental pluralism. Today, two trends—dramatic, sculptural forms and a Super high tech that exploits unprecedented advances in technology, both made possible by the computer—vie for drop-dead honors.

But I suggest you hold your bets. The lesson at Parsons is how little we understand and how poorly we judge without the help of the passage of time. How will we see the mavericks and innovators, the movements that may seem off-putting or inconsequential, a few decades later? One thing is clear: Don't throw anything away.

Wall Street Journal, February 16, 2006

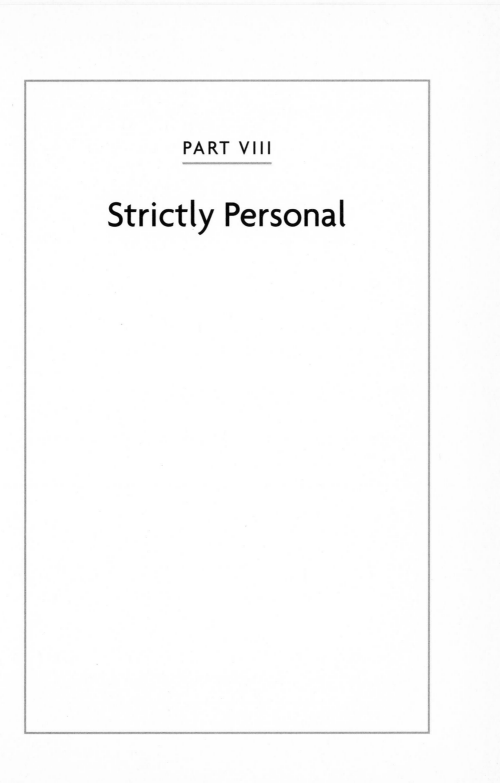

PART VIII

Strictly Personal

Growing Up in a Beaux Arts World

MANY OF MY EARLIEST AND MOST PERSISTENT architectural memories are of the Beaux Arts in New York, but I was unaware of it, like Molière's bourgeois gentilhomme who didn't know he was speaking prose. When I did become aware of it, I found out I wasn't supposed to like it. Alas, it was too late. Those buildings were as much a part of my life as my family, and I could neither dismiss nor neutralize my feelings toward them, which were intimately involved in the process of growing up.

By a curious coincidence, one of the institutions that taught me that they were all wrong now tells me that they're all right, and I'd be confused if I weren't delighted. The Museum of Modern Art, in a scholarly reversal of its own tradition as keeper of the flame of modern architecture, is currently featuring a large and beautiful show of nineteenth-century French academic drawings called The Architecture of the École des Beaux Arts (through January 4). The Beaux Arts style, in its variations from ornate French classicism to cool Roman and Renaissance revivalism, is to be found in this country's major monuments from 1890 to 1910 and later. The Architectural League has prepared a tour list, available at the museum, of some of the best local beaux arts buildings. In connection with these activities, I would like to present my own list. It might be called Beaux Arts buildings I have known and loved (or hated) in New York.

I grew up, all unwittingly, in a beaux arts structure called the St. Urban, whose style and substance were light-years away from today's architectural con game known as the "luxury" apartment house. All the milestones of my childhood and adolescence are colored by beaux arts experiences. I think of Grand Central Terminal, not in its present sad state, battling for its life, but as I remember it on Friday afternoons when we would take the Merchants' Limited—crisp white damask and roses in silver bud vases in the diner—to visit family in Boston. The trip began in the Grand Concourse, which seemed to hold all the nameless promises of pleasure and adventure of travelers past and present in its constantly moving, muted rhythms beneath the great sky-blue vaulted ceiling with its illuminated constellations. (Tomorrow, the universe.)

Grand Central's monumental richness and superb efficiency were accepted without question by New Yorkers; in fact, it was fashionable only to question its style, considered inferior to European models and somehow tainted with American utilitarianism. I can see now that it is absolutely one of the best things of its kind anywhere in the world. The façade from Park Avenue South is quintessential Beaux Arts—immense arched windows and paired, fluted columns rising building-height above the girdling roadway like a triple triumphal arch, fronted by the bronze Commodore in his astrakhan-collared coat directing taxis to the other side. It is hard to imagine New York without Mercury, Hercules, and Minerva atop Jules Coutan's monumental clock; it is part of the city's essential image and remaining elegance.

There were trips from Penn Station, too—McKim, Mead & White's Roman extravaganza of 1910 in cream travertine and pink granite, later soot-darkened, where the traveler debouched into the tepidarium of the Baths of Caracalla. It was demolished in 1966. "One entered the city like a god," Vincent Scully has written, ". . . one scuttles in now like a rat."

When I was allowed to roam New York by myself, I went first to the Museum of Natural History, where I spent spellbound days in the old J. C. Cady Wing of 1877, a dark, blackish brown pile later cleaned to a surprisingly frivolous pink. The blue whale suspended from the entrance ceiling became my friend. So did the building. When the museum built its new centerpiece in 1936, an archaeologically correct Roman monument in *retardataire* Beaux Arts by John Russell Pope, I hated it, and still do. Not because anyone told me to hate it (by then I knew), but because those pompous, forbidding, overscaled steps led to huge, cold, tomblike halls, vast, dim, dead spaces in which one felt depressed and diminished. This is a kind of building totally devoid of joy. I cannot make myself go there now, but I am glad that lots of other people do.

The world really opened for me across town, at the Metropolitan Museum. It was true-blue Beaux Arts (Richard M. Hunt, Richard H. Hunt, and McKim, Mead & White, successively, from 1895 to 1906), and its grandeur worked. The steps invited rather than repelled, in that formal Beaux Arts *marche*, or moving progression of spaces, that invited one into the high-ceilinged hall with its tapestries, chandeliers, and stray knights in armor or oversized antiquities. (I have never been able to reconcile myself to its current "restoration," a slick cross between IBM and I. Magnin glamour.) In the best Beaux Arts fashion, these spaces either beckoned you up the grand stairs (if you were young and supple) to the painting galleries or led you left or right, to the worlds of Egypt, Greece, and Rome. It is no exaggeration to say that this building shaped my life.

So did the Forty-second Street Library (Carrère and Hastings, 1898–1911), when my art studies began to take me there for research. Another beautiful beaux arts building became a friend. It made no pretense at chumminess; it was intended to impress; but, again, it worked. A sense-expanding spatial sequence from the arched and colonnaded portal to more marble and massive stairs and richly detailed rooms inside provided both grace and grandeur and suggested that man might be noble, after all. Or at least that he knew quality from junk.

Walks around town left indelible impressions. There was the New York Yacht Club on West Forty-fourth Street (Warren and Wetmore, 1889), a baroque extravaganza with flowing water carved below galleon-shaped windows—what child would not adore it? I was a post-postgraduate student before I knew that this was *architecture parlante*, defined in the Architectural League's guide as "architecture whose function is literally articulated by its form and decoration"—here ships and sea in stone.

A woman still does not enter New York's great beaux arts men's clubs, except as a pariah through designated areas. I remember visiting the University Club (McKim, Mead & White, 1889), a Renaissance superpalazzo, and making an instinctive architecturally propelled rush for the great, gutsy marble columns visible from the door. None of that, now. I was peremptorily turned aside into a pusillanimous "ladies" dining room. The insult was as much architectural as personal.

At the Battery, I found the U.S. Custom House (Cass Gilbert, 1907), forty giant columns around its sides, embellished with dolphins, rudders, tridents, and winged wheels, guarded by Daniel Chester French's *Four Continents*. Farther along, on Liberty Street, was James Baker's 1901 Chamber of Commerce Building, a particularly rich fruitcake of dormers and bull's-eye windows, colonnade and copper-crested roof, frosted with garlands. Delighted by their outrageous assurance, I adopted them both.

From my office window, as I write, my constant companion is a small beaux arts skyscraper directly across Forty-second Street. It is elegantly composed and decorated, with three elongated, vertical bands of round-arched windows dominating a delicate, five-bay arrangement, topped with a crown of carved stone. The street at its feet is porn-country; the neighborhood around it is a disaster area. But the finesse with which the building proposes that skill and order are not only justifiable but desirable is somehow reassuring. I raise my eyes for an architecture-break in a city that is as heartbreaking in its beauty as it is in its poverty and decay. It is still a city of dreams—promised, built, and broken.

New York Times, November 9, 1975

Personal Landmarks Along the Highway

IT IS THAT GETTING-OUT-OF-NEW-YORK TIME OF YEAR, and if you are driving on I-91 through Connecticut don't miss the Colt Firearms Building as you pass Hartford on your way to New England diversions. You can't miss it anyway; how many expressways offer a view of a deep cerulean-blue onion dome, gilt-trimmed and studded with stars, set on a crown of white columns, atop a large nineteenth-century brick factory with a miragelike twentieth-century Hartford behind it?

I have been watching that building, en route, for a good part of my life, and I find that these places seen in transit through a car window, with the changing vision of motion, have a special kind of image. The eye is really a camera, and the image is kinetic and transient, but timeless in the way that makes cinema a haunting art of transfixed, passing shadows. Perhaps because these buildings are a repeated and anticipated experience, such places and structures that may only touch our lives tangentially stay permanently fixed in the mind's eye.

But they change, from one year to the next. Over the decades I have watched the Colt Firearms Building (which instantly tells me that I have gotten to Hartford) transformed from a shabbly relic to renewed splendor, with growing general recognition of the fact that it is a superb example of what art historians now call industrial archaeology. This summer it is really something to see. An anonymous admirer, whose name is supposedly unknown even to Colt, donated five thousand dollars to put back the stars on the dome that have been missing for the last fifty years. The stars were part of the original building of 1857, which burned in 1864 and was reconstructed in 1874. They disappeared around 1920, probably for economy reasons.

Obviously, Colonel Colt was quite aware of the symbolic and status value of architecture. The Hartford Architectural Conservancy, in its notes on the building, tells us that he meant the exotic dome on its circle of decorous columns to be seen by travelers passing through Hartford by barge on the Connecticut River. Today they see it from the thruway, at high speed. They may miss the details—the gleaming gold ball at the top is surmounted by a casting of a rearing colt, and there are eighty stars. But the fine vernacular brick building, a prime example of typically pragmatic and handsome nineteenth-century American design, has even gained in visual impact.

I FIND, WHEN I think of it, and generally I don't, that I have a set of such landmarks—personal, transient, and indelible—that mark the stages of my journeys and the stages of my life. I wait for these particular places on trips year after year; they are all old friends. It is more important than I have ever consciously admitted that they should be where I expect to find them. If they are gone, I have a real and shocking sense of loss; if they have been refurbished, I am suffused with a surprising joy.

Sometimes I admire these buildings for years without knowing what they are or anything about them. They can be encountered on country roads or on those curious routes by which one is forced to leave large cities. They loom up along New York's potholed, poverty-blitzed avenues that turn abruptly onto bridges of surpassing beauty or on boulevards of oppressive banality; the city's exits and entrances are a surreal mix of scales and references, from graffiti praising Bessie Smith on the crumbling wall of a corner bar to pocket handkerchief gardens bordering a superhighway and anonymous public-housing wastelands where even grass and trees despair. The omnipresent urban glue is dust, litter, and weeds.

Just past the cemeteries on the approach to La Guardia airport, with their legions of carved angels like stone hiccups from the same mortuary sculptor's pattern, is the Bulova watch factory, a long, streamlined art deco structure that never ceases to be satisfying. Time stands still there in more ways than one; the building is a frozen custard of architectural optimism—these were the soft, rounded forms of the world of the future in the thirties—and the entrance clock no longer has its hands.

Driving along the superlimbo of Bruckner Boulevard, in an ambience of grubby small factories, Kansas Fried Chicken, and derelict housing, I have for years watched and loved a building that is the sole anchor for one's sensibilities in that grim stretch of road. It seems like a miraculously misplaced bit of Claude Nicholas Ledoux in the South Bronx.

This building is a severe and serene example of a kind of disembodied classicism, not grand enough to disdain its neighbors—it is no aloof white temple—but still able to be part of its surroundings with a plain sort of dignity. It is an extremely well-proportioned building, with a brick pediment and unadorned stone architrave, and a curious odd number (seven) of attached flat columns or pilasters along the front. These pilasters alternate stone and brick courses for a lively formality. Between them are large open bays topped by lunette windows framed in round arches of beautifully laid brick with proper keystones. This is a strong, simple design, and I have always bowed respectfully to it, in this surprising place, without knowing the building's name or purpose.

I FOUND OUT only recently, when the New York Landmarks Conservancy undertook an inventory of public buildings in the city, that this distinguished and workmanlike structure is a "grit chamber" built in 1936 by McKim, Mead & White, long after the famous principals were working members of the firm. A grit chamber is a sewage plant. Disposal trucks go through those classical bays. There are no limits to elegance.

Another building that I look forward to seeing on annual New England excursions is a factory in Beverly, Massachusetts. This is one of those structures that always elicited a pleased "there it is" long before I knew what it was. An early reinforced concrete-framed industrial building with great expanses of many-paned sash, it stretches far along a meadow with singular assurance and surprising grace. Impressive and pleasing proportions combine with the direct expression of structure to create an outstanding aesthetic.

Twenty years ago, when I was doing research in innovative concrete construction in the United States, I found an illustration of the United Shoe Machinery Plant in Beverly, designed by the pioneering engineer of reinforced concrete, Ernest Ransome. It was a picture of my building. And the dates were an astonishingly early 1903–5, putting it slightly in advance of the celebrated Detroit automobile factories by Albert Kahn. To find that the structure that so pleased my eye also rewrote an important chapter of architectural history has increased my contentment on every subsequent viewing.

These are some of my personal landmarks, and there are many more. I am catholic in my tastes, possessive and passionate in my responses. And response is the key word—the point of these buildings that become one's geographic and cultural signposts is that it is impossible to be neutral toward them. From high art to high camp, they are a source of satisfaction and delight. I am as fond of Violet's Lounge, a humdrum little house raised to spurious glamour with mauve plastic panels and a glittering silver sign at a busy intersection on Massachusetts Route 114 (I always wondered what Violet was like), as I am of the Bruckner grit chamber. Violet's Lounge disappeared last year. Sewage is forever.

New York Times, June 26, 1977

No Place Like Home

I FIND THAT I HAVE TO REMIND myself that New York is the center of the universe after several weeks in a New England town. It is not just that one is seduced by the insidious idea that small is beautiful, or that one builds up a false ideal of small-town virtues that may be largely in the mind, or that one confuses the reality of work with the unreality of vacation—it is that the living is easy. That means that compared to life in New York, every minute of the day isn't a hassle. Compared to life in New York, every encounter isn't a joust with survival.

The weather has something to do with it, of course; summer is the time when one sheds one's tensions with one's clothes, and the right kind of day is jeweled balm for the battered spirit. A few of those days, and you can become drunk with the belief that all's right with the world.

But the one thing that stands out, and that I do not really understand, is why the house where we spend those weeks is so much more comfortable than the apartment in New York. It is a rented house, to which we have returned for many years, so while we have done some rearranging and added a few personal touches, we had nothing to do with the design and furnishing in the first place. That it seems to work so much better is surprising, because we have devoted a fair amount of time to how our New York place looks and functions. We have selected the furnishings with care and planned layout and storage meticulously.

It is understandable, of course, that we are happier in a house where we can (and do) get up with the first colors of the sunrise and watch the gulls commute morning and evening over a harbor that turns from blue to pearl or steel with the changing weather. Or where one starts the day with a tour of the garden to see which flowers have bloomed or faded overnight.

But chiefly, it is not a house one worries about. It is an easy house that rewards affection and any kind of care. It is full of old things, and comfortable things, and shabby things—objects that have been used and loved or just discarded gently. Some of these things are useful, and some are not. (Still, I could not spare the framed membership certificate in the Warren G. Harding Memorial Association or the Grover Cleveland plate.) There is wicker, but it is not the kind of wicker that has surfaced fashionably and expensively; it is the kind with irretrievable dust in the crevasses. There are no loveseats or étagères, but a collection of old rockers—even one that kicks you when you come downstairs in the dark.

An assortment of tables has no relationship to known styles, periods, or purposes, but there is always one where you need it. The bric-a-brac ranges from Bennington and art glass to vintage Woolworth and early

Sunsweet, and it includes whatever you could possibly want at the moment you want it. Beds are high and old-fashioned and easy to make. The flagpole has a view of the ocean, and so does the laundry line. There is fresh mint for cutting outside the kitchen door, and friends supply parsley and basil.

The house is full of surprises, even after years of intimate association. This year I found a Thebes stool. I had not noticed it before because it has always been covered with Caruso records or old magazines. It was such a handy place to toss an afghan or sweater, in one of those convenient dark corners that new houses totally lack. The only reason that I know it is a Thebes stool now, or know what a Thebes stool is, must be credited to the Tutankhamen exhibition and an old issue of a British journal, the *Architectural Review*. It seems that a stool called the Thebes stool was in Tutankhamen's tomb and was copied endlessly in the twenties, at the time the great archaeological discovery caused fashion waves in clothing and homes.

The Liberty stool, by Liberty of London, was probably one of the best copies of the type. I am not sure, but there may have been other nineteenth-century versions, dating from those British arts-and-crafts episodes of earnest intellectual nostalgia. The process of reproduction and knockoff is going on again today with the latest Tutankhamen vogue. Our house version was clearly a product of the twenties, and after "restoration" with soap and water and scouring powder and the addition of a velvet cushion, it came out of the corner. This was the home furnishings event of the summer.

Every year brings similar projects. In summer houses, the caned seats of chairs constantly break through, and an entire instant decorating scheme can be set in motion by a search for cushions to camouflage them. One table (known as "the gaming table" because of its permanent shaker of alphabet cubes, for tossing on rainy days) listed relentlessly to port; it was a summer's job to break it apart and reglue it at right angles. Considering its dubious provenance, this was clearly a labor of love. Chairs are "upholstered" on impulse with mill ends and pins. Everything is relaxed, undemanding, and inviting. There is nothing new or showy or fashionable. The effect is as far from the British idea of tatty-chintz country-house status as it is from the trendy vacation homes featured in the fancy shelter magazines. I would say that the house has a certain kind of class.

The town has class, too. One of the loveliest sailing harbors in the world is surrounded by a pre-Revolutionary settlement that did much of its building by about 1820. The narrow Massachusetts streets are a casual treasury of Federal and Greek Revival, cheek-by-jowl clapboard houses on rising hills with gardens tucked between. It is all topped by a redbrick Ruskinian Gothic, Victorian town hall, which houses that archetypal American painting *The Spirit of '76*.

Old Town, as the original section is called, has had its share of buffeting by groupies, and geometrically increasing numbers of cars have made streets all but impassable and unparkable. The buildings are increasingly filled with boutiques. But the place withstands the invasion of twentieth-century lifestyles surprisingly well, and it has also resisted both Williamsburg and Disneyland influences. The blows of change are softened by installing traffic islands, where needed, of solid masses of petunias. Priorities are, properly, the availability of the first corn and the state of the tides, and important events tend to be ice-cream socials at the local historical mansion.

If there is anything here of the kind that makes New York go round—and there is a certain infiltration of the superchic, supercostly, overreaching for status—I have managed to steer clear of it. This is a home and lifestyle forever away from stainless steel and black glove leather. I have managed, in fact, to restore heart and soul here for another year's go at the great metropolis. There are country tomatoes and parsley in the city refrigerator. I cannot see the morning sky or the gulls skimming through the open porch (old houses have porches, with and without screens), and the hassle is on from the moment I arise. I think of that house as the single most beautiful thing that I know.

New York Times, September 29, 1977

Index

NOTE: Page numbers in *italics* indicate photographs